The Economics of Urban Property Markets

This book examines the relationship between the property market and the urban economy. The stimulus for this work was provided by the seemingly ever-accelerating process of urban economic change and the noticeable failure of existing studies to adequately explore the pivotal role that the property market plays in this process.

Drawing on institutional economics, the central argument of this book is that the property market as an institution is a mediator through which urban economic potential can be realised and served. In developing this argument, the book provides a critical realist ontological framework that advances understanding of the institutional structure of the economy and the complex interrelation between the institutional environment and human agency, as well as a holistic theoretical framework of urban economic change, where appropriate emphasis is placed on the specific mechanisms, processes and dynamics through which the built environment is provided. Arvanitidis also explores an institutional conceptualisation of property market efficiency, defined in terms of the ability of the market institution to adapt its structure and to provide the outcomes that the economy requires. To inform empirical research on the developed concepts, the book also offers a generic analytical approach specifying appropriate research methods and techniques for investigation along with a specific research design providing an operational framework that translates developed theory into empirical practice.

The book's primary contribution therefore lies in its delineation of a holistic research programme to conceptualise the property market as an institution and to explore its role within the urban economy.

Paschalis A. Arvanitidis is Assistant Professor of Institutional Economics at the Department of Economics, University of Thessaly, Greece.

Routledge studies in the European economy

1 **Growth and Crisis in the Spanish Economy, 1940–1993**
Sima Lieberman

2 **Work and Employment in Europe**
A new convergence?
Edited by Peter Cressey and Bryn Jones

3 **Trans-European Telecommunication Networks**
The challenges for industrial policy
Colin Turner

4 **European Union – European Industrial Relations?**
Global challenges, national developments and transnational dynamics
Edited by Wolfgang E. Lecher and Hans-Wolfgang Platzer

5 **Governance, Industry and Labour Markets in Britain and France**
The modernizing state in the mid-twentieth century
Edited by Noel Whiteside and Robert Salais

6 **Labour Market Efficiency in the European Union**
Employment protection and fixed-term contracts
Klaus Schömann, Ralf Rogowski and Thomas Kruppe

7 **The Enlargement of the European Union**
Issues and strategies
Edited by Victoria Curzon-Price, Alice Landau and Richard Whitman

8 **European Trade Unions**
Change and response
Edited by Mike Rigby, Roger Smith and Teresa Lawlor

9 **Fiscal Federalism in the European Union**
Edited by Amedeo Fossati and Giorgio Panella

10 **European Telecommunications Liberalisation**
Edited by Kjell A. Eliassen and Marit Sjøvaag

11 **Integration and Transition in Europe**
The economic geography of interaction
Edited by George Petrakos, Gunther Maier and Grzegorz Gorzelak

12 **SMEs and European Integration**
Internationalisation strategies
Birgit Hegge

13 **Fiscal Federalism and European Economic Integration**
Edited by Mark Baimbridge and Philip Whyman

14 **Financial Markets in Central and Eastern Europe**
Stability and efficiency
Edited by Morten Balling, Frank Lierman and Andy Mullineux

15 **Russian Path Dependence**
Stefan Hedlund

16 **The Impact of European Integration on Regional Structural Change and Cohesion**
Edited by Christiane Krieger-Boden, Edgar Morgenroth and George Petrakos

17 **Macroeconomic Policy in the European Monetary Union**
From the old to the new stability and growth pact
Edited by Francesco Farina and Roberto Tamborini

18 **Economic Policy Proposals for Germany and Europe**
Edited by Ronald Schettkat and Jochem Langkau

19 **Competitiveness of New Europe**
Papers from the second Lancut economic forum
Edited by Jan Winiecki

20 **Deregulation and the Airline Business in Europe**
Sean Barrett

21 **Beyond Market Access for Economic Development**
EU–Africa relations in transition
Edited by Gerrit Faber and Jan Orbie

22 **International Trade, Consumer Interests and Reform of the Common Agricultural Policy**
Edited by Susan Mary Senior Nello and Pierpaolo Pierani

23 **Economic Governance in the EU**
Willem Molle

24 **Financial Integration in the European Union**
Edited by Roman Matoušek and Daniel Stavárek

25 **Europe and the Mediterranean Economy**
Edited by Joan Costa-Font

26 **The Political Economy of the European Social Model**
Philip S. Whyman, Mark J. Baimbridge and Andrew Mullen

27 **Gender and the European Labour Market**
Edited by Francesca Bettio, Janneke Plantenga and Mark Smith

28 **The Economic Crisis and Governance in the European Union**
A critical assessment
Edited by Javier Bilbao-Ubillos

29 **Competitiveness in the European Economy**
Edited by Stefan Collignon and Piero Esposito

30 **The Contradictions of Austerity**
The socio-economic costs of the neoliberal Baltic model
Edited by Jeffrey Sommers and Charles Woolfson

31 **The New Economic Governance in the Euro-Area**
Armin Steinbach

32 **The Economics of Urban Property Markets**
An institutional economics analysis
Paschalis A. Arvanitidis

33 **South-East Europe in Evolution**
Edited by Hardy Hanappi

The Economics of Urban Property Markets

An institutional economics analysis

Paschalis A. Arvanitidis

Routledge
Taylor & Francis Group
LONDON AND NEW YORK

First published 2015
by Routledge
2 Park Square, Milton Park, Abingdon, Oxon OX14 4RN

and by Routledge
52 Vanderbilt Avenue, New York, NY 10017

First issued in paperback 2020

Routledge is an imprint of the Taylor & Francis Group, an informa business

British Library Cataloging in Publication Data
A catalogue record for this book is available from the British Library

Library of Congress Cataloging in Publication Data
Arvanitidis, Paschalis A.
The economics of urban property markets: an institutional economics analysis / Paschalis Arvanitidis.
pages cm – (Routledge studies in the european economy)
1. Cities and towns–Growth. 2. Real property. I. Title.
HT371.A78 2014
307.76–dc23 2014006420

ISBN 13: 978-0-367-66944-7 (pbk)
ISBN 13: 978-0-415-42682-4 (hbk)

Typeset in Times New Roman
by Wearset Ltd, Boldon, Tyne and Wear

To Dana, Martha and Kostantis,
. . . for being more than tolerant and supportive.

Contents

Figures

Tables

Preface

Real estate, real property, or, simply, property constitutes a major part of 'individual wealth' and is a substantial driver of the economy. This is because every activity needs space (property) for its setting and operation. Moreover, the property sector is so closely linked to the other sectors of the economy (e.g. the financial and construction sectors) that its performance greatly affects their performance and success, something that was made very clear in the recent economic crisis that afflicted the world.

However, limited research has been devoted to an understanding of the property market and to its relationship with the local economy. In attempting to do so, it is essential to consider not only property market outcomes, but also the property market process which gives rise to them. This is because it is through this process that property values are specified, information is generated and becomes available, legal interests are defined and enforced, uses are allocated and development and redevelopment are stimulated; thus, in general terms, the property market works to provide the spatial structures (real property) and legal interests (property rights) required for economic development. Developing a profound understanding of this process necessitates consideration of the institutional characteristics of the property market and the way these emerge, develop and evolve in relation to wider institutional structures and dynamics.

This book therefore sets out to explore in depth the relationship between the property market and the urban economy. The stimulus for this work comes from the seemingly ever-accelerating process of urban economic change and the noticeable failure of conventional economics to adequately explore the pivotal role that the property market as an institution plays in this process. Drawing on institutional economics, the central argument of this book is that the property market institution is a mediator through which local economic potential can be realised and served.

Owing to major philosophical and theoretical deficiencies in this field, the focus of this book is centred on the establishment of an appropriate philosophical framework, the development of a new theory and the specification of a research design for empirical investigation of the issues. The book's primary contribution lies in the development of a holistic research programme to conceptualise the property market as an institution and to explore its role and location within the urban economy.

Critical realist principles provide the basis for the development of the philosophical position of the study. These are combined with institutionalist insights to construct a three-layer ontological framework that advances understanding of the institutional structure of the economy and the complex interrelation between the institutional environment and human agency. The study then lays down a rich theory of urban economic organisation, placing explicit emphasis on the institutional mechanisms, processes and dynamics through which property is provided. The interrelation between property market process and the wider institutional environment is explored, particularly in terms of efficiency in providing the appropriate market institutions and property outcomes to support urban economic potential. From this discussion the institutionalist concept of 'property market purpose efficiency' is developed. Building on the philosophical and conceptual frameworks, the study explicitly addresses requirements for concrete analysis. To do this, it first lays down a generic analytical approach specifying appropriate research methods and techniques for investigation, and, second, sets up a research design providing an operational framework through which developed theory is translated into an agenda for empirical research. This research design provides a blueprint for prospective empirical studies.

Acknowledgements

Every text that finds a place in the pages of a book has a history. The text in this book has grown gradually over a number of years. Much of it was part of my PhD thesis at the University of Aberdeen (UK). Other parts have matured through my post-doctoral work and the teaching experience I have had, particularly here in the University of Thessaly (Greece). Traces of my previous work abound in this manuscript.

Although the book has undergone extensive revisions since I finished my doctorate, immense gratitude is owed to Geoff Keogh, my academic mentor and good friend, whose intellectual curiosity, unlimited patience and constructive comments have steered me through very difficult and testing times. Another person who deserves special mention is another dear friend, George Petrakos, who trusted my academic skills and generously supported me at the beginning of my academic career here in Greece, something he continues to do.

Many other people have influenced my thinking in diverse and often subtle ways; sometimes through a perceptive comment, sometimes through discussion. It is always difficult to single out particular individuals, but I should try, even at the peril of significant omissions. I therefore want to thank Craig Watkins, Robert McMaster, Alan Evans, John Finch, Bryạn MacGregor, Karen Sieraki, Norman Hutchison, Ioannis Theodossiou, Kostas Lalenis, Michel Zouboulakis, Christos Kollias, Nikos Kyriazis, Xenothon Paparrigopoulos and Apostolos Arvanitis. Needless to say, I must take full responsibility for any remaining errors, confusion or misunderstandings in the ideas presented here.

My editors at Routledge have been very supportive and ever helpful throughout this work. I gratefully acknowledge Terry Clague, who signed the book, Simon Holt and Emily Senior, who patiently watched me miss deadlines due to the joys and tragedies of life, and to Laura Johnson, who, thankfully, has pushed me over the end of the book's gestation. Without their encouragement and trust from the beginning, this book would not have been completed.

The book reveals my academic debt to a number of scholars, but especially to Geoff Hodgson and Tony Lawson, who, unknowingly, initiated me into the intellectual richness of original institutionalism and critical realism, respectively. I only hope that the book does not (overly) misrepresent their ideas.

Financial support for my doctoral study was jointly provided by Slough Estates plc and the Departments of Land Economy and Real Estate at the University of Aberdeen. Sir Nigel Mobbes and Professor Bryan MacGregor deserve special mention for making these funds available to me.

Last, but not least, I also thank my mentor and dear friend Jonathan (Mik) Smith, who has been very enthusiastic and supportive all the way. Mik has been kind enough to read most parts of the draft at very short notice and has offered helpful suggestions for making the text cohere better.

My wife, Dana, and my children, Martha and Konstantinos, have paid a heavy price for the writing of this book in absences, silences and sacrifices, but I cannot begin to speak of what I owe to their affection.

Paschalis Arvanitidis
Volos, Greece

1 Introduction

1.1 The research problem

This book sets out to examine the complex, but indisputably significant, relationship between the property market and the urban economy.[1] The stimulus for this work lies in the seemingly ever-accelerating process of urban economic change and the noticeable failure of existing studies to explore adequately the pivotal role that the property market plays in this process.

Over the last three decades or so, cities in Europe have witnessed a remarkable structural transformation at the economic, social and spatial levels, fuelled by changes in production relationships, developments in (tele)communication and transportation technologies, and European economic and political integration. In this environment, it became apparent that urban areas had to reinforce existing strengths and at the same time to develop new qualities to cope successfully with the often traumatic problems of structural adjustment and to maintain a secure basis for local economic development.

This process of urban economic change and spatial reorganisation has been examined by a wide range of studies in search of answers to the 'urban questions'. Using a number of philosophical, conceptual and methodological frameworks, these studies have offered a variety of interpretations and solutions to urban transformation. However, despite the fact that every socio-economic activity takes place on land or within a built structure, very limited research has been carried out to explore the relationship between urban economic change and the dynamics of property markets. The vast majority of studies either treat the built environment as a passive backdrop to economic change, or acknowledge the interrelationship between economic and spatial structures but simplify and underplay the complex institutional mechanisms that account for the provision of the built environment.[2]

Clearly, the nature of inquiry and the resulting explanations depend on the theoretical viewpoint adopted. Mainstream urban and property economics (e.g. DiPasquale and Wheaton, 1996; Harvey, 1996) stress the importance of market mechanisms, assuming that they operate in a more or less efficient way to bring supply and demand into a state of equilibrium. Trade defines property prices that can be taken as meaningful representations of value, and the built environment is put to the most valuable use and held in a form that most closely meets the various requirements of rational economic actors. However, the emphasis here is clearly on the demand side of the urban economy, with supply-side conditions being perceived as relatively unproblematic. The built environment is regarded as relatively malleable and the property market as a passive adapter to urban change. By taking this approach, conventional approaches largely neglect any property-related factors in urban economic organisation and change and therefore fail to provide a satisfactory explanation of the mechanisms and processes through which the built environment is provided and, perhaps more importantly, of the way it affects the course of the urban economy.

In contrast, other approaches view urban economic and spatial transformation as a reflection of the dynamics and processes of the evolving politico-economic system and therefore correctly place urban change and built environment provision in an economic and political context. Some of their explanatory determinants are structural, reflecting the nature and dynamics of capitalism (Castells, 1977; Harvey, 1985), while others place emphasis on the (inter-)active role of human agency (Healey, 1992). The analytical approach is essentially historical, focusing explanation on the way economic and socio-political structures are organised and interact dialectically with each other through human agency. These interpretations portray the city as a 'rational' economic, political and social entity in dynamic transformation, constantly searching for an equilibrium solution to all traditional urban problems (unemployment, poverty, physical decay, etc.) mitigating tensions in the economic sphere.

These approaches have been attacked on many grounds, including their deterministic or teleological system of explanation, their functionalist treatment of the built environment and their undue stress on structure or agency. In addition, none of these approaches has managed to effectively incorporate the complex nature of property market processes into their analysis of the provision of the built environment and to carry this analysis into an integrated urban economic theory. On these grounds, the dynamics and mechanisms of the property market, as well as its relation to urban spatial-economic transformation, remain largely unexplored.

There are, however, a few studies (e.g. van der Krabben, 1995; D'Arcy and Keogh, 1997; Ball, 1998) which explicitly place the property market (through which the built environment is defined, generated, transformed, used and traded) at the centre of their explanation. These draw on an eclectic mix of institutional economics. Institutional economics see the socio-economy as an integrated and dynamically evolving system which is constantly reproduced and transformed by purposeful and multidimensional human agency. This enables external pressures and internal institutional arrangements to be reconciled and tensions arising in economic relations, as well as in law, politics, culture and power structure, to be addressed. The potential for economic progress and success rests on the institutional context (described in economic, political, legal and socio-cultural terms), the associated organisational framework (economic actors, organisations and networks) and the ability of the system to adjust these structures to anticipate and accommodate changing conditions and circumstances.

In this approach, the property market itself is conceived as an institution, comprising a set of formal and informal rules, rights, norms, practices, conventions, cognitive frameworks, relationships and organisational formations through which property is defined, generated, used and exchanged. It acts, alongside other institutional structures, as a mediator through which the potential for economic change is realised. The effectiveness of the market to provide what economic actors require, in terms of both the physical and institutional aspects of property, affects the ability of the urban economy to accommodate pressures for change and promote economic potential. Thus the operation of the property market is seen as an important parameter in understanding economic performance and the development of cities.

Despite these theoretical advances in conceptualising the property market and its relation to the urban economy, our understanding of these mechanisms, processes, relations and dynamics still remains, at best, partial. For example, although the relation between the property market as an institution and the wider (urban) institutional environment is generally recognised, many of these links remain virtually unexplored and require further theoretical development before effective empirical research can be undertaken.

Three knowledge gaps and potential research avenues are apparent. First, despite the variety and diversity of institutional economics, no published research has systematically deployed its conceptual and methodological nuances and its perspective on urban economic development and the provision of the built environment. It therefore seems essential to explore the breadth and depth of institutionalist thought and to identify those elements which can be employed for the analysis of the property market as an institution and of its relation to the urban economy.

Second, a unifying and comprehensive conceptual framework is required to advance understanding of the complex mechanisms through which the built environment is provided in response to urban socio-economic processes and dynamics, and to translate this into an effective theory of urban economic development. This should involve the provision of an explicit ontological, epistemological and methodological perspective from which a clear research agenda for concrete analysis can be defined. Clarity on these issues is essential given the fact that institutionalist research can be, and has been, informed by a range of philosophical positions and analytical standpoints.

Third, empirical work is needed to investigate the processes of urban economic change and built environment provision and to consider their relations in specific urban settings. Such empirical analysis has a dual function. It serves to form new hypotheses about causal mechanisms and relations that have not been previously identified or adequately theorised. It also provides a basis from which the relative power of developed or competing theories can be assessed and validated in historically and spatially specific urban configurations.

1.2 Aims, objectives and research questions

The broad aim of this study is to theorise and investigate the operation of the property market and its role in the process of urban economic development. This aim is addressed through the following objectives:

1. To establish an appropriate philosophical framework that advances institutionalist understanding of both the wider urban socio-economic dynamics and the specific mechanisms through which the built environment is provided.
2. To develop a specific methodological framework, including the development of new theory, within which to consider the operation of the property market as an institution and its contribution to urban economic development.
3. To formulate a research design to guide empirical investigation on the issues.

These, in turn, suggest three sets of broad research questions which map onto the objectives and which define the path of inquiry of this research:

1. Which philosophical frames are available to social research and economics in particular? What are their epistemological and methodological bases? What are their shortcomings and their strengths? Which approach is the most appropriate to analyse socio-economic reality with particular emphasis on the processes and dynamics of the property market?
2. What explanations of economic transformation have been given by urban economic theories? What are their shortcomings and their strengths? Is it possible to develop a holistic urban economic theory that incorporates an explicit analysis on property market processes and outcomes? What is the relation between the property market as an institution and the wider urban environment? How does the property market influence the course of the urban economy? Which research approaches are suitable to explore these issues in concrete practice?
3. How can the developed concepts be incorporated into a research design and their relations explored in practice? In particular, which attributes best describe the wider urban institutional framework and which dimensions of the property market institution define the provision of the built environment? What kinds of information are required and which methods and techniques are more appropriate for empirical analysis? How should empirical analysis be structured and which specific relations and mechanisms should it focus on?

1.3 Organisation of the book

The arguments of this book are deployed in six chapters. Chapter 2 starts by examining the main philosophical traditions in the social sciences. This provides the basis to consider the analytical frameworks that are available in economics. The chapter discusses their conceptual underpinnings and methodological practices and critically assesses their deficiencies and limitations. This enables the identification of appropriate conceptual and methodological cornerstones for the development of a holistic framework that advances understanding of the processes through which the built environment is provided and the way it affects urban economic potential (developed in Chapter 4).

Chapter 3 reviews the extensive literature on urban economic change and the provision of the built environment to identify knowledge gaps and possible research agendas. It starts by outlining the processes, contextual trends and emerging patterns of urban socio-economic reorganisation, identified by researchers independent of their methodological stance. This essentially descriptive analysis of urban transformation is put under scrutiny on the basis of the theoretical interpretations provided by the main frameworks of economic thought. This discussion provides a range of theoretical insights into the transformation of spatial structures, the provision of the built environment, the operation of the property market and the role these all play in urban economic development.

Building on these insights, Chapter 4 develops a holistic framework to enrich the conceptualisation of the property market as an institution and to specify its links with the urban economy. In particular, drawing on the philosophical approach of critical realism, the chapter first delineates the ontological and epistemological underpinnings of the developed research programme. Next, key critical realist principles are combined with the institutionalist insights of economic organisation to construct a three-layer ontological framework discussing the institutional nature of urban socio-economy. Finally, a rich theoretical framework for the exploration of urban economic organisation is laid down, where emphasis is placed both on the wider institutional environment and on the specific mechanisms, processes and dynamics of the property market. The interrelation between the property market process and the wider institutional environment is explored, particularly in terms of efficiency in providing appropriate property market institutions and outcomes which support urban economic potential.

Building on the holistic research programme developed in Chapter 4, Chapter 5 provides an analytical framework that translates the developed theory into an agenda for concrete research and practice. A two-level research design is put forward. The first level examines in a conventional manner the relation between economic and property market outcomes, while the second provides an in-depth institutional analysis of the market process. To this end, the developed concepts are operationalised, the kind of information needed is determined, the appropriate techniques for data collection are identified, and the processes and methods for analysis are specified. This research design provides a blueprint for any empirical case study.

Chapter 6 concludes the book. Here, with reference to the overall research aims and objectives, the developed philosophical, conceptual and analytical frameworks are evaluated. This provides a judgement on the validity, reliability and generalizability of the overall framework and the associated research design. Finally, in the light of the key findings, directions and recommendations for further research in the area are provided.

Notes

1 This book is written mainly from the perspective of the commercial property market. However, the arguments raised are applicable to all property markets.

2 The term 'provision' is used throughout this book to signify the production, distribution, use, exchange and maintenance of land and built structures.

2 Philosophies and analytical frameworks

2.1 Introduction

Scientific inquiry in any academic discipline takes place within a framework provided by a philosophy on that discipline. These philosophical foundations, which are acknowledged either implicitly or explicitly by all researchers, provide the logical and methodological bases for any sound social research and the evaluation of the validity of the results so obtained.

This chapter begins by setting up the analytical assumptions and essential elements of philosophy in general and then proceeds to examine the four philosophical traditions in social science, namely, empiricism, positivism, humanism and structuralism. Their ontological, epistemological and methodological assumptions are discussed and their strengths and weaknesses are pointed out. Based on this discussion, the chapter then moves to examine three analytical frameworks that are available in economics: the mainstream, the structuralist and the institutionalist. Here, the conceptual postulates of each school are outlined and their goals, methodological practices and research designs are presented. The last section summarises the findings and concludes the chapter.

2.2 The philosophies in social science

Philosophy is a term not easily defined, even by philosophers. Katouzian (1980) argues that it involves the consideration and discussion of the logic and the methods of reasoning and argument, whereas Peet (1998: 5) describes it as "...an abstract way of thinking which employs logic to organise imaginaries, beliefs, and notions of purpose into formal systems of understanding". In this sense, philosophies are perceived as self-evaluating modes of understanding the world which involve the basic positions that people employ in their life to assess what is true and what statements can be made about reality. The aim is to gain insights into their social context, to comprehend other societies and to make sense of social change.

The essential features of philosophy are the ontological and epistemological assumptions which together provide the framework for defining the nature of knowledge. Ontology deals with the theory of existence, examining what really exists, as opposed to what appears to exist, but does not. By studying the kinds of things that exist and the way they relate to each other, it aims to provide answers to questions such as what the world must be like for knowledge to be possible, or what can be accepted as real or true 'facts'. Epistemology, on the other hand, involves the theory of knowledge aiming to provide answers to questions such as what constitutes valid knowledge and how it can be obtained. Ontology and epistemology are used to define the methodology, which represents a set of concepts, procedures and techniques that collectively indicate how argument and research are carried out within particular disciplinary boundaries.

In the social sciences and humanities a number of philosophies have been suggested and employed by researchers over time; these can be broadly summarised within four philosophical paradigms. These are empiricism, positivism, humanism and structuralism. It is important to highlight that, although a clear categorisation of the philosophical arguments is postulated here, in reality the boundaries between these traditions are not so evident and a certain amount of diffusion exists.

The material upon which this section is based include the work by Katouzian (1980), Johnston (1986, 1997), Cloke *et al.* (1991), Bunnin and Tsui-James (1996), May (1997), Peet (1998), Audi (1999) and Johnston *et al.* (2000).

2.2.1 Empiricism

Empiricism is the philosophy of science that accords a privilege to empirical observations over theoretical statements. The main principle is that knowledge comes from experience, based on the senses and particularly on direct observation. On this basis, emphasis is placed on the strategic role of scientific observation, where experience and introspection are given precedence over theoretical statements.

Its ontological argument asserts that the things that exist are only those which we can experience. Anything else, including values, beliefs, intentions and emotions, are rejected as metaphysical speculation. Accordingly, its epistemological assumption maintains that all knowledge can be gained through experience without any reference to theoretical statements. Empiricism asserts that testing is possible (through experience), assuming that reality can be observed and described in a neutral, objective and value-free manner that allows facts to speak for themselves. Based on this, its methodology concerns the collection, organisation and presentation of the experienced facts, where emphasis is placed on issues of accuracy.

The main strength of empiricism lies in its descriptive power and its ability to organise observed phenomena. This is actually the first step in the development of science, which allows the researcher to put things in context. However, its blind emphasis on description without any explanatory or analytical aspiration constitutes a significant weakness of the approach. Besides this, the assumptions of objectivity, truthfulness and neutrality on the part of the researcher have been heavily criticised.

2.2.2 Positivism

The philosophical foundations of positivism remain similar to those of empiricism. However, unlike empiricism, positivism seeks not only to describe experienced facts, but goes further to explain why they exist. This is done by developing empirical generalisations and statements of law-like character, which provide the basis for the formation of an overall theoretical structure.

The ontological position of positivism is that reality is present in appearances, which are independent of the observer. The world consists of agreed evidence that can be acquired through objective observation and direct measurement. Its epistemology consequently argues that knowledge is gained through experience, but this experience should be firmly established as verifiable evidence on which all researchers will agree. On these grounds its methodology is a hypothetico-deductive process towards explanation that is based on the verification principle. According to this, a statement is scientifically meaningful only when it is capable of verification.

Positivist science is a cumulative process, whereby knowledge is acquired in a structured manner so that every additional piece contributes to the general comprehension of the world. In this sense, scientific theories would be progressively unified and integrated into a single system of knowledge and truth. Investigation starts with the formation of a hypothesis. This is an empirical proposition of how things should be under certain conditions and assumptions and it is deduced from personal experience (empirical observations) and existing theories. The hypothesis is then tested against empirical data using probability theory and statistics. If the result is positive, a further scientific generalisation (or universal law) is provided, advancing explanation and prediction and improving the existing theoretical edifice.

This description of positivist science outlines the basis of a unified approach which, though developed almost entirely by and for the natural sciences, has been adapted for the social sciences. The assumptions on which positivist social sciences were built can be described according to Johnston (1986: 30–1) by one sentence: human society is organised in determinate ways as "…human behaviour is subject to the operation of laws of cause and effect, and the nature of these laws can be identified by the process of hypothesis-testing and verification against empirical evidence".

Since its inception, several standpoints have been established within positivism, all drawn on the same philosophical and methodological principles outlined here. In relation to economics and property-related research, two main strands of positivism can be identified: logical positivism and behaviourism.

Whereas positivism is the search for generalisations via a rigorous procedure, logical positivism asserts that this is the only path to knowledge, which provides a rational solution to all problems and, therefore, a sound basis for social engineering. Any statement which defies empirical verification (such as value judgements or ethical or moral positions) is rejected as either meaningless or tautological.[1] Concerning the ways of obtaining knowledge, logical positivism regards empirical observation as well as logical and mathematical/statistical analyses as the only methods of scientific discovery.

Behaviourism, on the other hand, is more interested in the examination, explanation and prediction of the behaviour of individuals and groups. Although consistently positivist (in the sense that it accepts that people are responders to exogenous stimuli), it appears sceptical of the deterministic perception of human behaviour and, particularly, of theories that espouse undetectable mechanistic explanations of how society works. On this basis, a 'normative' orientation to positivist analysis is introduced where emphasis is placed on processual rather than structural explanations. This is interpreted in methodological terms by more direct and systematic observations on human behaviour, using the inductive approach and employing empirical studies to 'measure' behaviour and examine how it came about.

The significance of positivism lies in the fact that it provides the basis for the development of laws and theories, advancing explanation by improving knowledge of society, rather than through accumulations of facts as with empiricism. Moreover, the ability to provide predictions enables the society to make forecasts and so to consider the means for managing social change towards certain ends. However, positivism has been fiercely criticised on a number of grounds. First, and similarly to empiricism, by artificially separating the observer from the observed and by asserting the value-neutrality of the former it creates a false sense of science objectivity. Second, it rejects any consideration of social, aesthetic, ethical and generally metaphysical questions, leaving no room for the consideration of values or how society is actually organised. In addition, the claim of the supply of universal, law-like theories has been contested on the basis of their ahistorical and aspatial nature. Moreover, by emphasising the use of mathematics, statistics and quantitative techniques it fosters a belief that there are technical solutions to all problems, which is hardly the case.

2.2.3 Humanism

Humanism is an umbrella term to embrace a range of philosophies in the social sciences which have been developed since the turn of the twentieth century (parallel with the structuralist philosophies; see later), in part as a reaction to the 'objective', mechanistic and deterministic view espoused by positivism. The essential feature of humanism is its anthropocentric approach to the social sciences. For Schiller (1907: 12), humanism represents a simple philosophical viewpoint that discusses problems concerning human beings "...striving to comprehend a world of human experience by the resources of human minds". As all of the intellectual materials available to make sense of the world are indelibly human attributes and products, this implies that the world itself is nothing but the sum of human experience, perception and consciousness.

The ontology of the humanistic philosophy asserts that what exists is that which people perceive to exist. Reality, therefore, is a social reproduction in which meaning arises out of human consciousness, perception and behaviour.

This informs an epistemological argument which maintains that knowledge is obtained subjectively through the curious instrument of the human mind in a world of meanings created entirely by individuals. Based on such philosophical positions the methodology of humanism involves the investigation of these 'personal' worlds with an emphasis on individuality and subjectivity, which are ascribed to both the observer and the observed. Such a philosophical approach necessitates a shift from the conventional reliance on the principles of statistical inferences towards a more 'sensitive', qualitative and hermeneutic analysis. The aim is not to advance a positivist type of explanation and predictive power, but to improve the understanding of humans and their behaviour through intuition and imaginative interpretation. This is achieved by utilising case studies (which are regarded as unique and idiosyncratic) and employing contextual interpretation of subjectively meaningful human action.

From the several strands that have been developed within humanism, pragmatism deserves special attention for its significant influence on economic thought. Pragmatism is a philosophical movement developed in the USA during the late nineteenth and early twentieth centuries by Charles S. Peirce and William James and, later, by John Dewey. It is based on the fundamental humanistic axiom that actions are structured by meanings which are subjective interpretations of the world, but it goes further to argue that these interpretations are evaluated in terms of their experiential and practical implications (James, 1907; Dewey, 1929). Choices are therefore made based on criteria of expedience and in the light of experience, providing a standard for the determination of truth in the case of statements, rightness in the case of actions and value in the case of appraisals. Knowledge, on these grounds, is perceived as the product of an activity directed to the fulfilment of human purposes and a true (or 'warranted') belief, concept or theory is known to be such by the consequences of its employment rather than by any ontological foundations.

The core idea of pragmatism comes from Peirce, who sees an intrinsic connection between rational cognition and rational purpose on the basis that the entire meaning of an idea is to be found in the totality of its 'conceivable effects': "Consider what effects, which might conceivably have practical bearings, we conceive the object of our conception to have. Then, our conception of these effects is the whole of our conception of the object" (Peirce, 1878: 294). This rule, known as the pragmatic maxim, remained unnoticed for twenty years, until it was taken up initially by James and later on by Dewey, giving to pragmatism a further direction and developing it as a determinate philosophical tradition.[2]

Approaching the fundamental philosophical questions of knowledge and truth, pragmatism maintains that thought and inquiry are psychologically and socially evolved modes of adaptation to experience, aiming at the resolution and adjustment of 'problematic situations' (James, 1907; Dewey, 1939a). Truth is, accordingly, what experience impels and compels humans to believe, judged by its purposive success in the course of human conduct to provide a basis for consistency, stability and certainty in human affairs. No truth is ever final, and knowledge should be always subject to further investigation, critical scrutiny and questioning aimed towards the resolution of practical problems that are 'urgent' and meaningful in actual life. This led to the deployment of the 'instrumental value theory' by Dewey (1939b), which views thoughtful action and inquiry as instruments or tools in producing ideas, beliefs, doctrines or theories for the overall betterment of human life.

Pragmatism has clearly the most interpersonal and evolutionary orientation of the humanistic approaches.[3] It postulates that society (whole) is prior to the individual (part) and so individual agency can be understood in terms of the behaviour of the wider social groups of which the individual is a part. The transitional conception that pragmatism holds for thought, experience and knowledge indicates also the ever-evolving nature of the social world, understood as the product of the ongoing interaction between humans and their social and physical environment. This process, although it manifests considerable spontaneity and fortuity (something that Peirce calls 'tychism'), is guided and informed by the 'practical instrumentality' of knowledge within a context of long-established social habits and institutions.

As regards its methodological implications, pragmatism stresses the need for openness, flexibility and plurality. On these grounds, the approach has not been tied to specific techniques, although Johnston (1986) asserts that a preference towards 'participant observation' is apparent. This involves the researcher becoming part of the society being studied in order to appreciate its beliefs and the way that these are being reconstructed in the context of the effects of their application.

Criticism of humanism is two-fold. The first criticism is largely positivist, arguing that humanist approaches are subjective and thus unscientific, with little relevance to the identification of objective conditions in the real world. The second criticism comes mainly from structuralism. It asserts that humanism gives excessive privilege to human beings in the sense that they are ascribed with too much freedom to act, whereas, in essence, their behaviour is very much constrained by existing social structures (such as class and gender) on which individuals have very little or no control. As a result, the humanist perception of the world is artificial and distorting.

2.2.4 Structuralism

The hallmark of structuralism is the principle that certain structures, which exist independently of human perception, set causal mechanisms that account for all observable phenomena in society. Consequently, any explanation for observed (surface) phenomena must be sought in these real, but unobservable, structures.

The ontology of structuralism assumes a stratified reality comprised by structures, causal mechanisms and empirical appearances. Structures and mechanisms are not directly observable since appearances reflect, but are the resultant of exercised forces (some of which could be counterbalancing). Such a stratified reality can therefore only be conceived in full, thorough thought processes.

In terms of epistemology this means that knowledge is not obtained through the accumulation of evidence, but by the development of theories which put together structures, mechanisms and appearances. These theories attempt to explain the driving forces of society and to enable an understanding of our experiences. Based on such positions, structuralist methodology involves the construction of theories which tentatively account for the forces giving rise to the observed phenomena, but which cannot be verified (or falsified) due to the complex, intertwined and often counteractive nature of the forces and the inexistence of conclusive, purely force-driven, empirical evidence. A real test is whether these theories continue to correspond to our experiences and can therefore form the basis for acceptable and viable practices. However, as theories are in essence not verifiable, they need to be continually redefined (in a dialectical interplay with experiences), acquiring new forms and transcending the limits of their previous formulations. In this sense, theories can be seen as open processes rather than as final products.

Structural approaches take a wide variety of viewpoints. With regard to economic and property-related research, three main strands are identified, differentiated by the degree of importance they ascribe to human agency. The first, Marxism, pays less attention to the individual. The other two strands, structuration theory and critical realism, acknowledge the mutual constitution of 'structure' and 'agency', although the former does not share with the latter the notion of the temporal priority of structure over the individual. On these grounds, both structuration theory and critical realism suggest a merger or dialogue between structuralism and humanism.

The philosophy of Marxism originates from the voluminous writings of Karl Marx and Friedrich Engels (Marx, 1959 [1844], 1970 [1859], 1973 [1857–1861]; Engels, 1946 [1886], 1947 [1876–1878], 1964 [1925]; Marx and Engels, 1956 [1844], 1970 [1846]). The Marxist philosophical basis (known as dialectical materialism) consists of two elements: materialism and dialectics. Materialism holds that all phenomena are essentially material. This means that matter and nature constitute an objective reality that existed long before, and still exists, outside and independent of human beings. Humans came to be through an evolutionary process of material development and perfection and, therefore, their minds, thoughts and consciousness flow out of, are created by, are dependent on, or are reflections or forms of matter. On these grounds, paraphrasing Marx, 'being is not determined by consciousness, but consciousness by being'. Putting it succinctly, materialism postulates the objective existence and interconnectedness of mind and matter, but it ascribes an ontological primacy to the latter over the former.

The Marxist view of the world is not only materialist, but also dialectical. This means that all natural and social reality is, and can only be understood, as a process (or, more precisely, as a complex of processes) where change is the result of a constant conflict between opposites arising from the internal contradictions inherent among the elements in all objects. In these terms, development is driven by three fundamental principles (or laws) of dialectics, namely, the interpenetration (unity and conflict) of opposites, the transformation of quantity into quality, and the negation of the negation. The first principle signifies that everything in existence is a unity of opposites, something which ascribes each entity with an internal auto-dynamic impetus for constant movement and change. According to the second principle, change occurs in small incremental quantitative developments that lead to abrupt qualitative leaps (transformations), whereby new, higher level entities or forms of reality emerge. The third principle indicates that this new higher level entity created, though being transcendentally different, retains some elements of the original form of reality from which it has emerged (while other original elements are totally obliterated). Therefore the first principle of dialectics discloses the source of development, the second the mechanism of development, and the third the direction and result of development. The overall process can be seen as a cyclical (or, rather, spiral) movement of thesis, antithesis and synthesis, where development proceeds in the following way. At the beginning it appears as a cohesive entity (thesis), which bears its own opposite (antithesis). The situation builds up by small accumulative changes, giving birth to a new entity (synthesis), which constitutes a higher, richer state of development as it contains elements of both its initial form and the unity of it with its opposite.

Carrying these ontological and methodological premises over to the social domain, Marxism presents 'the materialist conception of history' (Marx, 1970 [1859], 1973 [1857–1861]), also known as historical materialism. Historical materialism aims to uncover the structural laws of human society and historical development, arguing that their base lies in the material conditions of human existence (that is, the ways humans work on nature to produce the means of their subsistence). In the course of providing the material requirements of their life, humans enter into definite relations (such as property relations or division of labour) that correspond to the level and character of the means of production (called productive forces) of their time. The total sum of these production relations of society constitutes the economic base (called infrastructure) which provides the real foundation for the development of the state, law, ideology, culture, religion, morality and arts (which collectively constitute the superstructure). These elements comprise a complex structured whole that determines individuals' beliefs, preferences, objectives, choices, and so forth. In short, economic relations (infrastructure) are reflected in social practices (superstructure) providing definite forms of human consciousness and behaviour. Such a position, it is argued, does not imply economic determinism as it is the human agents who (though indirectly and within limits) maintain and modify these social practices through the (different) ways in which they interpret the economic conditions of their time.

Generally, for Marxism, the unfolding of history is the result of the conscious (and rational) behaviour of individuals determined by material (economic) considerations. The essential feature (and driving force) of the development and dynamics of the economic infrastructure is the idea of the dehumanisation or alienation of people from aspects of their human nature. This gives rise to determinant contradictions, materialised as conflicts (between capital and labour), struggles (between classes) and crises within (the capitalist) society. Marx adopts the dialectic approach on the resolution of such contradictions, where development proceeds in the commonly known spiral sequence of thesis–antithesis–synthesis.

Summarising, it can be said that Marxist analysis sees human society and history, thought and behaviour from an ultimately materialistic viewpoint (referring to matter or economic relations), where development follows dialectic processes. The major strength of this approach lies in its demonstration of the need for a new perspective in social research paying due attention to structural elements and dialectic dynamics. Marxism, however, has been criticised for an overly abstract and deterministic (structural) conception of human existence, which leaves little room for autonomy in consciousness, thought, behaviour and agency, for an excessive emphasis on material conditions and for a functional, mechanical and economistic understanding of history, society and economy.

Structuration theory, developed by Giddens (1979, 1981, 1984), attempts to steer a middle course between Marxist structural determinism and humanist voluntarism. It acknowledges that pre-existing structural practices determine human behaviour (missing from humanism), but argues that these structural elements are constantly defined, modified or sustained by human agency (ignored by Marxism). The starting point of structuration theory is the theorisation of human agents as knowledgeable of social practices (at a conscious or subconscious level), reflexive (continuously monitoring all social action), purposive (with conscious and unconscious motives and the ability to elaborate discursively upon them), powerful (with transformative capacity) and rational (with the ability to explain the reasons of their actions). In these terms, agency is defined as an intentional action, in the sense that actors are driven by motives and are able to reflectively monitor human conduct and rationalise their actions, which, nevertheless, is affected by the unintended consequences of (other or others') actions and the unacknowledged conditions of further acts to which these give rise.[4] This is referred to as the 'stratification model of action'.

Structuration theory assumes a stratified ontology comprised by systems, structures and agents. Systems consist of the totality of regular social practices which emerge in time and space as a result of reproduced relations between agents. Structures, on the other hand, encompass the recursively organised 'rules' and 'resources'[5] that humans utilise in their daily activities to produce and reproduce these social practices. Structures, unlike systems, do not exist in time and space, but have only a virtual existence (as 'memory traces' in socialised actors) in that they are drawn upon and reconstituted continuously in practice. As such, they would no longer exist if agency and interaction were to end.

Rather than being two distinct phenomena (i.e. a dualism), structuration theory regards structure and agency as mutually and symmetrically constitutive of each other (through recurrent practices), with neither of them having any ontological or analytical priority over the other (this is the celebrated notion of 'duality of structure'). This is because the rules and resources drawn upon in the production and reproduction of social action are at the same time the means of system reproduction. In a sense, structures are both media and products of human agency and of the social practices constituting social systems. Structure, therefore, is the channel (medium and outcome) through which a social system affects human agency and human agency affects the social system.

The process governing the continuity and transmutation of structures and, therefore, the reproduction of systems, is structuration. This is characterised as a 'dialectic of control', where structure rules are generated and reconstituted by agents engaged in power relations and provide the framework within which agents interact with each other to reproduce and redefine those rules and power relations. Although, in this context, abrupt transformation is not ruled out, emphasis is placed by Giddens on the important role that the routinisation of activities plays in providing a sense of personal security (called 'ontological security') that ensures social stability, order and continuity.

Structuration theory has been criticised on many accounts and, primarily, for its inability to transcend the two philosophical approaches that it set out to merge (Callinicos, 1989). Scholars have also questioned the robustness and validity of its conception of structure. Thompson (1984), for example, has disputed the clarity in explaining structure in terms of rules and resources, Kilminster (1991) for perceiving structure as internal to actors, and Guy and Henneberry (2000) for emphasising the constraining character of structure. Others have criticised structuration theory for oscillating between a hyperactivity of agency and a rigid coherence of structural properties (Johnston *et al.*, 2000), for collapsing agency into action (Philo, 1984), for collapsing structure into rules and resources (Johnston *et al.*, 2000), or for obscuring those dimensions of agency that fall within or outside the polar positions of intentional activity and reactive behaviour (Cloke *et al.*, 1991). Finally, a major strand of criticism comes from critical realists, mainly Archer (1995), who question the idea of the duality of structure and the single level of reality that it implies.

Critical (or transcendental) realism is a philosophical position closely associated with the work of Bhaskar (1975, 1979, 1986, 1989). The starting point in Bhaskar's philosophy is the distinction between 'transitive' and 'intransitive' objects. Antecedently established facts, theories, models and the like are considered as transitive objects in the sense that they are 'artificially' made into knowledge by the science of the day. Intransitive, on the other hand, refers to the entities, relations, mechanisms and processes that do not depend on human agency for their existence. These objects are neither observable events (as in empiricism and positivism), nor human perception of phenomena (as in humanism), but real structures which exist and operate independently of our knowledge, our experience and the (contingent) conditions which allow their manifestation. Our cognition, however, of these entities depends on the processes by which they are known (i.e. it is concept or human dependent). This is the celebrated notion of epistemological relativism, which critical realism shares with humanistic approaches.

Overall critical realism sees the (social and natural) world constituted by actual events, by our experience or perception of those events, and by the structures and mechanisms that underlie these phenomena. Reality is therefore stratified into three domains that are ontologically irreducible and unsynchronised with one another: the 'empirical', which is concerned solely with experiences and the world as it is perceived; the 'actual', which is concerned with events and experiences (accepting that an event may be interpreted in different ways by different individuals); and the 'real', which is concerned with structures and mechanisms that, although not directly observable, determine the events and their appearances. Thus critical realism maintains that the empirical is only a subset of the actual, which itself is a subset of the real.

In discussing the relationship between structure and agency in the social realm, critical realism puts forth a 'relational conception' and a 'transformational model' of social reality (Bhaskar, 1979; Lawson, 1994, 1998b). The relational conception assumes that all social forms, structures, systems, and so on, depend upon, or presuppose, social relations. The transformational model assumes that humans in their daily activities unconsciously reproduce, and occasionally transform, the structures governing their activities. Thus a social structure is the often unacknowledged, but unavoidable, precondition for individual action, as well as an often unintended, but inevitable, outcome of individual agency taken in total. However, neither element (structure or agency) can be identified with, reduced to, or explained completely in terms of the other.

Critical realism has been attacked on many grounds. Hodgson (1999a) has criticised the fact that, by downplaying the role of institutions (which are a special type of social structure) in determining human behaviour, it has fallen into causal dualism and agent indeterminacy.[6] Marxists have argued that the conceptual tools necessary to analyse the philosophical 'reality' put forward have not been made available. Others, such as Gottdiener (1987), have regretted the lack, on the part of the approach, of an explicit theory of social process and spatial organisation. Concerns have also been raised about the methodology put forward. Gottdiener (1987) and Harvey (1987), for instance, have questioned the distinction between constitutive structures and contingent conditions as arbitrary and practically unattainable (as factors constitutive of the powers of an object at one time may be conditional to their exercise at another). Others, including realists such as Allen (1983), Pratt (1995) and Yeung (1997), have acknowledged a shortage on the method side because, for all the sophisticated philosophy of critical realism, the methods made available to implement or practise the approach "basically consists of the sometimes unhappy mix of orthodox extensive research methods ... with relative untried intensive methods and a 'dash' of abstract theorising" (Cloke *et al.*, 1991: 168)

The methodology put forward by structuralism distinguishes between 'abstract' and 'concrete' analysis (Althusser, 1969; Marx, 1973 [1857–1861]; Aglietta, 1979; Moos and Dear, 1986; Sayer, 1992). Abstract analysis refers to the level of the 'real', making claims about the constitution of, and internal relations between, generative structures, their causal powers and their essential connection to the specific object of study. It represents a way of focusing on specific parts of reality (the most essential aspects of the phenomenon under investigation) to provide a conceptual framework that advances understanding of how and what essentially makes things happen. Abstract analysis is continuously and dialectically informed by concrete analysis. The latter concerns the factual level of experiences, the empirical domain. It involves the analysis of actual events aiming to discern the generative structures and mechanisms that are in operation, the actual contingent conditions under which they have been activated, as well as the manner of their joint articulation in the production of the specific event or situation in question. In this sense, 'the concrete' is seen as the combination of many diverse forces and processes that are actualised in historically and spatially specific configurations under contingently related conditions and, precisely due to this incidental nature, is only determinable through empirical analysis.

Concluding our discussion on structuralism, we must highlight that critical realism and structuration theory share some common philosophical views which represent a middle course, or a dialogue, between Marxism and humanism. They both accept a structuralist theorisation of the world (that explanation of manifest phenomena should be sought in the real 'deeper' structures) and acknowledge the mutual constitution of structure and agency. Moreover, in line with Marxism, they reject 'methodological individualism' (the notion that societies can be explained solely in terms of individuals alone) on the grounds that humans are essentially social beings. However, in line with humanism, they argue against Marxist 'methodological collectivism', as they retain a central place for powerful individual agency by insisting that the human agent is the actual mediator and regulator of all structural forces.

However, structuration theory and critical realism have some significant differences and they should be confronted as two competing, rather than as alternative, philosophical perspectives (Archer, 1995). A distinctive feature of realism is its multi-level or stratified ontology, in which levels are differentiated through the phenomenon of emergence.[7] On this basis, realists perceive human agency and social structure as two separate layers of social reality, each one with its own emergent properties and causal powers. The denial of emergence by structuration theory entails a single level of reality and, consequently, a single time frame in the constitution and operation of structure and agency. This prevents the incorporation of proper historic time in its analysis and has serious implications for the conceptualisation of structure and agency. For Bhaskar, but not for Giddens, human agency and social structure, although existentially interdependent, are essentially distinct; people and society are not conflated into a singular 'duality' and are not two aspects of the same process, but rather are radically different kinds of things.

2.3 The methodological frameworks in economic thought

Explanations for economic and spatial phenomena are sought by a number of different schools in economics, drawing on the philosophical perspectives presented in the previous sections. Generally, three major methodological frameworks can be identified: the mainstream or orthodox approach (a synthesis of neoclassical microeconomics with Chicago and Keynesian macroeconomic perspectives); the structuralist; and the institutionalist (Colander, 2000).

2.3.1 Mainstream orthodoxy: neoclassical economics

It is widely accepted that the neoclassical school of economic thought is currently the dominant programme in economics[8] (Clark, 1998; Dequech, 2008). This is evident from the fact that the vast majority of university courses are overwhelmingly grounded on neoclassical principles, especially for microeconomics (Gee, 1991; Davis, 2006). On these grounds, the term is widely used to describe the overall mainstream orthodoxy in the discipline (and in this sense it is applied henceforth).

The philosophical foundations of neoclassical economics are attributed to positivism and, in particular, to logical positivism (Katouzian, 1980). However, over the course of time, the school has showed a remarkable degree of adaptability that has enabled it to embrace and assimilate other methodological positions and viewpoints. Thus, in its present form, it comprises a strange fusion between logical positivism, the methodological thesis of Milton Friedman and the Popperian position on falsification.[9]

Following positivism, mainstream orthodoxy rejects history as a useless source of, not only economic, but of any kind of scientific knowledge (Katouzian, 1980). It also draws a clear distinction between positive and normative economics, the former concerning statements of fact and the latter statements of value. As normative questions cannot be settled solely by an appeal to observation, they are discarded as meaningless 'nonscience', confining neoclassical inquiry to positive issues. Such a stance is also supported by the view (established by Friedman, 1953) that a positive agreement among economists would help to clarify debate and even work towards the establishment of a wider, normative consensus.

Neoclassical economics borrows from positivism its hypothetico-deductive mode of explanation, more concisely known as deductivism (Blaug, 1980, 1992). This is described as a structure of logical arguments where attempts are made to explain an actual event, or a state of affairs, by deducing a statement about it (*explanandum*) from a set of initial conditions plus at least one universal law (*explanans*). Such a law is a statement of universal regularities or constant conjunctions of the form 'whenever event (type) x occurs, then event (type) y also occurs'.[10]

This structure of scientific explanations indicates that the operation 'explanation' involves the same rules of logical inference as the operation 'prediction'; the only difference is that explanations come after events, whereas predictions come before (Blaug, 1980, 1992). On the basis of this symmetry, which enables explanation and prediction to merge (in a sense to become two faces of the same coin), neoclassical economics disregards the former, placing due emphasis on the latter. Such a stance is also supported by Friedman (1953), who bluntly asserts that the ultimate goal of positive economics is the provision of theories (or hypothesis) that yield meaningful predictions, whereas the quality of the prediction becomes the sole criterion for the assessment of the theory's validity. Whether the assumptions on which these theories are based are realistic or not, Friedman claims, is of little concern, as they never are. The critical question is whether they are sufficiently good approximations for the purpose in hand, i.e. to furnish sufficiently accurate predictions.

Having accepted that correct predictions indicate valid explanations, scientific inquiry in neoclassical economics proceeds by tentatively accepting those theories that exhibit a high degree of correspondence to reality. Economic hypotheses must therefore be both empirically testable (the so-called empirical testability axiom) and verified against empirical evidence. The latter, however, is a tremendous (if not impossible) task, even if we accept that statements about single events can be safely generalised. Alternatively, it is much easier to show that a statement has not been refuted or falsified. This terminology belongs to Sir Karl Popper, who maintains that the hallmark of scientific theory is its potential falsifiability, and thus shifts focus from the process of verification to that of falsification.[11] Incorporating this element into its mode of explanation, neoclassical inquiry begins with a priori true, logical statements (conjectures, hypotheses) which are testable and subject to falsification. When empirical tests fail to falsify such a statement, the latter is tentatively accepted as a theory, until it is falsified or replaced by a better theory.

In this attempt to test *explanandums* and deploy theories, mainstream economics espouses the view that all phenomena of interest are inherently quantifiable and subject to numerical representation (Dennis, 1994). On these grounds, a quantitative content is developed to hypothesised relationships connecting economic variables (variables which represent economic events or states of affairs) through the application of mathematical symbolism, mathematical models and statistical methods (mainly econometrics). This wholesale use of mathematical reasoning, symbolism, axiomatisation and method of deductive demonstration (referred to as mathematical formalism) is a substantial element of mainstream economics (Lawson, 2006; Dequech, 2008).

To sum up, mainstream orthodoxy maintains that the goal of economics is to develop universal theories (i.e. generally applicable to all times and places) which yield 'correct' predictions. Only the predictions or observable implications of a theory matter to its truth, whereby observability entails objective, reproducible experiments. Scientists have nothing to say about non-scientific, normative judgements and values. A theory is false if, and only if, one of its experimental implications proves false. In a similar vein, the assumptions on which a theory is based are valid (realistic or not) only as far as the corresponding theory provides accurate predictions.

The methodological stance of mainstream economics has been fiercely attacked by the heterodox schools. The first major area of criticism concerns the validity of the distinction between facts and values and the rejection of the latter as part of the economics' subject matter. In this respect, researchers have argued that both hypothesis building and the selection and analysis of facts follow certain procedures that are products of the human mind and so are value-laden[12] (Myrdal, 1958; Hodgson, 1988; Lawson, 1997a). The second stream of criticism condemns the neoclassical preoccupation with law-like statements and universal generalisations, and the mechanical, ahistorical, atemporal and dehumanised world view that these entail (Veblen, 1898a; Hodgson, 1988; Lawson, 1995; Edel, 1996). The counter arguments highlight the need for a more realistic perception of the economy that takes into account the complex relations between, and the unpredictable behaviour of, free-willed human agents. Finally, concerns are raised about the method that neoclassical economics puts forth. Here, the use (or, arguably, misuse) of mathematics and statistics to express economic propositions and to deduce seemingly valid inferences about economic phenomena has been widely criticised for its illusory attempt to formulate essentially non-deterministic and non-mathematical propositions (such as human dispositions) solely by means of mathematical formulae (Dennis, 1994; Downward *et al.*, 2002).

Having identified the methodological postulates of the neoclassical school, the discussion now turns to the core assumptions (or axiomatic propositions) on which its theoretical apparatus has been based. It is important to point out that these assumptions should not be seen in isolation as they reinforce and support each other. These can be summarised under the following headings: methodological individualism; rational economic man; and equilibrium state.

Methodological individualism can be defined as the doctrine which asserts that all social phenomena should be explained at the level of the individual agent, or as being the aggregative consequence of the decisions and choices made by independent and autonomous individuals. In this sense, the isolated individual is taken to be the founding stone of society and economy, whereas theories about social entities are reduced to theories or statements about individuals and their properties. Such a methodological position presupposes that human behaviour is in practice immutable. This means that tastes, wants, needs and purposes are given, fixed and predetermined by exogenous (to the matter of investigation) preference functions, which are not of scientific interest.

Criticism of this principle comes from the heterodox schools of economics which, by rejecting the idea that society is solely the sum of individuals, put into question neoclassical explanatory supremacy on the isolated individual alone (Hodgson, 1988; Lawson, 1995). Explanatory power, they argue, should also be given to social structures (typically defined as sets of interactive relations between individuals), avoiding, however, ascribing to any of them (structure or individual) any primacy in the explanation. Instead, a synthesis is proposed where equal explanatory status is attributed to both individual agency and social structure.

The assumption of 'rational economic man' (or *homo economicus*) is the hallmark of neoclassical economics. The concept presumes that humans are inherently egoistic, self-interested actors with an ability to make judgements aiming towards the fulfilment of well-identified ends. These concern the maximisation of their profits, utility, welfare, pleasure or, in general, of the satisfaction of their preferences (Hargreaves-Heap, 1994). Such a notion supposes a number of preconditions (Hollis, 1996): first, that humans have distinct ends (preferences) which are not only given (i.e. are beyond the compass of the investigation), but also are clearly distinguished from means and unaffected by them; second, that agents are perfectly informed and conscious of all the alternative choices; and, third, that is possible for humans (both in terms of information availability and mind capacity) to calculate the probability of all possible outcomes to establish the expected value of their acts (Hollis, 1996).

Homo economicus has been subject to extensive criticism on the basis of the deterministic and unrealistic way that it treats economic agents. As regards the latter, it has been argued that maximising behaviour is impossible due to information deficiencies and the limited computational ability of the human mind (Simon 1982). In turn, with regard to preference determinism and means–ends distinction, it has been claimed that they are erroneous and misleading. This is because human preferences and objectives (ends) are not static, but constantly defined and redefined on the basis of the chosen means, established beliefs and conditions faced (Tversky and Kahneman, 1986; Hodgson, 1988; Kahneman, 1994).

The last axiomatic assumption of neoclassical economics is the equilibrium state of the economy. This refers to an inherent tendency of the economic system (in essence, a trait in human behaviour due to the methodological individualism postulate) to stabilise at a state where economic forces (usually supply and demand) are in balance (Gee, 1991). This notion is so fundamental to neoclassical economics that it is used not only as a heuristic device to simplify economic analysis or to benchmark and compare real economies, but also as a system of logic for reasoning and argumentation (Fischer, 1986). Thus standard economic theory explores the properties of equilibrium or the movement towards some state of rest as instances of successive equilibria. In standard neoclassical analysis it is assumed that equilibrium under conditions of perfect competition provides the optimal outcome given the scarcity of resources. The notion of equilibrium also implies an absence of information deficiencies and of problems in the transaction process. Thus the availability of required information qualifies human agents to maximise rationality and, consequently, enables markets to clear instantaneously and without cost, thereby moving to equilibrium states.

Arguments against the equilibrium state come again from the heterodox schools. An often-raised point is that such a preoccupation prevents economics from developing a truly dynamic and realistic explanation of the workings of the economy (Veblen, 1898a; Harvey, 1973; Lawson, 1989). Moreover, equilibrium analysis has been dismissed for the rather deterministic and ahistorical view of the economic processes that it entails, as it seems to imply that, with appropriate manipulation of external conditions, any equilibrium state is achievable (Ayres, 1962).

Overall, it should be clear that neoclassical economics suffers from a number of weaknesses and limitations. On these grounds, it is surprising that the school has managed, not only to survive for so long, but also to remain the mainstream orthodoxy in economics. Why is this so? Perhaps the answer lies in its ability to respond to criticisms by adapting itself and assimilating its critics (Arnsperger and Varoufakis, 2006), or perhaps there might be political reasons behind it, reflecting the effort and resources spent on its establishment (Katouzian, 1980). Whatever the explanation, it seems that the neoclassical school has asserted its scientific status and authority and has become an ideology.

2.3.2 Heterodox approaches: structuralism

Over the last three decades or so it has become evident that mainstream economics cannot adequately explain the profound series of global economic crises that has occurred since the 1970s. In addition, there has been a growing controversy in philosophy and social science regarding the usefulness and applicability of law-like models and an increasing interest in the historical and spatial peculiarities in understanding and explaining socio-economic states of affairs. On these grounds, it is not surprising that heterodox approaches to economics have enjoyed an ideological renaissance and increased influence.

This section outlines the conceptual and methodological underpinnings of another set of analytical frameworks available in economics, which can be roughly referred to as structuralist on the basis that they all assign explanatory power (admittedly to a different degree) to unobservable structural forces that lie behind socio-economic phenomena. These are the Marxist (and neo-Marxist), structurationist and critical realist frameworks.

a Marxist and neo-Marxist

According to scholars (e.g. Scott, 1991; Luithlen, 1992; Edel, 1996), four key concepts comprise the methodological foundations of Marxist economics: historical materialism; the mode of production; the class struggle; and the theory of value.

The concept of historical materialism states that the development and change of society are determined by dialectic (evolutionary) laws grounded in the provision of the material means of human existence. The materialist element of the notion emphasises that societies are formed solely for the purpose of the collective provision of the material requirements of life, whereas the material conditions shape human consciousness, thought and action. The historical element indicates that social development and change are the result of progressive resolutions to the determinant contradictions that characterise social life. In this sense, society at any point in history can be properly understood by examining the conditions and contradictions of earlier times, which constitute the framework within which subsequent structures have evolved. The evolutionary force that steers the development of human society is dialectics, which constitutes a continuous dialogue between 'theses' and 'antitheses'.

The materialist analysis of human society indicates that the economic infrastructure provides the real foundation upon which the political, legal, social and cultural superstructure rises. On that basis, Marxists argue that changes in social arrangements are driven by changes in the way in which production is organised. This is known as the 'mode of production', which consists of two elements. The first is the material forces of production, comprising the physical means of production (resources, instruments) and the human labour power. The second is the relations of production, which concern specific social relations between humans (individuals or groups, or both) engaged in the production process. These include relations of power and control, of association and co-operation, and of ownership over the forces of production. Social relations are primarily defined in terms of social class, which is a group of people with a common relationship to the means of production and some perception of their similarity and common interest (called class consciousness). Marx (1976 [1867, 1885, 1894]) identifies four modes of production (ancient, feudal, capitalist and communist), which correspond to distinct stages in the progressive development of productive forces and represent four unique stages in the evolution of society. Evolution, he asserts, occurs in a dialectic manner. The production relations, which initially encourage the development of the productive forces, eventually become an obstacle to their further development. This creates a conflict between the forces and relations of production, demanding a transition to (or 'synthesis' of) a new mode of production.

In addition to the above perception, social transformation and development are also conceived in relation to the notions of social class and 'class struggle'. For Marx, social class is not simply a passive category to which individuals are assigned; it is the basis from which the entire consciousness of the individual is determined. Regarding the relations between classes, they are viewed as antagonistic or in conflict, pervading all aspects of the social order. Class antagonism in all instances arises from the exploitation of one class by another. 'Exploitation' has a precise meaning in Marxist economics and is derived from Marx's 'labour theory of value'. In simple terms this states that the production of commodities (which are essential to human existence) requires the application of labour to the physical means of production and, on these grounds, labour is the only source of value.[13] Marx, although recognising labour as a commodity itself, argued that it is the only one of all the inputs in the production process that has the ability to create value in excess of its subsistence or reproductive requirements (usually attributed as wages). This is called 'surplus value'[14] (i.e. the difference between use and exchange value) and it is its appropriation by the dominant class that Marx defines as exploitation.

Of the different modes of production, capitalism is the most extensively discussed and analysed. Its class structure comprises the proletariat (the working class) and the capitalists (the dominant class). The proletariat has no access to the means of production and thus workers are obliged to sell their labour power for their livelihood. The capitalists have control over the material means of production and the power to allocate labour to specific activities. Their aim is to reinvest and enlarge their wealth and, by so doing, to accumulate more capital. This can only be achieved by creating profit, which is the difference between the capitalist's total costs of production (i.e. the sum of the workers' wages and the money paid to employ and renew or increase the means of production) and the revenue derived from selling the commodities produced. The economic mode of capitalism that Marx developed in *Capital* (Marx, 1976 [1867, 1885, 1894]) is based on two abstract and complex analytical positions that are considered next: the theory of capitalist exploitation and the contradictory laws of motion of capitalism.

The capitalist exploitation of the proletariat indicates that capitalists, in their continuous quest for higher profits and capital accumulation, turn to the only source of surplus value, which is labour. Capitalists' wealth therefore comes from appropriation of the surplus value produced by the proletariat. An increase in the exploitation rate can be achieved, according to Marx, in two ways: directly, through the increase of the absolute surplus produced (e.g. by increasing the number of working hours); and indirectly by reducing the necessary element of labour time in commodity production (e.g. through advances in production technology, which involves investment by the capitalist class). The appropriation by capitalists of the value created by the proletariat inevitably informs the antagonistic relation between the classes, ensures the class struggle and, ultimately, constitutes the dialectic determining the evolution of capitalist society.

Although surplus value is achieved in the commodity production sphere, it can only be realised in the realm of commodity exchange where forces of competition apply. This competitive nature of capitalism compels each individual capitalist to increase the rate of exploitation as that is the only way to increase profit and capital accumulation. Marxists regard competition between different units of capital as executing the 'inner law of motion of capitalism'. However this law is subject to internal contradictions, which provoke crisis, recession and destruction in the capitalist system. This runs as follows. Under ever-mounting competitive pressures and with recurring crises, capitalists are compelled to expel labour from the process of production and replace it with machines. However, this increase in the 'organic composition of capital'[15] impairs the potential for creating value and, accordingly, surplus value. As profit ultimately feeds from surplus value, the rate of profit will tend to decline. This 'tendency for the rate of profit to fall' inevitably brings the system into a crisis as declining profits are speedily transformed into a lack of demand, a curtailment in activities, financial disruption and, generally, a downturn in the economy.

In the 1970s and 1980s, a series of developments in Marxist analysis became so distant from the original Marxist approach that they were set apart from the latter, forming what some scholars called the neo-Marxist school (Bovaird, 1993). Neo-Marxists pay less attention to the anachronistic concept of 'class' and seek to develop explanations of economic problems outside the deterministic framework imposed by Marx's historical materialism. Their aim is not to construct a theoretical model for the comprehensive explanation of the dynamics of the capitalist society (as traditional Marxists do), but to examine how certain contradictions within capitalist social formations necessitate change in certain areas of the economy and society.

Marxists in general have interpreted economic crises as representing turning points in the development of the capitalist system. However, there is a divergence of opinion with regard to the precise nature and causes of the crises. Traditional Marxists, following Marx, maintain that the origins of the crisis lie in the internal contradictions that characterise the dynamics of commodity production in capitalist economies. Neo-Marxists, on the other hand, argue that crises originate in the sphere of commodity exchange (Scott, 1991). They question Marx's idea of the tendency for the rate of profit to decline and argue that, under conditions of mature capitalism, the tendency is actually for the rate to rise. This is justified on the basis that capitalism in its maturity enters a monopoly phase where capitalists would become 'price-makers' rather than 'price-takers'. According to this view, crises result from what is called the absorption problem or, more commonly, underconsumption, which is perceived as a failure of consumption spending to grow at the rate necessary to enable capitalists to realise profits. This, in simple terms, describes the situation in which the growth in total demand in the economy is insufficient to meet the growth in total output. As a result, the excess productive capacity provokes a decline in capitalist investment and thereby initiates a cyclical downturn in the level of output and employment.

Another point of divergence between neo-Marxists and traditional Marxists lies in the doctrine of historical materialism. By and large, neo-Marxists question the idea that the structure of society is simply a passive reflection of technical conditions in the economic sphere. In this sense, they reject the economic deterministic element of historical materialism. Instead, society is seen as a reflection of the continual interaction between the legal, political and social aspects of the superstructure, on the one hand, and developments in the economic sphere on the other. Moreover, neo-Marxists contest the traditional explanation of the distribution of income based on Marx's labour theory of value. Rather, they assert that income distribution is the outcome of class struggle within the bounds imposed by the prevailing distribution of power in society. Thus it is suggested that, as the pattern of income distribution is affected by changes in the power relations in society, it can change independently of the arrangements surrounding commodity production. On these grounds, although neo-Marxists accept class exploitation as an innate feature of capitalism, they deem that the rate of exploitation cannot be determined solely with reference to the economic base of society. Social and political factors are seen as equally important.

The analytical concern of the neo-Marxist approaches is to explain the structure of capitalist economies and to analyse how this changes over time. One of the most important themes of this work is related to the discourse of Fordism and the debate concerning what follows it. Although a number of schools have contributed to this analysis, the most comprehensive approach is provided by the French regulation school[16] (Murdoch, 1995).

Theorisation within the school starts by accepting Marx's proposition that capitalism is characterised by certain fundamental contradictions, which should be resolved, controlled or regulated for successful capital accumulation to occur.

Various solutions to this proposition have emerged through time and space. In these terms, history is perceived as consisting of relatively stable periods of economic expansion in which the organisation of productive activity is in some general state of balance with the organisation of consumption. Each such stage of capitalist reproduction is characterised by a distinctive 'development mode', consisting of a 'regime of accumulation' and an associated 'mode of regulation' (Jessop, 1994). The regime of accumulation is a complementary pattern of production and consumption structures and relations which is reproducible over a long period, thus ensuring capital accumulation. The mode of regulation is an emergent ensemble of mutually interdependent organisational forms, social networks, laws, norms, procedures and patterns of conduct which can stabilise its associated accumulation regime.[17] Although each mode of regulation provides a coherent framework capable of sustaining the associated accumulation regime for a long period of time, it also tends to block the fluidity or flexibility of market forces, slowing down productivity and hampering the creation of surplus value (Aglietta, 1979). Each regime thus ends in a crisis period of major instability and stagnation, revealing the unsuitability of the regime to serve accumulation. To overcome the crisis a new mode of development must be established, in which new ways of organising production and consumption are provided along with corresponding sets of supportive institutions, organisational forms, norms and social practices.

The mode of development that dominated the post-war period is known as Fordism. This was characterised by Taylorism,[8] (the mass production of standardised products, mass marketing and mass consumption) and was supported by collective wage bargaining (which gave rise to sticky downwards wages and rigid work relations), credit-based consumerism and a heavily intervening Keynesian welfare state able to adjust demand to the supply-driven needs of mass production (Aglietta, 1979; Dunford, 1990). This mode has been in crisis under the weight of its own contradictions, with symptoms including changes in consumer behaviour, wage disparities (caused by the globalisation of the economy and the increased mobility of capital), international financial instability and the world 'debt crisis', and socio-political turmoil (Jessop, 1997). However, much debate has arisen regarding the labelling of the successor phase: is it 'neo-Fordism', simply an updated form of the essentially dominant mode, or 'post-Fordism', arguably a radically new regime of accumulation with its emerging mode of regulation?

Alongside the lines of the neo-Fordism thesis, Piore and Sabel (1984) introduced the model of 'flexible specialisation'. It is claimed that, through the period of Fordist crisis, certain sectors and regions managed not only to survive, but also to outperform their competitors. These particular industries and localities seem to exhibit a number of key distinguishable common features, such as flexible specialisation, the production of quality goods, high inter-firm (input–output) links, strong collective and territorial identity, and social and economic cohesion (Tickell and Peck, 1992, 1995). These characteristics contrast with the individualistic rationale that runs through the previous development mode and place emphasis on the elements of trust and personal commitment missing from markets, which can provide some stability and insurance against uncertainty. On these grounds it is argued that a model can be developed by which the world and urban economy can escape from the crisis (Lizieri, 1991).

The post-Fordism argument acknowledges the importance of flexibility in production systems, but goes much further to suggest that a new mode of development is under way. The primary role in explaining change is assigned to the collapse of mass markets, focusing attention on the wide range of forms and hybrids of flexibly specialised production and their social and institutional supporting conditions (Hirst and Zeitlin, 1991). Jessop (1997) designates this new mode as a 'Schumpeterian workfare post-national regime', which is characterised by a production structure that rests on innovation (in product, process, organisation and market), knowledge (individual, social, tacit and latent) and information technologies, and is supported by a highly skilled and flexible labour force, increased flows of international capital, self-regulated markets and a neoliberally retrenched state. The spatial reflection of the post-Fordism mode is the emergence of a 'new', highly polarised, global geography driven by new, dynamic and growth-promoting 'spaces' of production (such as technological innovation centres and financial centres) (Lipietz, 1992).

One of the main advantages of the Marxist and neo-Marxist approaches to economics is their substantial analysis of the structure and dynamics of the capitalist economy, where due emphasis is placed on the way in which production is organised to serve capital accumulation, giving rise to (and dialectically driven by) contradictions and crises within the capitalist society. However, the approach(es) have been attacked on many fronts, including philosophical and methodological arguments.

Marxism has received profound criticism (even by neo-Marxists) for the functionalist and determinist approach it puts forward. Giddens (1981), for instance, condemns Marxism for espousing a too mechanistic understanding of the historical processes and dynamics[19] as a result of the explanatory supremacy that it ascribes to structures (and, in particular, to the economic infrastructure) to the detriment of human agency. This originates from Marx, who perceives human action to be driven by class imperatives or, more generally, by economic (or material) considerations. On this basis, Hodgson (1988, 1999a) identifies an analytical gap in Marx's understanding of human agency, where the failure to connect individual action with specific structures results in a failure to explain individual motivation and human agency per se. This compels Marxism, as Hargreaves-Heap (1994) and Hodgson and Samuels (1994) argue, to assume some kind of *homo economicus* agents, who rationally calculate and maximise their interests (of course, under the constraints imposed by social structures). According to this naive rationalistic perception, all the information necessary for agency can, in principle, be collected and processed as if in a single human head. Thus, once people understand the structural elements that determine their existence, they will act accordingly as if they were one person.[20] This leads to another criticism related to the conception of equilibrium that Marxism espouses. At the micro-level Marxists (and neo-Marxists) reject equilibrium as a theoretical standpoint and adopt disequilibrium analysis to examine the dynamics of capitalism. However, this is not the case in macro-level analysis, where Marx sees the socio-economic system moving towards the equilibrium of a class-less communist society, in which the sources of fluctuations and struggles are eliminated and society achieves a unified harmonious order (Ayres, 1962). It is on these grounds that Hodgson and Samuels (1994) criticise the Marxist dynamic conception of history as unrolling[21] and teleological, leaving minimal space for consideration of the unpredictable.

As regards the neo-Marxist approaches, they correctly highlight the significance of the socio-cultural context in understanding and explaining socio-economic phenomena and, in that sense, they strive to escape from the deterministic and mechanistic framework in which Marxism is trapped. However, due to their Marxian heritage, they still share with it the same world view, values and methodological perspective and, on these grounds, most of the criticisms developed in the preceding paragraph also apply to them. Thus, for example, it is not difficult to discern within neo-Marxist theories the presumption of a rational human agent, where action reflects individual calculable interests (albeit under the influence of given socio-political structures). In this sense, like Marxism, a utilitarian understanding of human agency is espoused, where action is seen as a result of the rational calculus of satisfaction.

b Structuration theory

Structuration theory is a social theory that seeks to provide an integrated framework for understanding society and societal change, rather than to analyse economic phenomena as such. In this sense it had a small impact on economic thought, although economic relations are implicitly examined through the analysis of the society as a system of domination and allocation of resources. However, structuration theory had a significant influence on social science (Thrift, 1983; Whittington, 1992; Phipps, 2001; Webster, 2011), especially in the analysis of the built environment (Healey and Barrett, 1990; Healey, 1992, 1994; van der Krabben and Lambooy 1993), and on these grounds it is pertinent to discuss briefly its main themes and to outline its methodology.

Building on the conceptual foundations of Giddens (1984), Dear and Moos (1986) have developed an integrated framework for structuration (Figure 2.1) that describes the process of production and reproduction of structures and, as such, the development of social systems. Agency (which is situated at the centre of the model) is defined by both the 'stratification model of action' and the 'dialectic of control'. The former indicates that agents are reflexively monitoring their actions (which are driven by motivation and rationality) while they are bounded by the unacknowledged conditions and the unintended consequences of other actions. The dialectic of control (represented by the bidirectional arrows) is the primary force mediating interaction between agents. As a result of asymmetric power relations, agents have different degrees of control within social interaction. The

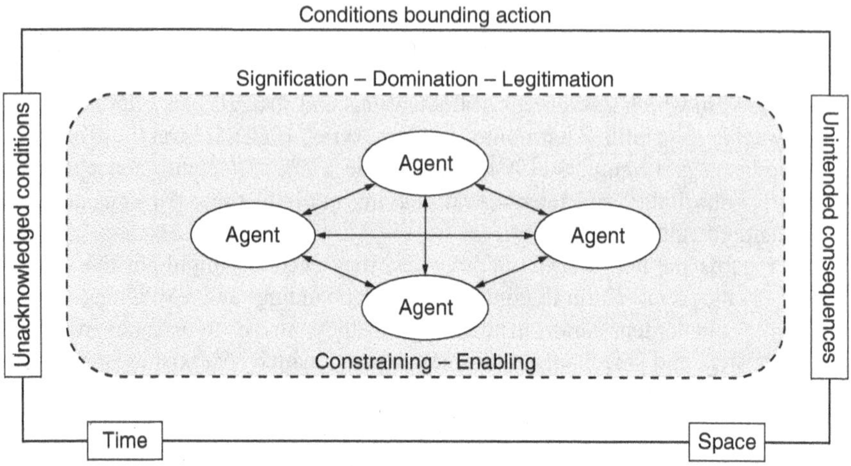

Figure 2.1 A model of structuration (source: based on Moos and Dear (1986)).

greater the knowledge a person has about the reproduction of and the relations within society, the greater is their ability to engage effectively in interaction (or, in other words, the greater is their power in the dialectic of control).

The outer line in the model depicts the social system presenting 'conditions bounding action'. These include the unacknowledged conditions and the unintended consequences of action (which comprise the 'stratification model of action'), as well as time and space considerations. Time bounds action in three levels: *duree* (immediate nexus of interaction among agents), *dasein* (the agents' lifetime) and the *longue duree* (the long-term reproduction of structures across generations). The influence of space to human agency is explored through the developed notion of 'locale'. This refers to the physical setting within which social groupings interact to produce and reproduce social systems (Giddens, 1981). This, however, should not be seen as an 'empty dimension' along which collectivities become structured, but as an essential element that is actively involved in the constitution of interaction.

Structure (the dashed line) is represented in the model as an intra-structure between social system and agency. It is both the medium and the outcome of social interaction, providing the rules that characterise the social system and thereby constrain and enable various forms of action. 'Signification', 'domination' and 'legitimation' are aspects (or dimensions) of structure which are manifested in all social interaction. Signification refers to the production and communication of meaning, domination to the use of power (political or economic) in interactions originating from the control of resources, and legitimation to the moral constitution of interaction (based on societal norms, values and standards). Structure and social interaction are a mutually constitutive duality (depicted by the grey area in the model).

To operationalise that model and to avoid the determination of either social structure or human agency, Moos and Dear (1986) (following Giddens, 1979) propose the method of 'bracketing'. This method, they argue, enables the separation of agent and system in analytical research, but without causing their disintegration. This is done by focusing attention on one part at a time without forsaking the other. Thus two sides of analysis are involved, namely strategic conduct and institutional analysis. Strategic conduct concerns how agents draw upon structural elements in social interaction. It focuses on understanding the rules and resources of the actors (including knowledge and power relations) and how these affect human agency (action and interaction) through the mechanisms of the dialectic of control. Institutional analysis focuses on how enduring, space and time specific, practices of social interaction affect the social system. These practices are analysed in terms of the modalities of interaction, which are communicative, political, economic and sanction/legal,[22] reflecting directly the structural aspects inherent in all human interaction.

Analysis in structuration theory is conducted in three levels (Moos and Dear, 1986). The first level, the concrete, concerns events that are time and space specific, empirical occurrences resulting from the production and reproduction of society. Events are further analysed in two ways, representing two extra levels of analysis at the abstract end, the contextual and the compositional. The first concerns agents and structures, examining the interaction between agents and their relation with structures (strategic conduct) and how these are involved in the constitution of social reality (institutional analysis). The second concerns the identification of the deep-seated abstract properties of the social system (emerged in the *longue duree* of social reproduction) that define structure and agency in interaction.

Overall it is evident that structuration theory exhibits a number of strengths. In the first instance it provides an important platform for addressing simultaneously the relationship between structure and human agency. This facilitates comprehensive explanation by placing equal emphasis on the roles of individuals and the effects of structures in the production, reproduction and transformation of society. Moreover, the approach is sensitive to time and space considerations in analysing society and societal change. However, certain concerns have also been raised. Dear and Moos (1986) highlight the difficulties in translating structuration theory into an agenda for empirical research and practice. Others see some structural limitations of the structuration theory. Its emphasis, for example, on rational action has been criticised as unrealistic (Hodgson, 1999a) and as leaving "...no conceptual space for passion and desire..." (Johnston *et al.*, 2000: 800). Further, the approach has been accused for eclecticism (Johnston *et al.*, 2000) as well as vagueness and confusion with regard to the determination of concepts such as institutions and locale (Dear and Moos, 1986). Finally, and in connection with the foregoing, structuration theory is seen to have an unusually weak understanding of culture (Guy and Henneberry, 2000), something which constraints the generalised contours of the theory.

c Critical realist perspective

It has been argued that critical realism has provided the methodological bases practised by a range of heterodox economists for well over a century (Fleetwood 1999). However, it was not until recently that serious attempts had been made to systematically assemble and present its underpinnings, theses and world view with reference to the economics discipline (Lawson, 1995, 1997a, 2003; Fleetwood, 1999; Downward, 2003; Downward *et al.*, 2006; Arvanitidis, 2013).

Within economics, critical realism has very much played the role of 'underlabourer', critically inquiring the mainstream orthodoxy and elaborating alternative perspectives as applied, or as of concern, to economic issues (Lawson, 1995, 1999; Lawson *et al.*, 1996; Fleetwood, 1999; Nielsen, 2002). This is because critical realism is intrinsically a philosophical position and, in particular, an ontologically oriented position. It presents a new way of seeing socio-economic reality, and, on these grounds, it advances discussion in economic philosophy and methodology, providing guidelines about how modes of reasoning and research might be fashioned in economics and other social sciences, such as management (Mingers, 2006), organisation theory (Tsang and Kwan, 1999), information systems (Mutch, 2002) and geography (Cox, 2013). Moreover, the fact that critical realism is "clearly compatible with a wide variety of theoretical and methodological approaches" (Outhwaite, 1990: 366) without prescribing to a specific ideology or political programme (Fleetwood, 1999), confers on this philosophical framework the status of a general platform, capable of embracing and ontologically enriching a wide variety of approaches in natural and social sciences, including economics (Sayer, 2000; Danermark *et al.*, 2002; Cruickshank, 2003).[23]

Critical realism, like all other structural approaches in economics, maintains that structures, powers, mechanisms and necessary relations lie behind and govern the flux of events in an essentially open and dynamic world. It is, however, the presence of certain contingent conditions that determines whether these causal powers are activated. Consequently, the explanatory concern is not with events, but with the structures and mechanisms that underlie and govern them. On these grounds, the objective of economics for critical realists is to identify and understand real structures and mechanisms and the ways in which they can act, so that events in, and states of affairs of, the economic process might ultimately be explained.

To achieve this, critical realism has put forward a rich methodological approach (Sayer, 1992, 2000; Lawson, 1997a, 2003), making use of two relatively distinct modes or types of explanation: theoretical and applied.[24] Theoretical or pure or abstract explanation is referred to the identification of underlying structures, causal mechanisms and their essential (internal) relations that govern the flux of economic phenomena with regard to the particular object of study. This mode of analysis is essentially retroductive. It entails refining and transforming existing conceptual resources into plausible theories of structures and mechanisms that account for the phenomena under study. These theories are then empirically assessed and reviewed and, when found to be empirically adequate (themselves explained in turn), are accepted as valuable parts in the continuous unfolding of explanatory knowledge.[25]

Applied or practical or concrete explanation, in contrast, is the mode of analysis used in studying the causal mechanisms, contingent conditions and the way in which they are actualised and interact with each other to produce identifiable (typically less than strict) patterns of phenomena in specific, real-life situations. This mode of explanation draws upon antecedently established knowledge of envisaged structures and mechanisms rather than revealing them. It entails the resolution of the event or situation of interest into its separate components and their redescription in theoretically significant terms. This is followed by the identification ('retrodiction') of possible determinative mechanisms, tendencies and conditions and the empirical elimination of the less probable ones. Such analysis can be articulated through the use of a variety of techniques of investigation, including both qualitative and quantitative research methods, usually by means of case study analysis (Yeung, 1997).

As argued in the preceding paragraphs, theories make claims about generative mechanisms and essential relations located in the real domain. Such claims must be interpreted as tendencies (Lawson, 1989). A tendency, in this sense, does not refer to something empirical, but to a 'real' transfactual "power that is being exercised whatever events ensue" (Lawson, 1997a: 23). As numerous (possibly countervailing) mechanisms may be simultaneously operative, such tendencies are not expected to necessarily give rise to observable regularities. However, when persistent regularities are observed, there are good reasons to suspect that some real causal mechanisms are in force. Such partial empirical regularities are seen as 'stylised facts' (Lawson 1989),[26] indicating "a conceptualised phenomenon – typically a broad but not universal generalisation about an event regularity – that is interpreted to hold in a way, or to a degree, such that the researcher regards as significant enough, given the context, that *prima facie* an explanation is called for" (Lawson, 1989: 65). Such stylised facts can serve both to form hypotheses (about particular causal mechanisms) and to assess and refine (on the basis of empirical support) the relative explanatory power of developed or competing theories (Lawson, 1997a). In that sense, pure and applied analyses become interlinked, reinforcing and complementing each other in the development of scientific knowledge.

d Evaluating structuralist approaches

Structuralist approaches have brought forward an essentially historical perspective to economic analysis. Marxists and neo-Marxists have developed a substantial theoretical system, but have been criticised on a number of points and especially for their deterministic and teleological view of economic processes and dynamics, and for their naive and rationalistic understanding of human agency. Structurationist and critical realist approaches have provided conceptual frameworks within which issues of human intentionality and purposeful behaviour can be properly addressed, but they both lack a coherent theoretical perspective as applied to economic matters. From these, realism has been appreciated for its ontological substance, which enables a clear differentiation between structure and agency, and its role as 'under-labourer', i.e. its ability to provide a wider philosophical platform to economic analysis that is compatible with a variety of theoretical views in economics.

2.3.3 Heterodox approaches: institutionalism

Institutional economics has been at the forefront of heterodox economic thought since the beginning of the twentieth century, offering criticisms to both neoclassical and Marxist economics. The school reached its zenith in the inter-war years in the USA, before being displaced by the neoclassical mainstream. This displacement was principally a consequence of the profound methodological shift in social sciences that favoured prediction (over understanding), mathematical formalism (over analytical description) and generalizability (over historically and spatially specific explanations), all of which are sustained by the neoclassical paradigm (Hodgson, 1998a). Viewed as inferior because it is technically less rigorous, its influence waned and, over the years, it became a more marginalised, less recognised heterodox part of the discipline and practice of economics.

However, since the late 1970s, institutionalism, as well as other heterodox approaches to economics, has seen a considerable renaissance. Today, institutionalist thought is rich in vigour and diversity. What brings together all these different approaches is the adoption of institutions as the centrepiece of economic analysis (Williamson, 2000; Samuels, 2000; Hodgson, 2000). However, while institutionalists have used the concept of institution to convey the idea that people's expectations, behaviour and interaction are shaped by and reflect humanly devised rules and regularities of behaviour, the word has never enjoyed a precise meaning. Some institutionalists have stressed the habitual and routinised mode of institutions. To Veblen (1919a), for instance, an institution is a set of norms and ideals which is imperfectly reproduced or internalised through habituation in each succeeding generation of individuals. To use his own words "...institutions are settled habits of thought common to the generality of man" (Veblen, 1919a: 239). Similarly, Hamilton (1932: 3) defines institutions as ways "...of thought or action ... which are embedded in the habits of a group or the customs of a people", Hodgson (1988: 10) as "...social organisation which, through the operation of tradition, custom or legal constraint, tends to create durable and routinized patterns of behaviour", Schotter (1981: 11) as general "...regularities in social behaviour ... agreed to by all members of society" and Bush (1987: 1076) as sets of "...socially prescribed patterns of correlated behaviour".

Other scholars have emphasised the constraining or enabling character of institutions. Commons (1934: 69), for example, defines institutions as "...collective action in control of individual action", North (1990: 3) as "...the rules of the game in a society or, ... humanly devised constraints that shape human interaction", Hodgson (2006: 2) as "systems of established and prevalent social rules that structure social interaction", whereas Matthews (1986: 905) views institutions "...as sets of rights and obligations affecting people in their economic lives" and Mirowski (1987: 1020) as "...transpersonal rules that endow individual economic actors with the ability to cope with interpretations of action and with change".

The scope of institutionalism consists of the theoretical and empirical examination of the institutional fabric of the economy. Analysis focuses not only on the conventional problems of resource allocation, income distribution and determination of output, prices, employment, etc., but also on issues related to the organisation and structure of the economy. It is argued that institutions have been developed to improve the smooth functioning of the economic system by providing a co-ordinative mechanism for economic action (North, 1990; Samuels, 1995). Institutions, however, are not regarded as transcendent mechanisms imposed by an external authority, but, rather, as social inventions, determined by prevailing interests and power relations over time (Hamilton, 1919). Hence institutions and, consequently, economic phenomena are seen as both evolutionary and dynamic.

Institutional analysis also takes explicit account of the interactive links that exist between economic institutions and other institutional arrangements in society (e.g. those embodied in law, politics and culture). As such, research focuses on the formation and functioning of institutions as part of the wider economic, political, legal, social and cultural environment they operate within (Hamilton, 1919; Kapp, 1976; Hodgson, 1988, 2000; North, 1990; Williamson, 2000).

Institutionalists generally question the idea that economics can or should be methodologically 'positive' in the mainstream sense (Veblen, 1898a; Kapp, 1976; Bush, 1991, 1993). They argue that any scientific inquiry with policy implications can only be conducted on the basis of value premises, where necessary value judgements provide the appropriate standards of evaluation. To put it plainly, questions must be asked before answers can be given, and questions are all expressions of our interest in the world. They are in essence 'value' positions which employ judgemental standards to provide a basis for identifying and choosing one option over another at every point. Having established that value premises and normative standards of judgement are intrinsic to any social scientific inquiry, institutionalists stress that, in fact, all economic theories are influenced, implicitly or explicitly, by value systems. What, on these grounds, signifies 'objectivity' in any economic analysis is a straightforward and clear statement of the value judgements used and commitment to keeping the path of inquiry open and subject to the identification and correction of errors (Myrdal, 1958, 1970). In meeting these requirements, institutionalism is one of the few schools in economics that has made serious attempts to explicitly incorporate values directly into their analysis.[27]

There are several strands of institutional economics, all of which emanate from the tradition pioneered by Thorstein Veblen, John R. Commons and others in the first decades of the twentieth century. The differences among these branches lie in the degree to which they diverge from neoclassical orthodoxy. According to Eggertsson (1990a),[28] these strands can be broadly categorised as neo-institutional, new institutional and old (original) institutional approaches; they are discussed separately in the following paragraphs.[29]

a Neo-institutional economics

Neo-institutionalists (such as Coase, Williamson, Alchian, Demsetz and North, before his 1990 book) effectively graft institutional content onto mainstream economics. Thus they extend conventional economic thought, but without challenging its basic behavioural assumptions (Eggertsson, 1990b). In particular, they are interested in explaining the organisational structure of the economy by taking account of the opportunistic behaviour of agents, information asymmetries and transaction costs, without jettisoning the conventional postulates of methodological individualism, economic rationality, or the predisposition of markets towards stable equilibrium.

Neo-institutional economics is, in essence, the study of transactions[30] (North, 1986, Williamson, 2000). The notion of transaction in this context is not confined solely to the transfer of goods and services in the sense of 'exchange', but includes the transfer of resources in the legal sense, namely the transfer of sanctioned rights (Coase, 1960; Demsetz, 1967). From this perspective, neo-institutionalists recognise that transactions in modern societies take place within a framework of rules and rights, which is not only economically, but also legally, politically and socially[31] determined and enforced. On this basis, they define their subject matter as the analysis of costs and procedures associated both with the exchange of resources[32] and with the creation, maintenance, use and change of a framework specifying and policing the rights that individuals have over resources, i.e. property rights (Coase, 1960, 1998; Alchian and Demsetz, 1973). Institutions, on these grounds, are defined as the formal rules, laws and regulations that define and monitor the property rights, plus the informal rules, norms and conventions that facilitate transactions between agents and ensure economic co-operation (North and Thomas, 1970).

The line of argument of the neo-institutional approach starts with the remark that transactions are costly (Coase, 1937, 1960). They are costly because agents have to expend time and resources to specify, assign, monitor, transfer and enforce property rights over goods or information. However, the importance of this assertion is not only that these costs exist, but that they are substantial enough to have significant effects on economic systems. In fact, given the dependence of the modern market economies on transacting, it is not surprising that, according to some estimates, transaction costs comprise as much as 50 to 60 per cent of net national product (Wallis and North, 1986; Dollery and Leong, 1998).

A thorough understanding of the nature of transaction costs requires an examination of the various contexts in which they appear. Considered in terms of holding property rights, transaction costs consist of the costs of defining the characteristics of resources plus the costs of specifying, assigning, utilising, policing and enforcing the rights over resources. Applied to the transfer of property rights, transaction costs include the costs of information (about prices and the characteristics of resources), negotiation, decision-making and contract enforcement (Furubotn and Richter, 2005).

Transaction costs analysis takes into account the institutional organisation of the economy. This is because, when it is costly to transact, institutions matter (Coase, 1937). On these grounds neo-institutionalists contend that institutions and their organisational structures have arisen and evolved to minimise the transaction costs associated with the running of the politico-economic system (North and Thomas, 1970). The working rule is that a low-cost tends to supersede a high-cost organisation (Williamson, 1985). This is seen as a movement towards a natural state of rest, or equilibrium, in which efficient outcomes and institutions prevail, and no individual is able to, or wishes to, make any adjustment to this situation.

Institutional change occurs (deliberately or spontaneously) as a result of the actions of autonomous individuals who economise on transaction costs. On these grounds the abstract individual becomes the basic explanatory element of economic organisation, attaching to neo-institutionalism the blotch of methodological individualism. Human preferences and tastes are, therefore, pictured as given and treated as exogenous to the matter of economic inquiry.

In line with the preceding discussion, the model of economic behaviour adopted by neo-institutionalism is described as 'maximising rationality under constraints' (Eggertsson, 1990a). According to this, individuals seek their own interests and maximise their utility under constraints imposed by the structure of property rights and transaction costs. People may break their word and they tend to interpret ambiguities to their own advantage. Such 'opportunistic behaviour',[33] it is argued, has profound effects on transactions and on economic organisation in general. To avoid the harmful consequences of opportunism, agents resort to either market relations or arrangements between and within organisations, depending on the circumstances. Whether a particular transaction is allocated to the market or to an organisational arrangement is a matter of cost minimisation (Williamson, 1975, 1985, 1993). This leads to the formulation of a theory of economic co-operation between the market and organisational hierarchy based on weighing internal and external transaction costs. On a similar basis, network organisation is recognised as a reflection of the concern to control transaction costs over space.

One of the key transaction costs is related to information. Information is necessary not only for transacting, but for any economic activity. However, in the real world information is substantially incomplete and people are never perfectly informed. This leads to a pattern of asymmetrically distributed information between the transactional parties that enables the holder of superior knowledge to use it opportunistically[34] (Alchian and Demsetz, 1972; Alt and Shepsle, 1998). On this basis, neo-institutionalists (and particularly Williamson

1975, 1985, 1993) recognise that contracts between agents are always incomplete or 'impure'. Generally, it can be said that information deficiencies affect the levels of risk or uncertainty in the market, revealing a potential for distortion in economic relationships (Demsetz, 1997).

This also raises issues of power relations acknowledging the significant role of the state and other institutional arrangements of a political nature in the efficient operation of economic institutions (North, 1981, 1986; Eggertsson, 1990a; Alt and Shepsle, 1998). The argument starts with the proposition that resource transactions and feasible forms of economic organisation are specified by a framework of rules and property rights that is politically determined and legally enforced. On these grounds, neo-institutional economics emphasises the importance of analysing the form and operation of the political and legal institutions and their organisational structures to understand economic organisation and, ultimately, the factors that account for economic growth and development (North and Thomas, 1970; North, 1981, 1986; Scully, 1988; Knack and Keefer, 1995; Henisz, 2000; Acemoglu *et al.*, 2002, 2005).

The philosophy underlying the neo-institutional approach falls within the spectrum of positivism and its methodology is closely related to the deductive-formalist model (Rutherford, 1994a; Furubotn and Richter, 2005). In this sense, neo-institutionalists are more prone than other institutionalists to use rigorous mathematical and econometric modelling to analyse the working of institutions and the role they play in the operation of the economy. Thus, although historical analysis of institutional phenomena has been undertaken by researchers within this strand of thought, neo-institutionalist empirical work exhibits a strong inclination towards quantitative, single-industry case studies and cross-sectional econometric analysis (Brunetti *et al.*, 1997; Lesmand *et al.*, 1999; Chong and Calderon, 2000; Djankov and Murrell, 2002; Menard and Shirley, 2005).

Notwithstanding its neoclassical assumptions, there can be no doubt that neo-institutionalism has made a useful contribution to economic thought. At the very least, the neo-institutional literature has made it clear to mainstream economists that institutions matter. Nevertheless, other institutionalist camps have levelled some valid criticisms. These critiques centre mainly on the assumption of economic rationality, arguing that it results in models which are logically inconsistent and fundamentally misleading (Furubotn and Richter, 2005). Original institutionalists (Hodgson, 1993a, 1998a; Rutherford, 1994a; Stanfield, 1999) criticise the whole set of neo-institutional assumptions drawn from neoclassical economic: the tendency towards equilibrium, optimizing behaviour and methodological individualism. This neoclassical legacy, they argue, takes inadequate account of the socio-cultural character and cognitive-enabling function of institutions and renders the neo-institutional conceptualisation insufficient and defective. Critics also take issue with neo-institutionalists for the institution-free state on which they base their theorising about the emergence and development of institutions, and for the efficient evolution and operation of institutions (of a neoclassical tinge) that they advocate (Granovetter, 1985; Hodgson, 1988, 1998a; Furubotn and Richter, 2005).

Moreover, even scholars sympathetic to neo-institutionalism, such as Eggertsson (1990a), have recognised that there are conceptual inconsistencies in the approach. The existence of information deficiencies within the market indicates that agents enter into trade with some gaps in their understanding of market opportunity and therefore they make decisions on the basis of some kind of imperfect, but satisfactorily 'adequate', information. Such a conception naturally leads to some form of sub-optimal, restricted (or bounded) rationality and thus towards the broader working framework of the new institutional approach (Furubotn and Richter, 2005).

b New institutional economics

New institutionalists (mainly North after 1990, but also Alston, Greif, Langlois, Matthews, Menard, Rodrik and Shirley) attempt a more fundamental departure. They start with transaction costs and property rights analysis, but go further to challenge the conventional assumptions of long-run equilibria and economic rationality. However, the elemental building block of their theorisation remains the abstract individual. Thus methodological individualism is retained assuming an exogenous explanation (in the sense that it is beyond institutions) of the factors that mould individual cognition, preferences and objectives (Hodgson, 1998a). Of course, institutions are acknowledged to affect individual behaviour, but only in terms of the choices, constraints and information presented to the agents. The principal conceptual framework that enables deciphering the environment and the moulding of preferences – and, indeed, the very individuality of those agents themselves – is provided by culture, which is treated as external to institutional structure.

North (1990, 1993a, 1993b, 1994) defines institutions as the formal rules and informal constraints that together shape human interaction. Formal rules refer to regulations prescribed and enforced by political, judicial and economic bodies through channels that are widely accepted as official. They are divided into political rules, which specify the hierarchy and structure of polity, and economic rules, which define the property rights in a society. Informal constraints, in turn, are socially prescribed rules (usually unwritten) that are determined outside formal or official channels to ensure human co-ordination. They include auto-enforced social conventions (such as following the rules of the road, speaking a language or using money; Young, 1996), self-imposed codes of conduct (such as ideology) and social norms of behaviour that are codes of conduct enforced by a second party (retaliation) or a third party (societal sanctions). Both formal and informal institutions are informed by cultural characteristics, although this is a very complex relation which is poorly understood (North, 1993b). It is acknowledged, however, that informal constraints generally become part of habitual behaviour and, on these grounds, they show tenacious survival ability and resistance to change. Therefore their change is much slower and indeterminate than that of formal rules.

New institutionalists argue that institutions and their organisational structures evolve to provide stability and order to human interaction. The rules and practices that emerge depend on the motivation of the actors, their power relations and the complexity of the economic, political, legal and social frameworks within which they operate. Such a complex environment calls into question the assumption of any tendency towards long-run equilibria and the conventional notion of economic rationality. In these terms, a framework of bounded rationality is introduced in which the choice criterion is more likely to be 'satisficing' rather than maximising (Simon, 1982). This concept of 'satisficing' behaviour is justified, not only on the basis of limited information, but also on the incapability of the human mind to perform all the necessary calculations that rational decisions presuppose, even if all the relevant information is available. As a result of both the complexity of the problems to be solved and the defective problem-solving 'software' possessed by the individual, uncertainty arises in human interaction (Heiner, 1983). The way to reduce uncertainty and achieve co-operative solutions is by developing institutions (North, 1990, 2005).

Institutions, however, not only structure economic interaction, making complex exchanges across space and time possible, but also affect, together with culture, the formation of the models that actors utilise to interpret the politico-economic environment (North, 1990). Thus the institutional framework influences the way that economic opportunities are being defined and, consequently, the way that decisions are made and the courses of action subsequently followed (Simon, 1991). Institutions therefore shape long-run economic performance (Matthews, 1986; North, 1993a, 1993b; Nelson and Sampat, 2001; Rodrik, 2008; Chang, 2011). In particular, institutions that promote productivity raising activities are conductive to economic growth, whereas those which are associated with redistributive or rent-seeking activities restrict economic growth.

New institutionalists argue that institutions, by providing a framework within which economic interaction occurs, influence not only transaction costs, but also the costs that are related to production, called transformation costs[35] (Matthews, 1986; North, 1990). However, nothing in this assertion implies that evolving institutions serve to minimise costs. North (1990, 1993b, 1994), in fact, emphasises that the institutional structure of any place and time can only be a 'mixed bag' in which some institutions reduce transaction and transformation costs, while others raise them. This is the case for three reasons. First, institutions have historically evolved as a result of the bargaining power of actors and not on the basis of a credible commitment to low-cost transacting (Matthews, 1986). Second, the complexity and volatility of modern economies, and the inert and stable character of institutions, mean that even if institutions established in the past are cost-minimising, there is little chance that they would still be the optimal solutions to the problems of the present (Furubotn and Richter, 2005). Third, as economic behaviour is determined within a framework of bounded rationality, inefficient institutions may persist as nobody has the knowledge, perceptual ability, power or motivation to change them (Heiner, 1983).

The new institutionalist framework offers two approaches to the efficiency question. The first questions the generic notion of conventional allocative efficiency and considers the issue with reference to a specific purpose or to the interests of a specific group of actors (North, 1990; Keogh and D'Arcy, 1999). It asserts that, instead of seeking a judgement on whether the economy as an entity is efficient, the assessment of efficiency should be constructed to capture 'efficiency for a purpose', or 'efficiency for a person'. However, the approach lacks an explicit value or welfare criterion for such an analysis, and this seems to be a significant omission.

The second, and more fully developed, approach views efficiency in a dynamic context related to the ability of the system to meet, cope with, and adapt to new problems as they arise[36] (North, 1990; Killick, 1995a; Syrquin, 1995). In these terms, an 'adaptive efficient' economic system displays tendencies to eliminate high transaction and transformation costs and generally provides an environment hospitable to economic growth. Thus the assessment of efficiency considers such characteristics as the willingness of a society to achieve co-operative solutions to complex exchange, "...to acquire knowledge and learning, to induce innovation, to undertake risk and creative activity of all sorts, as well as to resolve problems and bottlenecks of the society through time"[37] (North, 1990: 80).

New institutionalism recognises the interrelationship between institutions (i.e. the rules of the game) and organisations (i.e. the players of the game). Political and economic organisations are regarded as the main agents of change, as, by pursuing their objectives, they alter (or reinforce) the existing institutional structure. However, this is not a one-way relationship because institutional constraints also shape the form and objectives of organisations, determining the kinds of knowledge and skills that they seek and, in turn, the purposive activities they will be involved in (productive or redistributive) (North, 1993b, 1994).

New institutionalists argue that an understanding of institutional change necessitates an understanding of the nature and role of institutions. Institutions are characterised by relative stability and inertia, as their basic function is to ensure certainty and continuity in economic life, making possible complex exchange across space and time. However, changes in preferences (and ideas), expectations of the bargaining power of actors and exogenous shocks can affect the institutional structure if organisations (the agents of change) determine that altering the institutional arrangements at the margin might better serve their objectives.

New institutional economics argues that the path of institutional change is shaped by constraints derived from the past and by the (sometimes unanticipated) consequences of the innumerable incremental choices of entrepreneurs who continually modify those constraints to increase their returns (North, 1993b). Institutional change is thus seen as an incremental process in which thousands of small alterations contribute to fundamental institutional change and cumulatively determine the long-run direction of change.[38] This process is therefore 'path-dependent' in the sense that past institutional conditions set the possibilities, opportunities and boundaries for subsequent change (Langlois, 1986a; North, 1990; Jones, 1995; Syrquin, 1995). Path dependence, however, is more than the incremental process of institutional evolution. It is a consequence of the increasing returns characteristic of an institutional framework. The interdependent web of institutions and associated organisations tends to produce effects that further entrench its hold over society, at least in the short run (North, 1991; Greif, 2006). In short, path dependence means that history matters, for it is what accounts for the divergent paths that economies follow. Once a development path is set on a particular course, the lock-in and network externalities that arise from the symbiotic relationship between the institutions of an economy and polity and their organisations reinforce this course and make fundamental alterations of economic paths difficult (North, 1990, 1993b).

The philosophical and methodological traits of new institutional economics stem from positivism. The embracement of bounded rationality however, places it near to the behavioural end of the positivist spectrum (Khalil, 1994; Hodgson, 1997). On that basis, its research strategy involves the utilisation of both quantitative and qualitative techniques to investigate the evolving institutional framework and its political and economic organisation within the lines set up earlier. The focus is to describe the emergence, continuation and change in the relevant set of institutional rules, considering the strategic interactions between organisations and other endogenous and exogenous features, including beliefs and cultural characteristics. The appropriate methodology for such a task is, according to Greif (1998), 'historical and comparative institutional analysis' (HCIA) (a similar stance is taken by Langlois, 1986a, 1986b; Menard, 2001; Furubotn and Richter, 2005). In particular, this research mode employs: (i) historical techniques to explore the role of history in institutional emergence and development; (ii) comparative procedures to gain insights from the study of different times and spaces; and (iii) a mix of quantitative and qualitative analytical skills that enable reliance on context-specific micro-models for empirical analysis. For these reasons, the approach relies on case studies as the primary method of collecting information.

The essential element of the HCIA lies in its attempt to reveal both the forces that lead societies to evolve along distinct institutional trajectories and the sources of the difficulties that some societies face in adopting the institutions of more successful societies. More broadly, it indicates the importance of examining a society's institutions as products of a historical process in which past institutional and cultural features interact in shaping the nature of contemporary institutions and their evolution. A starting point for this analysis is the empirical identification of the institutions, organisations and related features (such as behaviour, beliefs and other socio-cultural features) that are relevant in the historical episode under consideration. On this basis, empirical investigation focuses on issues such as: (i) the costs of transacting, with particular regard to the functioning of political and economic markets; (ii) the formal rules in an economy and, in particular, political structure, property rights and the legal system; (iii) the informal constraints, i.e. the social rules that shape human interaction; (iv) institutional evolution and change, using the concepts of path dependence and considering the interconnectedness between informal and formal institutions; and (v) the organisational structure in a politico-economy, also considering issues of bargaining power between actors.

Although new institutionalists correctly emphasise the importance of institutions to the performance and evolution of politico-economic systems, they have been criticised for underestimating other important dimensions of institutions. Hodgson (1993a, 1997, 1998a) and Stanfield (1999), for instance, argue that new institutionalists are so strongly infused with a market mentality based on exchange principles that culturally and socially embedded institutions are not given appropriate consideration. Moreover, although the important role of informal institutions is recognised, new institutional theory is underdeveloped, as not only are informal institutions considered from a strictly functional market/exchange perspective, but they are also seen as no more than a set of supplementary constraints that support and reinforce the formal rules in defining the opportunity set in an economy.

Hodgson (1988, 1998a) also takes issue with new institutionalists for their exogenous (i.e. non-institutional) treatment of the factors that mould individual preferences and motives. As he notes, institutions not only constrain the choices and actions of agents, but also perform an enabling function. They provide a cognitive framework for the interpretation of the environment and the determination of preferences and purposes. This function of institutions is certainly overlooked in new institutional theorisation and this is one of the main reasons, in addition to its embrace of a methodological individualism position, that the approach faces difficulties in developing an endogenous theory of institutional change.

Finally, Field (1994) criticises new institutionalism for its tolerance of ambiguity and its willingness to absorb ideas from different theoretical traditions such as original institutionalism and conventional economics. He argues that this generates confusion within the approach and frustration in those trying systematically to make sense of their work. Indeed, it is not difficult to discern traces of misunderstanding and confusion within the writings of new institutionalism, as, for example, in North's (1990: 57) remark that "...no institutions are necessary in a world of complete information". This statement, apparently reflecting new institutionalism's mainstream heritage, seems to conflict with the bounded rationality claim that limitations in the computational ability of the human mind made institutions essential to support the mental frameworks needed to decipher the environment.

c Original (old) institutional economics

Both neo-institutionalists and new institutionalists have advanced economic thought by establishing that institutions do matter and should not be taken as given or exogenous to the economic system. However, their theoretical contributions rest on the acceptance of all (neo-institutionalists) or some (new institutionalists) of the core assumptions of mainstream economics. The irony, of course, is that the original institutional economics emerged largely out of a critique of orthodox assumptions (Veblen, 1898a).

In a reversal of fortunes, there are signs of renewal and revitalisation of the original institutionalism by subsequent generations of thinkers in the USA[39] and all over the world.[40,41] Their approach is grounded in the foundations laid down by Veblen, Commons and the other institutionalists of the 1930s (i.e. Ayres, Hamilton, Mitchell, and others) and, on this basis, it is generally identified under the label 'old' institutional economics. Although complete agreement on the philosophical, methodological and other substantive issues is missing, original institutionalism is united by an holistic 'investigatory mode' (Wilber and Harrison, 1978; Wisman and Rozansky, 1991) and by a certain set of preconceptions and beliefs grounded on the rejection of all mainstream economic assumptions (i.e. methodological individualism, maximising economic behaviour and static-equilibrium states) (Miller, 1978; Lind, 1993; Rutherford, 1994a; Hodgson, 2000). The latter also justifies its critical stance towards both the neo-institutional and new institutional approaches.

Original institutionalists recognise the complexity of economic life and stress the need for a holistic and societal approach. The economy, they argue, should be understood and analysed as an open system in continuous dynamic interaction with the cultural, social, political, legal and physical systems from which economic processes receive important impulses and upon which they exert their own influences (Veblen, 1904, 1919a; Hamilton, 1919; Kapp, 1968, 1976; Fischer, 1986). Hence original institutionalists view economic processes as embedded in social relations, economic institutions as only part of the wider set of socio-cultural institutions, economic agents as social beings and, in short, the socio-economy as an integrated system (Polanyi, 1957; Granovetter, 1985; Hodgson, 1988).

According to old institutionalism, society is more than a mere aggregation of autonomous individuals. It also comprises values, beliefs, customs and norms, which have cultural underpinnings and cannot be fully explained in purely individualistic terms (Veblen, 1919a; Ayres, 1962; Rutherford, 1994a, 1998; Hodgson, 1998a). Hence original institutionalists renounce methodological individualism which assigns ontological and explanatory primacy to an immutable, institution-free atomistic agent. Humans, they assert, are all born into and socialised within a world of institutions and therefore institutions affect individuals' behaviour in fundamental ways. Thus, recognising the durable and self-reinforced character of institutions, original institutionalism chooses institutions as the basic unit of analysis rather than the ahistorical and abstract model of the individualistic agent. However, the proposed model does not necessarily imply methodological collectivism, where individual behaviour is entirely explained by the institutional–cultural environment.[42] Although human behaviour is largely influenced by the economic, social and cultural framework, it is also adaptive and purposeful and individuals can also act to form and alter institutions (Hamilton, 1919; Commons, 1931; Samuels, 1995). Thus new institutions are created on the basis of new experiences and old ones fall away due to 'habitual disuse' and displacement (Veblen, 1919b). In that sense, individuals are both the producer and the product of their institutional environment, in a process of continuous interaction and evolutionary change.

Original institutionalists also reject the model of 'rational economic man', stressing the habitual and routinised character of human behaviour[43] and carefully placing it in a socio-cultural context (see, for example, Veblen, 1899, 1914; Commons, 1934; Dugger, 1979; Bush, 1987; Rutherford, 1994a; Samuels, 1995; Stanfield, 1999). The various actions that a person undertakes are so complex, and the amount of sensory data received so enormous, that they resort to habits or standard practices to diminish conscious thought and to reduce fatigue (Hodgson, 1988, 1997, 1998a). These practices, however, are defined within a cultural context as it is culture that legitimises and habituates some beliefs and actions, while discouraging others, so as to organise human life and ensure its regularity. On that basis, the multidimensionality of economic behaviour is recognised. Human rationality need not be the outcome of a conscious act of reasoning, but is often embodied in a socio-cultural and historical process (Veblen, 1919a; Bush, 1987; Hodgson, 1988, 1997). In a sense, the behavioural hypothesis of bounded rationality is, within original institutionalism, being expanded into what has been described variously as 'mixed rationality' or 'irrationality' (Zingler, 1974; Wilber and Harrison, 1978; Hodgson, 1988, 1998a) to include consideration of these culturally driven human actions that are performed, consciously or unconsciously (instinctively), in the pursuit of habits and the following of social rules.

The purpose of original institutionalism is to provide a realistic and dynamic approach to economic organisation. Higher priority is assigned to the accurate description of the socio-economic system and the process of ongoing historical change. For original institutionalists, economic change is the natural, never-ending process of a constantly evolving socio-economic system (Ayres, 1962; Hodgson, 1993a, 1994c; Rutherford, 1994a, 1998; Stanfield, 1999). On that basis, original institutionalists recognise that economic change is characterised by 'cumulative causation'.[44] Veblen (1919a: 74–75) writes: "The economic life history of the individual is a cumulative process of adaptation of means to ends that cumulatively change as the process goes on, both the agent and his environment being at any point the outcome of the last process". This means that, alongside the exogenous shocks to the system (i.e. the changing exigencies of the life process), endogenous institutions and purposeful human agency determine the course of socio-economic change in an accumulative, incremental way. However, such a conception does not imply any prejudgement either for the direction or the outcomes of the cumulative response. The socio-economy is seen as a complex and open-ended system where the variety of possibilities for interdependencies could account for widely differing outcomes (Veblen, 1919a; Kapp, 1976). Notably, this is distinctly different from the Marxian teleological perception of evolution that regards history as progressing through a series of predetermined states (Zingler, 1974).

In recognising the durable character of institutions, Veblen (1899, 1904, 1914, 1919a) and his followers view socio-economic change as a selection process akin to the broader Darwinian conception of biological evolution[45] (Zingler, 1974; Hodgson, 1988, 1999b, 2003; Wisman and Rozansky, 1991; a similar position is also evident in North, 1994). Institutions are regarded as the units and replicators of socio-economic evolution, in a similar way to genes in biology; they perform this function by virtue of their self-reinforced character, which allows them to sustain and 'pass on' (through habituation) their important properties as circumstances change through time. Veblen's (1899: 188) thoughts are again revelatory:

> The life of man in society, just like the life of other species, is a struggle for existence, and therefore it is a process of selective adaptation. The evolution of social structure has been a process of natural selection of institutions. The progress which has been and is being made in human institutions and in human character may be set down, broadly, to a natural selection of the fittest habits of thought and to a process of enforced adaptation of individuals to an environment which has progressively changed with the growth of community and with the changing institutions under which men have lived.

Moreover, Veblen institutions have a cognitive dimension: "the situation of today shapes the institutions of tomorrow through a selective coercive process, by acting upon man's habitual view of things, and so altering or fortifying a point of view or a mental attitude handed down from the past" (Veblen, 1899: 190–1). Elsewhere he notes that:

> What men can do easily is what they can do habitually, and this decides what they can think and know.... A habitual line of action constitutes a habitual line of thought, and gives the point of view from which facts and events are apprehended and reduced to a body of knowledge.
>
> (Veblen 1934: 88)

Hence original institutionalists (and, especially Hodgson, 1988, 1993a, 1998a, 2003) recognise the important role of institutions, not only in constraining individual behaviour, but also in providing the cognitive framework for interpreting sense data and transforming information into meaningful knowledge. This involves the creation and promulgation of conceptual schema and learned signs and meanings through which sense information is perceived and made meaningful by agents. On that basis, the institutional environment has a significant effect on our views of the world, influencing our preferences and expectations and moulding our behaviour. Moreover, the cognitive function of institutions explains not only their relative stability and capacity to replicate, but also their virtue in reducing instability and uncertainty in human affairs. The strong interaction between institutions and individual cognition can account for some significant stability in socio-economic systems, partly by buffering and constraining the diverse and purposeful actions of the agents (Hodgson, 1996) and partly by providing relatively reliable information regarding their likely behaviour to other agents (Hodgson, 1988, 2003).

One of the key forces in the process of cumulative causal evolution is 'technology'. Original institutionalists have been attentive to how the pace and direction of 'technological' advancement determines institutional change and socio-economic evolution in general. The beginning of such a perception is identifiable in the writings of Veblen (1899, 1904, 1914, 1919a, 1919b), who views the evolutionary mechanisms driven by a tension between the developmental force of human creativity and the repressive force of status emulation. This is frequently referred to as the Veblenian dichotomy and constitutes a central analytical tool in the Veblen–Ayres strand of American institutionalism (Miller, 1978; Dugger, 1979; Waller, 1982, 1994). In particular, Veblen distinguishes between two tendencies that are present to a different degree in all human socictics. Technological, industrial or instrumental frames of mind (and habits of thought and action) are connected to the intrinsic human propensity for 'workmanship', 'idle curiosity' and creative innovation, and refer to the ceaseless advance in scientific understanding involving the development of 'matter-of-fact' knowledge and reasoning from cause to effect. Institutional, ceremonial or pecuniary frames of mind (and habits of thought and action), in contrast, are regarded as related to the predatory aptitude of human behaviour, settled upon and habitually reproduced to serve 'invidious' or 'leisure class' interests, legitimising abstention from productive work, emulation, aggression and dominance as accepted schemes of life, and using the established status quo and traditions for their warrant. Thus, whereas the instrumental facets are considered as progressive, serviceable and conducive to economic development, the ceremonial facets are predatory, past-binding, resistant to progress and change, and thus impede or even undermine economic development. The result is an evolving socio-economic system, driven by status emulation, conflict and power relations, where, within the context of technological process and under the stress of the exigencies of associated life, old institutions break down and new ones are created in the continuous process of adaptation to changing circumstances.

Ayres (1951, 1961, 1962) builds on the Veblenian dichotomy (filtered through Dewey's instrumental value theory) to develop a general theory of economic progress. However, whereas in Veblen 'technology' and 'institutions' are categories into which behaviour could fit, in Ayres they become determinants of all behaviour and modes of evaluation with their own logic and method of validation (Walker, 1979; Bush, 1994). For Ayres, therefore, instrumental values become the criteria to assess economic progress in terms of the support and betterment of human life (Breit, 1973; Rutherford, 1981). These are validated through the consequences of their use, judged on their 'instrumental efficiency' in maintaining the causal continuity of the problem-solving process. On these grounds, Ayres argues that the values of freedom, equity, security, excellence, abundance and democracy have shown functional significance in terms of the life progress and, as such, are all 'true' values, essential for continued instrumental advance (Rutherford, 1981; Tool, 1994a). The ceremonial practices of a community, on the other hand, are based on an invidious mode of evaluation which prescribes status and warrants the exercise of power of one social group over another. This mode of evaluation is embedded in the myths, rituals, mores and ideology of the community and seeks to authenticate existing patterns of behaviour by reversion to claims of authority, immemorial practices, the word of God, and so on[46] (Breit, 1973; Walker, 1979). Following this track, Ayres (1962) comes to disregard the stabilising, and possibly beneficial, effects of ritual and to argue that progress occurs only when instrumentally warranted behaviour displaces ceremonially warranted behaviour in the conduct of human affairs. This makes him slip into a position of technological or instrumental determinism (Samuels, 1977; Walker, 1979; Waller, 1994).

Subsequent institutionalists within the strand (DeGregori, 1977; Samuels, 1977; Walker, 1979; Foster, 1981) refine Ayres's treatment of the instrumental–ceremonial dichotomy, breaking the association of the term 'institution' with ceremony. Foster (1981), for instance, maintains that institutions are socially prescribed patterns of behaviour which encapsulate both ceremonial and instrumental aspects interlinked in complex ways. This careful consideration of all behaviour as part of a social process not only eliminates the likelihood of employing the notion as a dualistic set of universal categories (Waller 1994), but provides the basis to connect the concept of instrumental efficiency with the institutional structure. Technological advance, Foster argues, changes the means available to satisfy instrumental needs and thus affects change both in the instrumental and ceremonial aspects of behaviour. Available means and behavioural aspects are more appropriate or less appropriate, adequate or less adequate to the task at hand, and are subject to evaluation through trial and error. Relative success is assessed in terms of consequences, although no final ends are envisioned. Means and ends are regarded as entwined and the means–ends process as a continuum (Miller, 1978).

Foster's conceptualisation of the dichotomy has led to a more explicit consideration of the dominance of the ceremonial versus instrumental aspects of particular behaviour and the impact of that dominance on both that behaviour and on the cultural and economic processes (see, for instance, the discussion in Bush 1987). From that basis, one of his students, Tool (1986, 1994b), has strengthened further the tie between the dichotomy and social evaluation processes by formulating the notion of the 'instrumental value principle'. His thesis is that the dominance of ceremonial warranted aspects of behaviour can induce the malperformance of institutions, which can cause substantive impairments in the provisioning process and the flow of real income.[47] On that basis he suggests a criterion for selecting among alternative institutional arrangements to achieve genuine progress in the community's problem-solving process (Bush, 1987). Tool (1994b: 408) defines his social value principle as: "…do or choose that which provides for the continuity of human life and the non-invidious recreation of community through the instrumental use of knowledge" and argues that it can provide the basis for considering when the existing institutional structure has become inadequate or inappropriate for the instrumental functions assigned, or when a new structure is needed, or both. Moreover, Tool (1994b), responding to criticisms from other institutionalists (Mayhew, 1987), asserts that the principle should not be given the status of eternal verity or exclusivity beyond that which inquiry continues to affirm. Each researcher in each inquiry context should continuously decide which choices are instrumental or ceremonial, and so are facilitative or destructive of the provisioning process.

The second strand of original (American) institutionalism can be traced to Commons, who takes a much more favourable view of the role of institutions than Veblen and Ayres. Commons (1931, 1934, 1950) sees institutions as problem-solving instruments that evolve out of a need for 'workability' in human interaction. They are seen as responses to the scarcity of resources and conflicts of interest (a dynamic process that involves human will and choice), so that requirements for order, certainty and security are met (Zingler, 1974; Rutherford, 1983). On that basis, Commons views institutional evolution as a process of collective action that involves both spontaneous acts and conscious efforts for design. The cumulative effect of collective action taken over time by the members of a 'going concern' (i.e. any type of community, such as a family, a firm, a union, or a whole state) is the provision of 'working rules', which not only 'control' but also 'expand' individual action. Working rules determine "...what the individual can, cannot, must, must not, may or may not do" (Commons, 1931: 650) and provide the basis to settle conflicts within the socio-economy, to establish order in economic life and, ultimately, to ensure economic progress (Ramstad, 1986; Bromley, 1994). Working rules are codified in the legal framework of statutes, decisions of courts and administrative bodies, or in the less formal sense of prescribed behaviour (i.e. customs) of going concerns.

Although Commons appears to have accepted the Veblenian dichotomy in his system of thought (Hamilton, 1953; Mirowski, 1987; Miller, 1998), his depiction of evolutionary dynamics emphasises the application of creativity to the design of institutions themselves more than the continual conflict between instrumental creativity and ceremonial inertia (Rutherford, 1983). On these grounds, Commons sees not only technology, but also organisational development as a vital evolutionary force (Bromley, 1994). Given these ideas, Commons' principal aim is to understand how the complex of working rules affect economic behaviour and economic outcomes, how these change and evolve over time and how to bring about expedient economic outcomes. To that end he emphasises the significance of equality and justice, acknowledging the importance of legal and political matters in the functioning of the economy, something which leads him to seek holistic explanations in the old 'political economy' fashion (Dugger, 1980; Ramstad, 1986).

As mentioned earlier, Commons attached high significance to issues of conflict, power and coercion in the development and function of working rules. These lines of argument are taken into further account by original institutionalists (Miller, 1978; Wilber and Harrison, 1978; Samuels, 1990, 1995), who highlight the implications of coercion, power structure and social control to institutions, institutional change and the functioning of the socio-economy in general. Moreover, it is evident that Commons' institutionalism has certain similarities with the new institutional approach. In particular, it is argued (Dugger, 1980; Rutherford, 1994b; Furubotn and Richter, 2005) that, although the perspective and the assumptions differ, both strands: (i) place emphasis on the transaction as a basic unit of economic analysis; (ii) recognise the significance of customs and ideology in the development of (working) rules; and (iii) highlight the importance of property rights, the legal framework, pressure groups and political institutions in economic organisation.

The philosophical underpinnings of original institutionalism owe a great deal to the American pragmatism of Peirce and Dewey[48] (Mirowski, 1987; Wisman and Rozansky, 1991). A fundamental postulate of pragmatism is that any conception of reality, truth, knowledge, etc., essentially involves the notion of a community. No universal, objective, secure or permanent anchor exists to guarantee true knowledge. Knowledge is therefore the outcome of a process of interpretation and conceptualisation of experiences by a self-identified community of inquiry, aiming towards the enhancement of generic 'workability' and 'serviceability' in the lines of thought and action to the overall betterment of human life on the whole. Thus the perception and interpretation of the world (and thus also reality) is, substantially, a socio-cultural process, where the community of inquiry is the basic epistemological unit.(Mirowski, 1987).

Having embraced such a philosophical position, old institutionalism espouses a holistic view of the world, where economy, politics, legal processes and social structures are conceptualised as an integrated, unified whole, or synthesis, and not as logically separated structures and processes (Mirowski, 1987). This holistic perception is couched in the belief that the whole is not only greater than the sum of its parts, and so is not deducible from its parts,[49] but also that the parts are so interrelated that their functioning is conditioned by the whole to which they belong (Rutherford 1994a). Along these lines, Wilber and Harrison (1978: 71) describe the old institutional approach to economics as holistic, systemic and evolutionary: it

> is holistic because it focuses on the pattern of relations among parts and the whole,... systemic because it believes that those parts make up a coherent whole and can be understood only in terms of the whole, [and] ... evolutionary because changes in the pattern of relations are seen as the very essence of social reality.

Meaning is therefore linked to the whole social context, and entities or activities are assumed to be truly comprehensible only through their interrelations with other entities or activities. This entails that an intelligible and relevant model of the economic system cannot be obtained by isolating the phenomenon of interest from its interrelationship with the overall social whole (Kapp, 1976). Indeed, at least in principle, one should investigate nearly the whole socio-politico-economic institutional framework to understand and explain one institution (Hamilton, 1919; Atkinson and Oleson, 1996).

The technique of investigation of original institutionalism is an amalgamation of history and comparative analysis, where historical situations or cases are systematically recounted and compared in an effort to discern a pattern or general element. This particular mode of research is called 'pattern modelling' or 'storytelling' (Wilber and Harrison, 1978; Wisman and Rozansky, 1991; Atkinson and

Oleson, 1996; Stanfield, 1999). At the heart of the pattern model investigatory mode is an inductive, empirical analysis based on evaluating and synthesising context-specific historical evidence. The mode relies primarily on case studies and ethnographic techniques for collecting information[50] (Wilber and Harrison, 1978; Dugger, 1979; Atkinson and Oleson, 1996).

The process of pattern modelling, which is described extensively in Wilber and Harrison (1978) and Ramstad (1986), proceeds as follows. Initially the investigator focuses on parts of the system and, through analytic observation, tries to identify recurrent themes and build typologies. These themes can be in the form of an accepted practice, a cultural norm or a particular mode of production. The researcher then moves to consider tentative linkages between themes and to construct tentative hypotheses about parts of the system based on these recurrent themes and their linkages. These are subsequently tested and validated (contextually) by consulting a wide variety of evidence and examining the plausibility of the initial interpretations. In this way, a complex picture of the subject matter gradually emerges, which provides the basis for the pattern modelling, i.e. linking all these validated themes into a network or a pattern. The pattern model is similarly tested by observing how well new evidence can be incorporated into or explained within it. However, as new evidence constantly emerges and as the system itself is evolving, both the model and the typologies are continually being revised and can neither be completed nor rigorously confirmed.

The method of original institutional economics is pluralistic, utilising both qualitative and quantitative types of data (Kapp, 1976; Lind, 1993; Whalen, 1996). This is because original institutionalists ascribe primacy to subject matter over method (Wilber and Harrison, 1978). However, researchers within the strand tend to rely more on the examination of qualitative empirical information of a historical and cultural nature and on descriptive rather than inferential use of quantitative information (Atkinson and Oleson, 1996; Stanfield, 1999). Moreover, a preference for the narrative rather than a mathematical format is evident (Wilber and Harrison, 1978; Van Staveren, 1999). Original institutionalists, however, do not stop at pure description. They also develop theory by examining cases for similarities and differences and they try to identify the critical or strategic factors controlling a situation (Dugger, 1979; Atkinson and Oleson, 1996). Theory development, nevertheless, is oriented towards explanation rather than prediction. This is achieved by relating a phenomenon to a set of other elements that together construct a unified system, and by identifying the process of change that drives the system. Accordingly, no theoretical statement can be generalised beyond the particular system to which it applies. Thus, for original institutionalists, theory describes local specificities, i.e. regularities relative to time and space, which are not presumed to exist throughout history or in different societies (Wilber and Harrison, 1978; Wisman and Rozansky, 1991).

As already noted, the methodological tenets of original institutionalism emanate from the philosophy of pragmatism. This relationship is at least partly explained by the historical origins of institutional economics. The pragmatist philosophical basis of institutionalism is a legacy from the age of Veblen and

Commons and can be understood as the result of lock-in or path dependence from the original formulation of the approach at a time (the end of the nineteenth and beginning of the twentieth century) when humanistic approaches and pragmatism were in their heyday, whereas others had not yet been developed.

Critical realism, for example, appeared much later (in the late 1970s) to provide an alternative conception and approach to social research by enriching the notion of social structure already available from structuralism (defined as a level of social reality which, though dependent on, is irreducible to human agency) with the main argument of humanism that social material is agent-dependent (i.e. determined by the way that human agents understand, interpret and conceptualise the world). From this perspective, society is perceived as produced and reproduced partly through the interpretations of human agents and partly through deeper causes not always recognisable by these agents. These deeper causes or social structures not only pre-date each individual (and thus have a temporal priority over the individual), but have emergent properties of their own which are marked by the existence of separate and additional causal effects on other parts of the system.

Stimulated by such developments in the philosophy of social science, contemporary original institutionalists have attempted to reconsider their philosophical bases. On these grounds, some (e.g. Bush, 1993) have suggested an intellectual recombination of the key elements of American pragmatism with modern philosophical realism. The argument is that Dewey's pragmatist philosophy – and Peirce's too, to some extent – was actually based on realist foundations, as the former was quite comfortable with the idea of external, pre-existent, and stratified reality (see also Delaney, 1999). Hodgson (1993b), commenting on the subject, argues that the two approaches indeed exhibit a number of ontological and epistemological similarities. Both, for instance, recognise that an understanding of the whole is necessary to comprehend the parts, and the parts and their relations have to be examined to understand the whole (holism). Both also accept that society cannot exist without the individual and the individual does not exist without the social whole, without this implying that the one is reducible to the other. Both finally acknowledge the significant effects of social reality on the individual, but also recognise that the world is interpreted and conceptualised by lay agents in their activities. Nevertheless, despite these common grounds, there are still many issues to be resolved and much work to be done to see whether pragmatism and realism can be really reconciled.[51]

As expected, most contemporary original institutionalists would question the necessity and feasibility of reconciling pragmatism and realism. Yet some scholars (such as Hodgson, 1988, 1998a, 1999a, 2000, 2003, 2006; Samuels, 1990; Adams, 1993; Van Staveren, 1999; Cumbers *et al.*, 2003; Schmid, 2008) have acknowledged the structural nature of institutions being receptive to philosophical arguments raised by the critical realist movement. In particular, it has been argued that institutions are not only "... 'subjective' ideas in the head of agents...", but also "... 'objective' structures faced by them" (Hodgson, 1998a: 181, 2006). This suggests that institutional structures, mechanisms and necessary relations lie behind and affect the flux of events in an essentially open world. Institutions, as all social forms, depend on human agency and social relations for their existence. Similarly, individuals depend on institutional structures for their socialisation, interaction and survival, and their behaviour is affected profoundly by the institutional context. Thus it is not only that institutions prescribe the behaviour and actions of individuals, but also that the actions of individuals are part of the process of the reproduction and transformation of the institutional structures. Yet neither element can be reduced to, or conflated with, the other. Although agent and institutional structure are connected in a process of mutual interaction and interdependence, they do not have the same ontological and explanatory status. Clearly, they have different qualities.

This critical realist tinge gives an interesting twist to the methodology of original institutionalism. The purpose remains the explanation of the institutional structures and their underlying mechanisms of change with regard to the economic phenomena under concern. However, the methodological apparatus now involves a combination of abstract theory, observation and analysis. Institutionalism works from 'stylised facts' and attempts to uncover the underlying institutional features of the system (including local cultures, political and legal structures, and so on) that account for adequate causal explanations. This requires analyses that are qualitative and quantitative, historical and comparative, so that the real causal linkages involved are outlined.

This should not be conceived of as naive empiricism. Facts do not speak for themselves. Nor does theory arise by induction from the data. All empirical inquiries presuppose a set of concepts and an implicit or explicit theoretical framework, which is essential for the perception and recognition of the corresponding facts (Myrdal, 1958; Miller, 1978; Dugger, 1979; Hulsen, 1998). For this reason the analysis of stylised facts requires the prior development of a conceptual framework that conjecturally specifies the 'constitutive' institutional structures, mechanisms and causal powers at work, discusses their particular relationships and provides the basis for the identification of tendencies or partial empirical regularities (the stylised facts in question). However, it is not possible to incorporate in this framework all the details and all the features of reality. To reduce complexity, a process of abstraction has to occur where the theorist identifies abstract descriptions of situations, phenomena or institutional features (i.e. 'ideal types'[52]) which underlie the key features that are deemed crucial for the purposes of explanation. On that basis, it is possible to construct and develop hypotheses concerning the key causal linkages behind the observed phenomena.

d Diverse traditions of institutional economics

It is evident from the preceding discussion that institutional economics is an extremely diverse set of approaches highlighting the significant role institutions play in the functioning of the socio-economic system. It embraces a wide range of conceptual standpoints (ranging from the transaction costs approach to the broader socio-cultural interpretation of institutional dynamics) and it can be informed by a variety of philosophical and methodological underpinnings (positivism, pragmatism and realism). Moreover, things are made more complicated by the fact that it is difficult to draw precise lines of demarcation, not only between the different strands within the paradigm, but also between institutionalism and other economic traditions. This plurality and diversity of the institutionalist paradigm does not, however, necessarily constitute a weakness. Actually, some researchers (Hoksbergen, 1994, 1998; Luker *et al.*, 1998; Samuels, 1998a, 1998b, 2000) have welcomed the heterogeneity and disciplinary richness of institutionalism, not only as an indication of maturity, but also as a sign of adaptation to 'the rising tide of postmodernism'.[53] In particular, they argue that institutionalism, by being open to interaction with other economic traditions and less rigid with regard to its ontological, epistemological and methodological assumptions, is in the process of coming to terms with the ideas coming out of the philosophical attitude of postmodernism. Additionally, others (Khalil, 1994; van der Krabben, 1995; Johnson and Nielsen, 1998; Guy and Henneberry, 2000; Cumbers *et al.*, 2003; Cheng, 2005; Buitelaar, 2007; Needham *et al.*, 2011) have demonstrated that, despite its philosophical pluralism, it is legitimate to articulate an eclectic mix of the theories that it encompasses to develop an appropriate framework for the analysis of the economic phenomena under concern.

2.4 Conclusions

It is generally acknowledged that philosophies structure social research. The importance of philosophical issues arises from the fact that every research procedure is inextricably related to particular perceptions of the world and cognitive approaches to it. On this basis, the effectiveness and intellectual quality of research methods must depend on philosophical justification.

This chapter has examined the main philosophical currents in the social sciences, highlighting the different disciplinary biases and ideological disputes encountered in social research. In particular, four philosophical orientations were considered (empiricism, positivism, humanism and structuralism) and their epistemological, ontological and methodological assumptions were discussed. On this basis, this chapter has provided the rationality and perspective to consider the prevailing paradigms in economics.

Three analytical frameworks are generally recognised in economics: the mainstream, the structuralist and the institutionalist. This chapter has considered the schools of economic thought associated with these frameworks and has discussed their world views, conceptual underpinnings and methodological practices. Additionally, their deficiencies and limitations were considered. The discussion started with the neoclassical paradigm. This is regarded as the mainstream orthodoxy in economics and is closely related to the positivist philosophical approach. This school, although it experiences a number of severe weaknesses and limitations, has exhibited a remarkable adaptability which has enabled it, by embracing and assimilating its critics (e.g. the Keynesian tradition), to dominate economic thought for more than a century.

From the heterodox approaches, a group of economic schools is generally informed by a structuralist philosophical perspective and comprises Marxist (and neo-Marxist), structurationist and realist traditions. Marxist and neo-Marxist approaches have provided some significant insights with regard to economic organisation, but have been challenged on a number of points and, in particular, for their deterministic system of explanation, their teleological view of economic processes, their rationalistic and utilitarian understanding of human agency, and their lack of a cultural perspective. Structuralist and realist approaches have developed conceptual frameworks through which the nature and role of human agency can be properly addressed. From these, critical realism stood out in virtue of its ontological substance, which enables a clear differentiation between structure and agency and its role as 'under-labourer', i.e. its ability to provide a wider philosophical platform as applied to economic analysis embracing a variety of economic theories.

Finally, another heterodox perspective of economic analysis is provided by the institutional paradigm. This is actually an extremely heterogeneous group of approaches, which are united by a relatively common set of beliefs and attitudes emphasising that institutions are indeed important determinants of economic organisation and should not be taken as given or exogenous to the economic system. This chapter has considered the different strands of thought within the paradigm, identifying their conceptual and methodological tenets, to provide the basis for the development of an eclectic theoretical framework presented in Chapter 4. It became evident that institutionalist research can be informed by various philosophical positions and analytical standpoints. In that sense, the institutional paradigm can be seen as a 'frame' embracing a variety of compatible approaches, theories and conceptual tools that are brought together on the basis of their merit in examining the institutional environment.

The next chapter builds on the current setting and reviews the literature on urban economics. In particular, it adopts the specific analytical frameworks developed here to provide a commentary on urban studies of economic transformation and property market analysis.

Notes

1 However, as Katouzian (1980) points out, the two most important criteria of logical positivism (i.e. verifiability and verification) are indeed value judgements, as they have not been rigorously tested and verified within the natural sciences, and it is very likely to be refuted if it were tested within the social sciences.

2 James, however, changed and, as Peirce (1905) himself saw it, ruined his pragmatism. For where Peirce saw in pragmatism a road to impersonal and objective standards, James gave it a personalised and subjective turn that heavily influenced the nature and course of the subsequent philosophical approach. For instance, Peirce's (1877: 12) assertion that "[t]here are Real things, whose characters are entirely independent of our opinions about them … [and which] we can ascertain by reasoning how really and truly are" would not be unconditionally accepted by many contemporary pragmatists.

3 However, differences on that matter are apparent between the founders of pragmatism. As Honderich (1995) highlights, James's pragmatism is psychologically personalistic, Peirce's is scientifically elitist and Dewey's is democratically populist.
4 In this sense, human history is created by intentional activities, but is not an intended project.
5 Rules are certain regularities (or generalisable procedures) applied in the reproduction of social practices. They could be procedural (dealing with how a practice is actually performed) or moral (concerning appropriate ways of carrying out social actions). Resources refer to the power to which agents have access in the course of social interaction. They are classified as material resources (i.e. the means of production) and resources of authority (stemming from the co-ordination of the activity of human agents).
6 However, Hodgson accepts that critical realism can be easily modified to overcome its limitations. What is needed is for it to embrace psychological, neurophysiological and biological explanations of (human) motives, and to strengthen the role of structure by adopting the institutionalist insight that institutions (and social structures in general) not only constrain, but also reconstitute and redefine human cognition and behaviour.
7 As Lawson (1994: 222) succinctly puts it, an entity, aspect or power found at one level is emergent if it has "arisen out of some 'lower' level, being conditioned by, and dependent upon, but not predictable from, properties found at the lower level".
8 However, a number of scholars (Colander, 2000; Colander *et al.*, 2004a, 2004b; Davis, 2006, 2008; Hodgson, 2007) have argued that neoclassical economics is in the process of being replaced as the dominant research approach in economics by a new mainstream pluralism.
9 Strange in the sense that these three methodological positions (positivist, Friedmanite, Popperian) are hardly compatible with each other (Hodgson, 1988).
10 According to Blaug (1992), such universal laws may be deterministic in form, by referring to individual events *y*, or statistical, by referring to classes of events *y*. In the latter case, statistical laws take the form 'in all cases where events *x* occur, events *y* also occur with a probability of *p*, where $0<p<1$'.
11 Friedman (1953) also subscribes to the falsification position, maintaining that a hypothesis is 'confirmed' when factual evidences fail to disprove it.
12 In fact, even verification and falsification are themselves value judgements.
13 Note that this is in contrast with the neoclassical theory of value, which states that not only labour, but also capital and land, make a contribution to value formation and are thus entitled to a return.
14 It is the difference between the use value and the exchange value of labour power, where the former refers to the total value that the commodity labour power creates and the latter to the costs paid for the reproduction or subsistence of the labour (wages).
15 The ratio of the capital that is invested in the materials and fixed costs (i.e. tools, machinery, buildings) embodied in the production of a commodity (called constant capital) to the capital which is invested in the purchase of labour power (i.e. wages) used in making it (called variable capital) is referred to by Marx (1976, vol. III [1894]) as the organic composition of capital.
16 Excellent reviews of the approaches of the regulation school, as well as its theoretical and methodological properties, are provided in Aglietta (1979), Boyer (1990), Jessop (1990, 1997) Brenner and Glick (1991) and Boyer and Saillard (2002).
17 The mode of regulation is generally analysed in terms of five institutional dimensions: the wage-labour nexus (concerning work organisation, wage formation, lifestyles and the ways in which the labour force is reproduced); the enterprise form (which refers to forms of organisation and competition between firms); the monetary constraint (i.e. the monetary and financial regime); the state (concerning forms of state intervention);

and the international regime (which refers to the arrangements and relations that link national economies together).

18 Taylorism generally refers to the application of scientific methods to the organisation of production. It involves the separation of production activities into their simplest constituent components and the linking together of these fragmented activities into precisely co-ordinated and closely supervised sequences (Dunford, 1990).

19 Hodgson and Samuels (1994) assert that Marx, although impressed by Darwin's evolutionary theory, did not assimilate Darwinian ideas in his social science because it was incompatible with the Hegelian notion of '*Zeitgeit*' and the classical Newtonian world view within which he was trapped. '*Zeitgeit*' or 'spirit of the times' is one of several names Hegel gave to '*Geist*' (translated variously as Spirit, Mind, Absolute Idea or God), expressing the concept of the sense or rationality in the order of things and the succession of one state of affairs after another according to some kind of lawful process. Such a perception is evident in Marx, who views the socio-economic system moving towards the equilibrium of a class-less society in which struggles and crises are eliminated. On this basis, communism refers to a unified social order in a state of harmony, where not only conflict, but also diversity of material interests and socio-economic forms, disappears. In contrast, when historical movement is perceived in terms of Darwinian evolutionary principles, it is not possible to predict the character and form of social change as they result from a process of natural selection among a population of entities exhibiting great diversity and variety.

20 For instance, it is argued that once the proletariat sheds its false consciousness and reflects rationally on its situation, it will be impelled to revolt against the capitalist system.

21 According to Hodgson and Samuels (1994), the Marxist understanding of historical processes can be more precisely described as *evolvere* (the Latin etymology for evolution) or unrolling, rather than by Darwin's theory of natural selection. This is evident, for example, in the supposed development from 'primitive' to 'full' communism, where it is perceived as a revolving movement returning to the original position, but at a 'higher' level.

22 Healey and Barrett (1990) and Healey (1992) suggest another classification of institutional analysis distinguishing between the material resources of production (i.e. property rights and information), the rules of institutional organisation (i.e. laws and customs) and ideas (or ideology).

23 For the application of critical realism to economics and economic methodology, see Lawson (1989, 1995, 1997a, 2003), Fleetwood (1999), Northover (1999), Downward (2003), Downward *et al.* (2002, 2006), Lewis (2004) and Castellacci (2006); to human geography, see Lawson and Staeheli (1990), Pratt (1995), Yeung (1997) and Gruffyd-Jones (2006); and to the analysis of the built environment, see Ganderton (1994), Guy and Henneberry (2000), Naess and Jensen (2002) and Lawson J. (2006).

24 It is interesting to note here that a similar approach is also evident in the writings of institutionalist Myrdal (1958: 156, 1970: 5), who identifies theoretical research as "…thinking in terms of cause and effects" and applied as "…thinking in terms of means and ends".

25 However, the relation between theory and empirical research should not be understood in terms of correspondence rules where theory is supposed to provide a set of propositions from which empirical forms can be logically deduced, but in terms of statements about causal connections between real objects.

26 Note also that Lawson in his latest writings (1997a, 2003) uses the term 'demi-regularity' or 'demi-reg' to convey virtually the same idea. Demi-regularity is defined as "a partial event regularity which *prima facie* indicates the occasional, but less than universal, actualisation of a mechanism or tendency, over a definite region of time-space" (Lawson, 1997a: 204).

27 This, according Randall (1978), is true for all institutionalists, even if some strands of

neo-institutionalism and new institutionalism tend to approach value questions in a rather implicit way.

28 Other scholars (Williamson, 2000; Richter, 2005; Rafiqui, 2009) also adopt a similar classification.

29 The discussion draws on a variety of sources, including Hodgson (1988, 1993a, 1998a, 1999b, 2000, 2004a), Eggertsson (1990a), North (1990, 2005), Maki *et al.* (1993), Hodgson *et al.* (1994a, 1994b), Rutherford (1994a), Samuels (1995), Furubotn and Richter (2005), Menard and Shirley (2005) and Chavance (2009).

30 It is interesting to note that, though from a different perspective and under different methodological assumptions, Commons (1931) also views the study of transactions (defined as the exchange of property rights) as the subject matter of institutional economics.

31 However, the discussion on the social character of rules and rights is incomplete and unsatisfactory (Hodgson, 1988).

32 'Resources' are used here in the wider sense and include both human labour and the goods and information that humans possess.

33 Williamson (1985: 47) defines opportunistic behaviour as the "...self-interest seeking with guilt".

34 This is also referred to as the 'principal-agent problem', describing a situation in which agents, on the basis of some informational advantages they enjoy, may act in a self-interest manner instead of serving the interests of their principals (Furubotn and Ricter, 2005).

35 Furubotn and Richter (2005) use the term 'optimization costs' to describe the totality of these costs.

36 This line of argument can be traced back to Veblen (1904, 1919b).

37 It should be noted that the approach has certain similarities with the emphasis on technological and instrumental advance found in the Ayresian tradition of old institutionalism (see later).

38 Although institutional change is overwhelmingly incremental, discontinuous institutional change can occur in the form of revolution. However, it is highlighted that revolutionary change is seldom as revolutionary as it appears on the surface and this is because, although it is relatively easy to change formal rules, it is much more difficult to alter informal constrains (North, 1990).

39 See, for instance, Stanfield (1980, 1999), Foster (1981), Tool (1986, 1988, 1993), Bush (1987, 1991), Neale (1987), Mayhew (1987, 1994), Rutherford (1994a, 1998), Samuels (1995) and Bromley (2006).

40 See, for example, Clark and Juma (1987), Foster (1988), Hodgson (1988, 1993a, 1993c, 1998a, 1999b, 2000, 2001, 2004a), Van Staveren (1999), O'Hara (2000), Thevenot (2001), Favereau and Lazega (2003), Orlean (2004) and Elsner (2012).

41 Hodgson (1994b) argues that institutionalism has never gained a significant foothold in Europe. This can be partly explained by the fact that, by the time that the USA became a prominent exporter of economic thought (after World War II), institutionalism had already been displaced from within the country by the neoclassical school. Additionally, the wide variety and heterogeneity of the school and its less coherent theoretical system (compared with that of Marxism or neoclassicism), though provided with a fruitful and productive pluralism within the USA, were substantial drawbacks for the successful export of institutionalism. Despite that, economic work of an institutional flavour can be found in Europe. Economists such as Kapp (1968, 1976), Myrdal (1958, 1970) and Polanyi (1944, 1957) all had close links with American institutionalism and made major contributions to the old institutionalist thought. For example, despite Veblen's earlier discussion, the idea of 'cumulative causation' was mainly developed by, and thus is more frequently associated with, Myrdal (Kapp 1976). However, although these figures exerted influence on the ideas of other prominent non-institutional economists (e.g. Nicholas Kaldor), none of them has left behind a salient institutional tradition in Europe.

42 Rutherford (1994a) and Hodgson (1998a), however, assert that the American institutionalism of the post-1940 period (and particularly the Ayresian tradition) seems to espouse an 'oversocialised' view of human behaviour, moving towards methodological collectivism and cultural determinism. This is evident, for instance, in some writings of Miller (1978), Waller (1988a), Mayhew (1994), and elsewhere. Such one-sided emphasis, Hodgson (1999a) continues, cannot be found in the original institutionalism of Veblen and Commons.

43 Old institutionalists use the terms 'habit' and 'routine' to demote any propensity by individuals to follow, usually unconsciously, certain patterns of behaviour (Hodgson, 1998a). This behaviour can be induced by personal rules or social norms, or both.

44 Note the similarity with the path dependence notion of new institutionalism on this point.

45 However, whereas the Darwinian notion of evolution is grounded in competitiveness, there has been an anti-competitive animus both in Veblen and in other old institutionalists (Hodgson, 1988, 1999b, 2002; Wisman and Rozansky, 1991).

46 It is interesting to mention that Ayres (1962: 184) uses the term institution to denote "...segments of social behaviour predominantly ceremonial in character".

47 According to Tool (1994b), this is manifested in: (i) extensive, protracted and involuntary unemployment; (ii) continuing and significant instability (in the market/prices); (iii) substantial gender, race, ancestry and ethnicity discrimination; (iv) pervasive and expanding environmental degradation; and (v) possession and use of economic power without accountability.

48 Both Commons (1934) and Ayres (1962) explicitly recognise the direct influence of Dewey in their institutionalism.

49 In the philosophical discourse this is defined as metaphysical or methodological holism and it holds to the thesis that with respect to some system there is no 'explanatory emergence', i.e. the laws of the more complex situation in the system are not deducible from the laws of the simpler or simplest situations(s) (Addis, 1999).

50 However, Lind (1993) and Rutherford (1994a) argue that old institutionalist work provides no evidence that the latter methods (and especially participant observation) are in common use.

51 Interestingly, critical realist Lawson (1997a: 242, emphasis in the original) seems to come very close to a clearly Peircean pragmatism stance by arguing that "[t]he *judgement* of the truth of a proposition, the criteria for deciding which propositions are to be held as (possibly) true, are necessarily intrinsic to the science (or social activity) concerned". However, this is as far as he goes, as he finally accepts that such judgements have necessarily to "be ontologically grounded or justified,... facilitating discovery and development in science as a rational, discriminating, and adequating process" (Lawson, 1997a: 243).

52 The notion of 'ideal types' is much associated with the work of Max Weber, who views it as a heuristic tool for ordering observations. However, it is worth emphasising that institutionalists (in common with realists – see, for instance, Sayer, 1992 and Lawson, 1997a) hold a slightly different perception on the issue. Commons (1934), for example, asserts that its usefulness lies in its ability to enhance understanding of phenomena, underlying structures and causal mechanisms by coping reality. In that sense it can be said that ideal types are not regarded as subjective classifications of an undifferentiated empirical reality, but abstractions which attempt to grasp precisely the generative mechanisms and causal structures that account, in all their complex and multiple determinations, for the concrete phenomena of the socio-economic realm.

53 Postmodernism is a movement in philosophy, the arts and the social sciences characterised by the acceptance of epistemological pluralism and scepticism towards the ideas of universal truths, grand theory or meta-narrative that signifies the modern era (Cloke *et al.*, 1991; Magnus, 1999; Johnston *et al.*, 2000).

3 Urban development and the property market

3.1 Introduction

The previous chapter dealt with the analytical frameworks that are available in economics, identifying their philosophical underpinnings, conceptual cornerstones and methodological practices. This chapter employs these analytical frameworks to discuss the issue of urban economic transformation. In line with the objective of the book, particular emphasis is placed on the production and reproduction of the built environment and the degree to which each framework takes such considerations on board when discussing urban economic development.

The chapter begins by examining the wider macro factors that affect the urban economy and outlining the contextual trends and emerging patterns of urban socio-economic reorganisation, as identified by a number of researchers independent of methodological stance. This descriptive (almost a-theoretical) analysis is followed by three sections discussing the theoretical explanations provided by the three economic perspectives, i.e. the mainstream, the structuralist and the institutionalist. The final section summarises the findings, setting an agenda for the development of a holistic framework that advances understanding of the function of the urban property market and its role in economic development.

3.2 Urban transformation: stylised facts, contextual trends and emerging patterns

Various scholars (Hausner, 1987; Bovaird, 1992; Castells, 1993; Hall, 1993, 1997b; Meijer, 1993; Bailly *et al.*, 1996; Lever and Bailly 1996; McIntosh, 1997; Atkinson, 2001; Thorns, 2002; Swyngedouw *et al.*, 2003; Kazepov, 2005; Arvanitidis and Petrakos, 2006; Turok and Mykhnenko, 2007, 2008; Ache *et al.*, 2008; Musterd and Murie, 2011) have surveyed and specified the driving forces and contextual trends shaping the recent transformation of European cities. Thus informed, this section highlights the main factors putatively influencing urban development, reports contextual trends and emerging patterns, and outlines the framework within which the current socio-economic and spatial changes are occurring in urban Europe. Although examined separately, these factors are interrelated, interacting with and reinforcing each other.

3.2.1 Technological revolution and information technologies

A key factor in urban economic transformation is technology. This is because technology affects not only the products developed, but also the processes by which they are produced. As such, technological developments have pervasive effects in the overall organisation of the economy and, consequently, in the whole spectrum of urban activities.

Hall (1993) and McIntosh (1997), for example, argue that, since the beginning of the twentieth century, developments in transportation and communication have played a crucial role in the pace and pattern of urban change. Put simply, improvements have lowered transport costs and widened locational choices. Future developments in these areas will substantially impact, among other things, accessibility and connectivity, thus continuing to affect the economic and spatial configuration of urban areas.

Similarly, other researchers (e.g. Castells, 1993; Short, 1996) have placed emphasis on information technology, maintaining that recent innovations in microelectronics and information processing mark the emergence of a major technological breakthrough. These innovations formed a nucleus for other fundamental developments enabling the full utilisation of the new technologies, with important implications for the economic and spatial structure of cities. For example, computer-aided manufacturing systems enabled the substitution of high technology for labour in manufacturing, improving speed, cost-effectiveness, flexibility and efficiency. In (tele)communications, advanced services such as e-mail, fax and the internet facilitated information exchange, offering locational freedom and enabling firms to diversify spatially (Gibson and Lizieri, 1999, 2001). Some scholars have gone as far as arguing that technological advances eliminate the need for face-to-face interaction, making cities, and, indeed, space itself, obsolete (Cairncross, 1997), whereas others have provided evidence of the increased importance of cities (Gaspar and Glaeser, 1998; Hall, 1999).

Equally important, however, is the effect that these technological developments have on all aspects of urban life. The new technological/informational revolution, like all major revolutions, provided a framework within which a number of other transformations have occurred. Referred to as changes in "...production and consumption, management and work practices, culture and warfare, communication and education, space and time" (Castells, 1993: 248), they engender a new economic organisation with its own social and spatial consequences (Nilsson and Schamp, 1996).

3.2.2 Globalisation of the economy

Economic globalisation has been widely discussed in the literature. Some scholars (e.g. Hall, 1993, 1997a; Amin and Thrift, 1994, 1995; Gordon, 1999; Groth, 2000) define it as a more intensive internationalisation of economic activities. As such, it is generally conceptualised as increased mobility of capital, labour, products, firms, information and ideas. Yet others (Lizieri, 1992; Castells, 1993; Budd, 1995, 1998; Sassen, 2001) assert that globalisation actually means something more than this, referring to an economy that works as a single unit on a global scale. It is an economy where capital and financial flows, labour and commodity markets, information, management and organisation are not only internationalised, but are fully interdependent worldwide, linking the globe into a 24-hour trading day and ensuring that changes originating in one part of the planet rapidly diffuse to others. It must be emphasised, however, that change does not occur everywhere in the same way and at the same rate, i.e. the process of globalisation is not geographically uniform. Indeed, the particular character of individual localities interacts with this large-scale general process to produce quite specific outcomes.

Independent of the definitional differences, all researchers agree that the emergence of the global economy is certainly associated with the economic deregulation and liberalisation of the financial markets. The starting point of these changes was the breakdown of the Bretton Woods international monetary regime (in 1971) which, accompanied by developments in information technology, enabled the internationalisation of financial transactions and the liberalisation of the world's major capital markets from the 1980s onwards.

Liberalisation and globalisation have significant implications for the economic and spatial organisation of cities. This is due to the fact that specific economic activities, like production and finance, have become less tied to particular geographical locations (Boddy, 1999; Lever, 1999). Certainly, the high mobility of these activities could affect, and in some cases undermine, the economic structure of some urban areas, while others could position themselves to take advantages of these possibilities, attracting international business, capital and labour (Jensen-Butler *et al.*, 1997).

3.2.3 European integration

A fundamental process affecting European cities is European integration (Cheshire, 1999; Groth, 2000; McCarthy, 2000). Seen as a process of economic and political unification and social cohesion between member states, it has spawned a number of actions (including the establishment of the single market, single currency and European citizenship) and common policies in key areas (such as regional development, transport, innovation and foreign affairs) over the years.

Whatever the future developments and the course of European integration, it is undeniable that the process heavily affects the economic, political and social underpinnings of European cities, with further implications for their spatial structures. For instance, the progress of the single market and monetary integration, with the removal of the technical and physical barriers to the free movement of both products and factors of production, has profound consequences for the economic, demographic and spatial fortunes of urban areas.

To start with, economic activities become more footloose, as obstacles to movement diminish and new opportunities to cut costs and increase returns (by gaining market share) open up. This has the effect of further increasing competitiveness between firms and underlining the competitive advantages of urban regions (Porter, 1990, 1996, 2003) in terms of providing a supportive environment for business clusters. In this context, arguments have been raised that territories, and not just firms, compete with one another to attract economic activities, investment, population, public funds or hallmark events, and to define a productive role for themselves (Gordon, 1999; Lever, 1999). Both attractiveness and competitiveness depend not only on 'hard' economic determinants, but also on 'soft' socio-political assets (such as policy effectiveness, public–private co-operation, quality of life, innovating capacity and institutional quality) (Camagni, 1999; Kresl and Singh, 1999). These factors drive competitiveness, but at the same time foster co-operation between places. Cities co-operate through specialisation and the exchange of goods and services, and as components in an urban system that increasingly transcends national borders (Begg, 1999). Co-operation is also evident in the articulation of common problems (such as social exclusion or environmental degradation), sharing experiences and establishing policy networks.

In addition to economic forces, there are also political forces at the European level exerting independent influences on urban development (Castells, 1993). For example, weakening national sovereignty and the reinforcing of other tiers of political organisation (namely, the supranational-European and the local-regional), have underlined cities as the prime loci of political and economic activity (European Commission, 1997; Harris, 1997), enabling direct financial support from the European Union to alleviate problems and improve urban conditions. In addition, some social implications of European integration can be hypothesised on the basis of the socio-cultural and ethnic multiplicity and heterogeneity characterising European member states. Thus Castells (1993) and Kunzmann (1996) argue that the advent of 'supranationality' blurs the significance of national identities, highlighting the importance of local, socio-cultural settings in the process of urban transformation.

3.2.4 Restructuring of economic organisation

Another trend that lies behind urban transformation relates to the structural reorganisation of the economy. One of the major manifestations of this process has been the rise of service activities (at the expense of traditional manufacturing industries), which now constitute the principal sector of the urban economy (Fielding, 1994; Nagle and Spencer, 1996; European Commission, 1997).

The shift in the urban economic base from manufacturing to service activities is not a particularly new phenomenon (Hausner, 1987). However, over the years, its intensity and scale have increased enormously, to the point that it now dominates all major urban economies in Organization for Economic Cooperation and Development (OECD) countries (Wolfl, 2005). This, however, does not mean that manufacturing has ceased to constitute an important sector of economic activity. Indeed, manufacturing production has continued to grow in absolute terms, albeit at a rate inferior to services and with a steadily decreasing proportion of the total resources used (Arvanitidis and Petrakos, 2006).

Many scholars have, however, argued that such a transition towards a service economy has changed the form and organisation of manufacturing production (Lever and Bailly, 1996; Nagle and Spencer, 1996; McCann and Sheppard, 2003). This reorganisation concerns both the types of goods produced and the way they are produced. In terms of what is being produced, there has been a marked trend towards greater product differentiation, bringing to the fore aspects such as design, marketing, distribution and, in short, a set of activities referred to as 'producer services' (i.e. services linked to manufacturing production). In terms of how goods are produced, the tendency (as noted earlier) is to substitute high technology for labour in the goods-producing processes. This has allowed attention to shift from physical production towards other areas previously regarded as of lesser importance (e.g. corporate and product planning, R&D, advertising, marketing and administrative control). Thus it is evident that service functions have become an important input to both physical production and to other activities ancillary to production, blurring the traditional distinction between manufacturing and services (OECD, 2000).

In addition to their growing significance in goods production, service activities in modern economies are becoming increasingly important in their own right (OECD, 2000, 2005). Whereas in the past they were regarded as non-growth-generating activities, they are now viewed as crucial to the performance of the urban economies, being not only tradable, but also highly responsive to external demand. Examples of this kind of service activities include consumer services (those related to education, health, recreation, etc.) as well as the tourist industry.

A key element of the development and function of the service economy is its direct reliance on the production, use and distribution of information and knowledge (Castells, 1993). On that basis, information and knowledge are becoming important productive resources in their own right,[1] critically determining urban economic performance and the potential for growth (Knight, 1995; Artelaris *et al.*, 2011).

In conclusion, it must be emphasised that the restructuring of economic organisation and the emergence of a service economy has important implications, not only for the socio-economic development, but also for the spatial development of urban Europe. This is because both the service economy in general, and the production and exchange of information/knowledge in particular, have specific spatial requirements that create different geographies and distinct urban spatial organisation.

3.2.5 Social trends and population dynamics

Cities are open systems; they may expand or contract, and their populations may become 'older' or 'younger'. Whatever the trend, it is argued that demographic and socio-cultural forces have a significant effect on the economic and spatial organisation of cities. One such important force concerns the increasing instability and heterogeneity of contemporary life, which affects the pattern of families and the structure of households (Blotevogel and King, 1996; Champion, 2001; Hadar and Pines, 2004). In particular, the archetypal 'two-parents-plus-children' nuclear model of one breadwinner has been replaced by single-person or single-parent households, unmarried cohabitation and increasing levels of the participation of women in the workforce. Moreover, these new types of households have a strong preference for large-city lifestyles.

These micro-level socio-cultural trends have been viewed in relation to wider macro-level demographic patterns. In particular, researchers (Ilbery, 1990; Dicken and Oberg, 1996; Lutz *et al.*, 2008) have highlighted the emergence of two trends: the ongoing decline in birth rates and the gradual increase in life expectancy, which, in combination, have led to the reshaping of the population age structure (a phenomenon known as 'ageing'). It is estimated that the number of people aged over sixty years will reach one billion by 2020 and almost two billion by 2050, representing 22 per cent of the world's population (Bloom *et al.*, 2010). These demographic trends affect the patterns of consumption, production, housing, employment, savings, insurance, investment and innovation, and, on that basis, have important social, economic and spatial implications.

With the overall decline in birth rates across Europe, the regional map of population change has become increasingly dominated by migration movements.[2] Cities play a key role as the loci of these activities. Scholars (Blotevogel and King, 1996; Mitchell, 2004; Turok and Mykhnenko, 2007) discuss these population movements under the heading of 'counterurbanisation'. In general terms it is argued that, in the 1960s and 1970s, populations were moving from larger cities to smaller towns and rural peripheries. By the late 1980s and 1990s, however, the phenomenon had developed more diverse and complex trends and a new picture of population patterns has emerged. Regions experiencing net out-migration and population loss are of two main types: (i) heavily urbanised areas, especially in north-west Europe, where urban decentralisation is reinforced by industrial closures and the decline of port-related activities; and (ii) low-income rural areas, particularly in peripheral Europe (Ireland, Scandinavia, the Mediterranean regions). Cases of net in-migration and population gain are less easy to generalise, but three main types of location are identified: (i) the hinterlands of major cities (e.g. London, Randstad, Copenhagen); (ii) some of the largest cities themselves, particularly those in Scandinavia and southern Europe; and (iii) 'sun-belt' regions, such as the 'souths' of England, Germany, Sweden and France, together with central and north-east Italy, the Mediterranean coasts of Spain and southern Portugal.

More functionally, the relationship between population change and the economy is reflected in the changing patterns of employment and unemployment. Concerning the latter, researchers agree that, despite extreme unevenness across Europe, urban unemployment has been rising since the 1970s to stabilise at today's high levels (European Commission, 1997; Crampton, 1999; Blanchard, 2006). In addition, changes in the pattern of employment along two major lines are reported: declining manufacturing employment and increasing service jobs. Regarding manufacturing, researchers highlight the significance of the decentralisation of manufacturing and routinised 'back-office' activities to smaller peripheral towns (discussed in detail later). With service employment, the evidence suggests a tendency towards spatial centralisation in large cities, although, in general, it is questionable whether this could redress overall job losses.

Moreover, the social structure of urban employment has also been investigated, highlighting the more varied and selective requirements of service-base employment, demanding flexible employment terms and conditions as well as a highly skilled and well-educated workforce (Fainstein and Campbell, 1996). This leads to the emergence of two distinctive social groups within the urban frame: high status, highly skilled, expensive professional personnel on the one hand, and low status, lower skilled, relatively inexpensive labour on the other (Mingione, 1995; Bailly *et al.*, 1996; Hall, 1999). The spatial implications of this polarisation are discussed, acknowledging that certain groups have an extended range of choices as to how they can (spatially) organise and fulfil their lives, with others having little or no choice, living excluded, marginalised lives and concentrated in declining industrial areas or other areas of economic decay and under-investment. The geographical significance of social polarisation manifests itself in phenomena such as 'gentrification' (Lees *et al.*, 2008; Lees and Wyly, 2010), transforming the socio-economic composition of whole neighbourhoods and often involving direct or indirect displacement of the indigenous populations.

3.2.6 Spatial implications of socio-economic reorganisation

Changes in technological, economic, political, social and demographic structures are generally reflected in the spatial structure of the cities housing them. An important role in this restructuring process is played by firms and other economic agents, which, through their locational decisions, determine the economic activity in cities and, in turn, the prospects for economic growth and prosperity.

Affected by the technological, economic, political and demographic changes described here, the geography of manufacturing activity has begun to undergo significant changes over the last few decades. Although researchers highlight different underlying causes, they all agree that technological advancements and organisational restructuring reduce the need for industrial plants to locate within urban areas. On that basis, the range and diversity of feasible industrial locations have been greatly extended, leading, since the 1960s and 1970s, to a movement of industrial activity out of the urban cores and subsequently away from large metropolitan areas (Nilsson and Schamp, 1996; McCann and Sheppard, 2003). The increasing environmental degradation and high costs related to urban centres have certainly played a significant role in these locational decisions.

Although the movement of manufacturing can be neatly described as deconcentration away from urban cores, service activities show a more complex and varied pattern of location. Thus, at the intra-urban level, a spatial separation of two types of activity has been recognised. High-level service functions, such as headquarter offices, remain concentrated at strategic locations in metropolitan areas (because of the importance of centrality-accessibility and their need for frequent face-to-face contacts), whereas routinised, low-level functions, such as back-office activities, tend to decentralise to take advantage of the qualities of peripheral locations. Unlike manufacturing, however, the latter activities seem to go to the suburbs of the same urban areas in which the front office functions are located. Similar locational patterns also hold for commercial, public administration, education and cultural activities. At the inter-urban level they have shown a high preference for a small number of large metropolitan areas, whereas at the intra-urban level they have moved from city centres to nodal points of high concentration located in the urban periphery or along main transportation routes.

The evidence so far suggests that some major metropolitan areas have managed to respond positively and to adapt to the underlying restructuring, experiencing economic development and prosperity. According to Meijer (1993) and Hall (1999), these cities are the national European capitals, together with the 'commercial capitals' of Europe (e.g. Milan, Barcelona) and some major regional capitals of large nation states (e.g. Edinburgh, Lyon). The concentration of administration/control (either private or public), financial, cultural and other high-level service activities reflects their economic success (Bosman and de Smidt, 1993; Rozenblat and Pumain, 1993; Sassen, 2001).

At the same time, not all cities have been able to adapt to the technical and sectoral changes and successfully generate or attract activities promoting economic growth. In particular, a number of cities with economic rationale centred in traditional manufacturing (mainly old industrial or port cities) have shown signs of economic decline associated with a common array of problems, such as declining investments, shut-down plants, considerable unemployment and out-migration (especially of skilled labour), declining revenues, ageing or obsolete infrastructure, rising crime levels and other indicators of social stress.

Additionally, the emergence of a third group of cities has been highlighted, which, although not representing historical growth points, have shown exceptional trajectories and developed into dynamic economic centres (Hall, 1993, 1997a; Batten, 1995; Lever and Bailly, 1996; Budd, 1998; Raco, 1999). These are generally small to medium-sized urban places able to attract people and firms, creating a new economic geography. Some are part of the growth belts of mega-city regions receiving inward flows of people and jobs and benefiting from the deconcentration processes. Others have prospered through specialisation in one or two service functions, such as R&D, hi-tech activities, or educational services (Hall, 1993; Batten, 1995; Nagle and Spencer, 1996; Budd, 1998).

Overall, it has become evident that cities are at the crossroads of an economic, political and social restructuring manifesting itself both functionally and spatially. This is an intrinsically complex process, reflecting the volatility, instability and uncertainty of the environment in which contemporary cities operate. As such, although it is relatively easy to identify *ex post* some key trends and emerging patterns, it is difficult to provide adequate explanations for mechanisms and causes, or to predict eventual outcomes (as neatly demonstrated by Kunzmann, 1996). Certainly, an adequate theoretical framework is crucial to expediting this. On these grounds, the following sections discuss the conceptual frameworks available from urban economics, identifying the viewpoints, theories and models used to analyse urban economic change and the provision of the built environment.

3.3 Conventional approaches to urban transformation

Conventional approaches to urban transformation focus their analysis on the laws of the marketplace. The central idea is that supply and demand relations define the urban economic and spatial structures, resulting in a form of stable urban equilibrium (Evans, 1985; Harvey, 1996). Accordingly, observed urban changes are ascribed to the decisions of rational individuals (consumers and producers), who react perfectly to price signals in seeking to maximise their welfare (utility/wealth) given certain budgets and preferences. In most of the conventional urban studies, supply-side conditions are seen as relatively unproblematic and emphasis is thus placed on the demand side of urban markets and their economic and spatial consequences.

Mainstream urban studies approach the mechanisms underlying urban change at the microlevel[3] by focusing on the changing determinants of the location, the property-related decisions of firms and households and the implication these have for the economic and spatial structure of the city (Anas *et al.*, 1998). On that basis, explanations of urban land use and value patterns are based on the assumption that all economic actors seek an equilibrium situation at which (*ceteris paribus*) costs are minimised, while profitability/utility is maximised. An important concept in the development of this kind of explanation is 'accessibility', an umbrella term referring to the comparative advantages of a particular urban location in terms of movement, transport costs and convenience. Two forms of accessibility are commonly identified: special and general (Ball *et al.*, 1998). Special accessibility refers to the economic advantages available to individuals or firms when they locate near to each other. These advantages called 'agglomeration economies' and are discussed later.

General accessibility places an emphasis on the requirements of firms and households to minimise movement costs. Given certain simplifying assumptions with regard to the centrality of economic activity, the structure of transportation costs (which vary with distance to the central market) and transportation technology, primacy is attached to the city centre location, assumed (historically) to represent the point of greatest accessibility. However, due to space scarcity, costs (land values) are highest in central locations and decrease with distance from the centre. Hence any rational location decision can strike a balance between the costs of centrality and the advantages of accessibility. On these grounds, trade-off models have been developed describing the location decisions of economic agents and, in turn, the patterns of urban land use (Alonso, 1964; Mills, 1972; Anas *et al.*, 1998). Location choice for firms, for example, is described as a straightforward trade-off of rent payable against distance from the centre. For households, although decisions tend to be more complicated due to non-monetary determinants of utility, the key mechanism remains intact: households trade-off transport costs to the centre against the extra space or quality of life offered elsewhere, simultaneously choosing between distance from the centre and the level of land rent. Social segregation within the city is also theorised, with more affluent households affording to locate either in the city centre (balancing high rents against accessibility) or at peripheral locations (balancing transport costs against locational amenities).

These trade-off models of locational behaviour provide the basis for understanding the allocation of urban space to economic activities and, in turn, explain the economic and spatial structure of the city and its dynamic properties. A fundamental theme in these traditional urban economic theories is the monocentric form of urban structure. This describes a pattern of urban land use with service activities outbidding other uses for central locations, followed by industrial and residential uses in successive zones. However, technological, economic and social changes (as described in the previous section) can erode the central location advantages of general accessibility, providing a new impetus to the location dynamics of specific user groups, with implications for urban change. Taking these parameters into account (and particularly the advances in transportation and (tele)communications technology and the rise of service economy), conventional urban economic studies have revised and extended their theoretical models in an attempt to explain the decentralisation and deconcentration of certain economic activities. On a similar basis, polycentric or network forms of urbanisation have been suggested for the analysis of urban structures, highlighting the emergence of multiple central places ('subcentres') within urban configurations as a result of the advantages of 'concentrated deconcentration' (Kloosterman and Musterd, 2001; Meijers, 2005).

Alongside the trade-off models of general accessibility, another way to explore urban dynamics at the micro-level has been through the changing nature of special accessibility issues. These are generally discussed under the term 'urban agglomeration economies', which refers to the external economies available in large concentrations of population and economic activity. Standard textbooks on urban economics (such as Goodall, 1972; Evans, 1985; Harvey, 1996; O'Sullivan, 2012) state that urban agglomeration economies arise due to the advantages of concentration or complementarity. The former takes the form of a ready supply of trained labour, common services and large market areas offered by the locality ('urbanisation economies'). The latter highlights the fact that some firms prefer to locate alongside others in the same industry to benefit from information and labour sharing, trading links and specialised inputs ('localisation economies').

Marshall (1920) is commonly credited with originating these ideas, setting out in the early twentieth century the basics of agglomeration economies with regard to industrial activities (Fujita and Thisse, 1996; Gordon and McCann, 2000). In Marshall's view, there are three principal reasons for industrial agglomeration. First, clustering facilitates a pooled labour market for workers with specialist skills, to the benefit of both firms and workers. Second, agglomeration generates demand on a scale facilitating the efficient provision of specialist inputs and services. Finally, knowledge and information flows between firms create 'technological' spillovers or externalities to the benefit of all firms.

A number of researchers have attempted to provide empirical evidence supporting the validity of agglomeration economies, relating them to urban economic growth and prosperity (for a review, see Rosenthal and Strange, 2004). For instance, David and Rosenbloom (1990) and Dumais *et al.* (2002) argue that industries with similar labour mixes enjoy the largest benefit from proximity, suggesting the importance of labour market pooling. Likewise, studies by Glaeser *et al.* (1992), Rauch (1993) and Henderson (2007) provide evidence for the importance of knowledge spillovers. Holmes (1999) established the importance of input sharing, whereas the findings by Rosenthal and Strange (2001) support the significance of all three Marshallian factors. In a similar vein, other researchers (e.g. Moomaw, 1981; Henderson, 1986, 2003; Bertinelli and Black, 2004; Glaeser and Gottlieb, 2009) have established that spatial concentration enhances productivity and economic growth.

All these studies agree that agglomeration forces tend to encourage the concentration of economic activity via 'circular causality', i.e. spatial concentration itself creates an environment that encourages further spatial concentration. However, there are counter-forces to agglomeration in urban activities. Excess concentration in cities brings negative externalities (or diseconomies) due to congestion, higher commuting costs, land scarcity, pollution, crime and social problems (Combes *et al.*, 2005). These constraints work as a dispersion or centrifugal force, impelling certain economic activities to move out of the urban agglomerations. On that basis, a number of researchers have attempted to explain urban economic change by focusing on the process whereby urban agglomeration diseconomies exceed the economies for certain manufacturing activities (see, for example, Moomaw, 1985; Hansen, 1990; Kanemoto *et al.*, 1996; Mano and Otsuka, 2000). From a similar perspective, other researchers (Rivera-Batiz, 1988; Guimaraes *et al.*, 2000) have examined the location characteristics of the service sector agglomeration economies, arguing that, despite the dispersal forces, the principle of urban agglomeration is still valid. Finally, there is another strand of the literature (Aji, 1995; Suarez-Villa and Walrod, 1997; Phelps and Ozawa, 2003) which, without contradicting the other studies, asserts that positive externalities, typically assumed to occur only in urban agglomerations, could emerge in other locations, explaining the centrifugal location decisions of certain industrial (such as hi-tech and R&D) and service (back-office) activities. Finally, some scholars (Sato and Yamamoto, 2005) have attempted to relate agglomeration (dis)economies to fertility decline and, accordingly, to demographic changes, positing that negative externalities reduce disposable household income and so the number of children they can afford to raise.

Parallel to these approaches, another recent strand of economic analysis focuses on the role played by both increasing returns to scale and the (imperfectly) competitive market structure to provide explanations for spatial agglomeration and the location of economic activity in space (Krugman, 1991a, 1991b; Fujita and Thisse, 1996; Tabuchi, 1998; Fujita *et al.*, 1999; Fujita and Krugman, 2004; for reviews, see Ottaviano and Puga, 1998; Fujita and Mori, 2005). Drawing on Marshallian theory, this literature attempts to reconcile conventional economic analysis with the spatial aspect of economies in developing formal models of spatial clustering and agglomeration in highly abstract terms. Moreover, this emerging tradition, commonly known as 'new economic geography', emphasises the role of external economies and agglomeration in explaining economic growth (Fujita and Thisse, 1996; Ottaviano and Thisse, 2004).

Although still in the early stages, this body of research has produced interesting findings, not only in advancing our understanding of agglomeration mechanisms, but also in enabling their integration with the trade-off theories outlined earlier. This approach, which also provides the basis to understanding the empirical patterns of concentration and deconcentration discussed in the previous section, is as follows. It starts with the acceptance of scale economies as a critical factor in explaining the emergence of agglomeration, but it goes further to argue that the spatial organisation of markets is characterised by a fundamental trade-off between scale economies and transport costs, within a general equilibrium framework. On this basis, it is asserted that very high or very low transport costs (or, more generally, 'trade costs') favour the dispersion of economic activities, while agglomeration emerges for intermediate values of these costs. In other words, it is suggested that the relationship between trade costs and the degree of spatial agglomeration of the economy is U-shaped. However, the difficulty of predicting the form and future of agglomeration economies is also recognised (Fujita and Thisse, 1996). This is because models of agglomeration economies may generate multiple equilibria (Krugman, 1991a), where "minor changes in the socio-economic environment … may result in very different geographical configurations" (Fujita and Thisse, 1996: 371). In other words, history matters for economic geography, as the initial conditions appear to be crucial in the selection of a particular equilibrium.

On the assumption that location decisions by firms and households reflect urban transformation and help to determine its economic performance, another set of studies has attempted to explain changes in spatial dynamics at a more macro-level, paying due attention not only to accessibility, but also to other less traditional (or 'soft') locational determinants. Espousing a more behavioural/qualitative methodological approach, but without challenging the main assumptions of the conventional economics, these studies (for instance, Bosman and de Smidt, 1993; Rozenblat and Pumain, 1993; Cheshire, 1995; Porter, 1996, 2003) highlight that, alongside the need for accessibility, other factors become increasingly important in the location decisions of certain (mainly service-type) activities and populations. On that basis, they conclude that the availability of amenities and the quality of the urban structure in general (described in infrastructure, environmental, social and functional terms) play a significant role in urban economic development.

Akin to the literature just discussed, another focus for the analysis of urban change has been the competitive macro-environment, in which cities operate engendered by opportunities and threats arising from European integration, internationalisation and economic restructuring. This literature (Cheshire and Gordon, 1995, 1996; Jensen-Butler *et al.*, 1997; Oatley, 1998; Begg, 1999, 2002; Cheshire, 1999; Lever, 1999; Rogerson, 1999; Turok, 2004) builds on the discussion of the locational requirements, but goes further to consider appropriate policy responses for sustainable urban economic development. Urban places that are capable of providing a range of specialised services and an accommodating regulatory environment underpinned by a high quality of life are argued as most attractive to mobile investments, funds or quality residents, and thus enhance their economic potential and growth. A wide range of policies enabling such comparative advantage is suggested, including city promotion and marketing, provision of locational incentives, development of infrastructure, or other forms of supply-side capacity-building. It should be noted at this point that an important issue has been raised in a number of these studies (e.g. de Smidt and van der Marc, 1991; Cheshire and Gordon, 1995). This is the critical role that the availability, quality and price of land and property could play in the locational decisions of firms and households and, therefore, in urban economic growth. However, this analysis takes into account only the property market outcomes (in terms of rents, yields, etc.), ignoring the market mechanisms and processes through which these outcomes are provided.

In addition to these theories, which focus their explanations of urban change on the location decisions of economic agents, another strand of analysis has examined the issue from the perspective of the overall economic activities thriving in the city. The theoretical model available to facilitate this discussion is described as the 'economic base' or 'export base' theory (Andrews, 1953). This theory postulates the hypothesis that urban economic prosperity depends on the amount of goods and services supplied to outsiders, i.e. on 'exports'. Economic activity is divided into 'basic', which produces goods and services for export, and 'non-basic', i.e. the production of goods and services for internal consumption. In the 'traditional' model, manufacturing activities are regarded as basic activities, whereas services are non-basic activities. However, financial, business and professional services are exportable and, in certain cases, the service sector may be the main exporter, with manufacturing playing a secondary, domestic role (Groth, 2000). Using this perspective, a number of studies (Hall, 1993, 1997a; Groth, 2000) discuss urban transformation, highlighting not only that economic growth necessitates the economic orientation of the city towards service activities, but also identifying certain non-basic economic activities (such as the tourist industry) that can provide a healthy basis for attracting and developing 'basic' activities.

Similarly, but at a more macro-level, another course of urban analysis has focused on the changing economic function of cities. Pioneering studies by Hall and Hay (1980) and van der Berg *et al.* (1982), followed by Cheshire *et al.* (1986), Cheshire and Hay (1989), Cheshire (1990, 1991, 1995), Cheshire and

Carbonaro (1996) and Cheshire and Gordon (1996), among others, provide an explanation of the process of urban development and change in Europe since the 1970s. Analysing aggregate demographic and economic data, some strong results have been obtained that show an interaction between the physical patterns of urban development and the changing economic function of European urban regions. Thus this body of research argued that European cities have followed a cyclical pattern of development evolved in three stages. The first is urbanisation, defined by industrialisation and spatial concentration. This is followed by decentralisation, which starts with the suburbanisation of the population to neighbouring areas and concludes with deindustrialisation and further deurbanisation of the population and employment (both manufacturing and services) to places further away. Finally, the halt or even reversal of these trends suggests that a phase of recentralisation or reurbanisation is under way, though the complexity and lack of uniformity across Europe are also recognised. To explain this, a process of cumulative causation is suggested, where cities with an environment capable of attracting and retaining skilled residents and service-type activities can cumulatively improve their living conditions and experience growth, while those with fewer advantages may see continuing decentralisation and decline. In these terms, urban change is viewed as a process of urban adjustment or reconciliation to the international macro-forces measured by the adaptive capacity of the local economic, political and social structures.

Although the main body of conventional analysis has concentrated on the demand side of urban markets, there are few studies which have examined urban transformation considering the supply side of the urban economy (see, for example, the discussion on territorial competition in Cheshire and Gordon, 1995). The general idea is that urban economic growth can be achieved by removing the perceived bottlenecks in the operation of factor markets. Of particular interest to the current research is a number of studies which have focused their attention on the land and property markets, examining the issue of property-led urban regeneration (see, for example, Turok, 1992; Imrie and Thomas, 1993; Carbonaro and D'Arcy, 1993; Jones, 1996; Jones and Watkins, 1996; McGuirk, 2000; Ball, 2004). Based on the assumption that economic expansion exerts pressure for more land and property, it has been argued that, by enhancing the supply-side conditions of the urban system, it would be possible for new development to be stimulated and economic growth to be achieved. It is important to highlight here that these studies address directly the issues of land and property development, initiating a discussion that has an advanced understanding of the links between property and urban economic regeneration. On that basis, the influence of the built environment and property market products on economic fundamentals has been clearly emphasised. However, very little attention has been paid by this literature to the property market mechanisms and the processes through which the functional requirements for property use, investment and development are directed. On these grounds, other researchers (e.g. Healey, 1991b) have argued that a more sophisticated understanding of the property market operation would be necessary.

It becomes evident from this discussion that conventional economic approaches to urban change place explanatory emphasis on the labour and capital markets, whereas land and property considerations are very marginal. This is because the built environment is assumed to be relatively malleable, with property supply adjusting smoothly to demand pressures. Therefore land and property markets are regarded as passive adapters to urban change. Property prices, determined by the forces of demand and supply in an urban equilibrium environment, are held to provide meaningful representations of value and property rights are assumed to be acquired by those who value them most highly. By this means, property is put to its most valuable use (optimal allocation) and held in a form that most closely meets the diverse requirements of users and investors. Accordingly, it seems that only a one-way relationship between the urban economy and the property market is recognised: urban property outcomes are explained with economic arguments.

Certainly, this theorisation is evident in the majority of property market studies. Consider, for instance, the analysis of the property market mechanisms at the micro-level. Generally, three functional components are recognised: use, investment and development (Keogh, 1994; DiPasquale and Wheaton, 1996; Ball *et al.*, 1998). These three submarkets are regarded as platforms on which market activities take place, resulting in the determination of price through the interaction of supply and demand. Adequate information flows efficiently between the submarkets, providing the basis for an immediate response and alignment, which results in market equilibrium. The working of such a model is neatly outlined in Keogh (1994)[4] and analysed in detail in DiPasquale and Wheaton (1996) and Ball *et al.* (1998) (Figure 3.1). According to these models, exogenous economic factors induce changes in either rental levels (use market) or required rates of return (investment market), which are reflected back to the investment and development markets triggering further changes and adjustment (e.g. through 'repackaging' of property rights or alterations in supply through development activity) towards a new equilibrium situation.

Accordingly, similar theoretical bases are apparent in the conventional property market analysis at the macro-level. Here, emphasis is placed on the effects that economic conditions have on the provision of land and buildings and the performance of the property market, whereas the reverse relationship is virtually disregarded. Generally, two strands of literature are recognised (Ball *et al.*, 1998). One attempts to investigate the dynamics and identify the economic factors that account for the performance of property market outcomes through the development of formal econometric modelling techniques. On these grounds, a quantitative framework for comparative property research across European Union national boundaries has been developed, where the performance of property market outcomes is analysed based on the economic fundamentals of demand and supply (Giussani *et al.*, 1993; Adair *et al.*, 1997; D'Arcy *et al.*, 1997a, 1997b; Egert and Mihaljek, 2007). For that purpose, macroeconomic indicators, as proxies of demand and supply[5] in European urban property markets, are used.

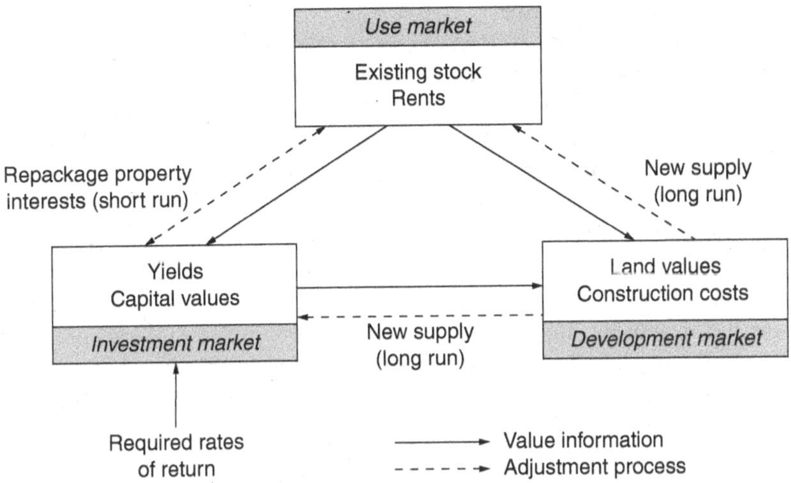

Figure 3.1 A simple model of the property market function (source: based on Keogh (1994)).

The other body of research (e.g. Barras, 1983, 1994; Royal Institution of Chartered Surveyors, 1994; Gordon *et al.*, 1996; Kaiser, 1997; Renaud, 1997; Wheaton, 1999) focuses on the way in which the cyclical pattern of fluctuations in economic activity impacts on property, generating short- and long-term cycles in the property markets. It is generally indicated that short-term property cycles are created by the economic or business cycles operating through occupier demand and affected by production lags involved in property supply, whereas longer term (or so-called Kuznets) cycles are determined by major technological and demographic changes. Interestingly, some studies within this area recognise the important role of property market performance in influencing macroeconomic dynamics (Ball *et al.*, 1996; Ball and Wood, 1996). Nonetheless, the literature espouses a deterministic and mechanistic approach to property market dynamics, marked by the view that these cyclical forces are "powerful and pervasive…" and thus "…inevitable" (Barras, 1994: 195), which limits its ability to understand the richness of the property market processes.

What becomes evident from the discussion in this section is that the conventional economic approaches seem to be inadequate on many grounds. Resting on unrealistic assumptions and idealised concepts, not only do they fail to incorporate property market processes (through which property outcomes are delivered and property interests are traded) into their theoretical frameworks, but they also misinterpret the relationship between the market and the urban economy. Moreover, when property market considerations are taken into account, the analysis lacks an appropriate behavioural and institutional context and, as a result, the idiosyncratic characteristics of property (such as heterogeneity, illiquidity, information problems, time lags between demand and supply, high transaction costs) are generally underplayed.

Before moving on to the next section, which reviews the structuralist discussion of urban transformation, it is important to mention that there are a number of property studies which, although they do not jettison the assumptions of conventional economic theorisation, highlight the importance of approaching the issues from a more behavioural perspective. On that basis, the broad institutional and behavioural context within which the property market operates is taken into consideration and its important role in influencing both property market outcomes and the urban economy is recognised. Thus, for instance, Sweeney (1993), Adair *et al.* (1994, 1997), D'Arcy *et al.* (1997b) and Lizieri (1997) highlight the increasing importance of local institutional factors and property market conditions in property investment decisions, whereas Jones Lang Wootton (1992) and Bruhl and Lizieri (1994) acknowledge the significant impact of the wider political, administrative and economic structures on the performance of urban property markets. Similar reflections can also be found in Worzala and Bernasek (1996) and Hutchings (1997), who examine the impact of European integration on the property market, asserting that it is not likely that a single European property market will evolve due to the different local conditions and institutional structures that exist within the European Union countries.

3.4 Heterodox approaches to urban transformation: the structuralist perspective

Some scholars question conventional economic analysis and, drawing on structuralism, espouse a more radical and structural approach to spatial development. This section sketches out their arguments, placing emphasis on issues of urban transformation and the production of the built environment.

Marx and Engels did not provide a systematic study of the role space plays in economy; spatial issues, however, were implicitly raised in the wider discussion about capitalism. As such, traditional Marxist analysis on urban development and decline has been formulated with reference to concepts of capital accumulation and class struggle (Saunders, 1981; Smith, 1984; Edel, 1992, 1996; Katznelson, 1992; Short, 1996; Harvey, 2008, 2012). According to these readings, cities are reflections on space of the uneven distribution of capital accumulation and their development is explained by reference to 'transfers' or 'flows' of surplus value from one place to another in an attempt to resolve the internal contradictions that characterise the dynamics of capitalism. On these grounds labour urbanisation is the result of industrial concentration in specific locations, with suburbanisation and gentrification constituting distinct geographical expressions of capitalism consumption and class inequality (Massey, 1984).

It is interesting to note that there are scholars who attribute to these trends the status of general laws governing the capitalist system, slipping, thereby, into deterministic modes of thought. For example, Mandel (1975) suggests a uniform, almost mechanical, process that produces spatial unevenness, even in the ideal case of homogeneous beginning:

> The accumulation of capital itself produces development and underdevelopment as mutually determining moments of the uneven and combined movement of capital. The lack of homogeneity in the capitalist economy is a necessary outcome of the unfolding laws of motion of capitalism itself.
>
> (Mandel, as quoted in Edel, 1992: 24)

On that basis, he maintains that the geographical transfer of surplus value and the uneven development of places are fundamental mechanisms of capitalism, necessary for the survival and strengthening of the system. In a similar vein, Smith (1984: 149) proposes a 'see-saw' theory of uneven development: "...capital attempts to see-saw from a developed to an underdeveloped area, then at a later point back to the first area which is now underdeveloped". Applying this theory to the urban level, Smith (1984) explains how mobile capital destroys and then gentrifies inner-city neighbourhoods.

One of the most significant and holistic contributions to the analysis of spatial development under capitalism comes from David Harvey. His early works (Harvey, 1973, 1978) lay the groundwork for the construction of a highly refined theoretical model (Harvey, 1982, 2010), which analyses capital accumulation with specific reference to urban dynamics and the built environment development process. This model is organised around three separate, but related, 'cuts' at a theory of capital crisis. The first 'cut' sees the crisis of overaccumulation (i.e. the production of capital in excess to the opportunities for its usage), which rests on the fundamental contradictions of capitalism (both between capital and labour and between individual capitalists and their class interests) and the tendency for the rate of profit to fall. Violent episodes of destruction of value, where capitalists turn on each other, but the labour ends up paying the social costs, are manifestations of this crisis. In the second 'cut', the role of the credit/financial system is introduced as a means of resolving contradictions in the process of production, with the state playing an important regulative role. However, such a solution is only temporary and eventually inflation and uncertainty rise and crisis once again comes to the fore. It is in the third 'cut' that the geographical element to the capitalist crisis is introduced, focusing on the system's spatial as well as temporal dynamics. For, he argues, the contradictions of capitalism are susceptible to a 'spatial fix' in which geographical expansion into new areas temporarily ameliorates crisis tendencies as part of the process of uneven development. In this way, capitalism is capable of 'switching' crises from one place to another, smoothing the overall process of accumulation, with inevitably devastating results for some places over others. However, for Harvey (1982, 1985, 2008, 2010, 2012), the problem for capitalism is that it never solves its crisis (it merely moves them around) and the more it develops, the more it tends to succumb to the forces of geographical inertia. Thus in overcoming crisis by "annihilat[ing] space with time", certain structures are created which ultimately act as barriers to further accumulation (Harvey, 1985: 37). The growth of productive forces therefore acts as a barrier to further geographical restructuring: "The more the forces of geographical inertia prevail, the deeper will the aggregate crises of capitalism become and the more savage will switching crises have to be to restore the disturbed equilibrium" (Harvey, 1982: 429). In this fashion, he argues, local crises build to create global crises.

Parallel to these approaches which analyse spatial dynamics in terms of capitalism contradictions, others (Soja and Hadjimichalis, 1979; Soja, 1980; as well as Lefebvre 1991) have placed due attention on the dialectic character of social–spatial relations. Soja (1980: 208), for example, asserts:

> The structure of organised space is not a separate structure with its own autonomous laws of construction and transformation, nor is it simply an expression of class structure emerging from the social (i.e. aspatial) relations of production. It represents, instead, a dialectically defined component of the general relations of production, relations which are simultaneously social and spatial.

Distinguishing between 'contextual space' as an objective form of the existence of matter and the 'created space' of social organisation and production, he argues that, although space itself may be primordially given, its organisation, use and meaning are products of social transformation. Thus by recognising a complex socio-spatial dialectic interrelationship, Soja automatically rejects the treatment of space as being a separate structure with rules of transformation independent of the wider social context. In that sense he calls for a concrete Marxist analysis where the socially produced space is not just an epiphenomenon, but instead its central element.

Akin to this approach, but more structural in nature, is that of Castells (1977). Like Soja, Castells sees space as an integral part of a general social framework. However, for Castells, any social form, like space, can be conceptualised as a concrete expression of each historical ensemble in which society is specified. As such, space is perceived as the reflection of the economic, politico-juridical and ideological structures which form it. On this basis, Castells argues that the social organisation of space can be understood in three ways: in terms of the determination of spatial forms by each one of the three aforementioned structures; by the structural combination of all three (with the economy setting the conditions under which the other instances of society systematically shape space); and also empirically, by the persistence of spatial forms created by earlier social structures. Analysing spatial organisation at the urban level, Castells views the city as an arena within which aspects of collective consumption (education, housing, transport and other infrastructure required for private production to be profitable) are undertaken for compliant labour power to be reproduced and a smooth and efficient functioning of the city to be achieved. As the state is involved in these kinds of provisions, issues of collective consumption become issues of political power encompassing the competing demands of various fractions of capital, consumers, residents and organised labour. This leads Castells (1977) to set questions regarding urban organisation, urban problems, urban politics and planning, urban struggles and urban social movements, which are seen as central issues of advanced capitalism.

Expanding this conceptual framework, Castells (1989, 1993, 1996), in his later work,[6] attempts to explore the restructuring of modern capitalism and to analyse its spatial implications, while paying due attention to the role of technology and the process of technological transformation. The argument is that the recent technological revolution, which is based on information technology, gives rise to a new economic order with its own social and spatial consequences. The result is epitomised in the rise of the informational city, which is seen as the urban expression of the whole matrix of changes and developments in the spheres of production, consumption and state intervention, and their subsequent structural contradictions. This formulation is used to explain both macro and micro urban organisation. For example, and with regard to the former, phenomena such as the reinforcement of the metropolitan hierarchy, the decline of old industrial regions and the emergence of new dynamic economic centres are attributed to the ability of certain areas to develop qualities that increase their informational as well as command/control/management capacities (see also Sassen, 2001). In terms of the latter, Castells argues that the informational economy has a structural tendency to generate a polarised occupational structure based on the informational capabilities of different social groups, which leads to 'dualization' of the urban social structure and subsequently to social segregation and functional differentiation.

A similar perspective to the urban geography of economic restructuring is provided by the regulation school. This approach links historical 'breaks' (i.e. distinct periods in capitalism development) to specific geographical patterns (Kratke, 1999). It argues that every historically evolved 'development mode' of capitalist socio-economy (i.e. the specific 'regime of accumulation' and the associated 'mode of regulation') corresponds to a distinct pattern of spatial organisation. The crisis and replacement of the Fordist mode of development is therefore the driving force in the current restructuring of socio-economic space, which is manifested, first, in the decline of 'old' industrial areas, second, in the selective concentration of advanced service activities to metropolitan regions and, third, in the creation of new dynamic (flexibly specialised) industrial spaces (Scott, 1988; Moulaert and Swyngedouw, 1989; Kratke, 1999). As such, urban areas in the process of decline are those trapped in the old, Fordist, regime, whereas those capable of flexibly organising their production structures and so to prosper are the spatial anchors of the new regime geography.

A significant theme brought out in the regulationist analysis on urban development is related to the mode of regulation. It was acknowledged that a key determinant of sustainable urban growth is the local milieu, i.e. the social environment of a locality "...resulting from the interaction of firms, institutions and labours, which leads to a common way of perceiving economic and technical problems and finding respective solutions" (Raco, 1999: 956; Maillat and

Lecoq, 1992). Despite the great potential this concept brought to the analysis of urban restructuring, it remained poorly developed in the regulationist writings. The underlying mechanisms and processes, for instance, by which the milieu functions were not specified and the cultural bases (values, attitudes and the like) of the social dynamics were not given proper consideration (Storper, 1995).

Acknowledging the structural character of the urban economy and the high explanatory power of human agency, other perspectives on urban analysis come from structuration theory and the critical realist school. The concern of the former was to develop a contextual theory of social actions that interpenetrate the time–space context. Space, in this context, is not regarded as an empty dimension along which social groupings become structured, but an integral part which is actively involved in the constitution of the socio-economic system. A similar treatment is also evident in the realist approach. Deeper structural elements shape the urban socio-economy, which, like any other open system, is comprised of time–space entities (such as social structures and institutions) whose causal powers are activated under specific 'contingent conditions'. These entities depend upon and are constituted through their spatial configurations, whereas these spatial configurations are the outcome of, and necessary condition for, human agency. Space, in this conceptualisation, depends upon human agency, but exhibits a degree of causal autonomy that makes it irreducible to the latter. On these grounds, spatial elements, rather than simply constituting a context of human activity, are distinct ontological objects that affect all domains of urban socio-economy.[7]

An example of the empirical application of structuration theory at the urban level is given by Dear and Moos (1986) on the basis of a model developed in Moos and Dear (1986). This model indicates that agents, defined by the institutional aspects of their locality, produce (intended and unintended) outcomes as a response to (acknowledged and unacknowledged) structural conditions. Five types of agents are recognised (politicians, bureaucrats, interest groups, influential individuals and ordinary citizens) and their strategic conduct is analysed in terms of power relations. In turn, institutional aspects are conceptualised on the basis of 'modalities of interaction', and concern manifestations of the language employed (communicative modality), the structure of power relations (political domination), the control of economic resources (economic domination) and the legitimisation of institutional action (sanction modality). To avoid focusing attention on one level of analysis (either structure or agency) at the expense of the other, Moos and Dear apply the method of 'bracketing'. Although the analysis takes place on a short to medium time span (*duree*), the outcomes determine the long-term reproduction of the system (*longue duree*).

It is evident from this discussion that structuralist urban theories correctly seek to locate urban change not only in an economic, but also in a political and social context. Their analysis is essentially historical, placing emphasis on the dynamics of change. In these terms, urban outcomes emerge out of a complex dialectical interaction between agency and structure, in the light of economic, political and social contradictions and conflicts that arise in the urban scene.

Some of the determinants of this process are structural, linked to deep trends that prescribe the socio-political evolution of capitalism (as emphasised by Marxist and regulation theories); others are historically and culturally specific (as indicated in the writings of Castells and Soja) and others are related to 'contingent' events and 'contextual' interpretations of individual agents (as highlighted by the realist and structuration theories). These readings portray the city as a rational economic, political and social entity which, although in dynamic transformation, is constantly searching for the equilibrium situation in which a rational solution to all traditional urban problems (unemployment, poverty, land use problems, physical decay, crisis of democracy) is afforded.[8]

Let us now move to examine how structuralist approaches treated the production of the built environment and the function of the property market. As noted, Marxist analysis was based on the concepts of capital accumulation and class struggle. Thus some traditional Marxist scholars (such as Massey and Catalano, 1978) placed due attention on the way power relations between capital, labour and landowners affect the processes and outcomes of the built environment provision. In particular, these studies focus on the struggle between landowners and other capitalists to capture the surplus value generated in the property development process. On this basis, analysis attempts to explain spatial structures and property market organisation as a result of the conflict between the various actors involved in property development (usually the 'local community' and the developers) (Ambrose and Colenutt, 1975) and the contradictions arising from the different forms of private landownership (i.e. former landed, industrial and financial) (Massey and Catalano, 1978).

In tandem with this perspective, other Marxist studies have placed emphasis on the circulation of capital to examine how surplus values move sectorally (from industrial production to other economic sectors) and geographically to generate more capital and to defuse tensions inherent to the capitalist system. Discussing this process with specific reference to the provision of properties at a micro-level, Boddy (1981) and Luithlen (1992, 1993) identify three circuits of capital movement: industrial, commercial and interest-bearing (Figure 3.2). In the industrial circuit, which concerns the construction process, money is exchanged for means (materials, labour) to be used for the construction of properties, which are subsequently sold to generate surplus value. In the commercial circuit (which refers to the development market), surplus value from the purchase and sale of properties goes to the developer, whereas the interest-bearing circuit (which concerns investments in the property market) involves the advance of money capital by financial institutions to both developers and contractors; which is subsequently repaid with interest. On these grounds, the provision of properties is seen as an event-sequence process where a property company secures short-term development finance from a financial institution for the purchase of land and for the arrangement of property construction, which is undertaken by a building contractor.

From a rather macro perspective, Harvey (1978, 1982, 1985, 2008, 2010) discusses how a portion of surplus value has to be invested into the built environment for its productive potential to be expanded. As such, he perceives the

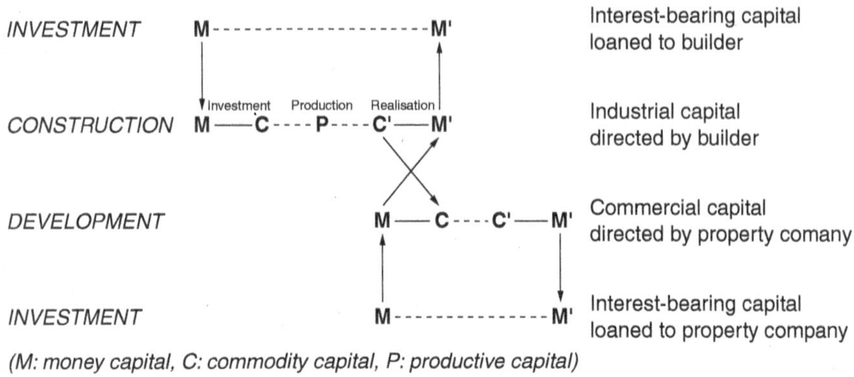

Figure 3.2 The provision of properties through circuits of capital (source: based on Boddy (1981) and Luithlen (1992)).

(urban) built environment as a financial asset (thus the built environment acts as capital) governed and specified by the movements of international, national and local capital aiming to reproduce and expand itself. On that basis, Harvey puts forward a model for the production of the built environment defining three circuits of capital. The primary circuit involves the production and consumption of commodities, which leads to the overaccumulation of capital and consequently to a crisis situation. To alleviate this, capital flows into 'fixed asset' and 'consumption fund'[9] formation, which collectively comprise the built environment and represent the secondary circuit. The level and direction of the capital transfer from the first to the second circuit is regulated by policies and institutions put forward by financial agents and the state. However, once again, capital accumulation comes to a halt. Thus a tertiary circuit is introduced where capital is forwarded to social investment, necessary for the reproduction of labour power (such as education and health), as well as investments in science and technology, aiming to develop the productive forces of society. Three points should be added here. First, the secondary and tertiary circuits, although very different in character, share an important common feature: they have the capacity to absorb surplus value for long periods (called 'temporal fix'). Second, there is an important spatial dimension in the model in the sense that capital switching may occur both within and between areas. Third, although the provision of the built environment occurs in the second circuit, the importance of considering the processes and links within and between the other circuits is apparent.

Evaluating Harvey's approach, Healey (1991a: 234) recognises the thoroughness of the model where due care is given not only to the "…complexity of the links between production (land and property for use), financial capital (land and property for investment) and the state (public policy) in 'driving' investment, disinvestment, development and abandonment of the built fabric", but also to the wider connections between the built environment, economic activities (such as investment) and social life, as well as to the temporal and spatial variations in the way capital flows into and out of property. In spite of these strengths, the few studies (Feagin, 1987; King, 1989; Beauregard, 1994; Charney, 2001) that have explored empirically Harvey's model provide weak support to the capital-switching argument. In addition, the focus of the model on the variable flows of capital into different types of activity at different points in time, without taking full account other social mechanisms and institutions that affect this process, remain one of its weak points (Leitner, 1994).

These Marxist approaches to the built environment have been attacked on many grounds (see Needham, 1994) and especially for the deterministic explanations they suggest, disregarding the purposeful role human agency plays in this process. Ball (1986) similarly criticises them for the functionalist way that they treat the built environment, where emphasis is placed mainly on the uses to which both property and its production are put (serving the interest of capital). Property development, for example, is regarded as unproductive capital, used to maintain mechanistically the rate of profit by restructuring the built environment. This leads to another criticism, put forth by D'Arcy and Keogh (1997), which concerns the lack of cultural perspective within these models. This is because, as Ball (1986: 453) notes, the built environment is actually "...treated as the physical framework around which other social processes take place rather than as an integral element of them".

A regulationalist account of the built environment and property market can be found in Lizieri (1991, 2003), Gibson (2000, 2003), Gibson and Lizieri (1998, 1999, 2001) and Smart and Lee (2003). This literature has pointed out that pressures for flexibility in economic organisation and for innovation in production (placed by the new regime of accumulation) have been transferred to the built environment provision, calling for modernisation and flexibility in all aspects of property: legal, functional and physical[10] (see also Harris, 2001). On these grounds, recent phenomena such as the employment of new construction techniques (that shorten the development process), the emergence of new property rights arrangements (in property use, investment and development, e.g. new lease and ownership practices) and the liberalisation of property financing have been explained. The key point that has emerged from this discussion is the importance attached, first, to the flexibility issue with regard to the property market and, second, to the role that the legal/property rights framework plays in the provision of the built environment. However, the latter has been treated in a rather incomplete manner, as other institutional arrangements that affect the function of the property market (i.e. political, social, cultural) were virtually ignored.

Drawing explicitly on structuration theory, another strand of structuralist approaches has stressed the complex role of human agency in the provision of the built environment. Perhaps the most significant contribution in this area is the so-called 'structure and agency' model developed by Healey (1992, but also Healey and Barrett, 1990), which explores the property development process by considering the interests, strategies, relations (networks) and roles (actions) of the involved actors, with reference to their resources, rules and ideology (values). Resources refer to the means of the production process, including finance, information, expertise and legal rights. Formal and informal rules govern the way these resources are utilised, whereas ideology informs the interests and strategies of agents influencing the dynamics of resource use and rule formation. Overall, resources, rules and ideology comprise the 'structure' part of the model, whereas interests, strategies, relations and roles refer to the variety of 'agency' involved in the development process.

To inform empirical inquiry, Healey (1992) proposes a four-level analytical framework. The first level introduces a mapping function to analyse the events that take place (including the inputs used and the outcomes provided) and to identify the actors involved. The latter provides the focus for the second level, at which roles (in production and consumption) and power relations are specified. At the third level the strategies and interests of the agents are assessed and related to their resources, rules and principles. Finally, the last level involves the description of the particular socio-economic circumstances and prevailing ideology that govern the development process.

Despite the huge data requirements and the lack of clarity about research methods, the model has inspired a number of studies exploring property development in the UK (Healey, 1992, 1994, 1995; Adams, 1994; Fisher, 2005) and other countries (van der Krabben and Lambooy, 1993; Parsa and Keivani, 1999; Keivani *et al.*, 2002; McGreal *et al.*, 2002; Zhu, 2005; Qian, 2007). However, it has been criticised on several grounds. Some have condemned it for mistreating the structure–agency duality in favour of the agency part and for downplaying the exogenous determinants of agency behaviour (Hooper, 1992; Ball, 1998; Ball *et al.*, 1988). Others have complained that, although it acknowledges the effects that social, political and economic institutions have on the development process, it does not pay due attention to the reverse relation and the dynamics behind institutional change (van den Krabben, 1995; Guy and Henneberry, 2000).[11] Finally, others have highlighted its inability to analyse the wider process of property market operation (due to the exclusive focus on property development at the expense of property use and investment) and to "carry the analysis of property market behaviour into an effective theory of urban change" (D'Arcy and Keogh, 1997: 689; Hooper, 1992).

A critical realist approach to the built environment provision is put forward by Ganderton (1994) in a three-layer stratified model analysing the land conversion process. The bottom layer ('deep structure') contains the mechanisms that drive land conversion, namely, power motivation and perception. The infrastructure constitutes the second layer, where rules and other social constructs are situated. Here, Ganderton identifies law and economy as the most fundamental elements (although he acknowledges that other elements could also be involved), which are connected both to each other and to the deep structure by bidirectional 'flows'. These flows are partly information and partly power-related and they are expected to vary through time in terms of rate and intensity. Both infrastructure and deep structure are connected to the superstructure, which concerns the events and experiences that are evident in the land conversion process. In particular, two sub-layers are identified here, one representing the planning procedure and the other representing the actors operating within the system; these are classified on the basis of certain characteristics, such as similarities in their purpose, role and power. Moreover, the model regards the planning procedure as a dynamic activity, which is understood vis-à-vis the power and roles of the actors involved.

An important concept that comes out of this model is the stratified ontology though which built environment provision is perceived. As such, important explanatory power is given to the purposeful human agency without this being conflated into a singular 'duality' with structure (as the 'structure and agency' model does). Similarly, structure, though existentially interdependent with agency, is ascribed its own 'emergent properties', which are not reducible to human perception or action. On the basis of this ontological separation, each entity is placed in a different layer of social reality and their causal powers and attributes are discussed with regard to the process of urban land provision. However, some important shortcomings are evident in the model. For instance, although proper emphasis is placed on the economic and legal determinants of the land conversion process, the analysis fails to take into account any social or cultural characteristics. Moreover, despite the fact that 'perception' is explicitly recognised as a fundamental quality of the deep structure, the model fails to carry this line of argument into a discussion on human rationality and behaviour. Finally, and in relation to the current research, this work focuses on the process of land conversion without examining the mechanisms, qualities and processes that describe the property market operation.

Summarising and evaluating the findings of this section, it can be said that structuralist approaches correctly seek to locate built environment formation and property market activity not only in an economic, but also in a political and social context. Marxist, neo-Marxist and regulationist analysis is essentially a dialectical–historical analysis, where concrete events are linked to abstract categories, thus providing an explanation for these events and, at the same time, infusing new meanings into these abstract categories. However, their interpretation of the production of the built environment (structured around the themes of social/class struggle and capital switching) falls into the twin pitfalls of functionalism and determinism. On this basis, they contrast with the structure and agency and the critical realist perspectives where the purposeful human agency is explicitly taken into account. However, it is evident that none of these approaches manages effectively to incorporate into its analysis of the built environment provision the complex behaviour of the property market, and to carry this analysis into an integrated urban economic theory. On these grounds, it is asserted that the dynamics and processes of the property market operation, as well as its relation to urban transformation, remain largely unexplored.

3.5 Heterodox approaches to urban transformation: the institutionalist contribution

Institutional economics is a dynamic and relational approach to economic organisation that does not confine itself to a particular spatial scale. As such, there is no specific strand of institutional analysis focusing particularly on cities. However, there are a number of studies on local and regional economic development that borrow heavily from institutionalism and can provide a starting point for the formation of a contemporary institutionalist urban analysis. On these grounds, the current section begins with a brief rehearsal of the salient attributes of the approach, giving emphasis to the urban dimension, and then goes on to review the studies that employ the institutional perspective to analyse local economic organisation, built environment provision and property market operation.

Institutional economics encompasses a wide variety of different strands, ranging from the transaction costs approach put forward by the neo-institutionalists, to the broader socio-cultural interpretation of original institutionalism. Each strand has elaborated its own theoretical and methodological tools for the analysis and explanation of (urban) economic organisation and change. The common element of all these approaches is the belief that it is the institutional environment with its organisational set up which accounts for the course and performance of the (urban) economy. In particular, it is established that alongside the economic characteristics it is also the political, legal and socio-cultural aspects that determine (urban) economic development. On that basis, considerable explanatory power is given not only to the laws of the marketplace, but also to institutional structures, to human agency and to the related issues of power, cognition, learning and knowledge development (Amin, 1999; Martin, 2000).

Neo-institutional economics is the strand of institutionalism that enriches conventional economic explanations with the analysis of transaction costs, property rights and the contractual arrangements through which the economy is organised. As such, it asserts that economic growth and efficiency at the local level are achieved by developing such mechanisms to co-ordinate economic action that minimise transaction costs (Lambooy, 1993; Martin, 2000). The market is the most apparent of these mechanisms and can function efficiently only when reliable formal (market-creating and market-securing) institutions are in place on the economic, legal, political and social fronts. These include clear and enforceable property rights and other credible arrangements that improve information flow, promote fair competition (through the rule of law) and reduce uncertainty in interactions between economic agents (World Bank, 2002). However, efficient provision and arrangement of these institutional qualities might be problematic. This, as Williamson (1985) argues, is mainly due to opportunistic human behaviour and to information deficiencies. In short, the argument states that information is asymmetrically distributed, something which enables the holder to use it opportunistically, creating a potential for distortion and uncertainty in a transaction. As a result, high transaction costs could persist, making it difficult to achieve efficient co-ordination via the market only. On that basis, economising on transaction costs (and the enhancement of co-operation and economic potential) can be achieved through other forms of (contractual) co-ordination, namely 'hierarchy' and 'network' (Lambooy, 1993; Coffey and Bailly, 1996). The former usually describes organisational structures within firms, or organisations in general (including public organisations), which are based on fiat and subordination, whereas the latter refers to relations between organisations based on common interests and co-operation. Similar arguments have also been applied to the urban level in an attempt to delineate the organisational structures and economic dynamics of cities (Bovaird, 1993; Phelps and Ozawa, 2003). Network organisation in particular is recognised at both the inter-urban and the intra-urban level, as a reflection of controlling transaction costs over space.

Apparently, network theorisation does not only contribute to a better understanding of the organisation of relations between economic agents in and among cities, but also profiles the city as the optimal and preferred environment for the production, acquisition and sharing of information and the development of knowledge (Lambooy, 1993; Coffey and Bailly, 1996; van der Berg *et al.*, 2001). On that basis, it is argued that network formation promotes the exchange of information, knowledge and innovative ideas between economic agents, creating an environment of co-operation and collaboration. Moreover, proximity and spatial co-presence seem to play an important role in the development of network relations due to the significance attached to the face-to-face exchange of information and to tacit forms of knowledge (Amin, 1999; Raco, 1999; Storper and Venables, 2004; McCann, 2008). Based on this, there has been a resurgence of interest in agglomeration economies (McCann, 1995; Wood and Parr, 2005).

Putting these pieces together, an outline of the neo-institutional perception of urban organisation can be provided. According to this logic, urban agglomerations emerge and develop as the efficient locus of economised transaction costs. The latter is achieved both by the establishment of a sound institutional framework (including property rights, rule of law and other legal and political institutions) that facilitates market relations and through the development of hierarchies and networks that connect economic agents and support a non-market basis for the advancement of modern economic activity. Based on these qualities, Lambooy and Moulaert (1996) describe the main features of the neo-institutional city as follows (see also Table 3.1). Economic organisation is based on transactions between rational (information-constrained) economic agents made possible by credible institutional arrangements (economic, legal and political), which regulate markets, hierarchies (organisations) and networks and facilitate information flow. These structures economise on transaction costs and are deemed to improve over time, leading the urban system towards more economic efficiency. Co-operation is envisaged both within and among cities on the basis of the common interests of agents (who economise on transaction costs). Medium or long-run equilibria are taken for granted and social relations are generally not articulated.

Table 3.1 Characterisation of institutional cities

The neo-institutionalist city Economic organisation is based on transactions between rational (information-constrained) economic agents made possible by credible institutional arrangements (economic, legal and political) which regulate markets, hierarchies (organisations) and networks and facilitate information flow. These structures economise on transaction costs and are deemed to improve over time, leading the urban system towards more economic efficiency. Co-operation is envisaged both within and among cities on the basis of common interests of agents. Medium or long run equilibria are taken for granted and social relations are generally not articulated.
The new institutionalist city The organisation and development of the urban economy are led by bounded rational economic behaviour and governed by a number of co-ordination and co-operation principles which are based on the exchange of information and happen through transactions undertaken by individuals, organisations and networks. Economic activity is determined by economic as well as political, legal and social institutions that are historically and spatially specific. Relations between actors remain, however, of an economic nature. Differences in economic performance between cities are attributed to different institutional arrangements and the credible commitment of each locality to adjust its institutional structures to allow an environment conductive to the structural changes and, thus, fertile to economic growth, to be provided. Long run equilibria are not precluded.
The original-institutionalist city The socio-economic system is considered as a unique (in space and time), dynamic, open-ended and constantly evolving whole; this means that aspects of reality (economic, political, social, cultural) at all spatial levels interact with each other. Plurality of behaviour is recognised in which the creative and purposeful human agency plays an active part in institutional dynamics, but is also determined by them. The continuous interaction between human agency and institutional structures leads to a wide variety in urban forms and economic activities. Contradictions in interests and behaviour as well as disequilibrium in the market are the rule. The essential dynamism that characterises the interplay between human creativity and ceremonial values accounts for urban transformation. Urban economic growth is seen as a conflictual and cognitive process by which the socio-economy manages to effectively advance the 'technological' challenges of its time.

Source: based on Lambooy and Moulaert (1996).

In a similar vein, the new institutionalist perspective on urban economic organisation incorporates the analysis of transactions, property rights, networks, etc., but adopts a more dynamic and less deterministic stance than neo-institutionalists. It acknowledges that, although institutions and their organisational arrangements are mechanisms which (by reducing transaction costs) provide certainty and order in human interaction and economic co-ordination, they do so with varying degrees of success. This is because: first, agents are bounded-rational and hence they lack the knowledge and the mental capacity to develop such efficient institutional structures; second, because those with the incentives might not have the power to do so (and vice versa); and, third, because the environment is so constantly changing that (the relatively stable – as *meant* to be) institutions might not continue to be efficient, even if they were so at some point in the past. As a result, the framework a place has at a point in time is always a 'mixed bag' of institutions. Some of these reduce transaction costs, promote co-operation and growth, and limit inequalities, whereas others allow free-riding and rent-seeking behaviour, sustain (if not enhance) disparities, and promote social and political instability and conflict (North, 1990, 1994; Rodríguez-Pose and Storper, 2006; Rodríguez-Pose, 2013). On these grounds, for urban economic growth and development to be achieved, societies need to fortify the former and combat the latter institutions, also developing mechanisms that infuse institutional flexibility and adaptability to endogenous and exogenous changes.

However, the path of institutional evolution is not independent of the initial institutional conditions prevalent in an area. As North (1990) neatly indicates, history matters and institutional change is 'path-dependent'. Yet nothing in this assertion implies a deterministic or teleological perception with regard to institutional or urban evolution. This is because it is the human agency (triggered by changes in opportunity sets) that plays a decisive role in shaping the course of institutional change and, consequently, the process of urban transformation. On that basis, urban economic development is associated with the credible commitment of the locality (represented by certain actors) to continually develop 'good' institutions and eliminate the 'bad' by adjusting and readjusting its framework (i.e. the formal economic, political and legal rules as well as the informal–social characteristics) to provide an environment hospitable to economic growth, i.e. an environment which enables co-operative solutions to be formed (North, 1993a, 1993b; Jaffe and Louziotis, 1996; Rodríguez-Pose and Storper, 2006).

Following Lambooy and Moulaert (1996), Table 3.1 outlines the characteristics of the new institutional city. Bounded rationality is the behaviour that underlies its operation. Like the neo-institutional city, transaction relations between individuals, organisations and networks are the essence of urban organisation. This is driven by co-ordination and co-operation imperatives on the basis of the adequate flow of information/knowledge. Economic relations and activity are determined by economic, legal, political and social institutions that are spatio-temporally specific. However, the power of the socio-cultural aspects as co-ordinative mechanisms is underestimated, with the assumption that they play a subordinate role to the essentially economic function of the city. The differences between cities with regard to economic performance and development are ascribed to, and explained by, different formal (economic, political and legal) and informal (social) institutional arrangements which determine (place boundaries upon) the rationality, incentives and actions of economic agents (Rodríguez-Pose and Storper, 2006). The credible commitment of the locality to adjust and adapt its institutional apparatus to the constantly changing conditions, providing a co-operative environment conductive to economic growth, is also seen as an important element of urban change and economic development. Once again, networks are formed within and among cities and the possibility of long-run equilibria is not ruled out a priori.

In contrast with both new and neo-institutionalists, the original institutional economics stresses the socio-cultural character of economic relations regarding the urban socio-economy as a complex, holistic, dynamic and open-ended system (Munro, 1995; Hayter, 2004). Innate and constantly interactive parts of that system are the economic, political, legal and social institutional structures, their cultural basis (values, mores, beliefs, habits, conventions, routines and the like) as well as the creative human agency (of individuals, organisations and networks) which constitutes the developmental force behind any change. The idea of transformation and the focus on the process of change at any spatial level are inherent to original institutionalism. This is because change is regarded as the natural, never-ending process of a constantly evolving socio-economic system (Klein, 1977; Adams, 1993). Furthermore, as economic action is considered to be embedded in wider socio-cultural relations (Granovetter, 1985, 1992), the multidimensionality of human behaviour is recognised and identified as 'mixed rationality' or 'irrationality'. This mixed rationality assumption and the evolutionary approach to economic organisation account for diversity in economic agents, interests and activities at all spatial levels. Contemporary economic patterns grow on the foundations of previous layers of urban development as a result of the interplay between 'technological progress'[12] and the 'ceremonial' (power-related) restraints of urban existence (this is the celebrated Veblenian dichotomy). As such, urban change is a cumulative causal evolutionary process where 'creative development' is filtered through 'regressive' values within society sustained by power-vested interests. In these terms, urban economic growth occurs when the constantly evolving urban socio-economic system develops (consciously or unconsciously) those institutional qualities that enable 'smooth' and successful advancement of the 'technological' challenges in an attempt to achieve 'workability' over time.[13]

The institutional/cultural environment, however, plays a multiple and complex role in the process of economic development. This is because it does not only constrain agency behaviour, but also provides a cognitive framework through which information is interpreted and transformed into knowledge. On these grounds, urban change is associated with a cognitive process by which information is apprehended, contextualised and turned into meaningful (i.e. matter-of-fact, problem-solving) knowledge which is, subsequently, shared and reproduced within the community. In that sense, learning is being built into the system (i.e. internalised), whereas both the individual agents and the collectivity as a whole become more expert. The scope for forging those place-specific cultural qualities that promote the development of this kind of collective knowledge[14] and action becomes apparent (Hodgson, 1989, 1996).

On the basis of these arguments, the main attributes of the original institutional city can, according to Lambooy and Moulaert (1996), be summarised as follows (Table 3.1). To start with, the socio-economic urban system is considered to be a unique (in space and time), dynamic and open-ended whole. This means that facets of reality (economic, political, legal, social, cultural, physical) at all spatial levels (local, national, supranational, international) interact dynamically to provide distinct urban patterns (Hayter, 2004). Plurality of behaviour within and between networks, organisations and individual agents is recognised, expanding economic relations beyond transaction/exchange boundaries. Creative human agency plays an active part in institutional (technological–cultural) dynamics, but is also determined by them. This continuous interaction between agency and institutional structures in economic, political and socio-cultural life gives rise to a wide variety of urban development forms. In contrast with the neo- and new institutional city, the city of original institutionalism is full of contradictions in interests and behaviour, as institutions reflect both co-operative and conflicting relations and processes far beyond the simple purpose of economic co-ordination. In spatial terms, there is far more variety and disequilibrium in place than the other institutional approaches suggest. The essential dynamism that characterises the interplay between 'technological' and 'ceremonial' aspects of institutional organisation (and the degree of ceremonial encapsulation) accounts for urban transformation. As such, urban economic growth is seen as a conflictual and cognitive process by which the socio-economy manages effectively to advance the 'technological' challenges of the time.

In tandem with the economics literature (which is essentially aspatial), some relatively recent work on local and regional development, urban planning and economic geography[15] employs the institutionalist perspective to enrich its understanding of regional economic organisation and to provide a basis for policy action that will strengthen the local economic potential and deliver economic success. Interestingly, the majority of these studies have a structuralist tinge, blending key ideas of the institutional economics and regulation school, sometimes under the philosophical umbrella of structuration theory. Thus, in a similar way to the work of Giddens, the interrelation between structure and agency is recognised, with human agency and institutional structures given equal explanatory power. Moreover, studies within this literature emphasise the emergence of more flexible organisational forms (such as industrial districts and learning regions), where economic actors (individuals, firms or groups of firms) are connected with each other through networks of economic, political and social relations established by the locality within which they live and operate. These networks of relations provide an environment where the development and exchange of information, knowledge (including tacit/latent forms), innovative ideas and experience is facilitated, entrepreneurial activity is boosted and local economic potential is generated (as neo- and new institutionalists maintain). However, it is acknowledged that these 'relational networks' are shaped not only by economic imperatives, but also by the socio-cultural characteristics of the locality. On these grounds, and in a fashion similar to original institutional economics, appropriate emphasis is given to the cultural basis of a place. Thus, for instance, the social values of trust, reciprocity and mutual understanding are identified as important elements in explaining both the network relations between economic actors and the underlying institutional framework.

As the work of Storper (1995, 1997) "represents one of the most sophisticated and influential contributions" to this literature (Cumbers *et al.*, 2003: 329), a special mention should be made of it. Storper, in a rather original institutionalist tone, argues that the potential for territorial development and prosperity lies in the quality of 'untraded interdependencies', which are cumulative–causation prone externalities rooted in the stock of informal rules, conventions, norms, routines and habits of the locality. These locally specific, difficult to imitate 'relational assets' not only generate positive externalities that attract firms, but also foster a capacity for advanced learning, making territories adaptable to endogenous and exogenous changes.

Turning to policy issues, scholars of this literature have argued that economic success at a local level can be achieved by advancing institutional characteristics and relational networks that "generate consensus on 'what kind of collective game to play' and how to play it,... providing a rich 'soil' in which individual projects, partnerships, and associations can 'grow' in flexible and innovative ways" (Healey, 1998: 1542). Amin and Thrift (1994, 1995) develop the concept of 'institutional thickness' to measure these qualities, identifying four constitutive elements: a plethora of civil associations and organisations, a high level of interaction between social groups, coalitions which cross individual interests, and a strong sense of common purpose. Healey (1998), in turn, prefers a more relational view of the 'institutional capacity', rather than treating it as a stock of assets. She develops the concept of 'institutional capital' which takes three (analytically distinct) forms: intellectual capital (knowledge resources), social capital (relational resources, such as trust, reciprocity and co-operative spirit) and political capital (which refers to the capacity for collective action). Empirical studies (Trigilia, 1992; Hudson, 1994; Raco, 1998, 1999; Coulson and Ferrario, 2007), however, have been reluctant to support the argument that high degrees of institutional quality are sufficient for establishing a secure basis for local economic growth, raising a number of methodological and conceptual concerns. On these grounds, some scholars, such as Paraskevopoulos (1998) and Amin (1999: 375), resort to the (new institutional) position that the critical factor for economic success is not merely the presence of relational networks and their supportive institutional framework, but mainly "the ability of places to anticipate and respond to changing external circumstances". Others, such as Farole *et al.* (2011) and Rodríguez-Pose (2013), acknowledge the great difficulties in assessing these instructional qualities in practice and, reiterating caveats raised in the wider economic development literature,[16] conclude that it is pointless to look for blueprint guidelines for institutional design and therefore policy intervention should have a strong local, bottom-up, flavour. Finally, others, such as Cumbers *et al.* (2003) and Gertler (2010: 2), point out that, although institutions exert an "undeniably pervasive" influence on local economies, this role is still inadequately theorised and poorly understood, making a case for further empirical research on the basis of comparative case study analysis.

Overall, this 'institutional turn' in economic geography and local/regional development studies has not only provided some significant insights, but it has also given a much clearer and sharper spatial dimension to institutional economics. However, scholars such as Cumbers *et al.* (2003) have been concerned with the selective manner by which certain ideas of (original) institutional economics were transferred in this literature, raising two points of criticism. First, the emphasis on the co-operative and collaborative relations between actors (over issues of divergence in ideology, unequal power, dominance and conflict) reflects the assumption that innovation and learning serve equally the interests of all groups in the locality, which is hardly the case. Second, the focus on the local level (over national or international levels) signifies a tendency to essentialise and reify the urban/regional scale over other geographical scales as an object of empirical enquiry and a site of policy intervention, ignoring the fact that economic development and policy formulation are open ended and contested processes operating across various geographical levels (regional, national and supranational). As such, it is argued that institutionalist studies of local economic development need to be informed by a much stronger sense of politics, assessing the specific ways in which places are produced and reproduced through the actions of particular social groups and institutions from a wider spatial political economy perspective informed by structuration theory and critical realism.

In looking explicitly at the functioning of property markets and their role in urban economies, institutional approaches signal the complexity of the issue and offer a holistic view. Emphasis is placed both on the demand and on the supply side of the urban system, and property is seen as a bundle of property rights in use, development and investment (Jaffe and Louziotis, 1996). Societies create, provide and maintain their built environment in relation to their needs, history, power relations, socio-cultural characteristics and material contexts (Samuels, 1999). Social values, norms and customs seem to play a significant role in this process. Property values, accordingly, emerge out of the institutional and organisational structure and cannot be simply reduced to prices (Hodgson, 1998a). In this context, a number of researchers have examined the processes through which the built environment is produced and reproduced, paying due attention both to the factors that influence the operation of the market and the relationship between economic change, spatial organisation and the property market process.

Espousing a rather neo-institutional viewpoint, a number of scholars have discussed the crucial role that information deficiencies and transaction costs play in the functioning of the land and property markets, affecting the price mechanism and the processes by which property is developed and allocated to users (Dokko and Edelstein, 1992; Alexander, 2001; Buitelaar, 2004, 2007; Needham and de Kam, 2004) as well as the perceptions and strategies of property investors (Geurts and Jaffe, 1996; D'Arcy and Lee, 1998; Fereidouni *et al.*, 2013). Similarly, other studies (Jaffe, 1996; Webster and Lai, 2003; Needham, 2006; van der Krabben, 2009; Musole, 2009) have drawn attention to the role that property rights' specification and allocation play in these processes (and especially in land use planning). In short, the arguments raised highlight the fact that property actors (both on the supply and demand sides of the market) are faced with significant transaction costs due to information shortages and other deficiencies of the institutional framework that defines property as an asset (called the 'property rights regime'). On these grounds, the wider institutional context within which the property market operates should be taken into consideration and its important role in influencing both property market outcomes and the urban economy should be recognised.[17] Overall, two important points come out of this literature. First, the property market exists within a wider economic, legal, planning and fiscal regime and, as such, all these elements affect its performance and investment opportunities. Second, the property market as a structure has two dimensions: one formal, encompassing all the rules and regulations which specify the rights and obligation related to property ownership, lease, transfer, use, investment and development; and one informal, comprising local social attributes and attitudes towards property (e.g. ownership) and market behaviour.

A similar perspective can also be found in the work of D'Arcy and Keogh (1997, 1998, 1999, 2002), who draw on new institutional economics to provide a systematic framework for the analysis of the property market structure and to explore its role within the urban economy. In particular, a three-level model is conceptualised to describe the market functions in use, investment and development. At the topmost level, the property market stands within the broad institutional environment, which comprises political, social, economic and legal institutions. At the next level, the market itself is regarded as an institution, including a range of characteristics that prescribe its structure, scope and function. These include formal and informal aspects of property rights allocation and enforcement in use, investment and development. At the bottom level, the main organisations that operate in the market (i.e. users, investors, developers, property service providers, financial service providers, and various related bodies and agencies) are examined in terms of the roles they play in the market function. The relations both within and between each level (e.g. between actors or between actors and institutions) are seen as interactive and capable of changing in response to actors' experiences and actions. What stands out in this work is the idea that the property market is an institution in itself, which is affected by the wider urban institutional environment within which it locates. Unfortunately, this is as far as it goes. The model refrains from exploring and unfolding further the complexity of this relationship, and, on these grounds, a thorough understanding of its nature is missing.

Interestingly, in another set of papers Keogh and D'Arcy (1994, 1999) use these ideas to examine how market operation affects market outcomes, addressing also the issues of market 'maturity' and 'efficiency'. The basic argument here is that, although wider socio-economic change represents the main determinant of property market performance, the level of maturity[18] exhibited by a given market structure will exert an independent influence on property outcomes. In these terms, it is asserted that the dynamic process of emergence, development and maturation seems likely to exhibit certain common features across property markets (an argument also raised in Jones Lang Wootton, 1992). However, maturation should not be perceived as a universal evolutionary process and therefore such an analysis should be supplemented with a detailed examination of the prevailing institutional characteristics to provide a more robust explanation of the observed outcomes. Additionally, Keogh and D'Arcy distinguish the concept of maturity from that of efficiency, arguing that mature property markets may exhibit characteristics which inhibit their efficient operation. In this context, they introduce a new concept to market efficiency, called 'bounded efficiency'. This is defined as a theoretical, but feasible, frontier representing the best potential market structure in the inevitable presence of institutional constraints (such as transaction costs and information deficiencies)[19] and other structural imperfections that characterise property (Evans, 1995). As such, the institutional constraints within, and the specific mechanisms by which, the property market operates contribute to an assessment of bounded efficiency, "...which in turn becomes the yardstick for evaluating actual market efficiency" (Keogh and D'Arcy, 1999: 2409).

However, the judgement of efficiency cannot be uniform across different groups of actors. This is because their interests and objectives may vary significantly, whereas the institutional structure is likely to reflect the bargaining power of certain actors. On that basis, Keogh and D'Arcy (1999) emphasise that an appropriate assessment of market efficiency should be constructed in partial terms, focusing either on the objectives of specific groups ('efficiency for a person') or on the advancement of specific purposes ('efficiency for a purpose'), rather than across the market as a whole. However, although this remark has a value on its own, further developments of the notion of market efficiency on these partial terms is missing from their work.

In evaluating the concept of property market bounded efficiency, it must be recognised that, although it is a static concept (as Keogh and D'Arcy themselves acknowledge), it neatly introduces the idea of an institutional environment and the restraints that it imposes on the operation of the market. However, specific methodological directions (in terms, for example, of what particular forms an empirical judgement of market efficiency would take) are not given, rendering the approach incomplete and ambiguous. Additionally, efficiency is primarily defined in economic terms, whereas social, cultural and political institutions are regarded only as constraining elements to market operation.

Apart from efficiency, D'Arcy and Keogh (1997, 1998, 1999) address explicitly issues of urban economic change and competitiveness, placing the property market in a central position. Their reasoning is based on the idea that the property market is a mediator through which the built environment is produced and reproduced to meet the requirements of economic actors for property use, investment and development. On that basis, it is argued that the property market influences the ability of the urban economy to accommodate pressures for economic change[20] and, in that sense, it acts as a filter through which these requirements pass and economic growth is achieved. In this attempt to assign property its proper explanatory role, the importance of understanding the mechanisms and nature of the 'property market process' is highlighted. This is the process which, among other things, specifies property values, generates information, defines legal interests, allocates uses, stimulates development and redevelopment, and generally determines the effectiveness of the urban system to provide the spatial structures (real property) and legal interests (property rights) that are required for economic development. A profound understanding of this process necessitates consideration of the institutional structure of the property market, through which property is defined in physical, economic, legal, political (power) and social terms, and an examination of how these institutions advance the functional requirements for property use, investment and development. On this basis the circularity of the argument is also recognised. Not only is the operation (and institutional basis) of the property market essential to understanding urban change, but it is also necessary to take into consideration the pressures for urban change that push against the prevailing property market institutions to be able to comprehend how and why the property market process has evolved. To illustrate the validity of these ideas and explore their analytical requirements, D'Arcy and Keogh refer to recent instances of urban change and competitiveness as experienced by selected case study cities in Europe. In that context, some key property market institutional factors are considered (such as property rights, the legal and planning framework, the organisation of service and information provision, or the development of the investment market), providing a basis for the explanation of urban change and a consideration of territorial competition strategies from a property market point of view.

A similar perspective for the analysis of the built environment is also found in the work of van der Krabben (1995, also van der Krabben and Lambooy, 1993; van der Krabben and Boekema, 1994). Van der Krabben starts by criticising conventional urban theories for their inability to theorise urban change properly on the basis of ignoring, first, the mutual relationship between spatial and economic phenomena and, second, the complex processes responsible for the 'provision of the built environment'.[21] On these grounds, he combines insights from both new and original institutional economics[22] to develop a framework for the analysis of property development and its effect on the urban economy. In particular, he maintains the new institutional ideas of transaction costs, property rights and institutional change, but infuses them with the original institutional emphasis on the socio-cultural nature of institutions and the plurality of human behaviour.[23] The theoretical frame put forward is as follows. Property market institutions (both formal and informal) and organisational structures are developed to resolve transaction cost problems that arise due to uncertainty in economic activity and they change in response to changes in prices, information costs, technology and preferences. This process is path-dependent, but is also heavily affected by the purposeful agency of the involved actors. The mixed rationality principle specifies their behaviour because, next to the politico-economic institutions, it is local traditions, habits, norms and social values (in short, socio-cultural institutions, which are dynamic and complex in nature and local in origin) that prescribe action, accommodate unavoidable uncertainty and contribute to the formation of expectations.

Informed by this position, van der Krabben turns next to provide an analytical framework guiding the empirical analysis of the property market structure and its spatial and temporal dynamics, which is subsequently applied in the Dutch housing market. In particular, the institutional organisation of the market is explored in terms of the actors involved, their rationalities and strategies, the relations among them (whether they are market-, hierarchy- or network-based), the role of the public sector, and the legal/planning and other formal rules and property rights that regulate the market. The next step in the analysis is to investigate the impact of this institutional organisation on the structure and outcomes of the property development process. The aspects examined include: the construction costs; property prices; profit margins; the number of transactions; the volume, type, quality and location of the new development; and the type, quality and ageing of the existing stock. Finally, the dynamics and temporal change of the organisation of the development industry are considered with reference to changes in relative prices, information costs, technology and preferences, also taking into account issues of path dependency.

This framework enables van der Krabben (1995) to evaluate the role and contribution of the property industry to the economic success of (Dutch) cities and, on that basis, to discuss issues of market efficiency. Interestingly, his case study reveals that the property market can both stimulate and impede urban economic growth, depending on how effectively supply responds to demand pressures. On these grounds, van der Krabben distinguishes between two forms of property market efficiency and discusses their characteristics. The first, called 'allocative efficacy',[24] employs a (rather vague) public or social criterion to assess market efficiency in terms of the stability of property prices and the socially acceptable (whatever this means) distribution of property rights. The second, called 'productive efficiency', focuses on the development side to assess the market in terms of the profits it yields to the developers, whereas aspects such as organisational structure, resources and the strategies of the actors are taken into account. These notions, although elaborate on the idea of 'efficiency for a person' or 'efficiency for a purpose' (raised in Keogh and D'Arcy, 1994, 1999), are static in nature and essentially neglect the full spectrum of interests and institutional aspects that characterise the property market.

Evaluating van der Krabben's work, it must be acknowledged that it provides useful insights into the institutional character of the property market, but it fails to see the whole picture when the market is but a part (and product) of the wider institutional environment. As such, not only is the relationship between the property market as an institution and the urban institutional environment simplified and underestimated, but also the plurality of economic, political, legal and socio-cultural issues involved in the operation of the market tends to be understated.

Ball (1998, 2002, 2006; also Ball *et al.*, 1998) suggests a more relational approach to property market analysis. Condemning Marxists for functionalism and neo-institutionalists for determinism, he argues that the structure and organisation of the built environment should be seen with reference to the specific (in time and place) social relations that account for its provision. This is defined as 'structure of building provision' (SoP), referring to the "contemporary network of relationships associated with the provision of particular types of building at specific points in time" (Ball, 1998: 1513). These relationships are embodied in the institutional and organisational aspect of the property market and can take both economic and non-economic forms. In that sense, an SoP is an institution incorporating the organisations, networks, rules, practices and all kinds of relations which account for a particular form of building provision. Each type of SoP is place and time specific and therefore is unique. Change in an SoP may come from a number of contingent sources, including market pressures, as well as changes in technologies, tastes, policies, or in the strategies of the actors involved. However, there is no a priori weighting of the importance of these potential influences and, as such, the evolution of an SoP cannot be prescribed in a deterministic manner. Indeed, it is argued that at any point in time there is "no contemporary rationale for the existence of a particular SoP – it just happens to be there (although it has a history and a future)" (Ball, 1998: 1514). This, of course, implies that the emergence and development of an SoP do to conform to economic efficiency requirements.

Examining an SoP empirically involves the identification of the social relations and economic roles of the involved agents and the relevant institutional factors which determine these socio-economic relations. Which institutions and relations should be included is a matter of research judgement depending on the questions asked (Ball, 1998). In that sense, the SoP methodology is a way of organising empirical material (including institutions), rather than a theory of property market phenomena in its own right. This is why "other theories are needed to understand particular research questions formulated within this framework" (Ball *et al.*, 1998: 131).

Although Ball (2003, 2006) has used this framework in empirical research, there is an issue with the contingent nature of the concept, making it difficult to identify 'what shapes what' and so to properly define an SoP (Guy and Henneberry, 2000: 2405), let alone to compare the SoPs of different urban contexts. Moreover, this emphasis on the unique nature of each SoP tends to underestimate the fact that common socio-economic trends have caused comparable experiences and responses across urban Europe, giving rise to similar evolutionary patterns and institutional contexts (Jones Lang Wootton, 1992). In addition, Guy and Henneberry (2000) criticise Ball, first, for maintaining a too clear division between the economic and the social realms and, second, for overlooking the cultural basis of agent behaviour (making the approach susceptible to mainstream economic rationality). Despite the criticisms, however, some important insights have been offered by this work, concerning the historical and local nature of the market institutions and the difficulty in identifying and exploring these characteristics in empirical analysis.

Building on the above criticisms, Guy and Henneberry (2000, 2002a, 2002b) put forward another research framework for the understanding of the property development processes informed by a number of sources. For instance, critical realism is called up for its unifying philosophical position[25] and its pluralistic methodological stance that supports 'abstract conceptualisation' alongside quantitative and qualitative empirical analysis, whereas the institutional paradigm is appreciated for its emphasis on the socio-cultural basis of structure and agency (original institutionalism) and its insights on the function of markets, organisations and networks (new institutionalism). Integrating these ideas, Guy and Henneberry recognise that the economic structure is part of the wider structural base of society and, as such, economic phenomena are not merely social, but deeply cultural manifestations. Each society legitimises and reproduces (through habituation) its own socio-cultural practices, providing the frames of reference (spatially and temporally specific) that underlie human rationality and inform purposeful action. On these grounds, variety in human behaviour, agency and economic activity is accounted for.

Carrying this discussion into the built environment provision, Guy and Henneberry assign involved actors with rationalities and behaviours that are not only economic, but also social, cultural and habitual in nature. However, agency is purposeful: actors constantly interact, struggle, exercise power, negotiate and co-operate, acting on and reformulating the institutional frames that define their existence. This makes property development a deeply contextual, dynamic and contingent process, defined by the "particular aims and objectives of development actors" and by the "shifting market [institutional] framework which may enable or constrain development strategies" (Guy and Henneberry, 2000: 2413). In these terms, a complex interrelationship between institutional structures and human agency is recognised, whereby "...one layer of agency can become, in another context, the next layer of structure and so on" (Guy and Henneberry, 2000: 2413).

Overall, Guy and Henneberry make a convincing case for an institutional turn in property research, where proper emphasis is placed on the socio-cultural base of institutional evolution and the complex interplay between agency and structure in this process. However, a number of weaknesses are evident. First, although socio-cultural considerations are correctly put to the fore,[26] this is done at the expense of the political and legal dimensions, which virtually disappear from the discussion. Moreover, the approach introduced is exploratory and general in nature. A number of important ideas are put together without formulating a solid theoretical framework. Subsequently, no specific analytical directions are outlined that could guide empirical study and provide a basis for sound research practice.

Finally, a rather general agenda for the analysis of the property market along the lines of original institutionalism has been put forward in a number of studies (e.g. McMaster and Watkins, 2006; Watkins, 2008; Needham *et al.*, 2011; Kauko, 2012).[27] Addressing different subject matters, these pieces of research do not provide a common methodological framework, but are mentioned here on the merits of their discussion about the institutional nature of the property market and its empirical investigation. Three of the points raised deserve special attention: first, in contrast with mainstream economics the strength (and weakness) of original institutionalism lies in its ability to advance a deep understanding of the processes underlying property market phenomena. Second, aiming towards such an understanding, emphasis is placed on historical and socio-cultural characteristics (values, beliefs, norms, conventions) deemed to (partially) structure agents' preferences, motivations (including coercion) and behaviour.

Third, detailed description through observation becomes important in understanding institutional structures, which is to be achieved through inductive, case study analysis.

Concluding, it becomes evident that institutional approaches provide valuable insights with regard to (urban) economic organisation, built environment provision and property market operation. In particular, they properly emphasise the important role that both the institutional set up (economic, political, legal, social and cultural) and its organisational frame (individual actors, organisations and networks) play in urban transformation and economic growth. In addition, and contrary to, conventional and most structuralist approaches, the significance of the processes through which the built structures are produced, exchanged, distributed, used and maintained is appreciated and examined with regard to the question of urban economic development. In this context the property market is perceived as an institution in itself, i.e. a set of formal and informal rules, structures, practices and organisational arrangements that specify the provision of property. It is argued that, alongside other institutions (political, social, cultural and economic), it acts as a mediator through which the potential for economic change is realised and served. This means that the operation of the property market (described in terms of property market outcomes and property market process) is an important parameter in understanding the economic development, change and performance of cities. Regarding the institutional nature of the property market, three points need special mention. First, the property market is itself part and product of the general institutional framework of an area and, in these terms, not only economic, but also political, legal and social institutions define its operation and change. Second, the property market is constantly evolving in a path-dependent manner, affected by trends and shocks which are endogenous or exogenous to the urban system. Finally, understanding of the institutional structure of the property market necessitates appropriate attention to the cultural factors that determine these institutions. However, despite these developments on the theorisation of the property market and its links to the urban economy, it is generally acknowledged that our understanding of these issues remains, at best, partial. For instance, although the connection between the property market as an institution and the urban institutional environment is correctly recognised, important aspects of this relation are still poorly understood.

3.6 Overview and conclusions

This chapter has examined the issues of urban economic and spatial transformation. It started by identifying the contextual trends and emerging patterns that affect contemporary cities, as identified by a number of researchers independent of their methodological or analytical stance. It was acknowledged that technological developments as well as economic, political, demographic and social changes affect the socio-economic organisation of cities, with profound implications for their spatial structures and the built environment. In turn, this descriptive (a-theoretical or multi-theoretical) presentation of urban reality was examined on the basis of the explanations provided by the three schools of economic thought. Emphasis was placed in this discussion on the issues of built environment provision and property market operation and the role they play in urban transformation.

A review of the conventional (mainstream) approaches to urban analysis reveals that the primary explanatory role is ascribed to market mechanisms, assuming that they operate in a more or less efficient manner to bring economic forces (supply and demand) into a state of equilibrium. Accordingly, urban economic and spatial transformation is explained on the basis of the decisions of rational economic actors who, in the face of exogenous changes, react perfectly to maximise their welfare. In that context, emphasis is placed on the demand side of the urban economy, whereas the supply side is regarded as relatively unproblematic. Indeed, it is assumed that the built environment is relatively 'malleable' and the property market works efficiently to supply land and property in accordance with demand. Given these assumptions, it is not surprising that the property market is seen as a passive adapter to urban change and, as such, theorisation of its operation has been, at best, marginal. Ultimately, it becomes evident that conventional approaches are unable to provide a sound theoretical basis for the consideration of both the property market process and its impact on the urban economy.

As regards the structural approaches, they correctly locate urban change and property market activity not only in an economic, but also in a political and social context. In that sense, urban economic and spatial transformation is explained on the basis of the inherent contradictions and dynamics of capitalism, where economic, political and socio-cultural forces interact dialectically to define and redefine socio-economic organisation, spatial structures and the built environment. Evaluating these approaches, it must be noted that Marxist, neo-Marxist and regulationist approaches place increased emphasis on these structural and historically specific determinants and, as such, they have been criticised for determinism and functionalism. Other structuralist theories (i.e. the structuration and realism perspectives), however, have been more open in their interpretation, recognising purposeful human agency as an equal contributor (next to structural determinants) to the processes of urban transformation and built environment provision. However, particularly in the context of this book, none of these approaches has been able to effectively theorise the functioning of the property market and to translate this into an integrated economic theory at a city–region level.

Finally, the last strand of the examined literature concerns the institutionalist responses to questions of urban change, built environment provision, and the role of property markets in these processes. These studies have put forward the idea that it is the institutional environment (defined in economic, political, legal, social and cultural terms), with its organisational structure, that accounts for the course and performance of the urban socio-economy. Additionally, and in contrast with all other economic approaches, the process through which the built environment is produced, used, maintained and traded was explicitly theorised and considered in relation to urban economic development. On this basis, the organisation and functioning of the property market were emphasised as important parameters in understanding urban economic performance and transformation. However, our knowledge with regard to these issues remains limited, as important aspects, qualities, dynamics and relations have not been adequately theorised and understood. This gives a high priority to theoretical work.

In the light of these remarks, a research agenda for the property market is suggested along the lines of the institutional paradigm. Three key arguments are put forward. First, economic pressures for urban change are inevitably mediated through the overall institutional environment (and its organisational structure) which determines the course and direction of the urban economy. Second, the property market as an institution is part and product of the overall urban institutional environment and, as such, economic, political, legal, social and cultural institutions affect its operation and evolutionary path. Third, the property market acts as a filter for economic adjustment, affecting the performance and development of the urban economy through its ability to efficiently provide the property outcomes required.

Notes

1 Although this must always have been the case, the difference between now and in the past is a matter of degree or intensity.
2 Hohenberg (2004) argues that a significant number of new urban dwellers come from abroad, rather than from the local countryside. Despite all the stress caused (due to a clash of cultures and difficulties of employment), these foreign migrants have provided much of the labour supply on which growth has drawn.
3 Mainstream urban economics generally identify the wider urban area as the main unit of analysis. From that perspective, micro-analysis looks within the urban level (intra-urban), whereas macro-analysis is generally focused at the urban system level (inter-urban).
4 A similar discussion is also provided in Nabarro (1990).
5 However, it must be mentioned that because of data problems, generally supply is often either ignored or is treated very crudely in these studies.
6 Some researchers (e.g. Bovaird, 1993) have argued that Castells's recent work increasingly deviates from his original (more traditional) Marxist position. On that basis, the influence of the neo-Marxist conceptualisation on his approach is evident.
7 Critical realists do not hold a uniform opinion with regard to the ontological status of space. Some scholars (e.g. Sayer, 1992; Yeung, 1997) view space as a mere component of deep structures, whereas others (e.g. Pratt, 1995; Peet, 1998) insist on its ontological differentiation, ascribing spatial configurations with particular causal and generative qualities.
8 Deviations from that model of long-term equilibrium can be found in some structurationist and realist contributions (e.g. Dear and Moos, 1986; Ganderton, 1994).
9 Fixed asset refers to the built environment used for production (e.g. roads, railways, industrial buildings), whereas consumption fund indicates the built environment used for consumption (i.e. housing, sidewalks).
10 This includes the location characteristics, external layout and internal configuration of buildings.
11 As such, Ball (1998: 1512) argues, institutions disappear from the focus of analysis, drawing this approach apart from institutionalist approaches.

12 Note here that, for original institutionalists, the concepts of 'technology', 'technological development', etc. have a wider meaning than is implied by the common use of the words and refer to the process, led by the developmental and organisational creativity of human agency, that arises out of the human proclivity for workmanship at the exercise of intellectual curiosity (Veblen, 1899, 1904; Ayres, 1962; Samuels, 1977; Bush, 1987). On this basis, and in contrast with neo- and new institutionalists, 'technology' is regarded as an endogenous variable to urban economic organisation and change.

13 This is what Bush (1987) terms 'ceremonial encapsulation'.

14 Knowledge, in this context, comprises information, views, experiences, technical knowledge, social knowledge (i.e. knowledge of people, attitudes, habits, practices), and latent and tacit knowledge (i.e. hidden, not explicitly known, difficult to expresses knowledge).

15 See Amin and Thrift (1994, 1995), Healey (1995), Storper (1995, 1997, 2005), Healey (1997, 1998, 2002), Raco (1998, 1999), Paraskevopoulos (1998), Amin (1999), Martin (2000), Vigar *et al.* (2000), Cumbers *et al.* (2003), Hayter (2004), Rodríguez-Pose and Storper (2006), MacKinnon *et al.* (2009), Rafiqui (2009), Gertler (2010) and Rodríguez-Pose (2013), among others.

16 Such as the problems with the measurement of institutions, their space–time specificity, and the endogeneity they show both with development and with other factors driving development (see, inter alia, Chang, 2007, 2011).

17 A similar argument was also raised in Jones Lang Wootton (1992) and Bruhl and Lizieri (1994).

18 Keogh and D'Arcy (1994) identify six principal characteristics of property market maturity: (i) accommodation of a full range of use and investment objectives; (ii) flexible adjustment of the market in both the short and the long run; (iii) existence of a sophisticated profession; (iv) extensive information flows and research activity; (v) market openness in spatial, functional and sectoral terms; and (vi) standardisation of property rights and market practices.

19 A similar concept is also put forward in Buitelaar (2004) with specific reference to the property development process.

20 Note that similar arguments were also raised in Healey (1995) and in van der Krabben (1995).

21 The term 'provision of the built environment' is attributed to Ball (1986: 455), defining "the production, exchange, distribution and use of a built structure". Van der Krabben (1995) extends this concept by adding the 'maintenance of a built structure' to this definition.

22 North (1990) and Hodgson (1988) are acknowledged as his sources of information.

23 Although van der Krabben (1995) uses the term 'bounded rationality', this is not done in a new institutional manner. Rather, he perceives human behaviour to be driven by habit-persistence and other socio-cultural characteristics (such as trust and moral values), coming close to the notion of 'mixed rationality'.

24 This would be more normally described as 'allocative efficiency'.

25 On that basis, Guy and Henneberry (2000) reject the structuration theory's notion of 'duality of structure' in favour of the critical realist concept of dualism.

26 Interestingly, Ball (2002), in a rather neo-institutional tone, criticises Guy and Henneberry (2000) for overemphasising the cultural nature of the market without having sound theoretical or empirical support.

27 Apart from Kauko, all others refer to the "original institutionalist" Richard T. Ely, founder of the land economy school at Wisconsin and Columbia (known as Columbia School).

4 Philosophical position and conceptual framework

4.1 Introduction

The previous chapter examined how the different paradigms in economics analyse urban economic and spatial transformation. In this way, we have seen which factors each analytical framework regards as significant in explaining urban change and also the role the property market is assigned in this process. Overall, it became evident that institutional economics stands out for its holistic and dynamic view of the world and the open-type explanations that it espouses. Scholars within this approach have theorised the property market as an institution, proposing an agenda for analysing urban economies with the property market in a central position. However, this is only how far this has gone. There are still important theoretical areas left unexplored or addressed at the margins. For example, although the relationship between the property market institution and the wider institutional environment has been recognised, many of these links remain virtually unexplored, requiring further theoretical development before effective empirical research can be undertaken.

The current chapter addresses these issues. It develops a unifying and comprehensive conceptual framework to advance understanding of the complex mechanisms through which the built environment is provided in response to urban socio-economic pressures and dynamics and translates this into an effective theory of urban economic development. This necessitates the provision of an explicit ontological, epistemological and methodological perspective with which a clear research agenda for concrete analysis can be defined. Clarity on these issues is paramount, as institutionalist research can be, and has been, informed by a range of analytical standpoints and philosophical positions.

The chapter is organised as follows. The next section constructs a philosophical framework to advance understanding of the institutional structure of the economy and to enrich the philosophical basis of institutionalism. To achieve this, key elements from institutionalism are subsumed into the philosophical platform of critical realism. The chapter then moves to deploy a theoretical framework of urban economic organisation and change in which appropriate emphasis is placed on the wider institutional environment and the specific mechanisms, processes and dynamics through which the built environment is provided. Such a theorisation enables a more refined conceptualisation of property market efficiency, defined in terms of the ability of its institutional structure to enhance urban economic potential.

4.2 A philosophical framework of socio-economic organisation

It should be clear by now that institutionalism is not a methodologically homogeneous school. It is rather a 'research programme' that accommodates a number of approaches, providing various conceptual and analytical standpoints and informed by a number of philosophical positions (Chavance, 2009). The linchpin of all these approaches is the position that institutions are important determinants of economic organisation and should not be taken as exogenous to the economic system (Samuels, 1995; Hodgson, 2000).

This heterogeneity and methodological pluralism does not, however, constitute a weakness. In fact, leading institutionalists (such as Stanfield, 1980, 1999; Samuels, 1995, 1998a, 2000; Williamson, 2000) have welcomed this conceptual and methodological richness as a manifestation of openness and maturity, whereas other scholars (e.g. van der Krabben, 1995; Guy and Henneberry, 2000; Cumbers *et al.*, 2003; Buitelaar, 2004, 2007; Cheng, 2005; MacKinnon *et al.*, 2009; Needham *et al.*, 2011; Arvanitidis and Kyriazis, 2013) have demonstrated that it is legitimate to articulate an eclectic mix of the philosophical positions, methodologies,[1] ideas and concepts available in the wider institutionalist literature to deploy a conceptual framework appropriate for analysing the phenomena under investigation.

On the basis of these reflections, this section develops an ontological framework that advances conceptualisation of the institutional structure of the economic system and facilitates understanding of the complex interrelation between the institutional structure and human agency. Once again, this is achieved by incorporating key elements from (original) institutional economics into the philosophical platform of critical realism. As indicated, critical realism presents advantages over other philosophical perspectives in discussing the institutional organisation of the economy. These mainly stem from its ontological arguments that, by dissociating institutional structure from human agency, allow analysis to be focused on the institutional qualities, mechanisms and causal powers that characterise the economic system. Moreover, the fact that the critical realism ontology (or meta-theory) is compatible with a variety of approaches in heterodox economics (Outhwaite, 1990; Sayer, 1992) renders its fusion with institutionalism generally both valid and feasible.

4.2.1 Philosophical foundations

Science never takes place in a philosophical vacuum; all research activity, independent of its specific subject matter, presupposes the adoption of a philosophical position. This is because it is impossible to generate or integrate knowledge without a clear perspective of how 'reality' is constituted and realised and what constitutes valid knowledge, as it is these ontological and epistemological assumptions that define appropriate methodologies and generally inform and guide the overall research process (Johnston, 1986; Blackburn, 1996).

As discussed in Chapter 2, the critical realist perception of the social world is based on three fundamental premises about social reality. First, the world is comprised of objects that are 'structured' and 'intransitive': structured in the sense that they cannot be restricted to the events of experience and intransitive in the sense that they exist and function independently of their identification and the knowledge of which they are the objects (Bhaskar, 1975, 1979, 1989; Lawson, 1997a, 2003; Archer *et al.*, 1998). Hence the world is constituted not only by events or states of affairs, and our experiences or perceptions of those actualities, but also by 'deep' structures, powers, mechanisms and their relations that, although they may not be directly detectable, nevertheless exist and govern the actual events as well as what we experience, understand and act upon.[2] Such a distinction between intransitive entities (such as structures,[3] institutions, mechanisms, processes) and transitive objects of knowledge (such as events, observations, theories, hypotheses[4]) precludes any anthropocentric definition of ontology (i.e. defining reality and existence on the sole basis of human perception and experience) and the subsequent collapse of the ontological into the epistemological domain (i.e. equating what exists with what can be known to exist). The latter also highlights the significance of ontological determination as an essential step in any social enquiry (Bhaskar, 1975; Sayer, 1992; Dow, 2002).

Furthermore, critical realism upholds a clear conception of the intransitive nature of social entities without underestimating the relativity and historical transitivity of our knowledge of them. Thus the idea of 'ontological realism' (the proposition that there are true entities which exist and operate independently of our knowledge of them) is complemented by an 'epistemological relativism', the thesis that the only way to know and express these entities is "via human mediation in cognitive discourse"[5] (Lawson, 1997a: 241). Note, however, that such an assertion does not imply that knowledge is infallible, nor that there is only one supreme or correct understanding of the world.[6] What is clearly maintained is that the world can be understood only through the available conceptual resources, where different standpoints provide different (yet valid to a degree) perspectives of the world, but do not determine the structure of the world itself. As such, a distinction between existential and causal interdependence is acknowledged, where intransitive social entities are seen as existentially independent of, but causally interdependent with, the processes by which they are known (Bhaskar, 1979).

On the basis of this conceptualisation, which distinguishes between our knowledge of these entities and the reality of their independent existence, knowledge is inevitably seen as the endless social activity of understanding these true entities. This implies that knowledge is never created out of nothing. Rather, it can only be a produced means of cognition, where revised understandings are achieved via the update or transformation of existing conceptions, hypotheses and insights on the basis of their 'practical' adequacy,[7] intersubjective intelligibility and acceptability, internal consistency, as well as coherence to the overall existing conceptual framework (Bhaskar, 1975, 1979; Sayer, 1992, 2000; Lawson, 1997a; but also Veblen, 1919a; Ayres, 1962; Samuels, 1990; Hodgson, 1997). In short, critical realism regards knowledge as both a social process and product, which is historically and culturally specific, symbolically mediated and expressed and, as such, not only fallible, but also theory-laden, practice-dependent and value-impregnated.

On this epistemic account, the vital task of social sciences is to advance knowledge, i.e. to (re)define and refine existing nominal conceptualisations (definitions, theories) in an attempt to expand and improve our understanding of the (continually active and transfactually enduring) intransitive entities and their properties, which account for the phenomena under investigation (Sayer, 1992, 2000; Blackburn, 1996; Lewis, 1996; Lawson, 1997a).[8] Certainly, new conceptualisations do not emerge out of nothing, or without a reason. They are forged out of old ones in an attempt to reconcile 'pragmatic' anomalies (i.e. inconsistencies between experience and theory and/or gaps in existing theoretical systems) through cognitive reflection. Thus a realist starts by shaping (i.e. critically deploying, reworking, reforming and refining) existing conceptual resources to determine a hypothesis of a mechanism or a set of mechanisms that accounts for the phenomenon in question. These theories are then assessed and reviewed in specific situations (in an essentially progressive, reflexive and iterative manner) and, if found to be pragmatically adequate (i.e. empirically realised or correspondent to reality), they are accepted as valuable parts in the continuous unfolding of explanatory knowledge. To achieve this, a variety of methods and techniques of investigation can be used, including both qualitative and quantitative research methods,[9] most commonly by means of case study analysis (Sayer, 1992, 2000; Yeung, 1997; Downward *et al.*, 2002; McEvoy, 2006; Davidsen, 2010).

The second core premise of realism relates to the 'stratified' nature of the social world. The notion of stratification enables the differentiation of reality into distinct domains or strata, which, though unsynchronised or out of phase (i.e. operating and changing within different time frames), are seen as interconnected with one another[10] (Bhaskar, 1989; Lawson, 1997a, 1997b, 2003; also Ayres, 1962; Hodgson, 1999a). What relates and connects one layer with another is the phenomenon of 'emergence'.[11] According to this notion, each level of reality exhibits entities or aspects which emerge from, depend upon, and are conditioned by entities found at another layer of reality. However, these entities have a degree of causal autonomy from the level from which they emerged by virtue of the real essences, intrinsic structures, complex interrelations and organisational potentialities of the stratum in which they exist (termed as 'organising relational structure') (Lawson, 2012). This autonomy prevents entities formed at a particular level of reality from being reducible to (and predictable from, or explainable in terms of) the entities of the other levels from which they have emerged (Kim, 1999). On these grounds, differentiation of one layer from another is established, reaffirming the lack of 'synchrony' between them. Moreover, this autonomy is marked by the existence of separate and additional causal powers and novel qualities (due to the organising relational structure) that are absent from the entities located in other strata of reality. In particular, these emergent entities have the ability to frame (i.e. to constrain, enable or simply to influence) and cause changes to important powers and dispositions of the basal layer from which they have emerged[12] (Lawson, 2012; Pratten, 2013). However, this causal effect, although it may alter (or even give rise to new) true dispositions and conditions, does not radically disrupt or destroy the intransitive subsistence and existential status of that level (Sperry, 1991; Lawson, 1997b). In that sense, some order is sustained at each level and, in reality, as a whole, alongside complexity, contingency, novelty, plurality, openness and dynamism[13] (Pratten, 2013).

Finally, critical realists insist on the 'transfactuality' and 'openness' of social structures. In short, the argument states that the underlying generative mechanisms, structures and institutions operate independently of the closure or, in other words, of the systems in which they occur (Bhaskar, 1975). Their powers are continuous and invariant, stemming from their (relatively durable) properties, and thus they constantly operate independently of both the conditions for their actualisation and their actual realisation. However, although these generative qualities are always present, they may be "possessed unexercised, exercised unactualized, and actualized undetected or unperceived"[14] (Archer *et al.*, 1998: xii), depending upon 'contingently related conditions' which determine whether, and, if so, which, countervailing mechanisms would be activated or released[15] (Dow, 2002). On that basis, the mechanisms and powers of the underlying structures should be seen and analysed as transfactual or 'universal', despite being expressed and manifested in more or less historically specific and highly differentiated forms. On that basis, Sayer (1992) acknowledges that, although the abstract analysis of mechanisms into which human agency is locked by specific structures may be more generally applicable, further empirical (concrete) research is necessary to establish the extent of their generalisation.

It must be highlighted at this point that this final premise of critical realism does not imply that entities of social reality are immutable. Indeed, as Bhaskar (1979, 1989), Sayer (1992), Archer (1995) and Lawson (1997a, 2003), clearly indicate, one of the defining features of the social world is its potential to change as a result of the conception, reflection and action of purposeful human agency.[16] Thus, as realists insist upon a stratified view of social reality, they accept that "there are properties and powers particular to people which include a reflexivity towards and creativity about any social context which they confront" (Archer *et al.*, 1998: 190). From this conception, the 'transformational model of social activity' emerges, emphasising that social life possesses a non-teleologically, but historically evolving character by virtue of the agents' potential continually to re-interpret, and collectively reproduce and transform, the social reality they confront (Bhaskar, 1979).

Given these three ontological principles and their qualifications, it is now possible to advance the discussion on the nature of social structures and their connection with human agency, providing a solid ontological basis for the consideration of institutional organisation. From the outset, the realist understanding of social structures, and social phenomena in general, entails a 'relational conception of the subject matter of the social sciences', arguing that all social entities (structures, institutions, as well as human agency) presuppose a social context and depend upon social relations for their existence. On this basis, it is valid to argue, first, that social structures would not exist without human activity and, second, that such human activity would not occur unless the agents engaging in it had a conception of what they were doing[17] (something which presupposes the prior existence of social forms) (Bhaskar, 1979; Archer, 1995). Such a conception can be held consciously or unconsciously (implicitly) by the human agents. On this basis, the concept-dependence, activity-dependence and space-time specificity of social structures is identified.

However, it is equally important to acknowledge at this point the intransitive dimension of social structures. Thus, although social structures depend upon agents' conceptions (which may be distorted, incomplete, inadequate, or simply *inappropriately* conceptualised due to their evolving character), they exist intransitively and therefore function independently of their *appropriate* conceptualisation (Bhaskar, 1989, Archer *et al.*, 1998). To sum up, it can be said that social structures are regarded as both the ever-present condition and the outcome of human agency (defined as perception, conception, reflection and action), where people both reproduce and transform the very structures that they utilise for their activities in a recursive and non-teleological manner (see Figure 4.1).

However, there is an important asymmetry here. At any moment in time, social structures are pre-given for humans who do not create them, but merely reproduce or transform them in their day-to-day activities (Archer, 1995, 2000). To put it another way, as individuals we do not make social structures: they pre-exist our birth, sustaining the properties and powers that have emerged as a result of the actions and behaviours of humans before us.[18] This means that social structures (although they exist – sustained or modified – as a result of the totality of human activities) always pre-date the individual and provide (transcendentally and causally) the necessary condition for human behaviour and action.[19] These causal powers testify to the reality of social structures, whereas their pre-existence establishes their relative autonomy as distinct objects of

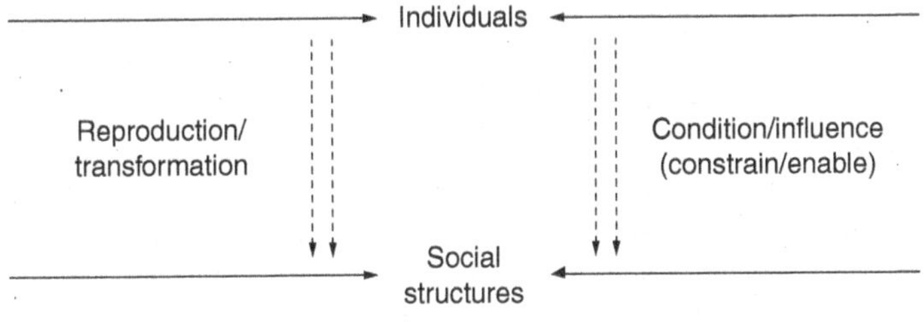

Figure 4.1 The transformational model of the structure/agency connection (source: based on Archer *et al.* (1998)).

scientific investigation. On this basis, the ontological (and methodological) 'separability' of social structure and human agency is recognised,[20] whereby it becomes clear that, by virtue of the different emergent properties and causal powers they possess[21] and the time frame they exist in, social structures and human agency belong in two distinct levels of social reality which are usually out of synchrony (Lawson, 1997a; Archer *et al.*, 1998) (see Figure 4.1).

It is evident from this discussion that a system of unifying concepts is required, designated the 'point of contact' between human agency and social structures. Such a mediating system, linking action to structure, is the enduring social relations that are conceived as holding between "*positions* (places, functions, rules, tasks, duties, rights, etc.) occupied (filled, assumed, enacted, etc.) by individuals, and *practises* (activities, etc.) in which, in virtue of their occupancy of these positions (and vice versa), they engage"[22] (Archer *et al.*, 1998: 221, emphasis in the original). A similar position is also evident in various institutionalist writings. Commons (1931), Granovetter (1985), Searle (2005) and Bush (2008), for instance, view institutional structures as defining, and being defined by, the correlative and reciprocal relations between individuals.

Given the realist conception of social structure developed so far, and the institutionalist theorisation elaborated in the previous chapters, it is now possible to move towards an understanding and definition of institutions as special types of social entities.[23] Lawson (1997a: 318) indicates a useful direction at this point, suggesting the term 'institution' should be used "to designate those systems, or structured processes of interaction (collecting together rules, relations and positions as well as habits and other practices), that are relatively enduring and identified as such". If we accept this, institutions are defined here as established rules or ingrained regularities of human life[24] that define agents' perception, thought, behaviour and expectations, providing certainty and order in social interaction and economic organisation.

Institutions, like all social entities, are products of human society, meaning that they exist, reproduced and transformed, only by virtue of it. On this basis, institutions do not exist independently of the activities, practices and relationships they govern, or the agents' conceptions (beliefs, values, etc.), mental attitudes (including habits and routines) and psycho-biological capacities (Veblen, 1899, 1904, 1914; Hamilton, 1919, 1932; Edie, 1922; Jensen, 1994; North, 1994; Thornhill *et al.*, 1997; Hodgson, 2006). However, institutions cannot be reduced to, or identified with, human agency. They are not only out of phase with the human activities they facilitate, but, as products of the processes and circumstances of the past, are "never in full accord with the requirements of the present" (Veblen, 1899: 191). Thus it becomes clear that they belong to a distinct layer of reality (as signified by the concept of dualism) with its own causal powers and emergent properties. Moreover, based on this notion of 'separability' between structure and agency, institutionalism, in line with the critical realist conceptualisation, warrants institutions with temporal priority (i.e. pre-existence), relative autonomy and causal efficacy over human agency. On that basis it can be argued with Hodgson (1998a, 2000, 2003) that institutions are simultaneously social structures 'outside' individuals and ideational representations 'inside' their heads,[25] which have the ability to mould the capacities and behaviour of human agency (groups as well as individuals) in fundamental ways.

The basic function of institutions is to create stable expectations of the behaviour of others and to ensure certainty and continuity in social and economic life. As such, they are characterised by relative stability, self-reinforcement and a capacity to replicate. Once they are in place and acted upon, they come to endure merely through being an outcome of the day-to-day activities of individuals 'going on' in life. On the basis of this continuity and persistence, institutions provide some kind of 'quasi-closure' in the agents' decision-making and, ultimately, to the overall, essentially open, socio-economic system[26] (Sayer, 1992; Lawson, 1997a; Mearman, 2006). However, this does not mean that they are immutable; they are human-made and changeable. In fact, institutions seem to evolve in a relatively slow, but dynamic and apparently incremental, fashion, a process characterised by 'cumulative causation' and 'path dependence' (Veblen, 1919a; North, 1990, respectively), through both non-deliberative (i.e. habitual and customary) and deliberative (typically legal) modes (Samuels, 1995). It is on that basis that institutional change is seen as a never-ending evolutionary process of adaptation to changing experiences, exigencies and circumstances of human life. Yet nothing in this assertion implies an economically efficient, deterministic or teleological perception with regard to institutional evolution. This is because it is human agency (characterised by variety in rationality and behaviour) in relation to other 'contingently related conditions' (such as unpredictable events and shocks) that plays a decisive role in shaping the course of institutional change.

On the basis of these arguments it is now possible to introduce a stratified ontological framework providing a robust basis for a holistic conceptualisation of the institutionalist understanding of urban socio-economy.

4.2.2 Ontological basis of the institutionalist socio-economic organisation

As stated earlier, the critical realist philosophical perspective is employed because of its ability to address the richness, multidimensionality and complexity of the socio-economic world, so far outlined as intrinsically structured, open, dynamic and characterised by emergence, 'irrationality', contingency, creativity and thus novelty. The resultant model, which can be seen in Figure 4.2, puts forward such an ontological interpretation, bringing together key insights from the wider institutional economics literature and the unifying philosophical approach of critical realism. In particular, a three-layered, interlocked, socio-economic reality is envisaged, whereby each level possesses unique properties and exhibits qualities that depend upon, and are conditioned by, the elements developed in other levels. On these grounds, the autonomy and differentiation of each level is sustained alongside their interconnection, interaction and interdependence.

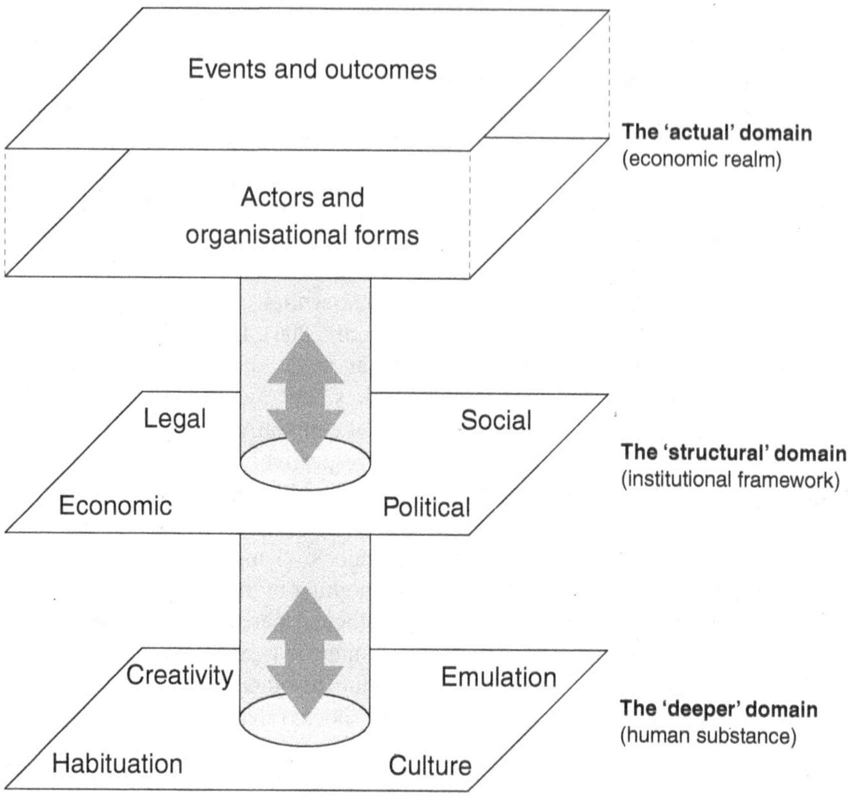

Figure 4.2 A critical realist interpretation of the institutional socio-economic organisation.

The bottom-most stratum is the level where the 'real' or the 'deeper' mechanisms and tendencies lie, intrinsically conditioning the 'run' of the whole socio-economy. Having subscribed to the 'relational conception of social entities' (the argument that structures/institutions and human agency are all entities that presuppose each other for their existence and co-evolution) and the fact that nothing whatsoever can happen (in terms of social forms, history, etc.) except by and through social/collective human action taken at some point in the past, it can be postulated that this layer should contain elements not directly attributable to either structure or current agency,[27] but to the universal traits of human nature. As such, it is in this stratum where the salient characteristics, tendencies and qualities of the human essence should be found. These collectively constitute the core make up, which is present to some degree in every human being, and which therefore rests on a broad basis of humankind. To be precise, however, it is necessary to take their non-static nature on board and to recognise that these basically behavioural propensities are profoundly inscribed (moulded, articulated, conditioned, actualised) by a long process of socio-cultural evolution.

On that basis, a position is espoused here according to which the properties and potentialities of the human being are neither predetermined solely by evolutionary biology, nor simply socially appropriated. Rather they emerge historically and through evolution from our relations with our environment which, although they embody the social aspect, are by no means reducible to it.

In that context, institutionalists (especially Veblen, 1899, 1914, 1919b; but see also Mitchell, 1910; Clark, 1918a, 1918b; Parker, 1918; Hamilton, 1919; Edie, 1922; Tugwell, 1922, 1930; and, more recently, Jensen, 1994; Twomey, 1998; Hodgson, 2004a; Cordes, 2005; Wolozin, 2005; Redmond, 2006) have postulated a number of deeper qualities, propensities or dispositions, all expressions of the invariant core of human nature, which blend, interact with and are interdependent on one another. These are considered to be the restless propellants that drive humanity along its evolutionary path by shaping cognition, beliefs, and the criteria of knowledge and reality, providing a basis to construct the canons of conduct which serve as guides and standards in socio-economic life. These are organised here within four wider rubrics: creativity, emulation, habituation and culture.[28]

The notion of 'creativity' (or 'technology'[29]) is utilised to encompass a variety of characteristics and impulsive aptitudes associated with human agency that are considered to be the developmental and progressive forces behind any economic, socio-cultural and technological processes that enhance the well-being of human life as a whole. Commons (1931, 1934), in this context, emphasises the human need for 'workability' that drives the development and provision of organisational solutions (i.e. working rules and institutions), establishing order and certainty in the course of economic life. Veblen (1899, 1914) along with Parker (1918) and Edie (1922), on the other hand, identifies the 'instincts' of 'workmanship', 'parental bent' and 'idle curiosity' as universal traits within human nature necessary to advance progress and to further human life as a whole. Workmanship refers to this gratifying and stimulating inclination humans have towards the accomplishment of some concrete, effective and collective end, which is also associated with preference for 'serviceability' or efficiency and an aversion to futility, waste or incapacity. In turn, parental bent reflects human (altruistic) solicitude for the life and well-being of the community at large (present and future) and greatly reinforces and overlaps with workmanship (Walker, 1977, Tilman, 1996). The idea of idle curiosity places emphasis on the human tendency towards experimentation, creative innovation, speculation and novelty. It is the basis for inquiry into knowledge for its own sake, which leads to new and improved ways of thinking and doing, something amply evident in the whole course of human evolution (Ayres, 1962; North, 1994).

Alongside creativity, institutionalists (e.g. Veblen, 1899, 1914, 1919b; Parker, 1918; Edie, 1922; Tugwell, 1922; Commons, 1931, 1950; Hamilton, 1953; Miller, 1978) have seen another proclivity of human behaviour towards unremitting emulation, possessiveness, acquisitiveness, antagonism and 'predation'. Moreover, such behaviour is regarded as accompanied by a taste for reputability, wealth and power, and is more readily inclined to self-interest seeking, pugnacity, self-assertion, coercion and aggression, inducing individuals to exploit and dominate other people. This tendency may stem from the conflict that humans are afflicted with on account of universal scarcity (Commons, 1931; Fusfeld, 1977), or from the comparison that is inevitably made between persons in terms of their efficiency or creativity (Veblen, 1899, 1914). In any case, it is important to point out that the socio-economic process bears the character of a struggle between people for the possession of goods, giving rise to this propensity for emulation and, in turn, to a number of social features and structures (such as status and power structures) which sustain and support this tendency (Parker, 1918; Searle, 2005). In modern economic life this propensity for emulation expresses itself in pecuniary emulation and competition to gain wealth, esteem and power.

These aforementioned human proclivities are conditioned by, and interact with, a less conscious mental propensity to form, acquire and follow habits (Veblen, 1899, 1914, 1919a; Mitchell, 1910; Parker, 1918; Edie, 1922). This is the Veblenian concept of 'habitual bent' or habituation, which is defined as the psychological predisposition to resort to previously adopted or acquired forms of behaviour in a particular class of situations[30] (James, 1890; Dewey, 1891, 1922; Clark, 1918a; Commons, 1924; Camic, 1986; Waller, 1988b). As such, it fosters non-reflective, self-actuating and mechanically repeated forms of action; in short, automatic responses to appropriate contexts or stimuli. Habituation is an essential part of our mental apparatus operating in various ways upon intellect. It removes conscious attention from the most ordinary and familiar details of daily life (physical or mental), helping the individual, by discarding unnecessary information, to cope with complexity and variability in the surrounding environment.[31] Thus, by conserving intellectual effort, habituation leaves the conscious activity of the mind free to handle new and perplexing situations requiring full consideration. On these grounds, habituation involves a degree of intentionality, as, at its simplest, conscious reflection is required to develop appropriate habits that (however imperfectly) economise on cognitive capacity. But this is not all. For Veblen and his followers, concrete habits act as filters of experience and the foundation of interpretation, intuition and deliberation. That is why Commons (1924: 359) asserts that "facts are facts as our habits ... deem them to be facts", to echo Veblen (1898b: 195) claiming that "a habitual line of action constitutes a habitual line of thought, and gives the point of view from which facts and events are apprehended and reduced to a body of knowledge".

The manner in which the above-mentioned proclivities might express themselves is dependent upon socialisation and culture (Veblen, 1899, 1914; Mitchell, 1910; Clark, 1918a; Edie, 1922; Camic, 1986; Jensen, 1994; Stanfield, 1999; Bergstrom, 2002; Cordes, 2005, 2007; Redmond, 2006; Bush, 2008). This is because these physio-psychological dispositions and capacities have been (and are being) formed in the course of a long process of social evolution and so are substantially socially and culturally articulated (Thornhill *et al.*, 1997). Attestation comes from a variety of sources. The anthropologist Geertz (1973: 68), for instance, testifies that "rather than culture acting only to supplement, develop, and extend organically based capacities genetically prior to it, it would seem to be an ingredient to these capacities themselves". Similarly, Ayres (1962: 52, emphasis added) views culture as a "phenomenon *sui generis*. It is not an epiphenomenon, a result of something else, explicable in other and noncultural terms", but rather "*the stuff* of social behavior, *the universe of discourse* of the social sciences, *the* aspect which the data of observation assume at that level of generalization". It is on these grounds therefore that 'culture' is perceived as simply an extension of human capability[32] and comprises the fourth element of this stratum.

Following Mayhew (1987) and Archer *et al.* (1998), we see culture as the collection of expressive forms of human conduct and related products of a community (mental, spiritual, intellectual, scientific, technological, etc.) which have been developed through time as a result of human socialisation (collective intentionality). These provide shared systems of meaning, frames of cognition, and modes of action and interaction between members that guide actors in their social and economic life.[33] Such forms and products are transmitted in society and acquired by the individual, sometimes even through unconscious imitation. Like habituation, once a cultural trait is acquired and internalised, it tends to trigger automatic behaviour, requiring no significant cognitive effort or reflection on the part of the individual. Hence the end product of culture is often the formation of social/collective habits that reduce uncertainty and establish social conformity (Redmond, 2006). However, culture should not be equated with habituation, as this characterises the individual, whereas the former involves a society or a group of people (Veblen, 1899; Commons, 1934; Camic, 1986).

It is important to highlight that, in the current context, culture should be understood historically. Therefore what differentiates culture from the institutional structures located in the higher layer is the time element[34] (see North, 1990, 1994; Archer, 1995). Although culture (both on its own terms and collectively with creativity and emulation) provides the basis for the development of the institutional infrastructure, it is the product of long past processes, whereas institutions are structural entities that define the cognition and behaviour of actors in the present.

This institutional environment is placed at the second ontological layer of socio-economic reality. It consists of institutions, i.e. the rules, rights, duties, norms, routines, relations, practices, conventions and cognitive frameworks by which the society is currently organised. These institutional structures are not reducible either to patterns of events, facts or outcomes explicable in human action terms (topmost level), or to the fundamental universal traits of human nature (bottom level). However, this structural reality depends for its existence on human agency, which is characterised by diversity in rationality and behaviour. In these terms, institutions are perceived here both as causal conditions and caused outcomes of collective human agency. Such a transformational conception of institutional structures, depending upon both human intentionality and other 'contingently related conditions' and material circumstances, provides the basis for recognising the open and contingent nature of the socio-economic world.

The institutional environment is multidimensional. Four key components are identified, although it is important to emphasise that these are necessarily interdependent and mutually reinforcing. Economic institutions refer to the structure of the economy. They concern the organisation of all markets (financial and asset markets, as well as markets for goods and services and factors of production) and all non-market mechanisms for the allocation of scarce resources, along with the environment in which economic expectations and behaviour are shaped. Political institutions broadly define the structure of the polity, its basic cognitive and decision-making structures, and the explicit characteristics of agenda control, specifying political rights and establishing a set of power relations. Legal institutions, in turn, deal with the broad legal setting, providing a general framework of legislation and mechanisms for its interpretation and enforcement (including criminal and civil law codes as well as the court system). Finally, the institutions that are socially constructed and enforced[35] to deal with issues of conflict and to enhance co-ordination and workability in the socio-economy are defined as social. They embrace cognitive frames (beliefs, ideologies), social conventions (customs, myths), codes of conduct (trust, reciprocity) and norms of behaviour (morals, social values) that are either self- or societally imposed.

It should already be clear that human capabilities, behavioural proclivities and the overall institutional framework set the parameters by which the socio-economy operates. By defining states of affairs, they structure action and interaction among actors, providing a degree of stability and predictability in socio-economic life (Veblen, 1919b; Commons, 1931; Polanyi, 1957; Kapp, 1968; Langlois, 1986d; Menard, 1995; North, 1990, 2005). Against this background, every situation presents a terrain of options and it is on this terrain that each actor pursues their own strategies. On these grounds, it is argued here that both the deeper layer of human qualities and the institutional environment are connected to the topmost 'actual' level, which concerns both the organisational[36] and factual outcomes that are evident in the socio-economy. In particular, the topmost level is envisaged as a two sub-layer structure: one representing the actors involved and their organisational forms (individuals, organisations, networks) and the other the concrete events and how these are actualised, experienced and understood by these players in their day-to-day life. Both the form of the organisational structure that comes into existence and the way it evolves are fundamentally influenced by the institutional framework. The transmission of 'information' from institutions to actors is carried out by culture, through which individuals learn the meaning and value of the sense data that is communicated. As Hodgson (1998a: 183) argues, information cannot be received unless agents have "...to some degree been enculturated through prior engagement with institutions". In turn, the way actors perceive events and outcomes has a retroactive effect on the organisational and institutional structure and, subsequently, on the mentality, behavioural propensities and qualities of these actors, and thus on the overall socio-cultural evolution.

The focus of this section has been the development of a holistic philosophical (ontological and epistemological) framework that advances the understanding of the socio-economic system along institutionalist lines. On this basis, it is now possible to deploy an integrated theoretical framework of urban economic organisation and change, where appropriate emphasis is placed on both the urban institutional environment and the property market institution.

4.3 Urban economy and the property market institution: a theoretical framework

A central argument of institutional economics is that pressures for urban economic change and development are mediated through the institutional structure and the consequent organisation of society.[37] Therefore the institutional environment affects the performance and course of the urban economy. A part and product of the institutional environment is the property market itself, which in its own terms, through the provision of property market outcomes, influences the performance, change and development potential of the urban economy. In short, the argument states that the effectiveness of the market to generate what is required in terms of property (both physical and institutional aspects) has a specific effect on the ability of the urban economy to accommodate pressures for change and thereby to achieve economic development. However, before examining the processes and qualities of the property market it is essential to consider what 'market' is.

Although central to the economics discipline, the concept of market is rarely and vaguely defined in the literature (Menard, 1995; Hodgson, 1998a). Mainstream economics describe it as the abstract space of exchange in which buyers and sellers interact to determine prices,[38] or as a network of persons linked to carry out transactions in any commodity (Black, 1997). Certainly there is a degree of vagueness and looseness in both definitions which subsequent writers have not been inclined to rectify as, for too long, 'the market' has been taken for granted (Hodgson, 1988).

In contrast with conventional approaches, institutional economics argues that it is not adequate to define the market simply as a place or network wherein transactions occur. Rather, this process involves contractual agreements for the transfer of property rights, a framework which defines, assigns, monitors and enforces property rights, plus mechanisms for the establishment and communication of prices and other information pertinent to the transaction (Rosenbaum, 2000; Chang, 2002; Furubotn and Richter, 2005). In this context, the market is defined as a set of institutions that enable commodity exchange by providing mechanisms to structure, organise and legitimate these activities. In short, the market, is "a metaphor for the institutions that form, structure and operate through it" (Samuels, 1995: 572), or simply an "organised and institutionalised exchange" (Hodgson, 1989: 174). Some institutions, Hodgson (1988) argues, are associated directly with exchange in an elemental sense (e.g. the economic and social aspects). These would be present even if a formal market did not exist, as is the case in illegal or 'black' markets. Others focus on the development of the formal mechanisms of the market and the co-ordination of exchange in an organised manner (e.g. the legal and political institutions).[39]

Accordingly, we define the property market as an institution concerned with the provision, use, and transaction of property. It comprises a wide network of (formal and informal) rules, rights, norms, practices and conventions, plus their associated organisations, through which property is defined, generated, used and exchanged.

The property market institution is subject to a number of qualifications. First, it should not be seen as a segregated entity as it operates within, and in interaction with, the other institutional structures of the wider environment. Therefore it is the economic, political, legal and social institutions that holistically determine its structure and operation. Nevertheless, an approach is espoused here where the property market is put in a distinct position in the institutional frame. Such an analytical separation is essential to understand and study its qualities (which constitute the focal point of this study) vis-à-vis the overall institutional structures. In short, it is argued that, although the property market has an independent substance ('persona') to be studied, it cannot be examined out of the institutional context from which it emerges and with which it interacts.

Second, although property rights are tradable and portable, the location of the land and buildings to which these relate is firmly fixed. Inevitably, property transactions are place-specific and the market institution reflects this, in a sense that it has an ingrained social, yet evolving, character. The former emphasises the socio-cultural basis of its institutions, while the latter stresses their dynamic nature (by virtue of changing circumstances and local responses). On this basis it is possible to understand why institutional characteristics vary from one local market to another and from one time period to another.

Third, the property market is not a single or cohesive entity, but a collection of diverse yet interrelated submarkets (Watkins, 2001, 2008), distinguished according to use type (e.g. residential, commercial), ownership type (freehold, leasehold), development level (undeveloped land, buildings), location (e.g. London, Hong Kong, downtown, outskirts) and quality (prime, secondary). Generally, each one of these submarkets has distinctive institutional characteristics and is driven by different economic fundamentals (Seabrooke *et al.*, 2004). Nonetheless, the framework developed here should apply to all property submarkets in the place under consideration.

Fourth, the property market, in common with all institutions, does not exist in a power vacuum. It takes form in a setting circumscribed by considerations of 'workability', alongside material scarcity, sovereign authority and power relations. Different actors have different interests and different abilities to impose these on the market structure. The property market institutions thus reflect power dynamics that are embedded in the particular context.

Lastly, we should highlight the cognitive dimension of the market. Its institutions not only impose constraints on agency, but also have an enabling function. They colour actors' perception, interests and judgement, providing a conceptual framework for the interpretation of information, the formation of preferences and expectations and the moulding of their behaviour.

To understand the operation of the property market and its role in the urban economy, it is vital to consider not only the property market outcomes, but also the property market institutions which give rise to them. It is these institutions which, inter alia, specify property values, define property rights, generate information, stimulate development, allocate uses and generally determine the ability of the local economy to provide those property outcomes (both built structures and property rights) that are necessary for economic development. Moreover, the circularity of the argument has to be acknowledged, as it is the assessment of the quality and quantity of market outcomes (events, market activity indicators and organisational forms) that may feed back into the property market institution, modifying its structure and path and, perhaps, triggering changes in the wider institutional framework. In that sense, both the property market institution and the overall institutional environment may themselves adapt in response to pressures for urban change.

As discussed in Chapter 3, conventional property studies largely ignore the role property market institutions play in the functioning of the market. As such, they examine market performance on the sole basis of direct indicators of market outcomes (e.g. rents, capital values, yields, vacancy rates). Similarly, market participants and urban policy-makers commonly use these indicators in arriving at property-related decisions. However, the ambiguity of these value signals has been acknowledged, as high (or low) values could be associated with either competitive success or competitive threat to the urban economy, depending on the latter's characteristics (D'Arcy and Keogh, 1998, 1999). Additionally, the cyclical pattern of property values undermines these indicators, as it is not a straightforward matter to assess whether these figures represent a meaningful measure of property worth, or whether they are just transitory and reflect the current position in the property cycle. Property market outcomes, therefore, should be considered as a function of the prevailing economic dynamics at a point in time, plus the influence ascribed to the property market process. Property market process, in turn, is seen as a product of the property market institutions, which are shaped by the overall institutional environment.

Figure 4.3 organises and diagrammatically presents these arguments, setting up a theoretical framework where urban (local) economic change is related to both the wider institutional environment and the specific institutions of the property market. At any point in time, external dynamics (unpredictable shocks, changing circumstances and long-term trends), alongside internal (institutional) conditions, exert pressures for change at the urban level towards economic development. These have certain requirements in terms of property market outcomes (built structures and property rights). The actual course taken is determined by the overall institutional environment, of which the property market institution is both a part and a product. On that basis, the property market institution is seen as a filter for economic adjustment, specifying the process through which property is determined and traded, and delivering property outcomes which are suitable (or not) to support economic change and development. The issue of how effectively the property market operates in supporting urban

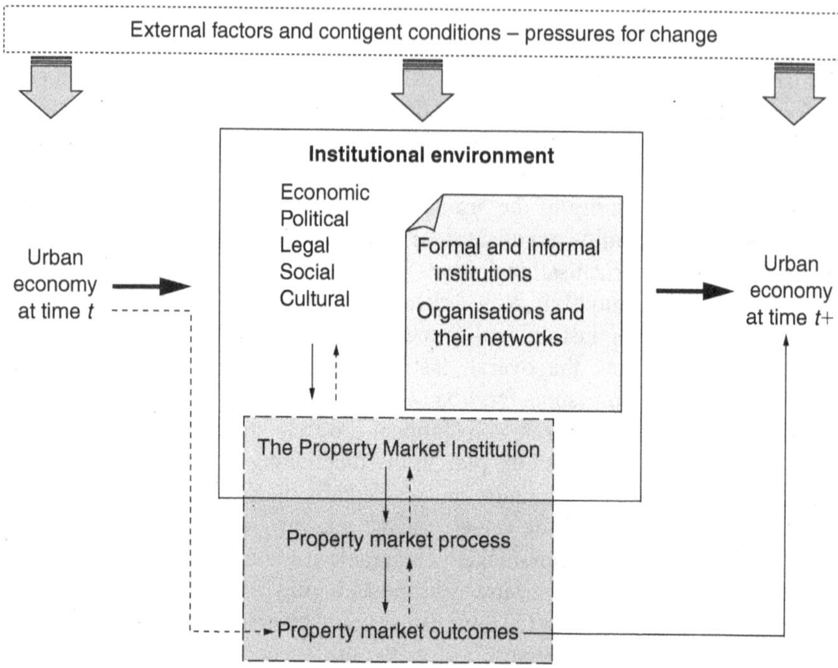

Figure 4.3 Urban economic change and property market institution.

economic development raises questions regarding the efficiency of the market. Expanding on the developed framework, the following section explores this topic examining the overall process of property market operation.

4.4 The efficiency of the property market

The concept of property market efficiency is inadequately developed and theorised in the literature, as "many researchers and most participants in real estate markets would consider the idea of an efficient real estate market to be a paradox" due to the number of peculiarities and imperfections that it exhibits (Gau, 1987: 1–2). However, over the years the issue has attracted increasing attention, accumulating a number of studies (e.g. Guntermann and Norrbin, 1991; Darrat and Glascock, 1993; Evans, 1995; Graff and Webb, 1997; Clayton, 1998; Keogh and D'Arcy, 1999; Kleiman *et al.*, 2002; Rosenthal, 2006; Kholdy and Sohrabian, 2008; Hjalmarsson and Hjalmarsson, 2009; for reviews, see: Gatzlaff and Tirtiroglu, 1995; Anderson *et al.*, 2000; Maier and Herath, 2009). The present section reassesses the debate around property market efficiency and draws on institutional economics to propose a new perspective.

4.4.1 Conventional approaches to property market efficiency

The mainstream property economics literature approaches the issue of market efficiency from two perspectives: allocative efficiency and informational efficiency. Allocative or Pareto efficiency is about making the best use of available resources (e.g. land, labour) to deliver the maximum amount of output (e.g. built structures) at the lowest cost, given current technical knowledge. A market is efficient when it is not possible, by reallocating resources, to produce more of this goal without accepting less of another (or to make at least one person better off without making anyone else worse off). Such a conception presupposes a perfectly competitive market in equilibrium, i.e. a market characterised by a large number of rational actors, homogeneous products, freedom of entry and exit, and perfect information. However, the property market is notorious for its imperfections. Standard property textbooks (e.g. Fraser, 1993; Harvey, 1996; Ball *et al.*, 1998; Evans, 2008) and other studies on the subject (Evans, 1995; Keogh and D'Arcy, 1999) make such a case in terms of the indivisibility, heterogeneity and illiquidity of property, the externalities that arise in the market, as well as the transaction costs and information deficiencies evident in property trade. On this basis, it is asserted that the property market should, at best, be seen as "ninety percent efficient" (Evans, 1995).

One particular market failure that has been paid special attention in the literature is related to information. As discussed, information is costly, asymmetrically distributed and, generally, it is not possible to assess its full value before its acquisition. This means that information is always imperfect and participants enter the market with only some part of the potentially available market knowledge. To take this into account, a more realistic conception of market efficiency has been put forward, where optimality is envisaged even when perfect information is missing. Thus an organised market can be considered as efficient as long as the relevant information is effectively capitalised into market prices (Jensen, 1978; Grossman and Stiglitz, 1980). Moreover, such informational efficiency is regarded as necessary for allocative efficiency, as prices that reflect fully the available information provide meaningful representation of values, and thus are accurate signals for the efficient allocation of resources (Fama, 1970).

This concept of informational efficiency, known as the efficient market hypothesis, was originally developed by Fama (1970) to examine efficiency in financial markets. It states that a market is efficient when it adjusts rapidly enough for asset prices to fully reflect all known information. Three forms of market efficiency are acknowledged. 'Weak form' efficiency requires all financial data to be capitalised into the asset price immediately and without any time lag. Accordingly, a market that does not exhibit significant correlation between price movements in one period and in a preceding period is regarded as weak form efficient. 'Semi-strong' efficiency concerns a market that capitalises all publicly available information, such as company accounts and reports, agent's reports and economic forecasts. Evidence in this case rests on the smooth path of price movements as they absorb the relevant market signals. 'Strong form' efficiency requires that prices reflect all information, whether publicly available or not, including insider information. Evidence here rests on the inability of insiders to yield above-normal risk-adjusted returns. The efficient market hypothesis has been extensively tested in stock markets. Empirical work in the 1970s provided supporting results, but more recent studies have questioned these findings, disputing the conventional use of efficient market hypothesis (Maier and Herath, 2009). In addition, scholars (e.g. Shiller, 1990, 2005; Akerlof and Shiller, 2009) have argued that cultural and behavioural aspects (such as participants' sentiments or psychology), rather than economic rationality, play an important role in pricing and should be taken into account when discussing efficiency issues.

With particular focus on the property market, two main approaches to informational efficiency have been adopted. The forecasting approach asserts that evidence for the support of efficient market hypothesis lies in its inability to predict future prices. Alternatively, other studies place emphasis on the existence of discernible rules and strategies for trading property. In this case, the ability to outperform the market, once transaction costs are taken into account, is regarded as evidence rejecting market efficiency. However, number of studies is fewer and the results are less conclusive (if not contradictory) compared with those dealing with the financial markets (Maier and Herath, 2009). In this situation it is impossible to make a clear judgement about whether the efficient market hypothesis constitutes a robust approach in considering property market efficiency.

Criticism of the application of both allocative and informational efficiency to the property market has come from a number of sources (e.g. Evans, 1995; Gatzlaff and Tirtiroglu, 1995; Ball *et al.*, 1998; Keogh and D'Arcy, 1999). Pareto efficiency is considered ambiguous because of the multiple optima which it implies. Further, the costs involved in shifting the market towards a more 'efficient' situation are substantially downplayed, if not totally ignored. As regards the efficient market hypothesis, it focuses on information to the exclusion (at least explicitly) of the operational and allocative aspects. In addition, substantial objections refer to the intrinsic characteristics of the property market as well as the overall methodology of the efficient market hypothesis. With reference to the former, it is argued that the approach is rather inconclusive, as it does not take into appropriate consideration the transaction costs and information deficiencies[40] which are the norm in the market. This latter criticism highlights the fact that any test of efficient market hypothesis is, in fact, a dual test with market equilibrium. This creates a number of problems in terms of the interpretation of the results and the inability to provide definite measures of the degree of market efficiency, even in the context of financial markets. The situation becomes much more critical in the property market, where the assumption of equilibrium is undermined due to decentralised trade, costly information and long time lags in property supply. Last, but not least, two general shortcomings present in both conventional notions of efficiency should be added. These refer to the use of naive and ideal benchmarks to judge market efficiency and to the failure to properly address the issue of property market process. As a result of the latter, the essential characteristics of property as a physical, legal and social entity are substantially disregarded.

4.4.2 Institutionalist approaches to property market efficiency

Discontented with the rationale and superficial treatment of conventional approaches, the institutionalist literature attempts to provide a more refined and pragmatic conceptualisation of property market efficiency, taking into account the process through which the market operates. Generally, three notions are put forward. The first is that of bounded efficiency developed by Keogh and D'Arcy (1999). As discussed in Chapter 3, this is actually a static assessment, where the degree of efficiency of the market in question is evaluated in comparison with a theoretically feasible frontier, which represents its best potential outcome (i.e. optimum in a sense) in the inevitable presence of the idiosyncratic property market characteristics and its institutional and organisational aspects. A significant achievement of this concept is that it elaborates the idea of an institutional environment, with all the constraints that this imposes on the efficient operation of the market. Moreover, it makes clear that efficiency is a contingent notion so, instead of seeking a judgement on whether the 'property market' in general is efficient, assessments should be constructed with reference to 'efficiency for a purpose' or 'efficiency for a person'. However, specific methodological directions, in terms, for example, of what specific value criterion should be used, or what empirical forms this concept should take, are not provided, rendering the approach incomplete and ambiguous. Moreover, efficiency is primarily defined in economic terms, whereas social, cultural and political aspects of the market operation are generally disregarded.

The second concept comes from van der Krabben (1995, especially chapters 6, 8, 9), who puts forward a dual assessment of property market efficiency. The first assessment, called 'allocative efficacy', assesses the outcomes of the development process on the basis of a value criterion set up by the public policy to reflect social considerations. On these grounds, efficiency is attained both when there is sufficient supply at relatively stable property prices, and when property rights are socially acceptable and equally distributed. The second assessment, called 'productive efficiency', concerns the way these outcomes are provided and is judged on the basis of profitability from the property producers' point of view. Evidently, these notions, although they elaborate on the idea of 'efficiency for a person' or 'efficiency for a purpose' and introduce an explicit value criterion, remain too close to the traditional rationale of efficiency. They are basically static in nature and neglect, to all intents and purposes, the institutional character of the property market. Moreover, as van der Krabben himself points out, there are further problems in the empirical application of this two-fold assessment, as the criteria put forward are open to various, often contradictory, interpretations.

The third institutionalist approach to market efficiency confronts the issue from a dynamic perspective, considering the process of institutional change and the ability of the market system to cope with and meet the challenges that the evolving socio-economy places on it. In these terms, the notion of adaptive efficiency is introduced, asserting that a (property) market can be seen as efficient if it displays tendencies to eliminate transaction costs and generally provides an environment hospitable to economic growth (Keogh and D'Arcy, 1999). The initial development of this conceptualisation is attributed to North (1990: 80) who, in a wider context, views adaptive efficiency as concerned with the willingness of the system "to acquire knowledge and learning, to include innovation, to undertake risks and creative activity of all sorts, as well as to resolve problems and bottlenecks of the society through time". In these terms, an adaptive efficient economy is defined as one which, over time, supports and is based upon an institutional framework which provides a wide menu of alternative choices for organisational innovation, so that a smooth adaptation to changing economic and social circumstances is achieved (North, 1993b). This interesting concept puts forward a dynamic assessment of institutional (and market) qualities, but remains largely underdeveloped.

4.4.3 Property market operation and efficiency considerations

Institutionalist conceptualisations of property market efficiency, though methodologically underdeveloped and incomplete, have provided some useful insights. First, as the property market structure emerges out of dominant economic and social interests, an appropriate approach to market efficiency requires reference to an explicit value or focus criterion.[41] Second, emphasis is shifted from the outcomes that the market produces to the way the market operates towards a specific purpose or a particular viewpoint. Third, a dynamic dimension is introduced, highlighting the need to assess market efficiency with reference to the changing economic, political, legal and social conditions.

Elaborating these arguments, the efficiency of the property market is perceived here with reference to the accomplishment of a particular purpose, which is the support of urban competitiveness for local economic development.[42] This defines purpose efficiency of the property market as the 'credible commitment', 'serviceability' or 'effectiveness' in providing these property outcomes that the urban economy requires. An efficient property market, therefore, is expected to deliver sufficient property outcomes to meet requirements at the prevailing price level. In that sense, substantial time lags in property development, erratic market behaviour or the lack of the information base necessary to support comprehensive market choice, all of which give rise to the mismatch and volatility of land and property values, could be interpreted as indicators of the market's inability to respond to economic imperatives and, therefore, as 'stylised facts' of purpose inefficiency.

Before developing further this idea of purpose efficiency, it is important to point out a number of general qualifications indicating the contingent nature of the concept. First, the purpose efficiency of the property market is a necessary, but not sufficient, condition for the realisation of economic potential. Other factors alongside the property market can affect, though to different degrees and directions, the course of the urban economy. Second, property market institutional mechanisms mediate between the requirements for property and the actual products provided; therefore the concept of purpose efficiency shifts the emphasis from property products to the property market process, while the central question becomes how well that process works in providing what the economy requires. Third, the concept of property market purpose efficiency does not prescribe a specific institutional configuration. It proposes, however, a conceptual point of reference to determine whether 'problematic' property market institutions exist and, if so, the directions for their revision. Any proposed institutional transformation will, of course, advance some interests and undermine others. In this sense, purpose efficiency might not coincide with the perceptions of efficiency held by different actors in the property market (called 'person efficiency'), as the latter are specified by their own characteristics, objectives and needs. Finally, regarding property market institutions as part and product of the wider institutional environment implies that the purpose efficiency of the property market should be seen in relation to the overall urban institutional context. On the basis of all these considerations, purpose efficiency is conceptualised in terms of the ability of the market institutional structure to respond appropriately to the wider institutional conditions. An appropriate response refers to the provision of such quantity and quality of institutions that the overall institutional environment allows and requires.

In examining the essential implications of the last qualification and developing the approach further, two interrelated notions prove helpful. These are the concepts of 'uncertainty' and 'flexibility'. Questions of uncertainty are central to economic theorising, as uncertainty is a pervasive fact of economic reality and life on the whole (Keynes, 1921, 1936; Knight, 1921; Schmidt, 1996). "Indeed most of the fundamental economic and political decisions that shape the direction of polities and economies are made in the face of uncertainty" (North, 1994: 363). On that basis, the approach to urban economic development and property market organisation envisaged in this study is based upon recognising, understanding and managing uncertainty, alongside the necessity for adaptability and change.

a Uncertainty

Uncertainty refers not only to a lack of information regarding the parameters of a problem, but also to a lack of knowledge about the fundamental nature of a problem and the possible outcomes. The former, called 'parametric uncertainty' or risk, describes a situation where the determination of an event's likelihood is possible, though costly, either through calculation a priori (i.e. based on purely general principles), or from statistics of past performance. The latter, called 'structural', 'true uncertainty', or uncertainty per se, refers to the case where there is no scientific basis to form any calculable probabilities because these are numerically indeterminate or simply do not exist.

Overall uncertainty refers not only to ignorance of what can be known by a study of the collected data, but also to ignorance tied to the unknowable. "It is a world of change in which we live, and a world of uncertainty. We live only by knowing *something* about the future; while the problems of life, or of conduct at least, arise from the fact that we know so little" (Knight, 1921: 199, emphasis in the original). The reasons for this are manifold. First, it is the open-ended, dynamic and contingent nature of the socio-economic reality (on account of the instability and complexity of both external conditions and internal elements) that precludes the predictability of events and aspects of reality (Lawson, 1985). Moreover, the situation becomes more complicated when the human factor is taken into account. Agents' behaviour is not only constrained by the limited computational and cognitive abilities of the human mind (Simon, 1982), but also by the unacknowledged and unintended consequences of the actions of other (purposeful and perhaps 'irrational') agents (Schmidt, 1996).

From that perspective, where uncertainty is seen as ubiquitous as well as inherent and structural to the system, it becomes clear that the future can never be fully anticipated or known. This has significant implications regarding our confidence in the future, the formation of expectations, and the overall course and working of the socio-economy.This is something which is evident in the appearance of 'irrational' instances of optimism or pessimism, even in cases where there are no solid reasons for such views (Keynes, 1936; Hodgson, 1988; Shiller, 2005). This leads to the assertion that uncertainty reflects the conditions under which economic dynamics are understood, appreciated, expressed and thus developed and, in that sense, mirrors the overall climate of the socio-economy. To put it in simple words, it is argued here that the level of uncertainty reflects the degree of agents' confidence with regard to the conditions and processes of the socio-economic system.

In this world of uncertainty, wherein agents have nevertheless to act, 'rules of thumb', 'conventions' and 'norms' are used as substitutes for the knowledge that cannot be attained (Heiner, 1983; Lawson, 1985; Hodgson, 1988). Without these "institutionally conditioned conceptual frameworks, an uncertain world would present a chaos of sense data" in which it would be practically impossible for agents to make decisions, act and interact with each other (Hodgson, 1988: 205). On this basis, it is argued that institutional structures play a functional role in the reduction of uncertainty by providing a basis for belief, perception, expectation and decision-making, and thus a degree of stability and predictability in human affairs (Hamilton, 1932; Ayres, 1962; Lawson, 1985, 1997b; Hodgson, 1997, 2003; North, 1990).

Some qualifications about this conceptualisation are, however, required. Although any institutional configuration reduces uncertainty to a degree, different institutional structures reduce uncertainty with different degrees of success. It is almost axiomatic that uncertainty can never be totally eliminated. This is due to three reasons. First, institutional structure can never be 'perfect', partly because institutions are the result of the limited nature of human mental ability and power relations, and partly because they are products of processes and circumstances from the past and are subject to institutional lock-in and path dependence. Second, because of the complexity and dynamic character of socio-economic reality and the unpredictable nature of human behaviour, fortuitous changes (external or internal) are always possible. Third, uncertainty (and especially other people's uncertainty) may be beneficial for some groups as it can generate opportunities for profits (Knight, 1921). Finally, it is important to keep two further things in mind. First, institutions generally reduce uncertainty, but probably more for some groups than others. This, of course, is related to the power relations between agents. Second, sometimes the cost of reducing uncertainty may be higher than the value of reducing uncertainty.[43]

The degree of uncertainty that exists in an institutional environment is determined by both external and internal (or, in critical realist terms, 'extrinsic' and 'intrinsic') conditions. In particular, three dimensions can be considered. One is the conformity between the exogenous changes–conditions (e.g. technological changes, wars, economic upheavals) and the associated institutional–organisational adjustment. Important parameters here are the complexity and degree of volatility of the external conditions and the ability of the institutional structures to adjust to these conditions. Another is the harmony between the institutional structures (e.g. between the political, economic and social structures). This refers to the situation where institutional changes in one structure necessitate changes in another (or others). Last is the harmony within institutional structures (e.g. the economic, or political, or social structures). This refers to congruity between the institutions of the structure as, for example, between formal and informal institutions.

Thus it is possible to argue that the degree of uncertainty in an urban system reflects the quality of its institutional structures and, in particular, the degree of institutional adaptability to the external conditions and pressures (in short, their potential to adapt) and the degree of congruity between and within the institutional structures and dynamics (or how well institutions adjust). To put it plainly, the degree of adaptability and congruity of the institutional structures determines the level of uncertainty within the socio-economic system.

Reflecting the concept of uncertainty back into the analysis of the property market, it can be said that such uncertainty is also affected by the idiosyncratic characteristics of property and this compels market actors to rely on the institutions and expectations set by the immediate economic, political, social and cultural environment. Thus the overall degree of uncertainty in the property market system rests on its institutional structure defined by the general urban institutional environment (e.g. its social, cultural, legal, political and economic aspects).

b Flexibility

Economies are generally in a state of flux, buffeted by developments in the rest of the world, shifts in the composition of demand, technological and institutional changes, or by other external and/or internal shocks. This complexity and volatility of external conditions generates uncertainty in the institutional environment and justifies the necessity for institutional adaptability (North, 1990;

Killick, 1995a, 1995b). In fact, Hamilton (1932: 86) argues that "the life of an institution depends upon its capacity for adaptation". The quality necessary for the successful adaptation of institutions to the changing conditions is institutional diversity. To put it in another way, it is argued that an appropriate degree of institutional 'variety' is essential to cope with external and internal volatility and complexity and to thus reduce uncertainty (Heiner, 1983; Nelson and Sampat, 2001; Hodgson, 1988, 1996).[44] Variety here refers to the 'widening' of institutions in response to change. This is the case where the needed adaptability is achieved not only by the creation of a new institution or by replacing an old institution by a new one, but also by broadening the existing institutional base in such a way that it can serve new interests without upsetting those that have so far made use of it.[45]

Generally, institutional variety is positively associated with economic development[46]; however, it should not be taken as desirable in itself without reservation. Certainly it has a cost, as resources are required to achieve and maintain it. Moreover, although variety is desirable when environmental volatility is high, excessive variety increases complexity, undermining the requisite institutional stability and certainty. Undue lack of variety, on the other hand, is also detrimental because it fosters inertia and encourages long-term rigidities which can lead to economic stagnation. However, it must be acknowledged that rigidities are not always detrimental and certain rigidities are necessary in the running of complex systems such as the urban socio-economy. In that sense, desirable institutions are those establishing sufficient stability for growth while not obstructing change. To achieve this delicate balance, it can be argued that a system (such as the property market) should exhibit the degree of variety sufficient to deal with all the potential variation (uncertainty) in its environment. In that sense, order and relative stability at the macro-level are reinforced alongside, and arise from, variety and diversity at the micro-level (Langlois, 1986d; Hodgson, 1988). In addition, such heterogeneity at a micro-level is deemed necessary, both for the system to reproduce itself through time and for macro-dynamics to be successfully sustained. On this basis, stability is more closely related to the general level of the institutional environment, whereas variety and flexibility pertain to narrower and more specific contexts, such as the property market itself.

In these terms, the role of market (and not only the property market) institutions in relation to urban economic development should be seen as an attempt to manage and buffer the effects of uncertainty at the urban level by providing a flexible and secure framework that enables easy adjustment to the contingencies and exigencies of economic processes (Goldberg, 2004). A prospective way to accomplish this is through the development of 'institutionalised variety'. Institutionalised variety refers to plurality in property market institutions and provides the necessary flexibility and diversity for the property market to manoeuvre successfully, both exploiting and contributing to overall institutional certainty and stability. The same caveat (as in variety in general) applies here: institutionalised variety comes at a cost and thus its appropriate degree is defined on the basis of the uncertainty that it faces.

4.4.4 Institutionalised variety and purpose efficiency of the property market

In the light of these arguments, it is now possible to evaluate the property market in terms of its credible commitment to urban competitiveness and success. The question is how efficiently the property market operates in providing the right quality and quantity of property market institutions so that urban economic potential is enhanced and economic development is achieved. This institution-building is seen in the context of the wider institutional structures and dynamics. Thus, based on the assumption that each urban economy, subject to its institutional volatility and incongruity, exhibits a certain amount of institutional uncertainty, the purpose efficiency of the property market is conceptualised in terms of the market's ability to respond appropriately to these wider institutional conditions by providing whatever degree of institutionalised variety the overall institutional environment allows and requires. The ability to explore the property market institution-building with reference to the wider institutional conditions and dynamics constitutes the main strength and novelty of the concept.

Figure 4.4 illustrates diagrammatically the notion of property market purpose efficiency. A purpose efficient property market delivers the property products that the economy requires at the prevailing price by harmonising its institutionalised variety to the level of uncertainty which the wider institutional environment carries. This is represented conceptually by the line *AA*. In particular, for a specified level of institutional uncertainty, the line indicates the respective level of institutionalised variety that is most appropriate in supporting economic potential. Less institutionalised variety (area of under-investment in Figure 4.4) creates undesirable rigidity in the operation of the property market. This means that the market cannot respond effectively to economic circumstances and institutional changes by providing the property products that are required. This weakens urban economic potential. Examples of such urban property markets can be found in countries which have recently opened up their economies (e.g. eastern European cities) and on that basis exhibit considerable institutional

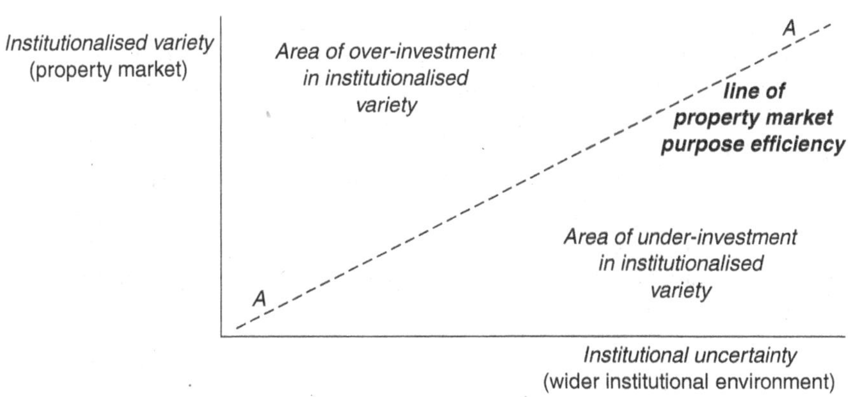

Figure 4.4 Purpose efficiency of the property market.

uncertainty, while their property markets have not yet developed the appropriate institutional framework required to facilitate economic adjustment (e.g. property rights in land and property are not clearly defined or properly enforced).

From a similar perspective, the achievement and maintenance of excess property market institutionalised variety, i.e. more than is required by the overall institutional conditions (area of over-investment in Figure 4.4) is also problematic. Such excessive variety impairs urban economic potential by incurring unnecessary costs and the expenditure of society's resources, and also by creating unnecessary complexity that is potentially detrimental to the requisite level of certainty and flexibility. Examples of such urban property markets may be found in mature economies that have developed complex market institutions[47] which are highly sophisticated, but rigid and resistant to adjustment or reformation in response to changing socio-economic conditions (for example, due to powerful established vested interests).

The graphical representation in Figure 4.4 should be seen as a conceptual device demonstrating the essential (intrinsic) relation between the property market as an institution and its wider institutional environment, where the notional balance of their qualities is hypothesised to be a necessary condition for property market pupose efficiency. Theory suggests that there is a positive relationship between institutional uncertainty and institutionalised variety, i.e. greater institutional uncertainty demands greater institutionalised variety to achieve property market pupose efficiency and vice versa. Clearly the detailed characteristics of the property market pupose efficiency (with reference to the conceptual line *AA*; these are its form, position, slope, etc.) will depend on the specific features of the market in question.

The characteristics of institutional balance (the conceptual line *AA*) may vary with time, location and circumstance. This is because each socio-economy has its own culture, institutions, organisations and power relations that are temporally and spatially defined and require time specific, locally flavoured explanations and solutions. This means that the appropriate degree of institutionalised variety for a given level of institutional uncertainty may be different across time and space owing to the quality of the available institutional base (i.e. the institutionalised variety already built) and the costs associated (and benefits foregone) with this particular institutional configuration. For example, emerging markets might lack some fundamental property market institutions (e.g. related to property rights speciation or enforcement, or related to information provision) and so even 'small' changes in institutional uncertainty will necessitate substantial developments in institutionalised variety for required property products to be provided. As the markets become more mature, they develop a substantial institutional base which makes it possible to compensate changes in institutional uncertainty with relatively smaller changes in institutionalised variety. On that basis, property markets which are at the initial stages of institution-building, or those characterised as 'emergent' in cross-sectional analysis, might be represented conceptually by a steeper purpose efficiency relationship (steeper line *AA* in Figure 4.4) than the same markets in the long run and to 'mature' markets.

The notion of purpose efficiency also provides a conceptual basis for the consideration of the evolutionary dynamics of the property market. Here, emphasis is placed on the market's ability to continuously adapt its institutional structures to accommodate changing conditions in the wider institutional environment. A truly purpose efficient property market should be able to match its institutionalised variety to the wider institutional uncertainty. However, even in the case of a market which is purpose efficient (i.e. on the line *AA*) at a point in time, conditions might change, requiring a movement to a new position. When uncertainty in the wider institutional environment is increased, the market should respond accordingly by delivering greater degrees of institutionalised variety, in order for required products to be supplied and economic potential to be supported (case b_1 in Figure 4.5). An example here might be a property market which, in response to internationalisation and the increased institutional uncertainty it bears, develops a framework of property rights that accommodates a wide variety of objectives in property use, investment and development (e.g. introduces real estate syndication or real estate securitisation, such as equity REITs).

Likewise, where overall institutional changes reduce uncertainty, an excess of property market institutionalised variety generates unnecessary complexity, wastes resources and incurs excessive opportunity costs; an appropriate response should be to reduce institutionalised variety (case b_2 in Figure 4.5). An example of this is a property market that, in response to lowered institutional uncertainty (e.g. as a credible legal framework develops or political stability is established), manages to restrain certain institutional aspects of the property market (e.g. the informal, non-professional networks of information provision) which impair its ability to effectively deliver the required property products.

Questions arise regarding the institutional adjustment process as conditions change. If the market is initially purpose efficient (e.g. point *b* in Figure 4.5) and there is a change in the degree of uncertainty in the wider institutional environment, we should be interested in the speed and path of institutional adjustment and whether or not it is capable of restoring the market to purpose efficiency.

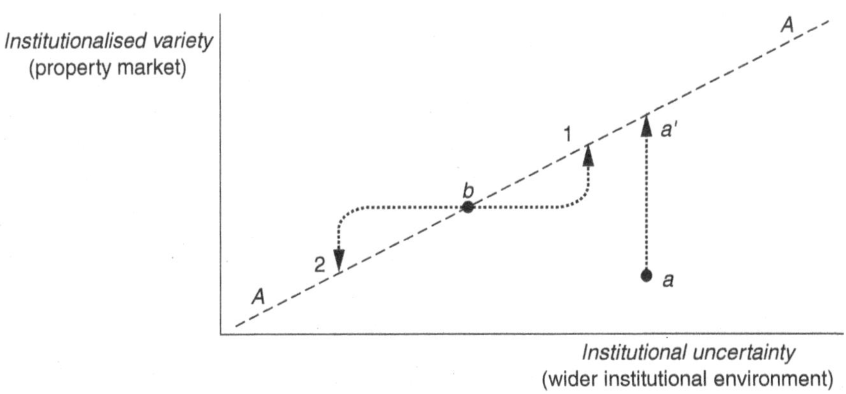

Figure 4.5 The relative conception of property market purpose efficiency.

If the market is initially purpose inefficient (e.g. point *a* in Figure 4.5), and this is the more likely case, we might again ask whether this is a temporary phenomenon and whether there is likely to be an institutional adjustment process that will secure purpose efficiency.

Various factors may restrict adaptation and the establishment of institutionalised variety in the short run. For instance, the property market as an institution carries a strong path dependency (with a tendency towards 'lock-in'), where the scope for change is defined by the existing institutional structure. The situation becomes more complicated when power relations and vested interests are taken into account. In a sense, as property market institutions crystallise into reputable usages, they create in their defence "vested interest, vested habit and vested ideas and claim allegiance in [their] own right" (Hamilton, 1932: 87), making them difficult to change. This also suggests that developed property market institutions (actual institutionalised variety) and market possibilities (to purpose efficiency) become contextualised, necessitating solutions that are political and policy oriented in nature and lie in the hands of policy-makers and other power brokers.

However, apart from the rapidity (or the time lag) with which property market institutions may adjust in response to changes in institutional uncertainty, the nature of decisions associated with institution-building should also be taken into account. As the costs and benefits of institutional change cannot be known in advance,[48] any investment in institutionalised variety must always be 'speculative'. This implies that the appropriate mix of institutions necessary to supply the required property products might not be delivered simply because the actors have a distorted perception of what its actual costs and benefits would be.

Undeniably, history and dynamic processes cannot conform to any simple graphical representation. In that sense, the notional balance between institutionalised variety and institutional uncertainty is not teleological, and so it should not be supposed that any suggested movement would or is 'bound' to occur. The dynamic process of institutional change might not, therefore, result in property market purpose efficiency. Institutionalised variety might fall short of, or overshoot, the efficient uncertainty–variety balance (lying above or below *AA* in Figure 4.5), while the range of purpose efficient solutions might itself change (i.e. a shift in *AA* in Figure 4.5).

This has certain implications in terms of policy. As argued, the concept of property market purpose efficiency can shed light on the qualities of the property market institution and its intrinsic relation with the overall institutional environment. This helps to clarify thinking in terms of what policy decisions are possible to shift the market towards a desired position. Two sets of choices seem to be available. The first targets the property market institutional structure directly, attempting to bring its institutionalised variety in line with the prevailing level of institutional uncertainty (in Figure 4.5, operating to move from a point such as *a* towards the line *AA*). Such policies could include, for example, setting up agencies to facilitate property-related information provision, or redefining legal interests to cater for changes in property actors' needs and tastes (in use, investment or development). The second set of choices targets the overall institutional environment within which the property market as an institution operates. Here, policies focus on the reconfiguration and realignment of institutional structures, paying attention to the implications these would have in terms of property requirements and the operation of the market (indirect effects, represented by a shift in the purpose efficiency relationship *AA* in Figure 4.5). Such policies may be designed, for instance, to strengthen legal efficiency and enforceability, to regulate financial markets, to increase political credibility and actors' transparency, or to provide certain economic stimuli. Obviously the latter set of policies has a much wider scope and far-reaching implications, not only for the property market, but also for other areas of economic significance.

In conclusion, it must be stressed that property market purpose efficiency is a conceptual device which enables the consideration of property market institution-building with reference to wider institutional conditions and dynamics. Turning the concept into an effective strategy, however, presents a challenge. This is because it is difficult to observe directly what a purpose efficient property market would look like in reality, and so to identify the criteria that give an objective fix to the concept. However, purpose efficiency might be indirectly measured through indicators that reflect the mismatch between property requirements and property delivered, such as the degree of property market volatility in otherwise matched property market institutional structures, compared across markets or across time. However, a lack of long runs of reliable data (even for the most mature markets), or consistent data across markets, makes it difficult to empirically verify the conditions of purpose efficiency with our current state of knowledge. Moreover, the place and time specificity of the balance between institutionalised variety and institutional uncertainty creates an additional complication for any attempt to explore their relation through comparative, cross-sectional research.

This leads to the suggestion that attention should be focused on analytical indicators of institutionalised variety and institutional uncertainty that aid description of the property market institution and the wider institutional environment within which it operates, facilitating further exploration and understanding of their intrinsic relation. Such indicators can provide a basis for the evaluation of the quality of the property market process with reference to the wider institutional structures at various points in time, as well as for comparative assessment between different markets. However, when used as comparable analytical devices they have to take account of local circumstances. This is because the same external forces and institutional conditions could, in different urban contexts, lead to different types of institutional uncertainty, giving rise, in turn, to different property market configurations in terms of the mix of institutions developed.

4.5 Overview and conclusions

This chapter provides a holistic conceptual framework: first, to advance our understanding of the institutional nature of the property market, its relation to the wider institutional structures and its contribution to urban economic development; and, second, to lay down the cornerstones upon which an operational agenda for empirical research can be put forward in Chapter 5.

Based on the argument that a philosophical position is a crucial and significant part of any social research, the chapter started by delineating its ontological and epistemological assumptions to develop an integrated philosophical framework along critical realist and institutionalist lines. In particular, key principles from the philosophical approach of critical realism were combined with the institutionalist insights of economic organisation to construct a three-layer ontological framework for discussing the institutional nature of urban socio-economy. It was argued that the deeper tendencies, capacities and qualities of human essence (understood as creativity, emulation, habituation and culture) condition the institutional environment (described in economic, political, legal and social terms) that constitutes the terrain upon which events, facts and organisational outcomes are actualised and manifested. In these terms, institutions were defined as established rules and ingrained regularities of human life that, by moulding agents' perception, thought and behaviour, provide certainty and order in social interaction and economic organisation.

In tandem with this stratified ontological reality, the chapter also specified the epistemological foundations of the research. It was argued – along critical realist lines – that although intransitive entities (e.g. institutions, mechanisms) exist and govern actual events, as well as what we experience, understand and act upon, the only way to know and express these entities is through cognition and reflection. In this sense, intransitive social entities are perceived as causally interdependent with (although existentially independent of) the processes by which they are known. Knowledge is seen as the endless social activity of understanding and expressing these true entities and, as such, is historically and culturally specific, theory-laden, practice-dependent and value-impregnated. On this epistemic account, the vital task of the social sciences is to advance knowledge, i.e. to (re)define and refine conceptual resources in an attempt to extend and improve our ability to understand the structures and mechanisms that account for the phenomena under investigation. To achieve this, emphasis was placed on theory development as the fundamental first step in carrying out social research.

Having adopted such a philosophical stance, the chapter proceeded to lay down a rich theoretical framework for urban economic organisation and change, where appropriate emphasis was placed on both the wider urban institutional environment and the specific institutional mechanisms, processes and dynamics through which the built environment is provided. Moreover, the interrelation between property market process and the wider institutional environment was explored in terms of efficiency in providing appropriate property market institutions to support urban economic potential and urban competitiveness. On these foundations, the chapter developed a new institutional concept of market efficiency, called 'property market purpose efficiency', describing a property market that is capable of adapting its structure: matching its 'institutionalised variety' to the level of 'institutional uncertainty' the wider environment exhibits. From this perspective, order, stability and adaptability at the macro-level are reinforced alongside, and arise upon, variety and diversity at the micro-level to increase urban competitiveness and deliver economic growth.

The strength and novelty of the property market purpose efficiency concept reside on its ability to view efficiency in both holistic and dynamic terms. The former highlights the fact that property market institutions are part and product of the overall institutional environment and so any comprehensive discussion of efficiency should take these issues into account. The latter introduces a time dimension. It was argued that pressures for change are filtered through the institutional environment, determining evolutionary dynamics and the potential for adaptation. A property market that is truly purpose efficient over time is able to effectively adapt its institutionalised variety to the wider institutional uncertainty. However, the property market as an institution carries a strong tendency towards 'lock-in', where the scope for change is defined by its existing institutional complexity. In addition, power relations, vested interests and the 'bounded' rationality of various market players come into play. From all this a number of important questions arise: how quickly will market adjustment take place and what things have to happen to allow it to occur? The adopted position was that market possibilities (purpose efficiency) and the current institutional aspects of the market (realised institutionalised variety) become contextualised, necessitating solutions that are political in nature and lie in the hands of policy-makers or other power brokers.

In conclusion, it must be stressed that the current work sets out to shed light on the institutional mechanisms and processes of the property market and to clarify thinking in terms of the nature of the choices available to shift the market towards a desired position. These have certain policy implications. In particular, the conceptual device of property market purpose efficiency provides a theoretical basis for considering the enhancement of urban competitiveness through intervention in the property market. However, as the relationship between the property market and the urban socio-economy is neither simple nor straightforward, it is argued that such a policy should pay due attention to the local conditions and peculiarities.

The explanatory research programme argued for in this chapter is holistic, theory-based, value-laden and critical, but also entails a significant empirical component. Chapter 5 builds upon the developed conceptual framework to explicitly address, given the philosophical position, the requirements for concrete analysis. In particular, it first lays down a generic analytical framework specifying the appropriate research methods and techniques for investigation and, second, outlines a blueprint for future empirical research providing an operational frame that translates developed theory into empirical practice.

Notes

1 It must be emphasised, however, that these philosophical (and so methodological) positions should be compatible and communicable to each other.
2 Lawson (1995) neatly illustrates this with an example from the physical world: the falling of an autumn leaf. He points out that, not only does the leaf goes down, and this is experienced as falling, but this is in fact a complex movement specified by real mechanisms (such as gravitational, aerodynamic, thermodynamic, electromagnetic and other interactive forces) and their relations.
3 Although the critical realism literature does not provide a consistent definition of structure (Parsons 1999), most realists (see, for instance, Sayer, 1992; Lawson, 1997a) employ the concept of structure to describe more or less socially embedded sets of relations through which social objects, positions or practices are interdependently constituted (e.g. those of master and slave, landlord and tenant, employer and employee).
4 These are regarded as transitive objects in the sense that, although they refer to states or properties of intransitive entities, they are, in essence, products of thought or outcomes of human discourse and are based on some predefined conceptual framework (Sayer, 1992).
5 To those who, on the basis of this assertion, would argue that it is unnecessary or misleading to believe that there are intransitive entities if their existence can only be postulated in thought, Sayer (1992: 67, emphasis in the original) replies that "what we see gives us reasonable grounds for supporting [the notion] that the world is not our own invention even though the *concept* 'world' undoubtedly is.... For it is precisely because the world does not yield to just any kind of expectation that we believe it exists independently of us and it is not simply a figment of our imagination."
6 Moreover, the admission that knowledge is fallible does not mean that all knowledge is equally fallible (Bhaskar, 1979; Sayer, 1992; Samuels, 1998b).
7 Practically adequate is knowledge which corresponds to reality (Sayer, 1992). Note that this 'practical' or pragmatic evaluation of knowledge is similar to that developed by the pragmatist tradition.
8 Note that institutionalists (such as Veblen, 1898a; Myrdal, 1958, 1970; Miller, 1978; Samuels, 1990) hold a similar position. For instance, Myrdal (1958: 156) defines theoretical research as a process of establishing "the causal relations between elementary factors in the social process" whereas in empirical research these causal relations "are transposed into *purposeful* relations" (emphasis in the original). Theory, therefore, must always come before any empirical research.
9 The purpose of statistical and econometric analysis in realist inquiry is not to develop universal laws, but to support theories or explanations proposed by the retroductive mode of inference (Sayer, 1992). However, some researchers (e.g. Downward *et al.*, 2002; Finch and McMaster, 2002) have argued that traditional econometric methods are based on assumptions that contradict fundamental philosophical tenets of realism and should be avoided. On that basis, emphasis is placed on the use of non-parametric statistical techniques in interpreting and analysing stylised facts.
10 Realists seem to perceive the notion of stratification in two complementary dimensions. The first dimension (which comes directly from Bhaskar's writings and is equally applicable to both the social and natural realms) highlights the distinction between the three ontological domains: the empirical, the actual and the real. The second dimension, which is more relevant to social analysis, emphasises a view of reality consisting of hierarchical ordered levels where the lower level tends to be more enduring and less open to change, and provides the conditions for the higher level. Although this perspective is relatively underdeveloped and subject to an ongoing debate (concerning, for example, which levels exist and how they relate), a very general and simplified, but, for the purpose of the current discussion, sufficient way of describing the ordering between some of the most important levels is: social,

psychological, biological and molecular or chemical (Pinkstone, 2002; Davidsen, 2010). Note that a similar line of argument can also be found in some original institutionalist writings such as Ayres (1962) and Hodgson (1999a, 2000, 2003).

11 For more detailed discussions on the notion of emergence, see Hodgson (1998b), Kim (1999), Bedau and Humphreys (2008) and Pratten (2013).

12 This is the idea of 'downward causation' which, Hodgson (1999a, 2000, 2003) argues, constitutes a key insight and defining characteristic of the original institutionalism.

13 This quality also safeguards against the danger of structural determinism as developed, for example, in some structuralist or American institutionalist writings.

14 A power is possessed by an entity by virtue of its intrinsic structure; it can be exercised unactualised due to the counterbalanced interference of other exercised powers, or actualised if it is not deflected by the effects of other powers.

15 As such, depending on conditions, the operation of the same mechanism, tendency, etc., can produce quite different results and, alternatively, different mechanisms may produce the same empirical results (e.g. an effect such as the loss of jobs may be caused by either the introduction of a new technology or by failure to introduce it, the latter being due to a reduction in competitiveness and closing down) (Sayer, 1992).

16 Following Lawson (1997a, 1997b), agency is differentiated from action in the sense that the former refers to the intrinsic powers and capabilities of human beings, whereas the latter refers to their exercise.

17 This is a fundamental insight borrowed from the pragmatist tradition (see, for instance, Peirce, 1877, 1878).

18 It is in this sense, i.e. by reference to the past activities, positions, practices and concepts of former (even deceased) human agents, that both the activity-dependence, concept-dependence and space–time specificity character of social structures can be affirmed and validated (Archer, 1995; Lawson, 1997a).

19 It is worth pointing out that original institutionalists seem to uphold a similar position here (see, for example, Bush, 1987; Samuels, 1995; Hodgson, 1998a, 2003; as well as Dewey, 1922). Commons (1934: 45), for instance, writes: "we do not start as isolated individuals – we start in infancy with discipline and obedience, and we continue as members of concerns already going". Similarly Veblen (1899: 191) argues:

> (t)he institutions ... under the guidance of which men live are in this way received from an earlier time; more or less remotely earlier, but in any event they have been elaborated in and received from the past. Institutions are products of the past process, are adapted to past circumstances, and are therefore never in full accord with the requirements of the present.

20 This is the celebrated notion of dualism.

21 Interestingly, Hodgson (1999a, 2000) highlights that some properties and causal powers at the human agency level emerge as a result of psychological, neurophysiological and biological (evolutionary) activity (a similar point is also made by Ayres, 1962). On these grounds, following Veblen, a conception of human agency is put forward where instinct, habit and reason all play a necessary and mutually dependent role.

22 Note, once again, that these relations, though they depend upon the concepts that agents hold (consciously or unconsciously), exist independently of their appropriate conceptualisation (Archer *et al.*, 1998).

23 A similar argument is also developed in Langlois (1986c) and Hodgson (1999a, 2000).

24 A distinction between rule-following and routinised behaviour is identified on the basis that the former is drawn upon in the course of action, whereas the latter drives mechanical action (Lawson, 1997a). However, these two are certainly interrelated, as rules are nothing more than meaningless statements if they are not embodied in the customs and habits of the community (Hodgson, 2006).

25 It is important to acknowledge that institutional structures can exist without being adequately conceptualised by agents, or without being conceptualised at all. This is because it is through human actions taken in totality that they come about and endure, whether or not individual agents have an awareness that, or precisely how, this is so.

26 As such, discernible (partial) event regularities may become evident and lend themselves with an ontological justification to empirical analysis.

27 This means agency attributed to the behavioural capabilities and action of present actors.

28 There is neither consensus with regard to the number of specific proclivities that are native to humans, nor any hard and fast way of sorting them out. This is why institutionalists (Veblen, 1899, 1914; Parker, 1918; Edie, 1922) have come up with varying taxonomies. The grouping envisaged here draws heavily on the writings of Veblen, but, like all taxonomies, is in essence arbitrary, as Ayres (1921) has highlighted. Moreover, this sort of classification is not all-inclusive. The significance of the list is that it brings within a small compass some of the paramount human dispositions which (arguably) define economic conduct.

29 In general, institutionalists use the concept of technology to define what, in the current context, is recognised as creativity (see, for instance, Ayres, 1962, 1966; DeGregori, 1977; Samuels, 1977; Bush, 1987). However, the latter is preferred here as it discourages the association of the notion with the common understanding and everyday use of the term technology.

30 It should be noted that Veblen draws on pragmatist philosophers to embrace a concept of habit that is twisted from its customary use. For Veblen, habituation, rather than the mere recurrence of specific activities, is a capacity, a proclivity to act in a particular way, which may or may not be actualised in current behaviour (Hodgson, 2004a, 2004b). Interestingly, a similar perception on habituation (i.e. as a propensity instead of a behaviour) is also held in critical realism (see Bhaskar, 1975).

31 Although we are "automatically prompted to *think*, *feel*, or *do* what we have been before accustomed to think, feel, or do, under like circumstances, without any consciously formed *purpose*, or anticipation of results", habituation is accompanied by awareness and consciousness of some kind (James, 1890: 112 emphasis in the original; Clark, 1918a; Dewey, 1922; Tugwell, 1922), as attention is immediately activated when something unexpected comes about to interrupt the habit in operation.

32 Interestingly, contemporary studies in evolutionary psychology have come to similar conclusions, arguing that human groups tend to acquire certain views and assumptions about the nature of the world and human action by virtue of human-universal psychological mechanisms (Tooby and Cosmides, 1992).

33 In this sense, culture is seen as a web of shared meanings external to each of its members, but internal to all collectively (Hollis, 1996).

34 Interestingly, Archer (1995) espouses a similar dualistic approach in cultural analysis by differentiating between cultural systems, the corpus of historically developed 'intelligibilia' (knowledge, beliefs, values), and the socio-cultural relations that exist between individuals and groups at a point in time.

35 On account of the social relations in which humans are engaged (Granovetter, 1985, 1992).

36 Following Hamilton (1932), Ayres (1962), North (1990) and Menard (1995), the distinction between institutions and organisations is highlighted here, where institutions are the 'rules' and organisations the 'players of the game'. However, broad organisational forms can be thought of as institutions, to the extent that they define or induce particular regularities or rules to organise socio-economic activity. On these grounds, organisations have been defined as special institutional arrangements

> designed to make possible the conscious and deliberate co-ordination of activities within identifiable boundaries, in which members associate on a regular

> basis through a set of implicit and explicit agreements, commit themselves to collective actions for the purpose of creating and allocating resources and capabilities by a combination of command and co-operation
>
> (Menard, 1995: 172)

or, more generally, as groups of individuals bound together by some common purpose (North, 1990, 1994). As such, firms, trade unions or professional bodies are regarded as economic organisations; political parties and legislatures as political organisations; universities as educational organisations; and churches and clubs as social organisations.

37 As discussed, the organisational structure of a society is the outcome, and reflection, of its institutional environment. Thus, from here on, the label institutional environment will refer to the whole institutional and organisational structure.

38 Cournot (1897), for instance, regards the market as a "region in which buyers and sellers are in such frequent intercourse with each other that the prices of the same goods tend to equality easily and quickly" (as quoted in Hodgson, 1988: 173; and Menard, 1995: 168).

39 Note, however, that this distinction might not be as hard and fast as it seems.

40 In regard to the information deficiencies, for instance, Keogh and D'Arcy (1999) outline the situation where evidence to support the efficient market hypothesis could reflect a false consensus in the market where participants share the same, but nevertheless inaccurate, information.

41 It should not be forgotten that institutionalism is one of the few schools in economics that explicitly acknowledged and incorporated normative standards of judgement in its inquiry as a basis for choosing one datum or option over another at every point (see Myrdal, 1958, 1970; Kapp, 1976; Miller, 1978; Tool, 1986).

42 A similar argument has been put forward by D'Arcy and Keogh (1997, 1998) and Goldberg (2004) on the basis of the growing globalisation and integration of the property markets.

43 A similar rationale underlies the remebiableness criterion (see Williamson, 1996).

44 In a similar vein is Hodgson's (1988: 168, 256–8) 'impurity principle' and 'law of requisite variety', arguing that, for a stable outcome to be attained, the variety of a system must be at least equal to that of the activity which it is directing. Consequently, to minimise the chances of disruption, an open system has to contain sufficient variety to deal with all the potential variation in its environment.

45 Contemporary examples from the property market are: lease-and-leaseback, real estate securitisation, REITs, etc.

46 According to Dosi (1988), Nelson (1994), Killick (1995a) and World Bank (2002), the plurality and heterogeneity of institutions are major determinants of sustained economic growth. A similar argument is also put forward by Gibson and Lizieri (2001) with reference to the property market institutions.

47 Such as subprime mortgage-backed securities or closed professions that opportunistically control the limited, and often inaccurate, market information.

48 A similar case is investment in information, where it is not possible to know its actual value before the information itself is acquired (Keogh and D'Arcy, 1999).

5 The research approach

5.1 Introduction

Chapter 4 outlined the philosophical underpinnings of this research programme to develop a theoretical framework that conceptualises the property market as an institution and explores its role within the urban economy. Chapter 5 builds on this framework to address explicitly the issues of concrete analysis. In particular, it provides an analytical basis to guide empirical research on the property market as an institution and its relation to the urban economy.

The chapter is organised into two main sections. The first starts by laying down the epistemological and methodological premises of this project to provide a generic (within the area of inquiry) research approach indicating the appropriate methods and techniques for empirical analysis. The second main section explores how the specific theoretical framework, developed in previous Chapter 4, can be operationalised and translated into empirical practice. Two levels of design are envisaged and issues of information requirements and methods of data collection and analysis are discussed. This research design provides a blueprint for empirical studies in this area.

5.2 From philosophical principles to methods of investigation

Any research activity is inextricably related to particular perceptions of the world and cognitive approaches to it as it is these ontological and epistemological assumptions that underlie and inform appropriate research principles and practices. On this basis, choosing an appropriate methodology requires going to these philosophical underpinnings.

Chapter 4 laid down in detail the ontological and epistemological foundations of this research project in accordance with a critical realist philosophical perspective and an institutionalist understanding of socio-economic dynamics. In particular, an intransitive, transfactual and stratified ontological reality was proposed (described by deep qualities of the human essence, institutional structures and empirical appearances) alongside an epistemological interpretation which recognised the historical transitivity of, and causal interdependency on, our knowledge of these entities. In line with this epistemic account, our objective is to advance knowledge, i.e. to (re)define and refine conceptual resources in an attempt to expand and improve the understanding of the qualities, mechanisms, processes and dynamics of the property market as an institution and its interaction with the wider urban institutional framework.

According to critical realism, causal powers can be exercised without being actualised and so the associated mechanisms may not give rise to detectable effects when, for instance, these powers are offset by the operation of countervailing mechanisms. This is because, as a general rule, the social world is inherently open and structured, comprised of complex systems (such as the property market) that are exposed to outside influences, interact with each other (in a holistic manner) and are subject to internal dynamics (at least due to transformative human agency).[1] As a result, stable and recoverable patterns of events (i.e. regularities) are not common in the social sciences, as they presuppose closure, something only possible in experimental situations. Lawson (1997a) identifies two conditions for closure which provide the required experimental insulation for constant empirical regularities to occur: the extrinsic condition of closure and the intrinsic condition of closure. The first insulates the object of study from upsetting external influences, whereas the latter safeguards it from internal disturbances so that only one outcome is feasible.[2] Although such closure is impossible, as a totality, in the social world, there are cases of partial, or quasi, or local closure (i.e. historically and spatially specific) due to physical and biological constraints and institutions (values, beliefs, habits, customs) that people develop (consciously or unconsciously) to cope with the structural uncertainty they face (Bhaskar, 1979; Lawson, 1997a). As such, discernible (partial) event regularities may actualise and make themselves available, with an ontological justification, to empirical analysis (see following discussion).

Whether addressing some conceptual issues or looking into empirical phenomena, researchers informed by critical realism seek explanations in terms of underlying structures, powers and mechanisms. To achieve these, critical realism sets forth two relatively distinct modes of analysis or types of explanation: theoretical and applied (Sayer, 1992, 2000; Lawson, 1997a, 2003). Theoretical (or pure, or abstract) explanation concerns the theoretical identification of underlying structures, powers, mechanisms and their essential relations governing the flux of phenomena related to the specific object of study. This mode of analysis is "characteristically retroductive" (Lawson, 1997a: 221). It starts with the issues under scrutiny and, drawing on the available conceptual resources and valuation criteria (agreed to by the relevant scientific community), it seeks to elaborate plausible theories of structures and relations (some of which are as yet unobserved or even unobservable) that support their explanation. Causal powers and mechanisms are thereby set out and their operation is explored and elaborated. This is done by 'abstraction' and 'metaphor' (or analogy).

Abstraction is a process through which a conceptual model is developed (identifying structures, powers, mechanism, relations) by focusing on certain features (regarded as real or essential) to the temporary bracketing of others (regarded as transient or less significant). This is not to reject the existence and influence of the ignored elements, but to temporarily relegate them to the fringes of attention (Mearman, 2006; Lewis, 2011). However, the researcher should never lose sight of the overall context from which features are abstracted and brought into close focus. Seen thus, abstraction is in contrast to isolation, which employs idealisation and omission techniques to eliminate the general background from the process[3] (Hodge, 2008).

Let us now turn to the metaphor/analogy technique. In developing theoretical models that advance existential hypotheses about 'real' entities (yet unobserved or even unobservable), it is useful to adopt terms from the existing literature as they are able to communicate a conceived concept in a sufficiently precise and meaningful way. To do this, scientists make use of metaphors (Lewis, 1996). A metaphor is most commonly described as a figure of speech that allows us to speak about one thing in terms of another, where there is some similarity or analogy between the two.[4] In this way, a metaphor enables us to conceptualise and understand the unknown (called 'tenor') in terms of the familiar (called 'vehicle'). Because metaphor works through the interaction of two different contexts, it not only capitalises on existing ways of seeing things, but it may acquire emergent cognitive content by projecting its subject in a unique and novel way (even by simply calling attention to properties hitherto unnoticed) and generating new perceptions, insights and avenues of inquiry (Lewis, 1996).

Although the retroductive process is fairly straightforward, the key issue of concern is how we can evaluate the relative strength of a putative theory and select among alternatives. Epistemological relativism leads critical realism to adopt a non-foundational position (Davidsen, 2010). Instead of a single test procedure or some decisive evaluation criterion, 'judgemental rationality' is to be used; here, competing explanations are assessed according to their explanatory power (Lawson, 1997a, 2003). This idea highlights the need to take into account all aspects relevant to the task, theoretical (such as theory consistency and coherence) as well as empirical (i.e. practical or pragmatic adequacy and explanatory breadth and depth), and to pass a credible judgement which, nevertheless, remains open to critical assessment. Proposed explanations are therefore reviewed and assessed in a reflexive and progressive manner and, when found to be theoretically consistent and empirically adequate (themselves explained in turn), are accepted as valuable parts of explanatory knowledge.

Moving to the applied (or practical, or concrete) explanation, this operates at the empirical level to explicate the generative mechanisms and the contingent conditions which account for the observed phenomena in specific, real-life situations. This mode of explanation is "characteristically resolutive and retrodictive" (Lawson, 1997a: 221; Fleetwood, 2001). It starts with the resolution of an empirical event or situation of interest into distinct components and the redescription of these components in theoretically significant terms. Next, it proceeds with the specification of plausible causal mechanisms and the elimination of the less probable ones, to the formulation of a hypothetical model (i.e. causal framework) that accounts for the phenomena under investigation. Finally, it turns to contextualise, refine and evaluate (of course, in a corrigible manner) the proposed model further, by empirically exploring its explanatory power in other (similar, broader, narrower, or different) contexts. Such analysis is conducted on empirical data (of a much wider range than those of orthodox economics) through the use of a variety of investigation techniques in a manner based on triangulation – see following discussion (Sayer, 1992, 2000; Danermark *et al.*, 2002; McEvoy, 2006; Downward and Mearman, 2007).

As argued earlier, theories make claims about generative mechanisms that exist by virtue of the nature of structures and their essential relations. Such powers should be understood as tendencies (Sayer, 1992; Lawson, 1989, 1995, 1998a; Fleetwood, 2001). A statement of a tendency is thus not a conditional statement about something empirical, but an unconditional, transfactual statement about a causal mechanism that "is being exercised whatever events ensue" as a result of the powers of structures and their relations (Lawson, 1997a: 23). As a number of (possibly counteractive) mechanisms may be in force at the same time and place, such tendencies are not expected, in general terms, to give rise to strict regularities at the level of events.[5] However, when some persistent regularities are evident in a time-space (i.e. a case of local closure), there are good reasons to believe that some causal powers are in operation. Thus, to the extent that any manifest phenomenon appears to reveal some degree of uniformity, generality, or persistence, albeit by no means complete in these respects, it would signal that some enduring generative mechanisms are at work.[6]

These partial empirical regularities are referred to as 'stylised facts' (Lawson, 1989, 1995) or as 'demi-regularities' (demi-regs, for short) (Lawson, 1997a, 2003). A demi-reg, therefore, is "a partial event regularity which *prima facie* indicates the occasional, but less than universal, actualisation of a mechanism or tendency, over a definite region of time-space" (Lawson, 1997a: 204). It is, in fact, a conceptualised phenomenon of a tendency that is robust enough "to hold in a way, or to a degree, such that the researcher regards as significant enough, given the context, that an explanation is called for" (Lawson, 1989: 65). Examples of demi-regs from the economics literature include phenomena of cumulative causation and path dependency, such as cases of technological lock-in (e.g. the QWERTY layout in typewriter and computer keyboards, see David 1985) or of the spatial concentration of population and economic activities (agglomeration economies), as well as patterns of persistent differences between otherwise similar (in terms of history and conditions) cases, such as in growth rates or in productivity records between regions or countries, or in employment positions and wages between women and men.

Lawson (1997a, 2003) argues that the latter demi-regs, called 'contrastives', are of special interest to economics as they look like conditions of experimental control (i.e. they provide some kind of system closure) and are widely in evidence. Contrastives stand out from the mass of observable reality, pointing out unanticipated, puzzling, surprising or implausible relations of some kind (whether primarily historical, spatial or social) and alerting researchers to the existence of powers hitherto unknown, unnoticed or even taken for granted.[7] For these reasons they direct researchers' attention to a subset of key mechanisms (rather than the totality of the causal factors, a task which is almost unattainable), enabling the formation of hypotheses about particular causal mechanisms which prima facie account for the outcomes observed (Pinkstone, 2002). Of course, both the contrastives that attract attention and the explanations developed will depend upon, and reflect, the particular viewpoint, understanding and interests of the individual researcher or the research community they belong to. Hence different observers or research communities may place emphasis on different aspects of the underlying causal situation, advancing (all together) scientific knowledge in an interdisciplinary and holistic way[8] (Lawson, 1997a, 1999).

Generally, demi-regs are of major significance and interest to economics, giving rise to genuine doubts (in the Peircean sense) and providing a starting point (though not the only one) for scientific inquiry. In particular, demi-regs can serve to both form models/theories about putative entities, relations and causal powers which may account for the specific outcome observed (in an abstract, retroductive fashion) and to assess (on the basis of empirical support) the relative explanatory power of developed or competing models/theories. On these grounds, theoretical and applied analyses become intertwined, reinforcing and complementing each other in the development of scientific knowledge.

Overall, the epistemological and methodological positions outlined here provide the foundations on which the investigation of the institutional texture of urban property markets can successfully be conducted. The methodological perspective put forward regards theoretical conceptualisation, applied explanation and empirical analysis as interlinked.[9] Research starts with the formulation of a theoretical framework (using abstraction and analogy) where underlying structures, causal mechanisms and essential relations are identified with regard to the particular object of study. (Chapter 4 has provided such a conceptualisation with regard to the property market institution and its relation to the urban economy). Applied research follows, where the operation and effects of the causal mechanisms are examined in specific, actual situations, vis-à-vis the contingent conditions which account for their actualisation. Analysis at this stage involves the identification, resolution, redescription, contextualisation and, eventually, understanding (in theoretically significant terms) of the partial empirical regularities (demi-regs and contrastives) that are related to the particular subject matter (i.e. the property market as an institution) in specific time-space contexts.

The methodological approach advocated in the current research programme is interdisciplinary and pluralistic.[10] The former indicates that property economics should draw upon and integrate knowledge and methods offered by other disciplines (such as political science, sociology, anthropology, psychology, history, geography), whereas the latter highlights the use of various forms of inference and techniques of investigation (on the basis of the scope and objects of the inquiry) with no a priori predominance of some over the others. Moreover, our methodological stance is also eclectic and critical. This means that the methods employed are those that are deemed most appropriate not to seek out event regularities and generalisations from which to declare universal laws (as mainstream economics does), but to corroborate explanations and theories that contribute towards a proper understanding of the 'real' structures and their relations which account for the phenomena under study. As these causal entities are contextual and historical in their realisation, understanding refers to the process of constructing a unifying system and identifying the role of these entities within the system and in its course of evolutionary change. In doing so, the historical and comparative research approach seems most appropriate due to its ability to establish causal explanations in a holistic manner (see following discussion).

Turning to the question of which specific types of method to be employed, we argue for both qualitative and quantitative approaches[11] (a between-method triangulation) by means of case analysis. Such a practice represents a polyvocal approach to research (Philip, 1998), provides a holistic picture of the phenomena under investigation (Bryman, 1992, 2001) and enhances the research validity of the study (Yin, 1998, 2003). Qualitative techniques focus on the description and interpretation of the issue under examination, providing contextual richness, depth and density. Quantitative techniques, in turn, work at the level of events to identify interesting demi-regs and to assess the capacity for the broader applicability of observed patterns in data (Downward and Mearman, 2007). In this sense, statistical and econometric techniques (especially non-parametric techniques) serve as a complement to qualitative analysis, provided that the former are more critically applied and cautiously interpreted than is usual in mainstream economics (Downward *et al.*, 2002; Castellacci, 2006).

Recapitulating, it is argued that, due to the complexity and multidimensionality of the phenomena under study, the research questions set out in this research project would best be answered by employing a predominantly qualitative methodology with supplementary quantitative evidence and analysis when appropriate (as suggested in Bryman, 1992, 2001; Denscombe, 1998; Silverman, 2000). The proposed research approach is HCIA, which relies on case studies for collecting and analysing information. It is to these that the discussion now turns.

5.2.1 Historical and comparative research

The historical and comparative approach is a powerful research method in the social sciences as it can address a wide variety of research problems (Mahoney and Rueschemeyer, 2003). According to Neuman (1994), this method is most appropriate for identifying factors (or combinations of factors) that give rise to specific outcomes, as well as for comparing entire social systems or institutional structures (such as urban socio-economies and property markets), to see what is common across societies and what is unique and how these change over time. Moreover, it can be used to develop theory or to strengthen conceptualisation by applying developed theory to specific cases to assess it or to illustrate its usefulness.

The historical and comparative research approach is characterised by an ability to shift between a specific context and a general comparison, something which enables it to combine sensitivity to particular historical and cultural contexts with theoretical generalisations. A researcher examines specific contexts, notes similarities and differences, and then generalises. They then look again at the specific contexts using the generalisations in an attempt to improve both understanding of the cases and the generalisation itself. Here the approach to causality is more contingent than deterministic (Neuman, 1994). 'Combinational' or 'concatenated' explanations are often used, which differ from a linear causal explanation, as the logic is more 'A, B and C appeared together in time and place, then D resulted' instead of 'A caused B, B caused C, and C caused D'.

The historical and comparative approach intensively examines a limited number of cases (or even a single case study) in which social meaning and context are critical, using predominantly qualitative evidence. However, quantitative data may also be used to supplement qualitative data and analysis. The researcher may start with a conceptual framework outlining the assumptions and organising categories that help them to 'view' the world, to 'package' observations and to search for evidence. Next, they locate and gather micro-level evidence and begin to organise data, conducting a preliminary analysis by noting low-level generalisations or themes. Finally, after most of the evidence has been amassed, the researcher refines and evaluates the concepts used, organises the evidence into a coherent whole and moves towards a general explanatory model based on both collected evidence and logical reasoning – even though the latter might not be reflected empirically. Neuman (1994) identifies four types of relevant evidence that can be collected: primary sources (documents, memos, official reports, newspaper or magazine articles), secondary sources (the writings of specialists who study primary sources), running records (files or existing statistical documents maintained by organisations) and non-source-based knowledge (knowledge based not on primary or secondary sources, but on logical reasoning).

As regards the study of institutions, HCIA combines historical research with comparative analysis. In particular, it attempts to reveal the forces that lead societies to evolve along distinct institutional trajectories, to understand the developed institutional organisation and to explore the adaptive ability of institutional structures to the changing conditions and opportunities, by evaluating and synthesising micro-level historical and comparative studies over time and space with an explicit reliance on context-sensitive conceptual models (Greif, 1998; Stanfield, 1999; Morgan *et al.*, 2010).

HCIA research recognises that institutional structures are a complex mixture in which informal, implicit, institutions interrelate with formal, explicit, institutions to create a coherent whole. It also indicates that the study of the institutional environment should consider the interrelations between the economic, political, legal and socio-cultural aspects of the particular societies under consideration. These are seen as products of a historical process in which past institutional features and contingent conditions interact in shaping the nature of contemporary institutions and their evolution. In this sense, institutional change is seen as a natural, never-ending process of a constantly evolving socio-economic system reflecting both external circumstances and internal changes in beliefs, cognition, knowledge, rationality or shifts in the power of the actors.

A starting point for the analysis is the identification of the respective institutions, organisations and related features (such as transaction costs, the bargaining power of actors, cultural characteristics, beliefs) prevailing in the particular historical episode under consideration (North, 1993a, 1993b, 1994; Greif, 1998). A hypothesis regarding the relevance of a particular institution is formulated based on the developed conceptual model and the available evidence at a micro-level (Greif, 1998).

The means of collecting and organising information in the HCIA is the case study (Wilber and Harrison, 1978; Dugger, 1979; Atkinson and Oleson, 1996; Stanfield, 1999; Downward *et al.*, 2002; Woodside, 2010).

5.2.2 Case study research

A case study is an empirical inquiry that looks into complex phenomena within their real-life contexts, in which there are many more variables of interest than data points and the boundaries between the phenomenon and the context are not clearly distinguishable (Hamel *et al.*, 1993; Yin, 2003: 13; Easton, 2010; Woodside, 2010). On these grounds, institutionalists such as Stanfield (1999: 236) think highly of the case study as an approach which can provide rich specifications of the activities, rules, cultural underpinnings and cognitive frameworks "that comprise human behaviour unfolding in an institutional context".

The case study relies on many of the same techniques as the HCIA, but adds two more possible sources of evidence: direct observation and interviews. As such, Yin (2003) argues that case study inquiry relies on multiple sources of evidence, with data needing to converge in the form of triangulation. Here triangulation refers to the case where evidence from three (or more) different, but coincident, sources is required to establish a robust fact (data triangulation).[12] However, such a perspective does not deny the possibility of methodological triangulation, in which multiple research techniques are also employed to investigate the phenomena under study (Yeung, 1997; Silverman, 2000; Bryman, 2001; Woodside, 2010).

As in HCIA, the development of a conceptual framework prior to the collection of data is an important step in carrying out case studies[13] (Easton, 2010; Woodside, 2010). The appropriately developed theory is not only essential to defining the appropriate research design and data collection, but also becomes the main vehicle for generalising the results. This role of theory is characterised by Yin (2003) as 'analytic generalisation', in which the previously developed theory is used as a template with which to compare the empirical results obtained from the case study.

According to its purpose, Yin (1998, 2003) distinguishes three main types of case study research: exploratory, descriptive and explanatory. An exploratory case study is initial research looking for patterns in the data and formulating questions for further inquiry. It mainly addresses 'what' type questions. Descriptive case studies take this further and try to obtain information on the particular features of an issue, aiming to answer 'how' type questions. Finally, explanatory case studies continue this even further by trying to analyse and explain 'why' something happens or happened.

The selection of the particular case(s) starts with the definition of the 'case' to be studied, called the 'unit of analysis' (Yin, 2003). The choice of the appropriate unit of analysis is related to the primary research questions and the conceptual framework that have been set out at the beginning of the investigation. Once a general definition of the case has been established, other clarifications in the unit of analysis become important. These concern the specification of the temporal and geographical boundaries that define the extent of the case and thereby the limits of data collection and analysis. As an added complication, the case study may also have one (or more) subunits of analysis, called 'embedded units of analysis', within the main unit, something that generates "significant opportunities for extensive analysis, enhancing the insights into the single case" (Yin, 2003: 46). Moreover, the study may contain more than a single case, leading to the development of a multiple case study design. Here, the selection of cases is based on theoretical, rather than statistical, sampling, and follows a replication logic in a manner similar to multiple experiments. This means that the theoretical framework specifies which cases are most appropriate for the study, whereas each case is carefully selected so that it produces either similar (a literal replication) or contrasting (a theoretical replication) results. In a similar manner, the choice of the number of cases follows the same logic, reflecting the number of replications that are deemed sufficient for the study. Here, of course, statistical criteria regarding sample size and similar matters are not applicable.

In analysing case studies and reaching conclusions within the HCIA, institutional economics suggest the employment of the 'story-telling' and 'pattern modelling' techniques (Wilber and Harrison, 1978; Wisman and Rozansky, 1991; Atkinson and Oleson, 1996; Stanfield, 1999), where institutionally rich 'cases' (i.e. instances, situations, events, contexts) are descriptively analysed, recounted and compared in an effort to discern (and to identify their place within) a wider pattern of relationships. This mode of research is couched in the holistic understanding that institutions are truly comprehensible only through their interrelations with the other institutions that collectively comprise the overall institutional environment. Consequently, at least in principle, the whole range of social, political, economic and legal institutional arrangements should be investigated to understand and explain one institution. This interpretative effort is very different from the conventional scientific procedure of isolation and reduction. Pattern modelling is intent less on reducing the variables and relationships than on expanding them. It is an effort to bring into focus relations, connections and constitutive mechanisms that are not evident in conventional comprehension[14] (Stanfield, 1999).

5.2.3 Generalisability and research quality

Before we conclude this section on research approaches, let us briefly discuss issues of generalisability and overall research quality. Leading theorists of critical realism, such as Bhaskar (1975), Sayer (1992, 2000) and Lawson (1997a, 2003), have argued that generalisability lies "in the hidden essence of things" (Bhaskar, 1975: 227) and so "causal powers of objects are generalizable to other contexts as they are necessary features of these objects" (Sayer, 2000: 21). However, as contingent (local) conditions are always in play, causal effects might not actualise in all contexts, calling for further research to establish the extent of their actualisation, and so of their generalisability.[15] To that end, other scholars in the same field (Yeung, 1997; Downward *et al.*, 2002; Easton, 2010) have pointed out that generalisability should not be approached as a matter of statistical generalisation (generalising from sample to population), but as a matter of analytical generalisation in which theory dictates which cases should be examined, and cases are subsequently used to represent, illustrate, refine and generalise to a theory. Researchers can therefore be confident that a theoretically postulated explanation of a phenomenon applies to other members of a larger population of which the original cases are an example,[16] if research into some of such cases (or even into a single case) leads to the verification (empirical realisation) of the same causal explanation. Such a perspective, Yeung (1997: 62) asserts, "helps avoid much decontextualization of objects in statistical methods and facilitates the choice of valid objects for investigation and retroduction".

A similar stance is also taken by other authors on research methodology. Yin (2003: 32–3), for instance, writes that cases are not 'sampling units', but theoretically guided choices, and so the method of generalisation is not statistical but analytical, "in which a previously developed theory is used as a template with which to compare the empirical results" obtained. In these terms, if two or more cases are shown to support the same theoretical proposition, then replication can be claimed. From a similar perspective, other scholars (e.g. Frankfort-Nachmias and Nachmias, 1992; Silverman, 2000; Bryman, 2001; Flick, 2009) argue for analytical as well as for purposive 'sampling' (i.e. sampling guided by time and resource constraints) and for the employment of certain tactics (see later) by which the generalisability and the overall quality of empirical research can be enhanced.

According to this literature (e.g. Lincoln and Guba, 1985; Silverman, 2000; Bryman, 2001; Yin, 1998, 2003; Trochim and Donnelly, 2008), the overall quality of the type of research advocated here (i.e. HCIA based on case study) can be assessed on the basis of four concepts: construct validity, internal validity, external validity and reliability. Construct validity concerns the extent to which accurate operational measures have been established for the concepts developed; internal validity (or credibility) regards whether causal conclusions can be drawn; external validity (or transferability) deals with the extent to which results can be generalised or transferred to another context or setting; and, finally, reliability (or dependability) refers to the extent to which the study can be replicated in the sense that the results can be confirmed and substantiated by others. Table 5.1 lists a number of recommended tactics covering the four quality concepts, also indicating the most probable phase of research in which each tactic usually applies. What follows is a short discussion on these tactics (based

Table 5.1 Tactics for high quality historical and comparative institutional analysis case studies

Quality issues	*Tactics to use*	*Phase applied*
Construct validity	Use multiple sources of data, i.e. triangulate Establish chain of evidence Have key informants review results	Data collection Data collection Composition
Internal validity (credibility)	Do pattern matching Do explanation building Do historical diachronic successive analysis Use logic models	Data analysis Data analysis Data analysis Data analysis
External validity (transferability)	Use theory in single cases Use replication logic in multiple cases	Research design Research design
Reliability (dependability)	Use case protocol Develop case database	Data collection Data collection

Source: based on Yin (1998, 2003).

mainly on Yin 2003) suggesting how these could be applied in the different stages of the research process.

The research design is, in fact, an action plan that guides the research process from the development of the research questions to the empirical study and, ultimately, to the arrival at conclusions. In this sense it affects all key stages in the research process, including data collection and analysis. To achieve high quality in the research design phase (external validity), two strategies have been suggested: the use of theory and the use of replication logic (in multiple cases). The employment of a conceptual framework that identifies causal powers and relations is essential, not only because it enhances quality in the research design, but also because it sharpens theoretical thinking. Within a single case, theory informs data acquisition and elaboration, whereas in multiple cases it additionally helps designate appropriate cases for examination. To this end, replication logic should be applied in a manner similar to experimental reasoning, in which certain cases are chosen because they are expected to provide similar results, whereas others (deliberately contrary) are used for contrasting purposes.

In the data collection phase, suggested strategies include: the use of multiple data sources; the establishment of a chain of evidence; the use of a protocol; and the development of a database. The most important advantage of using multiple sources of evidence is the accomplishment of converging lines of inquiry (thus constituting triangulation)[17] enhancing the generalisability of the research findings. To achieve this, information should be sought from various sources, such as documents, archival records, interviews and observation, and analysed using available techniques. Establishing a chain of evidence requires a traceable progression of consistent reasoning from initial research questions to ultimate study conclusions. This means that each successive step in the research process should be consistent with the previous step, in the sense that the move from one step to another should be validated with clear reference to methodological procedures and the resulting evidence. The case protocol is an important component of case research safeguarding its quality and reliability. The protocol is more than a simple instrument outlining the study questions; it also contains the procedures and general rules to be followed in data collection, including, for instance, directions for reframing these questions in the field (if needed). The case database is the means of organising the evidence (both primary and secondary) not only during, but also after the data collection phase. To arrange and cite the fieldwork and other material, a narrative can be used. One way of organising the narrative is to follow the sequence of topics or questions specified in the case protocol. However, a serious mistake here would be to construct a database that keeps the various sources of evidence segregated (e.g. the information from interviews separate from the documentary evidence). Synthesis across evidence from different and multiple sources addressing the same topic or theme is the main function of the database, with the result being a new narrative or new tabulation based on such synthesis.

Data analysis consists of inspecting, categorising, tabulating, recombining, processing, studying and interpreting the amassed data to address the objectives of the research. To successfully accomplish these tasks, an analytical framework is required which, by following the theoretical propositions developed, determines the appropriate methods for data elaboration and analysis. Four dominant analytical techniques can be used, which also address the issue of research quality (internal validity): pattern matching; explanation building; time series analysis; and logic models.

Pattern matching seeks to find order in the data by identifying whether the evidence collected from the case fits into a theoretically postulated pattern. When a large amount of data is available, statistical techniques can be applied. However, comparison need not necessarily involve quantitative or statistical analysis, as such formal methods could stifle interpretative discretion. In fact, Yin (2003) argues that even simple techniques, such as eye-balling, are sufficiently convincing to draw firm conclusions. A special type of pattern matching deserving separate attention is explanation building.[18] To 'explain' a phenomenon is to stipulate a set of causal links about it reflecting the theoretical propositions developed. To do this, the researcher begins with a number of research questions and a framework of concepts and relations. They then probe into case data, examining how well the 'model' fits the actual evidence and adjusting the model to reflect the evidence better. Next, in repeated iterations, they use the data from other cases to reflect on the refined model and the relations, mechanisms, dynamics, etc., it postulates. At each stage the evidence and the theory inform each other, enabling further refinement of the model and its concepts until it successively becomes more accurate. An important aspect in explanation building is to take into account possible rival explanations (specified in the theory) exploring whether they can be sustained on the basis of the case data.

Time series analysis explores the temporal dimension. Here, a series of data points (drawn from the case research) is compared to a theoretically postulated trend (or to rivals). A mismatch between the two can raise suspicions that some (as yet unidentified) causal mechanisms are in operation. Similar analysis can also be carried out in a chronological sequence, which constitutes a special type of time series. It is argued that arraying events into a chronology enables the investigator to determine causal relations over time, due to the fact that the basic sequence of a cause and its effect cannot be temporally inverted (Sayer, 1992). The logic model combines pattern matching and time series analysis as it deliberately stipulates a complex chain of events (a pattern) over time (a time series). The strength of the logic model is its requirement of an explicit conceptualisation of the event chain (reflecting the theory), which is sufficiently detailed so that operational measures can be provided for each step. Data collection is then designed to cater for these operational measures. If the data acquired are supportive of the initial chain, and no rivals can be substantiated, the analysis would claim a causal effect between the first and last event in the chain.

It is clear that the research programme put forward here is holistic, critical and theory-laden, but also contains a significant empirical component. Hence a generic research approach has been formulated (in this section), indicating the methods and techniques of investigation pertinent to the ontological, epistemological and methodological premises of this work. Having completed this, Chapter 5 now moves to explore how the specific theoretical model of the property market explanation for urban economic change set forth in Chapter 4 can be operationalised and explored in concrete practice.

5.3 Formulating a research design

This section develops an operational model of urban economic development with the property market in a pivotal role and puts forward an agenda for concrete research on the issues. To that end, a research design is laid out providing a blueprint for empirical analysis and practice.

The proposed operational model is deployed at two supplementary levels (summarised in Figure 5.1, following the line of argument of Figure 4.3). The first level examines how the urban economy performs over time, taking into account the external conditions and internal (institutional) dynamics that affect its course. In addition, a property market element is introduced into the explanation. This is property market outcomes, which, as discussed, reflect the ability of

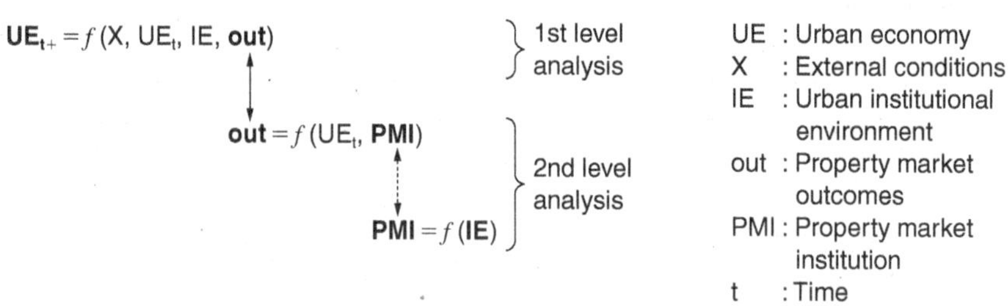

Figure 5.1 An operational model of urban economic change and property market analysis.

the market to accommodate demand pressures and thereby to support urban economic potential. However, such an analysis takes no account of the property market function and its deeply institutional character and therefore is simplistic, partial and, in a sense, conventional. Hence a second level of analysis is set up in which market outcomes are the result of the prevailing economic dynamics filtered through the property market institution, which determines the process and mechanisms accounting for these outcomes. As a result, research now focuses on the property market institution, defined in terms of market institutional characteristics (formal and informal) and organisational arrangements, which mediates between the urban economic requirements and the actual property products provided. This institutional structure of the property market, however, is not autonomous; it is part and product of the overall urban institutional environment, necessitating a closer look at this relation. The operationalised concepts of institutionalised variety and institutional uncertainty explore the qualities of the property market institution and the urban institutional environment, respectively, to facilitate analysis of their relationship. Such analysis enables an assessment of the urban property market as an institution with reference to the wider institutional structures across time and space.

What follows is a description of the research design at each stage. This includes the provision of operational definitions of the concepts used (i.e. how they can be measured in practice) and a discussion of the data requirements and methods of analysis and interpretation.

5.3.1 First level design

The proposition here is that both the urban institutional environment and the property market determine urban economic development. With regard to the latter, however, attention is paid at this level to the output it produces. It is argued that major fluctuations in property market indicators (e.g. rents, capital values, yields) signify a mismatch between the demand for property, coming from the urban economy, and the actual supply of property (in terms of both built structures and property rights), which is provided by the market. This suggests a property market which is less capable of delivering the appropriate mix of outcomes that the economy requires at the prevailing price levels (at least in the short to medium term), something which constitutes a threat to urban economic potential. Research at this level starts by examining the performance of the urban economy over time, before moving on to explore the factors and dynamics that affect its course and, finally, introducing a property market element into the explanation.

To assess the urban economic performance over time, available economic data sets can be used. These could be conventional economic indicators at the urban level (such as various measures of GDP, employment or unemployment), which are made available by various international, supranational and national organisations, statistical offices and agencies (such as the World Bank, the International Monetary Fund, the OECD, Eurostat). Analysis of these data should provide a picture of the magnitude and volatility of the urban economy and, on this basis, an indication of its robustness (or weakness). Analysis here could be very technical (using advanced statistical and econometric methods), but, as argued earlier, even simple techniques (such as eye-balling) might be adequate to provide some valuable insights. Thus, for instance, plotting a chronological series of economic data could reveal the direction of the urban economy and the structural breaks in the course taken, triggering thinking about possible causal mechanisms and generating ideas for further investigation.

Having outlined the urban economic trajectory, an attempt should be made in the next step to understand the pattern of change by examining which factors and dynamics have affected its course. The discussion may start by considering the explanations offered by conventional approaches to urban economic change. However, the study should move a step further to examine how the urban economy is influenced not only by external forces (e.g. globalisation, European integration, technological developments, economic crises), but also by internal institutional conditions and dynamics (i.e. political, economic, legal and social pressures and changes). For this purpose, substantial events with economic, political, legal and socio-cultural implications should be chronologically arrayed and examined in relation to the urban economic trajectory. Analysis may be based on rigorous statistical methods (such as time series intervention analysis), although relevant qualitative techniques can also be used to provide conclusive evidence, also allowing for interpretative discretion.

At the final step of this level, an attempt should be made to improve our understanding of urban economic performance and change by introducing a property market dimension to the explanation. The underlying hypothesis is that the property market affects the urban economy through the outcomes it produces. Here again, standard quantitative indicators of property market outcomes (e.g. rents, capital values, yields) at the urban level can be used, which can be provided by property agents and related organisations [e.g. Jones Lang La Salle (JLL), CB Richard Ellis (CBRE), Royal Institution of Chartered Surveyors (RICS) and the International Real Estate Federation (FIABCI)].

Analysis of the property market data series may take several forms depending on the objectives and availability of data (see Ball *et al.*, 1998). Investigation may start with exploratory data analysis in which property market outcomes are descriptively analysed in an attempt to discern the broad pattern of property market dynamics. This analysis can reveal overall trends, cyclical patterns (seasonal effects) and turning points which may constitute structural breaks in the series. In addition, spectral analysis can be carried out to describe how variations in the time series may be accounted for by cyclic components. In turn, intervention analysis can be used to measure the impact of some shocks or events on the behaviour of the data series. Finally, explanative analysis can be employed to assess the relationship between the property data series and the urban economic data series and to identify the direction of causality. Making use of highly sophisticated statistical and econometric techniques, such analysis can be quite rigorous. However,a lack of reliable long runs in property data (even for the most mature markets) precludes their inclusion in empirical work. Given this, researchers rely to a great extent on qualitative analytical techniques, which are more flexible and allow a certain degree of discretion in interpreting the complex dynamics of the property market (Guy and Harris, 1997). In these circumstances, the data on property market outcomes may simply be mapped against economic indicators and plain statistical measures of correlation may be used to discuss the observed relationship and to reflect on the market ability (or 'credible commitment') to support economic potential. If the property market cycle runs ahead of (or at least in parallel to) the economic cycle, then a claim can be made that the market exerts an independent influence on the economy. In turn, a higher volatility of property indicators would imply some failure on the part of the market to accommodate in time the kind of demand placed upon it, and by extension to promote economic development.[19] This inability signifies a degree of institutional deficiency which would be examined at the next level of analysis.

5.3.2 Second level analysis

This level aims to expand our knowledge of the institutional character of the property market and its relation to the wider urban institutional environment. The underlying assumption is that the institutional structure of the property market determines market outputs and therefore affects urban economic potential and robustness. However, as property market institutions are part and product of the overall institutional environment, it is essential to consider the organisation of the former in terms of the qualities of the latter. With this in mind, research at this level turns to identify the institutional characteristics of the property market (collectively described as 'institutionalised variety') and to explore their development with reference to the qualities of the wider institutional structures and the degree of uncertainty that they exhibit ('institutional uncertainty').

As most of these characteristics are qualitative in nature, the analysis will rely mainly on qualitative information (of a historical kind) and on the descriptive rather than inferential use of quantitative data. On these grounds it is argued that a deep understanding of the institutional fabric of the property market, and of its relation to the wider institutional environment, would be achieved by employing primarily qualitative techniques to analyse both qualitative and quantitative information.

In accomplishing these objectives, this section starts by discussing how the key concepts of institutionalised variety and institutional uncertainty can be analytically defined and operationalised. This discussion provides the basis on which to address the kinds of data that need to be collected and the respective methods of analysis.

a Operationalisation

It is generally accepted that, although it is relatively easy to identify the broad institutional attributes of an economy and its property market, it is hard to distil them into a concrete operational model for empirical practice (Jaffe and Louziotis, 1996; Ball, 1998; D'Arcy and Keogh, 1999; Rodrik, 2008; Gertler, 2010; Rodríguez-Pose, 2013). This, however, constitutes an essential part of the research process as it addresses important questions, such as, inter alia, what indicators can be used to measure the employed concepts, what kind of data should be sought and how meaningful analysis can be accomplished. Thus, building on the theorisation in which the function of the property market as an institution is perceived along the lines of the variety–uncertainty thesis, this section focuses on the operationalisation of the concepts involved. First, it reflects on the idea of purpose efficiency, before moving on to consider the institutional attributes of the property market and the wider urban environment within which it operates.

What is required for the operationalisation of purpose efficiency is to identify some objective criteria that would permit an assessment of whether a property market is able to provide on time the property products that the economy requires at the prevailing price levels. This, of course, cannot be measured directly. It can be indirectly assessed through independent indicators that reflect the correspondence between the required property products and the actual products delivered. Such indicators could be identified by means of comparative analysis across markets or across time. However, the lack of long runs of reliable data or consistent data across urban markets makes it difficult to empirically verify the conditions of purpose efficiency at our current state of knowledge. Nevertheless, the developed concepts of institutionalised variety and institutional uncertainty are not without value; they can be used to assess the qualities of the property market institution and the wider institutional environment and to explore their intrinsic relation. In this situation, research focuses on the development of analytical indicators for the aforementioned concepts. Such indicators provide a basis for the evaluation of an urban property market (as an institution) at various points in time, as well as for comparative assessment between different markets.

With regard to institutionalised variety, the purpose is to specify common themes/categories that describe the institutional structure of the property market across different urban contexts. One area of research which can provide the basis to develop such initial themes is that of property market maturity. The concept of property market maturity has been comprehensively discussed and codified in Keogh and D'Arcy (1994) and subsequently used by various researchers (see, inter alia, D'Arcy and Lee, 1998; de Magalhaes, 2001; McGreal *et al.*, 2002; Chin and Dent, 2005; Sajor, 2005; Chin *et al.*, 2006) to assess the institutional aspects of urban property markets and to understand their influence on market outcomes. Table 5.2 outlines the characteristics of property market maturity.

It is clear that the indicators of property market maturity adequately reflect the qualities of the property market process (D'Arcy and Keogh, 1997; Keogh and D'Arcy, 1999). On this basis, they can be used for the analysis of the property market institution and, especially, of the institutionalised variety concept. However, the notion of market maturity should not be applied without careful consideration. A couple of points should be noted. First, it is essential to

Table 5.2 Characteristics of property market maturity

1. Accommodation of a full range of use and investment objectives, through the development of diverse property products
2. Flexible market adjustment in both short and long run, implying effective trade and the ability to react to new information and opportunities
3. A sophisticated property profession with associated institutions and networks, generally regulated by law and/or professional codes of practice
4. Extensive information flow and research activity, serving the requirements of a flexible market and frequently developed as an adjunct of professional activity
5. Market openness in spatial, functional and sectoral terms, allowing market participants to operate across boundaries and aiding the transmission of information throughout the market
6. Standardisation of property rights and market practice, meeting the need for greater certainty about the nature of the property interests traded in the market, in an environment where the range of tradable property rights has become much broader

Source: based on Keogh and D'Arcy (1994).

highlight that maturity is an interesting idea which pinpoints some important institutional aspects of the property market. Second, although some literature has perceived maturity as the final stage in property market evolution (at which each market will eventually arrive), this need not be the case. In fact, maturation could be seen as an open-ended evolutionary process in which markets develop (generate, acquire, reinforce, discard) certain characteristics to function within the wider environment in which they are located. This brings us to a third point. Although maturation reflects on the efficient function of the market, maturity should not necessarily be equated with efficiency, as certain maturity characteristics may inhibit successful market operation, depending on the wider conditions and dynamics. On this basis, the broad institutional environment within which the market operates and, in particular, the level of uncertainty that it is able to accommodate (this is the essence of the idea of purpose efficiency) have to be taken into account.

Turning to the issue of institutionalised variety, it becomes evident that the indicators of maturity correspond to qualities of flexibility, diversity and certainty and, as such, they fit well within the concept. In particular, the first maturity factor ('development of diverse products') addresses directly the issue of diversity in property products, while the fifth ('market openness') highlights the necessity of institutional and organisational variety within the market. In turn, the third and sixth factors ('existence of a sophisticated property profession' and 'standardisation of property rights and practices') safeguard requisite certainty within the market. Finally, the second and fourth characteristics of maturity ('flexible adjustment' and 'flow of information') address, respectively, the needs for market flexibility and information plurality/variety.

Overall, the indicators of property market maturity constitute a solid starting point for the operationalisation and development of institutionalised variety.

However, variety means something more than maturity and so further elaboration, modification and enhancement of the indicators of the latter are deemed necessary. To that end, a number of remarks seem pertinent.

The globalised and liberalised regime in which economies perform implies higher degrees of factor mobility (compared with the past) and therefore an increase in the number of property actors (e.g. users, investors, developers, service providers) operating at the urban level. This leads us to propose an extension to the third maturity factor so that these aspects of plurality and variety can be properly addressed. Thus, for instance, apart from one sophisticated property profession, property market diversity may necessitate the plurality of property service providers, or even the development of an interdisciplinary network of property experts, driven by competitive opportunities. The latter could ensure high-quality specialist advice, reduce the tendency for the supply of information to become monopolistic (with implications for the power relations between property professionals and other actors) and lower transaction costs (due to competition).

Similarly, we can point out a number of additional characteristics of the property market that are deemed to advance the operational definition of the institutionalised variety concept. Thus it can be argued (Schulte *et al.*, 2005; Adair *et al.*, 2006) that acts which increase market liquidity and transparency, along with secured property rights, enhance both flexibility and certainty and thus reflect greater institutionalised variety. Likewise, plurality of legal rights and financial instruments in property and other indirect property investment vehicles promote variety in the property market (Wallace and Williamson, 2006; Falkenbach, 2009). In contrast, attributes related to rigid lease structures, restrictive forms of tenure, onerous obligations of occupation or high costs of transaction impose inflexibilities on the range of use and investment objectives and should be seen as restrictions to market variety (Dale, 1997; Lizieri *et al.*, 2000; Crosby *et al.*, 2003; Hamilton *et al.*, 2006). In turn, it can be argued (Adair *et al.*, 1998; Ronald, 2004; Wallace and Williamson, 2006) that strong and immutable cultural attributes, conventions and vested habits (e.g. attitude to, and status of, property ownership, close-knit nepotistic/clientelistic networks) may inhibit market flexibility, whereas other social characteristics and informal institutions (e.g. 'secondary' market development or the informal provision of information) might endow the market with additional manoeuvrability.[20] Other factors that should also be examined in considering institutionalised variety include the organisational structure of the market and, in particular, the degree and range of involvement of non-domestic actors and funds, not only in use, development and investment, but also in financial and property service provision (Wallace and Williamson, 2006; Falkenbach, 2009).

Putting these attributes together we arrive at a list of themes under which the most essential characteristics of property market institutional structure can be classified (presented in detail in Appendix I). All these characteristics and the developed themes provide a general sense of reference and guidance in approaching empirical instances in terms of single-case or cross-case comparative research.

In that sense, they define how data collection, analysis and overall discussion on the institutional structure of the property market can be organised. Ten themes have been identified, although some overlap between themes and characteristics may be apparent due to the intertwined nature of institutions and the phenomena under study. These are:

1. diversity in use and investment objectives;
2. market openness and transparency;
3. market flexibility;
4. information flow and research activity;
5. property rights and transaction costs;
6. standardisation of market practices;
7. flexibility in cultural traits;
8. plurality of immediate actors;
9. diversity of financial service provision; and
10. plurality of property service providers and professionalisation of the market.

The first theme ('diversity in use and investment') assesses the quality of property market institutions in terms of the market ability to accommodate a full range of objectives in property use and investment. For this to be achieved, the clear definition, specification and assignment of legal rights in property use, investment and development are required that match the diverse interests of all property actors. These, in turn, may be associated with the establishment of distinct, but interconnected, property submarkets, defined in terms of legal interest, sector or location.

Qualities that advance market diversity are 'market openness and transparency', 'market flexibility' and an extensive 'information flow and research activity', which refer to the second, third and fourth themes, respectively. Market openness can be analysed along various dimensions: 'spatially', discussing the degree of participation of non-local actors and funds; 'sectorally', examining the extent to which non-property (i.e. other asset) players are involved in the market; and 'functionally', assessing the actors' ability to adjust their objectives in the light of changing circumstances. Additionally, other qualities, such as market liquidity (i.e. the ability to quickly convert properties into cash with the minimum loss of value) and transparency (i.e. the availability of information on property prices and supply), are also incorporated in this theme. Market flexibility, in turn, focuses on the ability of the market to respond to changing conditions and opportunities and to overcome any imposed constraints. Suggested indicators here concern assessments: first, of the adjustment ability of the development process in both the short and long run; and, second, of the restrictions imposed by relevant regulating systems, such as the tax and planning regimes. Finally, the fourth theme examines issues of information flow and research activity (in terms of availability, quality and diversity). Information flow refers to the availability and quality of historical data and the provision of information databases. Research activity can vary from basic qualitative assessments describing the overall state of the market to rigorous quantitative analysis that explains the performance of market indicators and relates them to wider economic variables. The key issues here are the degree of establishment of an adequate information base and the type of organisational structure (e.g. formal versus informal) that emerges with regard to the provision and dissemination of information.

Other important dimensions of the property market as an institution include the structure of the 'property rights and transaction costs' involved (theme five), the extent of the 'standardisation of market practices' (theme six) and the 'cultural traits' of the market (theme seven). The first of these themes explores the prevailing forms of ownership and tenure, also examining issues such as obligations of occupation, security of tenure and costs associated with property transactions. The second looks into the degree and type of practice standardisation (e.g. formal versus informal), considering the initial conditions and their evolutionary path as well as issues of transparency, cultural embeddedness and the degree of institutional fixity (immutability). Moreover, such a discussion provides a basis for reflecting on whether such practices lead to increasing conservatism and rigidity in market mechanisms. Finally, in the seventh theme, an explicit attempt is made to explore some of the cultural characteristics of the market and to reflect on how these might affect the market process. In this way, the established conventions, habits and norms associated with property market activities, and attitudes towards property, should be examined.

The last set of property market institutional characteristics refers to the organisational structure of the market. In particular, theme eight, 'plurality of immediate actors', investigates the composition of the market in terms of the key participants in use, investment and development, discussing their organisational form and degree of complexity or sophistication as well as their power characteristics. Theme nine, 'diversity of the financial service provision', in turn, explores the composition and structure of the market in terms of the key actors in property finance, examining the main practices of raising capital for (and from) property and the role of financial institutions in that respect. Finally, in theme ten, 'plurality of property service providers and professionalisation', the market structure is analysed with reference to the service providers and professional bodies that operate within it. Issues considered include the form, regulation, manpower, educational base, social status and power characteristics of these organisations, as well as their role and the nature of their involvement in the market process.

Turning to the wider institutional environment within which the property market operates, the section identifies some key operational measures of the quality of its structures, which has been defined as institutional uncertainty. These can guide empirical research (through single or multiple case studies), acting as a means of uncovering the variety of forms that the phenomena to which they refer can assume. Discussion is organised under four themes/categories (a detailed presentation is provided in Appendix II): (1) economic uncertainty; (2) political uncertainty; (3) legal uncertainty; and (4) socio-cultural uncertainty.

To describe the quality of economic structure at the urban level, a number of indicators can be used. The mainstream economics literature commonly utilises standard urban economic indicators measuring, for instance, the performance and volatility of GDP, growth, productivity and unemployment. In that sense, it is argued that poor economic performance (e.g. prolonged recession, high unemployment) or high volatility, or both, is generally associated with increasing levels of economic uncertainty (Brunetti and Weder, 1997, 1998; Kliesen and Ricketts, 2013). From a similar perspective, other researchers utilise composite measures of 'competitiveness' to assess the quality of the urban economic structure in terms of its ability to achieve sustainable growth – mainly by providing a positive environment that enhances the competitiveness of local enterprises (Jiang and Shen, 2010; Ni, 2012; Kresl, 2013). Higher urban competitiveness is identified with lower degrees of structural uncertainty. Other measures of economic uncertainty focus on classifications of 'economic risk' and 'business environment risk', as discussed in Geurts and Jaffe (1996) and Jaffe and Louziotis (1996), or on assessments of 'economic freedom'[21] as developed by the Fraser Institute and the Heritage Foundation – see Appendix III (Gwartney *et al.*, 1996, 2005, 2010, 2013; O'Driscoll *et al.*, 2000; Hall, 2013). It is asserted that high risk in economic or business environments and low scores in economic freedom are associated with institutional environments that exhibit increased levels of uncertainty. More recently, other researchers have devised fairly simple indicators to assess economic uncertainty, such as the frequency of internet searches (Dzielinski, 2012), arguing that in conditions of increased uncertainty agents respond by intensifying their quest for information.

Additionally, assessments of the degree of 'entrepreneurship, innovation and risk-taking behaviour' and the existence, form and organisational structure of underground economic activity ('black markets'), provide an indication of the economic culture and thus a basis for assessing economic uncertainty. Other measures employed highlight the significance of issues such as the diversity of local economic activity and the strength of its local base (i.e. the degree of dependence on international capital and investment activity), as well as the organisational structure of the wider business and financial environment. Particularly with regard to the latter, attention should be focused on the degree of development and sophistication of asset and financial markets (e.g. in terms of actor plurality, variety of financial vehicles and restrictions imposed) and the general performance of the (local) stock market. It is hypothesised that risk-taking behaviour, entrepreneurial and innovative activity, and the complex organisation and development of financial and business-related markets are more likely to occur in environments characterised by relative certainty (EOS Gallup Europe, 2000). In contrast, a high level of black market activity is expected to be positively related with economic uncertainty, at least in regard to formal institutions (Singh *et al.*, 2012).

As regards political uncertainty, Geurts and Jaffe (1996) utilise an index of 'political risk' to capture uncertainty at the political level. Political risk indicates the probability of economic loss due to government actions that could hamper, curtail or preclude investment activities. In addition, political risk assessment considers the possibility of unfair administration, widespread corruption, nationalisation and expropriation threats and, conceivably, even the prospects of political revolution. From a somewhat different perspective, the wider institutional literature (e.g. Ayres, 1962; Tool, 1986; Stanfield, 1999; Henisz, 2000; Arvanitidis and Kyriazis, 2013) highlights the view that political uncertainty can be assessed with reference to the degrees of 'political pluralism' (as indicated, for example, by plurality in political parties) and 'participant democracy', or by paying due attention to issues such as political conflict and the power characteristics of the prevailing socio-political groups (including pressure groups or repressed minorities).[22] It is asserted that low political pluralism and participant democracy or high degrees of political conflict reflect a political context characterised by high uncertainty. Other indicators used to assess the quality of the political structure refer to the 'form and stability of local and national governments' and the degree of 'participation in international blocs', which have been discussed in Brunetti and Weder (1997), Svensson (1998) and Henisz (2000). Political stability and high participation are expected to mirror a political environment of low uncertainty.

Examining uncertainty attributed to the legal environment, indicators consider the strength of 'third party enforcement' and the degree of 'property rights establishment'. On that basis, it can be argued that prevailing variables of 'legal security', 'bribery and corruption', 'arbitrary expropriation' and degree of 'protection of intellectual property rights', which have been discussed in Geurts and Jaffe (1996), constitute appropriate measures of the quality of the legal structure. The legal security (or rule of law), protection of intellectual property rights and arbitrary expropriation variables capture the level of confidence people have that they and their property would be adequately protected. Thus it is suggested that high levels of security and protection and a low likelihood of expropriation are most likely to be associated with lower degrees of uncertainty (Lewis, 1955; Brunetti *et al.*, 1997; Brunetti and Weder, 1997, 1998). The bribery and corruption variable, in turn, signals a weak legal framework and it is hypothesised that high degrees of it are related to increased uncertainty (Shleifer and Vishny, 1993; Hodgson and Jiang, 2007; Lambsdorff, 2007; Goel and Ram, 2013). In addition, another variable that is used to describe legal uncertainty is the 'degree of influence of international law' (e.g. European Union directives), which has been suggested in Keogh and D'Arcy (1994). It is expected that the greater the influence of international law, the greater is the legal certainty.

An alternative way to analyse legal uncertainty has been discussed in Wood and Williams (1992), who argue that the degree of uncertainty attached to the legal structure is related to the type of legal system adopted at the national level (see also Posner, 2004). In particular, it has been asserted that the common law system exhibits lower degrees of uncertainty relative to the civil or codified law systems, as the former provides better protection to investors, stronger law enforcement, shorter durations in the resolution of disputes, is more flexible and is less susceptible to corruption. A number of studies (e.g. Levine and Ahmed, 1998; La Porta *et al.*, 1999; Mahoney, 2001; Djankov *et al.*, 2002) have supported these arguments, whereas others (Joireman, 2004; Graff, 2008) have taken a rather critical stance, asserting that common law countries are not significantly superior in terms of the rule of law.

Measurements of socio-cultural uncertainty can consider qualities such as the strength of 'social values' (e.g. in relation to freedom and equality) and 'work ethics', 'quality of education' and 'quality of life'. It is expected that high levels of these aforementioned qualities would be generally associated with lower levels of socio-cultural uncertainty (Weber, 1930; Ayres, 1962; Granato *et al.*, 1996). In addition, indicators describing 'socio-cultural diversity' (ethnic, linguistic or with reference to religion or faith) can provide some evidence about socio-cultural volatility and uncertainty based on the argument that uncertainty can be generated within cultural diversity if there are 'violent' groups or intense ethnic conflict. Thus cultural diversity without conflict implies lowers uncertainty, whereas cultural diversity and conflict indicate increased uncertainty (Coleman, 1990; Easterly and Levine, 1997). Trust and social capital (Bourdieu, 1986; Coleman, 1990; Putnam, 2000) are other social characteristics used to assess the quality of the socio-cultural environment and its implications for growth (Knack and Keefer, 1997; Zak and Knack, 2001). Trusting societies are expected to be more knowledgeable, more co-operative (due to lower transaction costs) and to exhibit lower degrees of socio-cultural uncertainty (Granovetter, 2005; Nooteboom, 2007; Akcomak, 2008).

b Data collection

The nature of HCIA case research and the essentially qualitative character of institutions imply that mainly qualitative information should be used to guide inquiry on the phenomena under study (Wilber and Harrison, 1978; Dugger, 1979; Wisman and Rozansky, 1991; Stanfield, 1999). However, appropriate quantitative information should also be sought (based on the criteria of data availability and quality) to provide corroborative evidence in support of the developed arguments.

As regards information on the institutional structure of the property market, the available data sources include academic documents, formal studies and other reports about the market, published by the public sector or by private organisations, institutions and property agents. In addition, primary data may also be gathered through field visits to enrich, validate and 'triangulate' this evidence. To that end, direct observation techniques, interviews and focus groups can be used. As regards the first of these, it is argued that its value rests on the assumption that the conditions of the built structures and the observable vigour of property development indicate something about the climate in the economy and the conditions of the property market. As regards interview methods, these should be conducted with relevant experts (e.g. prominent property agents, investors, urban policy-makers, planners or economists) and structured around the set of themes developed earlier in this section (see also Appendix I). Moreover, due to the nature of the concepts under study, it is argued that a more in-depth insight into the topics can be achieved using an open-ended interview structure and following a conversational and informal approach, as these allow the respondents to provide a fresh and detailed commentary on the institutional organisation of the market (May, 1997; Denscombe, 1998).

As to the wider institutional environment, both qualitative and quantitative data can be used to assess the degree of uncertainty it embodies. The urban economics literature, as well as official reports and documents, published by governments, organisations (such as the European Union, the OECD, United Nations Educational, Scientific, and Cultural Organization and the United Nations) and agents, are some of the principal sources for such information. In addition, enrichment and 'triangulation' should be sought using primary data collected through direct observation and interviews with key informants. Once again, the importance of an open-ended, informal and conversational interview structure should be stressed as it enables rich information to be collected.

c Analysis

The analysis consists of inspecting, describing, synthesising, categorising, evaluating or otherwise processing evidence collected from representative cases[23] (Atkinson and Oleson, 1996). The suggested methods consist of an amalgamation of HCIA and case study techniques, where context-specific, historical information is systematically organised, studied, interpreted and compared in an effort to discern a pattern or general explanation that fits both the original case(s) from which information comes, as well as other cases exhibiting similar characteristics (even though their particular details may vary). The aim is to identify the institutional attributes of the property market (through which property outcomes are delivered) and to explore their emergence, development and evolution with reference to wider institutional structures and dynamics. The key to this particular mode of analysis (called pattern modelling or story-telling) is to approach the phenomena under study in a holistic and dynamic fashion, focusing on those critical factors that are most important in explaining the particular issue(s) under consideration.

The point of departure for the analysis is the identification of initial themes exploring the concepts developed in the theoretical framework. The relevant literature provides the basis to develop such analytical themes and specific indicators (see earlier discussion and Appendices I and II) describing the institutional organisation of the property market and the qualities of the overall institutional environment. These are summarised under the umbrella terms 'institutionalised variety' and 'institutional uncertainty', respectively. The next step involves the appraisal and further refinement of the themes[24] on the basis of specific case evidence using HCIA and case research techniques. Here, the analysis could focus separately on each part of the system (i.e. on each institutional structure or on the property market institutions) in an attempt to achieve more polished and precise assessments of the concepts involved. Using logical reasoning, comparisons and contrasts, the original themes should be evaluated and refined. Initial categories might be discarded and others might emerge through synthesis and reorganisation, or on the basis of new, empirically based, evidence.

On the basis of these refined themes, the researcher should then move to consider the linkages and relations between the developed concepts, organising evidence into a coherent whole (i.e. pattern model) and reflecting back on the developed theoretical framework[25] (Dugger, 1979). In this way, the emerging holistic picture of the phenomena will provide the basis for further development, refinement and validation of the general explanatory model. However, as the system is dynamically evolving and new evidence constantly emerging, both the themes and the model should continually be revisited, and revised if necessary, as they can never be either fully completed or entirely confirmed (due to epistemological relativism). Validation in this respect consists of refining and expanding the model further on the basis of empirical evidence and explaining or verifying additional cases (Wilber and Harrison, 1978; Dugger, 1979).

Elaborating more on the analysis of the property market as an institution, it is argued that research should start with a single-case analysis, working on two fronts. The first front should concern an attempt to understand the historical evolution and to specify the current development of the wider urban institutional structures, which, as argued, define the property market process. Such an analysis will also provide a basis for assessing the quality of the overall institutional environment. The second front should comprise an explicit analysis of the institutional organisation of the property market, identifying its current structure and its evolutionary dynamics. In terms of the latter, efforts should be made not simply to point out historical changes and structural breaks, but, more importantly, to understand the causes of these changes and sketch out the process of transformation with reference to the overall path the property market institutions have taken. This is relevant to the concept of 'path dependence', in which initial institutional conditions set the boundaries for manoeuvrability and define the possibilities for subsequent institutional change. Specific techniques applicable here to define causal effects over time are story-telling and chronological (time series) analysis. The former refers to a narrative format in which historical incidents (treated as detailed stories rather than single data points) are connected through qualitative analysis and logical reasoning, whereas the latter defines causality on the basis of chronological sequence. As such, substantial urban events of economic, political and socio-cultural importance should be chronologically arrayed and examined in relation to events and changes that occurred in the institutional configuration of the property market.

In addition to this discussed analysis, the researcher should also explore further the relation between property market institutionalised variety and wider institutional uncertainty. The underlying argument is that the property market is able to respond efficiently to economic imperatives when its institutions are in line with the wider institutional environment. In other words, the institutionalised variety the market develops should correspond to the overall uncertainty that the wider institutional structures carry. A rival idea, introduced by Jones Lang Wootton (1992), is a naive interpretation of the property maturity concept in which property market institutionalised variety only increases in response to economic imperatives, without matching the wider institutional conditions.

To empirically examine the quality of the property market as an institution and its relation to the overall institutional environment, two composite analytical indicators have been developed. The first, referred to as 'institutionalised variety', provides a concise assessment of the institutional structure of the market focusing on the degree of variety its institutional attributes exhibit. It is produced by 'summing up' the individual scores of 'variety' for each institutional aspect of the property market in question. The second, referred to as 'institutional uncertainty', evaluates the conditions and quality of the wider institutional environment (and thus its needs and requirements) in terms of the uncertainty that its structures carry. It is produced by 'summing up' the single uncertainty indicators of each institutional structure.

These composite analytical indicators provide a basis for exploring the evolution of the property market as an institution across time. In particular, and taking into account issues of path dependency, the researcher should examine whether changes in the level of property market institutionalised variety correspond to changes in the level of uncertainty of the wider institutional environment. Story-telling and time series modes of analysis can be used in an attempt to unravel this relationship and understand the evolutionary dynamics of the property market.

In addition to the single-case analyses described so far, a cross-case comparative analysis should also be conducted to draw conclusions in a more holistic manner and to reflect on the developed model that describes the complex relationship between the property market as an institution and the overall institutional environment. The indicators of property market institutionalised variety and the overall urban institutional uncertainty should be examined across cases in this respect, providing a basis for making analytical comparisons identifying which combination of characteristics relate to similar empirical patterns of economic significance. To that end, the discussion may also attempt to reflect on whether a lack or excess of particular institutional aspects has affected the institutional quality of the property market in terms of its ability to respond adequately to economic imperatives and thus enhance urban economic potential. On the basis of the cross-case comparative analysis some trans-historical, trans-cultural or trans-territorial regularities can be identified, leading to the establishment of generalisable conclusions. As in single-case analysis, the available methods here include story-telling and time series techniques.

5.4 Overview and conclusions

Building on the philosophical and theoretical frameworks laid down in Chapter 4, this chapter has explicitly addressed issues of concrete analysis, putting forward an operational agenda for empirical research.

The chapter started by summarising the epistemological and methodological position of the proposed research programme to deploy a generic research framework specifying suitable methods and techniques for investigating the phenomena under study. The methodological approach put forward is interdisciplinary, pluralistic (involving both qualitative and quantitative perspectives) and holistic, but also eclectic and critical. The purpose is not to seek out event regularities from which to claim universal laws, but to corroborate explanations that contribute towards a proper understanding of the causal structures, mechanisms, institutions and their relations.

The HCIA is regarded as the most appropriate approach for this kind of social research. It has been argued that such a combination of historical techniques (to explore the dynamic processes of institutional change) and comparative procedures (to gain insights from different contexts) enables the establishment of theoretical generalisations and the achievement of rich understandings of local institutional contexts. The collection and organisation of information for the HCIA is achieved by means of case research. In interpreting cases and reaching conclusions within the HCIA, the institutionalist techniques of 'story-telling' and 'pattern modelling' are employed, where historical situations are recounted and compared in an effort to discern a wider pattern of relationships. In an attempt to safeguard quality and attain generalisability, appropriate tactics throughout the different stages of the research process have been provided.

Focusing on the particular empirical requirements of this project, the rest of the chapter has set out a specific operational model to translate the developed theory into an agenda for empirical research and practice. On this basis, a research design has been formulated that provides a blueprint for prospective empirical studies. Concrete analysis of urban economic development with the property market in a pivotal role is perceived on two levels. The first examines the robustness of the urban economy, taking into account the external conditions, internal dynamics and property market products that affect its performance. Here the relationship between the urban economy and the property market is explored by examining whether the observed market outcomes match those required by the urban economy. It is asserted that major fluctuations in property market indicators signify a mismatch between the economic demands placed on the property market and those products actually delivered by the market. This suggests a property market which is less credible in providing the appropriate mix of outcomes (both built structures and property rights) that the economy requires at the prevailing price levels (at least in the short to medium term), something which constitutes a threat to urban economic potential.

The second level of analysis focuses on the property market process which is responsible for the actual property outcomes provided, to enrich knowledge of the institutional character of the property market. As the property market institutions are part and product of the overall urban institutional environment, the analysis starts by exploring the characteristics of the latter. In this approach, historical situations (treated as detailed stories) and pivotal incidents are critically analysed to provide a rich understanding of the evolutionary dynamics and current development of urban institutional structures. Their quality is assessed in terms of institutional uncertainty. The institutional characteristics of the property market are then examined and their evolution and current structure explored with reference to the wider institutional environment. An attempt is then made to understand the causes of institutional change and to sketch out the process of transformation with reference to current dynamics, past tendencies and the overall path that the property market institutions have taken. The quality of the property market as an institution is assessed in terms of institutionalised variety. Such analysis provides the basis to explore further the relation between the property market as an institution and the wider institutional environment and to reflect on the emergence, development and evolutionary dynamics of the market.

In detailing the second level design, the chapter proceeded with the operationalisation of the developed concepts of institutionalised variety and institutional uncertainty and a thorough discussion of the types of information that need to be acquired, as well as possible methods that can be used for data collection, analysis and interpretation. On this basis, a wide range of explanatory aspects of both the broad institutional environment and the property market institutional characteristics have been identified (from the relevant literature), reflecting on the nature and extent of institutional uncertainty and institutionalised variety, respectively. These provide a general resource for reference and guidance in approaching empirical instances, acting as a means of uncovering the variety of forms that the phenomena under study can assume.

Notes

1 Lewis (2011) illustrates this issue by drawing on the quantity theory of money. He argues that a series of financial innovations in the early 1980s led to fluctuations in the amount of money that people in the UK wanted to hold and, as a result, the empirical direct relationship between money supply and the price level (i.e. the quantity theory of money) proved to be highly unstable. In critical realist terms, these financial innovations disturbed the (intrinsically open) economic system upsetting the "most robust of economic event regularities" (Steele, 2005: 147).

2 In mainstream consumer theory, closure is introduced with the *homo economicus* hypothesis (Lawson, 1997a). This postulates that individuals have given preferences (they have only one intrinsic state), that a unique utility maximum is feasible (there is only one possible outcome for each internal state) and that society consists of a single representative individual (with a Gorman form indirect utility faction).

3 Lawson (1997a) uses the metaphor of a football game to illustrate the point. Isolation, he argues, is like zooming in on one (individual) player and omitting all the others and their interactions (the background context). Such analysis might enable the prediction of certain actions (e.g. whether or not a goal would be scored), but is insufficient to provide a proper understanding of the game and its key aspects. These can be achieved through abstraction, which, while focusing on a single player, simultaneously acknowledges the contextual background and the system's openness (both extrinsically, in recognising the interactions between the players, and intrinsically, in distinguishing the motivations of the individual player).

4 Note that such similarity or analogy should not necessarily be factually accurate (or proved not to be thereafter). A stable referential link can be established and sustained as long as the relevant scientific community accepts its veracity, even in the face of significant changes in the corpus of scientific theory (Lewis, 1996).

5 As an illustration, consider the case of the demand curve. For critical realists it represents a graphical heuristic that captures the transfactual tendency of demand, without denoting a strict negative relationship between price and quantity. Under this transfactual understanding, an observed event of a higher price and higher quantity (Veblen good) would be interpreted as the result of background noise or countervailing powers (e.g. institutional/cultural characteristics).

6 This, however, does not imply that a hypothesis about a mechanism and the outcome that it could produce can be rejected simply because expected empirical patterns are not observed (Sayer, 1992; Dow, 2002). Theories make their claims at the abstract level about causal powers that exist by virtue of the 'intrinsic nature' or 'real essence' of structures. These powers may or may not be exercised or actualised. In these terms, a case is made for further investigation in terms of countervailing tendencies and contingent conditions (Lawson, 1997a).

7 Adding to the example of the demand curve mentioned earlier, an observed event of a positive partial relationship between price and quantity, seen in contrast to the expected pattern represented by a typical, negatively sloped, demand curve, would surprise the researcher, urging them to seek explanations and to hypothesise mechanisms hitherto unnoticed. It is in this respect that Veblen (1899) pointed out issues of social power and prestige (conspicuous consumption) and Akerlof (1970) highlighted problems of information asymmetry and adverse selection.

8 In these cases in which the causal explanations provided are in competition, judgemental rationality (see earlier) should be employed, where competing theories would be assessed on the basis of their relative explanatory power (Lawson, 1997a, 1999).

9 Such an approach is supported by both institutionalists (e.g. Veblen, 1898a; Myrdal, 1958, 1970; Miller, 1978; Dugger, 1979; Samuels, 1990; Hodgson, 1998a; Hulsen, 1998) and critical realists (e.g. Sayer, 1992, 2000; Pratt, 1995; Lawson, 1997a, 1999, 2003; Yeung, 1997; Downward, 2003).

10 Institutionalists (e.g. Miller, 1978; Dugger, 1979; Lind, 1993; Luker *et al.*, 1998; Stanfield, 1999; Sugiura, 1999; Williamson, 2000; Ostrom, 2007; Chinitz, 2013) and realists alike (e.g. Sayer, 1992, 2000; Yeung, 1997; Pinkstone, 2002; Davidsen, 2010) support such a viewpoint.

11 Although, traditionally, quantitative approaches are linked to positivism and qualitative approaches to humanism and behavioural social sciences, such an idealised methodological dichotomy is rarely reproduced in actual empirical practice. For instance, references to hypothesis, testing, generalisations and regularities abound throughout the qualitative research literature. From the same perspective, other researchers (e.g. Brannen, 1992; Bryman, 1992, 2001; Creswell, 1994; Philip, 1998) have argued that linkages between methodology and epistemology should not be viewed as strict and that epistemology should inform rather than dictate methodological choices. On that basis, the combination of qualitative and quantitative approaches is regarded as perfectly legitimate methodological practice, especially for the consideration of complex social phenomena.

12 According to Yin (2003), the use of triangulation in social sciences is exactly analogous to that in geometry (i.e. to define a point in space with the convergence of measurements taken from two other distinct points). This process of cross-checking different kinds and sources of evidence serves as a means of 'contextual validation' and evaluation of "the plausibility of one's initial interpretations" (see Wilber and Harrison, 1978: 76; Dugger, 1979: 905). For an analogous discussion on triangulation from the critical realist perspective, see Yeung (1997) and, to a lesser extent, Sayer (1992).

13 Of course, initial conceptualisations may change as the research progresses.

14 A similar approach is also evident in realist research (see Sayer, 1992, 2000; Pratt, 1995; Yeung, 1997; Jones and Murphy, 2010).

15 In this sense, generalisability requires a degree of invariance (or 'closure') in the world.

16 However, care should be taken in making claims of cases being members of wider populations (Bryman, 2001). This, Downward *et al.* (2002) argue, applies equally to positivist research, which nevertheless generally presumes that the characteristics of a population are well understood such that samples can be drawn in an unproblematic way.
17 Its significance has been acknowledged by both institutionalists (e.g. Wilber and Harrison, 1978; Dugger, 1979) and critical realists (e.g. Yeung, 1997; Downward *et al.*, 2002).
18 Some scholars (e.g. Neuman, 1994) refer to this technique as 'successive approximation'.
19 Support for the argument comes from a variety of sources. In fact, both the urban economic and property market literatures assert that steeply rising or falling rents (or other property market indicators) constitute threats for the economy (because they reveal that there is too little or too much space available, respectively), whereas stable rents indicate a well functioning property market, attuned to current property requirements and supportive of urban economic potential (Royal Institution of Charted Surveyors, 1994; Ball *et al.*, 1996, 1998; Ball and Wood, 1996; D'Arcy and Keogh, 1997; Jensen-Butler *et al.*, 1997; Henneberry, 1999; Henneberry and Rowley, 2000; Gibb and Hoesli, 2003; Peng *et al.*, 2008; Kim, 2011).
20 However, it is important to acknowledge that space for other interpretations has to be allowed when dealing with these kinds of features (i.e. socio-cultural).
21 Economic freedom is defined as the absence of constraints in the economic system beyond the provision of institutions necessary for citizens to protect and maintain liberty itself (Gwartney *et al.*, 1996; O'Driscoll *et al.*, 2000).
22 Researchers acknowledge that, although political institutions do matter for growth, it is unclear whether classification in terms of democratic or authoritarian regimes can capture the relevant difference (Przeworski and Limongi, 1993; Alesina and Rodrik, 1994).
23 As discussed earlier, theoretical and purposive sampling provides the basis for the choice of the particular cases following the 'replication' logic. A single case study, however, may also be used (Sproull and Tamuz, 1999).
24 Note, however, that this should be understood as a continuous process, taking place not only in data analysis, but also in the data collection stage.
25 Although this process differs from that put forward by some original institutionalists (e.g. Wilber and Harrison, 1978), Dugger (1979) legitimises such a research approach on the basis that it has been followed by Veblen and other leading institutionalists. He notes, for example, that Veblen himself first constructed an essentially theoretical pattern model describing the pecuniary–predatory canons of conduct under modern capitalism (Veblen, 1899, 1904) and subsequently he elaborated, tested and extended it through specific case studies (Veblen, 1918a, 1918b).

6 Overview and conclusions

6.1 The trajectory of the inquiry

This book has explored the operation of the property market, arguing that it acts as a mediator through which urban economic potential can be realised and served. To understand the pivotal role that the property market plays in this process it is essential to consider not only the market outcomes, but also the market institutions which give rise to them. It is these institutions which, inter alia, define property rights, specify property values, stimulate property development, allocate uses, generate information, regulate transactions and generally determine the ability of the urban economy to provide those property outcomes (both built structures and property rights) that are necessary for economic development. This is the basis for claiming that the book contributes significantly to the development of a holistic research programme to conceptualise the property market as an institution and to adequately explore its position within the urban economy.

Although urban and regional economics have long been acknowledged as an independent discipline with a substantial research activity, few studies have examined the effect the built environment has on local development, and even fewer have explored the role the property market plays in this process. Clearly, the nature of inquiry and the questions posed depend on the theoretical viewpoint adopted. Mainstream urban economic approaches assign primary explanatory power to the law of supply and demand, assuming that it operates in a more or less efficient way to bring the urban system into a state of equilibrium. From this perspective, emphasis is placed on the demand side of the urban economy, whereas the supply-side conditions are seen as relatively unproblematic. As such, the built environment is regarded as relatively malleable and the property market as a passive adapter to urban change. By taking this stance, mainstream economics largely neglects any property-related factors in urban economic organisation and change, thus failing to provide a satisfactory explanation of the mechanisms and processes through which the built environment is provided and (perhaps more importantly) of the way it affects the urban economy.

Structuralist approaches, in turn, give explanatory primacy to the inherent contradictions and overall dynamics of the capitalist system, assigning a functional role to the built environment. Urban outcomes are perceived to emerge out of a complex dialectical interaction between agency and structure in the light of the economic, political and social contradictions and conflicts that materialise in the urban scene. Some of the determinants of this process are structural, linked to deep trends that prescribe the socio-political evolution of capitalism (as emphasised by Marxist and regulation theories); some are historically and culturally specific (as indicated in the recent writings of Castells and Soja), whereas others are related to 'contingent' events and 'contextual' interpretations of individual agents (as highlighted by the realist and structuration theories). These approaches have been attacked on many grounds, including their deterministic or teleological explanation of the urban dynamics, their functionalist treatment of the built environment and their undue stress on either structure or agency. In addition, none of them has managed to incorporate the complex (institutional) nature of the property market into its analysis of the provision of the built environment and to carry this analysis into an integrated urban economic theory. This results in the dynamics and processes of the property market operation, as well as its relation to urban transformation, remaining largely unexplored.

Institutional economics sets forth an evolutionary, holistic and socio-cultural approach to urban transformation, in which considerable explanatory power is ascribed to the institutional set up (described in economic, political, legal, social and cultural terms) and the associated organisational frame (described in terms of individual actors, organisations and networks). Viewed thus, the urban socio-economy is seen as a complex, open-ended and dynamically evolving system, which is constantly reproduced and transformed by purposeful, but bounded-rational human agency in an attempt to reconcile external pressures and internal (conflict-oriented) dynamics. The potential for urban economic success rests on the 'conductivity' of the institutional configuration developed and its ability to anticipate and flexibly adapt to changing conditions and circumstances. A part and product of the institutional context is the property market itself, which, on its own terms, affects the potential for urban economic development. As such, and in contrast to all other economic approaches, the complex institutional and evolutionary character of the property market is recognised and its role in explaining urban economic transformation is explicitly acknowledged.

It is evident from the preceding discussion that institutional economics is the approach best qualified to analyse the property market process and provide a comprehensive theory of urban development, placing the property market in a central position. However, two major areas of knowledge deficiency have been identified. The first concerns the specific characteristics, relations, mechanisms and dynamics of the property market as an institution, calling for further theoretical development before effective empirical research can be undertaken. The second reflects the fact that institutionalist research has been informed by a wide range of philosophical and analytical standpoints, necessitating the provision of an explicit ontological, epistemological and methodological perspective from which a clear research agenda for concrete analysis can be defined.

In this situation, the broad aim of this project was to lay down a holistic research programme that advances the understanding of the property market as an institution and explores its role in the process of urban economic development. To meet this aim, specific objectives have been identified and addressed:

1 to establish an appropriate philosophical framework that advances institutionalist understanding of both the wider urban socio-economic dynamics and the specific mechanisms through which the built environment is provided;
2 to develop a specific methodological framework, including the development of new theory, within which to consider the operation of the property market as an institution and to explore its contribution to urban economic development; and
3 to formulate a generic research approach indicating the appropriate methods and techniques of investigation and a specific operational model with a research design that provides a blueprint for empirical study.

The rest of this chapter is devoted to a discussion about how these objectives have been accomplished. In particular, the next section provides an overview of the philosophical position and the theoretical framework developed, critically discussing the arguments put forward and assessing their significance. The following section revisits the analytical framework and associated research design to evaluate their strengths and weaknesses and to point out possible deficiencies and limitations in any prospective application. Finally, the chapter concludes by assessing the importance of the research programme developed and provides directions for further research.

6.2 The conceptual framework: philosophical tenets and theoretical developments

The salient achievements of this study are: first, the establishment of a robust philosophical basis within which the institutional analysis of the property market can be carried out; and, second, the formulation of a new theory that advances the understanding of the institutional nature of the property market process and explores its role in urban economic development. Such a framework, however, cannot be developed *ex nihilo*. Knowledge can only be a produced means of cognition, in which more informed understanding is achieved via the revision, update and reorganisation of existing conceptions and insights on the basis of their inter-compatibility, intelligibility, consistency and practical adequacy to the task in hand. As such, the provision of the philosophical and theoretical foundations on which a sound framework can be built requires the evaluation of both the philosophical world views in the social sciences and the methodological approaches in economics, as well as a distillation of the key conceptual elements of institutionalist thought.

The four most prominent philosophical approaches in the social sciences are empiricism, positivism, humanism and structuralism. In assessing their world views, empiricism has been rejected for its lack of explanatory and analytical power. Positivism has been rejected for the mechanistic, ahistorical, law-like theoretical explanations it provides and humanism has been rejected for its excessive emphasis on human agency at the expense of other social and structural considerations. Structuralist philosophical approaches, on the other hand, particularly those that have managed to overcome structural determinism by infusing arguments of human intentionality and purposeful behaviour into their theorisation, have been appreciated for their ability to deploy a sound philosophical basis for social and economic analysis. Among these, critical realism stands out by virtue of its ontological substance that enables a clear differentiation of 'structure' from 'agency'.

These philosophical approaches dictate the analytical frameworks developed in economics. Generally, three major frameworks are recognised: the mainstream, the structuralist and the institutionalist. Mainstream orthodoxy is largely associated with the neoclassical school of economics, informed by a positivist philosophical approach. The school, despite the remarkable resilience and adaptability to criticism which has enabled it to dominate economic thought for more than a century, has exhibited severe weaknesses stemming from the unrealistic core assumptions[1] it espouses, its deterministic and ahistorical world view, and the distinction between facts and values with the (alleged) rejection of the latter from its agenda.

With respect to the heterodox approaches, a number of economic schools draw on structuralist philosophical arguments, among which are Marxism, neo-Marxism, structuration and critical realism. Marxists and neo-Marxists have provided some valuable insights with regard to economic organisation, but have been challenged on a number of points, particularly for a deterministic, mechanistic and teleological view of historical processes and dynamics, and for what critics see as a naive, rationalistic and utilitarian understanding of human agency. The latter criticism has led structurationists and critical realists alike to develop conceptual frameworks within which the nature and role of human agency can be properly addressed, but their lack of a coherent theoretical perspective to economic matters raises concerns about their ability to define a clear agenda for applied research in economics. Critical realism, however, has been appreciated for its role as 'under-labourer', i.e. its ability to inform economic inquiry by providing a wider philosophical platform compatible with a variety of different theoretical interpretations.

Turning to institutional economics, it became clear that the school comprises a heterogeneous group of approaches united by a common set of beliefs emphasising 'institutions' as the most important determinants of economic organisation that should not be taken as exogenous to the economic system. However, although the concept of the institution has been used to convey the idea that people's expectations, actions and conceptions of the world are shaped by, and reflect, both humanly devised rules and regularities of human behaviour, the word itself has never enjoyed a precise meaning. An exploration of the different strands of thought within the school reveals that institutionalist research has been (and can be) informed by various (different, but largely commensurable) philosophical positions and analytical standpoints. In this sense the institutionalist 'paradigm' can be seen as a 'frame' or 'shell' embracing a variety of compatible approaches, theories and conceptual tools brought together on the basis of their efficacy in examining the institutional environment.

Dissecting the nuances of institutionalist thought identifies three major strands: the neo-institutionalist, the new institutionalist and the original (old) institutionalist. Neo-institutionalists effectively graft institutional content onto mainstream economics, without, however, questioning the core assumptions or the philosophical bases of the latter. Their approach to economic analysis places emphasis on the study of the costs associated with the exchange of resources and the organisation of an institutional framework that defines the property rights of individuals over resources.

New institutionalists, though positivist in essence, attempt a more fundamental methodological departure, challenging the mainstream assumptions of rational economic man and long-run equilibria. By incorporating an analysis of transaction costs, property rights and bounded rationality, they argue that the function of institutions and their organisational structure is to provide a secure and orderly environment, enabling interaction and co-operation between economic actors and the enhancement of economic potential. What develops, however, depends on the initial institutional arrangements, the power relations between actors and the capability of the system to adjust flexibly to changing conditions and circumstances.

Original institutionalists criticise both neo- and new institutionalists for their reluctance, first, to reject the full set of mainstream economic assumptions and, second, to take into appropriate consideration the cultural and social context within which institutions emerge and evolve. Drawing on pragmatist philosophical arguments, they stress the socio-cultural character of economic relations, putting forward an agenda for a holistic and societal approach. The economy, they argue, is a complex, constantly evolving open-ended system in dynamic interaction with the cultural, social, political, legal and physical levels of reality. As such, original institutionalists view economic processes as embedded in social relations, agents' behaviour as socially and culturally driven, and the socio-economy as an integrated system. In this context, institutions play complex and multiple roles, not only constraining agent behaviour, but also providing a cognitive framework through which information is interpreted and transformed into meaningful knowledge.

Building on such a knowledge base, it becomes possible to develop a framework that advances the conceptualisation of the institutional structure of the urban system and enriches understanding of the complex interrelation between economy, institutional environment and property market institutions. To achieve this, key elements from both new and original institutional economics are combined and integrated within the philosophical platform of critical realism. As indicated, critical realism presents advantages over the other philosophical perspectives in discussing the institutional organisation of the urban socio-economy. These mainly stem from its ontological arguments that allow the dissociation of the institutional structure from human agency and acknowledge the separate identity and causal powers of institutions without undermining their agent-dependent nature. This is important because it enables a neat identification and analysis of the institutional qualities, mechanisms, causal powers and relations that characterise the urban fabric in general and the property market process in particular. Moreover, the fact that the realist ontology is compatible with a variety of economic theories renders its fusion with institutionalism generally both valid and feasible.

In delineating the realist philosophical arguments, six fundamental premises about social reality were emphasised. In concise terms these are:

1 the 'intransitivity' of social structures, i.e. the argument that structures, institutions and mechanisms exist independently of their identification and knowledge of which they are the object;
2 the 'stratification' of the social world, i.e. the differentiation of social reality into distinct domains, or strata, which, although unsynchronised, are interconnected with one another;
3 the 'transfactuality' of generative qualities, i.e. the argument that mechanisms are always active, independent of whether they are being exercised, actualised or perceived;
4 the 'relational conception of the subject matter of the social sciences', i.e. the argument that all social entities presuppose a social context and depend on social relations for their existence;
5 the 'transformational model of social activity', i.e. the argument that social reality possesses a non-teleologically evolving character by virtue of the agents' potential to re-interpret, and collectively reproduce and transform, the structures they utilise and are shaped (constrained/enabled) by;
6 the 'temporal priority and separate identity of structure over agency', i.e. the argument that at any moment in time social structures pre-exist the individuals who do not create them, but merely reproduce or transform them in their substantive activities.

These philosophical principles provided the basis for the development of a stratified ontological framework discussing the institutional organisation of the urban socio-economy. In particular, a three-layer, interlocked reality has been identified describing the complexity, multidimensionality and dynamic character of the socio-economic world. It was argued that deeper tendencies, capacities, 'instincts' and qualities of the human essence (understood as 'creativity', 'emulation', 'habituation' and 'culture') condition the institutional environment (differentiated in economic, political, legal and social terms), which, in turn, constitutes the terrain on which organisational arrangements are manifested and socio-economic events are actualised. In these terms, institutions were defined as ingrained regularities or established rules of human life that, by moulding agents' perception, thought and behaviour, provide certainty and order in social interaction and economic organisation.

In unveiling the nature and essence of institutions, a number of qualifications apply. Institutions are the products of human agency, meaning that they exist, are reproduced and are transformed by virtue of it. Yet neither element can be reduced to, or conflated, with the other. The fact that each individual is generally born into, and moulded by, a world of pre-set institutions proclaims the temporal priority (i.e. pre-existence), relative autonomy and causal efficacy of institutions over human agency. On that basis, the ontological (and epistemological) separability of institutions and human agents is recognised, placing institutions in a distinct layer of reality with its own emergent properties and qualities. Once institutions are in place and acted upon, they come to endure merely through being an outcome of the day-to-day activities of individuals 'going on' in life. In that sense they are characterised by relative stability, continuity and self-reinforcement. However, institutions are not immutable; they are human-made and changeable. In fact, institutions seem to evolve in a relatively slow, but dynamic and, apparently, incremental fashion, a process characterised by 'cumulative causation' and 'path dependence'. It is on this basis that institutional change is seen as a natural, never-ending evolutionary process, where old institutions are dismantled and new ones developed in the continuous process of adaptation to the changing experiences, exigencies and circumstances of human life. Yet such a conception does not imply any economically efficient, deterministic or teleological view with regard to institutional evolution. This is because it is human agency (characterised by variety in 'rationality' and behaviour, as well as limited computational and mental ability) in relation to other 'contingently related conditions' (such as unpredictable events and shocks) that plays a decisive role in shaping the course of institutional change.

Developing such an institutionalist understanding made it possible to formulate a rich theory of urban economic organisation and change, placing explicit emphasis on both the wider institutional environment and the specific institutional mechanisms, processes and dynamics through which the built environment is provided. The main argument is that pressures for economic change and development are mediated through the overall urban institutional framework.[2] In this sense, alongside the wider external circumstances and conditions, it is the economic, political, legal and socio-cultural institutional structures of the locality that define the course and performance of the economy. Part and product of that institutional environment is the property market itself, defined as a set of institutions concerned with the 'provision of the built environment'.[3] In particular, it comprises a wide network of (formal and informal) rules, rights, norms, practices, conventions, cognitive frameworks, mechanisms and relationships through which property is defined, generated, used and exchanged. In this way, the property market as an institution acts as a filter for economic adjustment by delivering (or not) what the urban economy requires in terms of property (land, built structures and property rights and interests).

This institutional definition of the property market gives rise to a number of insights. First, the property market as an institution has an ingrained social and dynamic character. This emphasises the socio-cultural aspect of the market process (and of property in general, e.g. related to issues of status and symbolism), but recognises the market's continuously evolving nature (by virtue of changing circumstances and local responses). On this basis, it is possible to understand why property market institutions vary from one locality to another, or from one time period to another. Second, the property market, like all institutional structures, does not exist in a power vacuum. It takes shape in a setting circumscribed by considerations of 'workability' and 'efficiency', alongside material scarcity, uncertainty, sovereign authority, power relations and vested interests. Third, it is essential to emphasise the cognitive dimension of the market. Such institutions not only impose constraints and barriers to human agency and interaction, but also have an enabling function. They colour agents' perception and judgement, providing a conceptual framework for the generation, interpretation and transmission of information, the formation of preferences and expectations, and the moulding of their behaviour. Fourth, the analytical separation of the property market from the wider institutional environment is deemed essential to understand and study its institutional qualities, but does not imply that the property market as an institution should be seen as a segregated entity. In short, it is argued that the property market, although having an independent 'persona' to be studied, cannot be examined in the absence of the wider institutional context from which it emerges and with which it interacts.

The issue of how effectively the property market operates in providing an appropriate mix of outcomes so that urban economic potential is enhanced raises questions regarding the 'efficiency' of the market. Building on the conceptualisation outlined so far, a new institutionalist approach to market efficiency has been developed, called 'property market purpose efficiency'. The argument started by challenging the conventional measures of property market efficiency. It was argued that both allocative efficiency across the property market as a whole, and the narrower treatment of informational efficiency in the investment market, provide flawed and ambiguous judgements of market efficiency. This is because: first, they assess efficiency with reference to idealised benchmarks (Pareto optimality and full information); second, they do not take into account the intrinsic characteristics[4] and dynamic process of the property market; and third; they are artificially dissociated from important operational issues.

Institutionalist attempts to articulate more refined and pragmatic conceptualisations of property market efficiency (mainly those of van der Krabben and Keogh and D'Arcy), though remaining methodologically underdeveloped and incomplete, have provided useful insights. Three important conclusions were drawn. First, as the property market structure emerges out of dominant economic and social interests, an appropriate response to market efficiency requires reference to an explicit value or focus criterion. Thus, instead of trying to seek a judgement on whether the property market as a whole is efficient, the assessment of market efficiency should be constructed with reference to 'efficiency for a purpose' or 'efficiency for a person'. Second, emphasis was shifted from property products to the property market process, while the central question became how well that process works in terms of a specific objective or from the viewpoint of a particular group of actors. Third, a dynamic approach was introduced, suggesting the need to assess the adaptability of the property market process as economic, political, legal and social conditions change. Expanding on these arguments, the efficiency of the property market has been approached here with reference to the accomplishment of a particular purpose, i.e. the achievement and maintenance of urban economic potential. This addresses the purpose efficiency of the property market as the 'effectiveness', 'serviceability' or 'credible commitment' of the market in providing those outcomes that the urban economy requires. In short, an efficient property market is expected to deliver an appropriate mix of property (at the prevailing price levels) that meets the requirements placed upon it.

In an attempt to avoid possible misconceptions regarding property market purpose efficiency, it is important to point out a number of general qualifications. First, property market purpose efficiency is a necessary, but not sufficient, condition for the realisation of economic potential. Other factors alongside the property market intervene in, and affect in various degrees and directions, the course of the urban economy. Second, the notion of property market purpose efficiency does not prescribe a specific institutional configuration. It provides, however, a conceptual point of reference to determine whether 'problematic' property market institutions exist and, if so, gives directions for their revision. However, it is inevitable that any subsequent institutional transformation will, of course, advance some interests and undermine others. Third, the concept of property market purpose efficiency takes into appropriate consideration the structural peculiarities and idiosyncratic imperfections of the market and puts forward a conceptual benchmark that is realistic, pragmatic and feasible. In this sense, a property market can be purpose efficient even in the inevitable presence of high transaction costs and information deficiencies, which are conventionally seen as the classic causes of market failure. Finally, conceptualising the property market as part and product of the wider institutional environment implies that property market purpose efficiency should be viewed holistically. In this sense, the purpose efficiency of the property market is conceptualised in terms of the ability of the market to develop such institutional mechanisms and qualities as the overall urban institutional environment allows and requires.

Clearly, further development of the notion of property market purpose efficiency requires reflection on the function and qualities of the institutional structures. This line of reasoning starts by acknowledging the open-ended, dynamic and contingent nature of socio-economic reality, the limited computational and perceptual ability of the human mind, and the purposeful and potentially 'irrational' nature of human behaviour, all of which are held responsible for the ubiquitous and inherent 'uncertainty' that characterises economic reality and life as a whole. In this context, 'workable' institutions are those that provide a sound basis for perception, expectation and decision-making and, therefore, predictability and certainty in human affairs, while also being able to adapt flexibly to changing conditions and exigencies. To achieve this, institutional structures need to sustain a balance between institutional stability and certainty on the one hand,

and flexibility and adaptability on the other. Translating this conceptualisation to the subject matter of this study, two theoretical devices have been developed: 'institutional uncertainty' and 'institutionalised variety'. Institutional uncertainty assesses the quality of the wider (urban) institutional arrangements[5] and reflects how effectively the urban socio-economy adapts to external pressures, resolves internal incongruities and provides a secure economic environment. Institutionalised variety evaluates particular institutions, in this case the property market, in terms of diversity and plurality in mechanisms, processes, organisation and products provided. It is argued that this affords the market with the necessary flexibility, diversity and manoeuvrability without reducing the overall institutional certainty and stability. Such a micro-level variety is deemed necessary both for the system to reproduce itself over time and for macro-dynamics to be successfully sustained. Thus macroeconomic order and relative stability are reinforced alongside, and arise from, variety and diversity at the micro-level.

Putting the arguments together, property market purpose efficiency is understood with reference to the market's ability to match 'institutionalised variety' to the level of 'institutional uncertainty' that the wider urban institutional environment carries. Less institutionalised variety creates undesirable rigidity in the property market process, constraining its ability to provide the required property outcomes and thus weakening urban economic potential. Similarly, the achievement and maintenance of excessive institutionalised variety is also detrimental to the economy as it incurs unnecessary costs and complexity, undermining the requisite level of certainty and flexibility.

The strength and novelty of property market purpose efficiency reside on its ability to view property market efficiency in both holistic and dynamic terms. The former highlights the fact that property market institutions are part and product of the overall institutional environment, demanding that any comprehensive discussion on efficiency should take these issues into account. The latter introduces a time dimension, arguing that pressures for change are filtered through the institutional environment, determining the evolutionary dynamics of the property market and its potential for adaptation. A property market that is truly purpose efficient over time should be able to adapt its institutionalised variety in line with changes in the wider institutional uncertainty. Yet the property market as an institution carries a strong path dependency and 'lock-in', where the scope for change is constrained by its existing institutional complexity. This situation becomes more complicated when power relations, vested interests and the 'bounded' rationality (due to limited information on the costs and benefits of choices, as well as to the incapability of the human mind) of various market players are taken into account. From all this a number of important questions arise: will market adjustment take place; how quickly; and what things have to happen to allow it to occur? The adopted position is that market possibilities (purpose efficiency) and the current institutional aspects of the market (realised institutionalised variety) become contextualised, necessitating solutions that are political in nature and lie in the hands of politicians or other power brokers.

Closing this section, a final point should be made. The arguments developed here with regard to the property market can be extended to efficiency debates regarding other markets. Overall, this institutionalist approach advances the concept and analysis of efficiency, not only for markets which are generally seen as less efficient (e.g. the labour market), but even for those expected to exhibit high levels of efficiency (conventionally understood), such as the equity market.

6.3 From philosophical principles to a research design

The philosophical framework that the study adopts has not only ontological, but also epistemological and methodological implications. Its epistemological perspective indicates that although real structures, powers and mechanisms exist independently of the way they are manifested or experienced, the only way to understand and express them is through 'human mediation in cognitive discourse'. On this account, the objective for any social inquiry is to (re)define and refine conceptual resources in an attempt to reveal, specify and improve understanding of the structures, institutions and mechanisms, and the ways in which they (inter-)act in a seemingly open and intrinsically dynamic and interrelated social world for events and states of affairs to be properly explained. In turn, the methodological strategy that is put forward regards theoretical conceptualisations, applied explanations and empirical research as interlinked. Research is based on the formulation of a theoretical framework (using abstraction and metaphor) where underlying structures, causal mechanisms and essential relations are identified with regard to the particular object of study. Applied research is also involved where the operation and effects of the causal powers are identified and examined in specific, actual situations, determining whether these powers are being 'possessed unexercised, exercised un-actualized, or actualized undetected'. Analysis at this stage is based on the identification of empirical tendencies, represented as demi-regs and contrastives, which are deemed to be meaningful manifestations of the effects of causal mechanisms. Proposed explanations are therefore reviewed and assessed in a reflexive, progressive and essentially iterative manner and, when found to be theoretically consistent and pragmatically adequate (i.e. empirically realised or correspondent to reality),[6] they are accepted as valuable parts in the continuous unfolding of explanatory knowledge.

Translating this analytical mode to applicable methods and techniques of investigation, a holistic and pluralistic, but also critical and eclectic, research approach has been espoused, combining both qualitative and quantitative perspectives.[7] The purpose is not to seek out event regularities from which to claim universal laws, but to corroborate explanations that contribute towards a proper understanding of the causal structures, mechanisms, institutions and their relations. As these causal entities are contextual and historical in their realisation, understanding in this context refers to the process of constructing a unified system and identifying the role of the entities in the system and in the ongoing process of evolutionary change. In these terms, and due to difficulties in quantifying essentially qualitative variables such as institutions, research relies less heavily on statistical techniques, emphasising the use of HCIA. The collection and organisation of information for HCIA is achieved by means of the case study method.

The HCIA case research employs historical techniques to explore the dynamic processes of emergence, evolution and organisation of institutional structures, and comparative procedures to gain insights from different contexts. It is characterised by an ability to shift between a specific context and a general comparison, something which enables it to combine sensitivity to particular historical and cultural contexts with theoretical generalisations. In interpreting cases and reaching conclusions within HCIA case research, the institutionalist techniques of 'story-telling' and 'pattern modelling' are used, where historical situations are recounted and compared in an effort to define a wider pattern of relationships in a holistic manner.

In an attempt to safeguard quality, appropriate strategies throughout the different stages of the research process have been provided. It is important, however, to bear in mind the limitations and weaknesses that the approach entails. By virtue of its essentially qualitative and holistic nature, research relies on analytical description and emphasis on the context. On the surface, some of the detail may appear irrelevant and, indeed, there is a risk of the researcher becoming too embroiled in descriptive detail. However, a fairly detailed account of what goes on in the setting being investigated is important because it provides a rich and contextual understanding of the institutional attributes and dynamics. In that sense, institutional aspects and changes that may initially appear inconsistent can make perfect sense when the wider context within which they occur is taken into consideration.

Another problem relates to the vast amount of information (both qualitative and quantitative) that is required for the examination of the phenomena under question. This, in addition to questions of information availability that may arise, attaches a subjective element to the research. Inevitably, the researcher inquires, selects and focuses on specific aspects of socio-politico-economic life and their findings may rely heavily on their views about what is significant and essential. In this context, what signifies 'objectivity' is an explicit statement of the value judgements used and the commitment to keeping the path of inquiry open and subject to the identification and correction of errors.

Another particularly important issue refers to whether it is possible to generalise the findings of the research across different societies and contexts. In general terms, empirically established knowledge of the causal powers and essential qualities of a mechanism (here, the relations, dynamics and effects of the property market institutions) is more widely applicable to other cases that represent similar theoretical conditions. Therefore it follows that generalisability is not a matter of 'statistical generalisation' (generalising from samples to the population), but a matter of 'analytic generalisation', in which examined cases are used to illustrate, represent and generalise a theory. This means that 'verified' causal/structural explanations are expected to apply to the majority of similar cases, although the particular details of the context being examined might be too specific and could, on their own terms, hardly form part of a generally applicable theory or a description of the phenomenon in general terms.

Turning to the particular requirements for concrete analysis of the property market, a specific research design has been laid down. In particular, a two-level operational model has been provided, translating the developed theory into an agenda for empirical research. At the first level, urban economic transformation is analysed and the relationship between urban economic and property market outcomes is explored, reflecting on whether the observed market outcomes match those required by the urban economy. It is asserted that major fluctuations in property market outcomes signify a mismatch between the demand for property, coming from the urban economy, and the actual supply of property (in terms of both built structures and property rights), provided by the market. This suggests a property market which, at least in the short to medium term, is less capable of providing what the economy requires at the prevailing price level, something which constitutes a threat to urban economic potential. Investigation starts with 'exploratory data analysis', where economic and property market outcomes are descriptively analysed in an attempt to identify and picture the broad patterns of economic and property market dynamics. Subsequently, this relationship is explored further using formal statistical methods corroborated by qualitative analytical techniques allowing for discretion in the interpretation of the data.

The second level of analysis focuses on the property market process, which is held responsible for the actual property outcomes provided, to enrich knowledge on the property market as an institution and its ability to enhance urban economic potential. As the property market institutions are part and product of the overall urban institutional environment, the analysis starts by exploring the characteristics of the latter. Here, historical situations (treated as detailed stories) are discussed and interpreted and pivotal incidents are chronologically arranged and critically analysed to provide a richer understanding of the evolutionary dynamics and current development of the urban institutional structures. Their quality is assessed in terms of the institutional uncertainty they are imbued with. The institutional characteristics of the property market are then analysed and their evolution and current structure are explored with reference to the broad urban institutional conditions and dynamics. Here, an attempt is made not simply to point out historical changes and structural breaks, but, more importantly, to understand the causes of these changes and to sketch out the process of transformation with reference to current dynamics, past tendencies and the overall path taken by property market institutions. Overall, the quality of the property market institutions is assessed in terms of institutionalised variety. This analysis provides a basis for further exploration of the relation between the property market as an institution and the wider institutional environment and to reflect on the emergence, development and evolutionary dynamics of the system.

In detailing the second level design, a wide range of aspects describing the wider institutional environment and the property market institutional characteristics have been identified (from the relevant literature), reflecting on the extent of institutional uncertainty and institutionalised variety, respectively. These provide a general resource for reference and guidance in empirical research and act as a means of uncovering the variety of forms that the phenomena they refer to can assume. Attributes of the quality of the overall institutional environment have been organised under four themes/categories: economic uncertainty, political uncertainty, legal uncertainty and socio-cultural uncertainty. In turn, aspects of the institutional structure of the property market have been classified in terms of diversity in use and investment objectives, market openness and transparency, market flexibility, information flow and research activity, property rights and transaction costs, standardisation of market practices, flexibility in cultural traits, the plurality of the immediate actors, diversity of the financial service provision, and the plurality of property service providers and professionalisation of the market.

It is important to emphasise that evaluation and further refinement of these qualities should be sought at the concrete stage of research. Thus, on the basis of empirical evidence and through logical reasoning, comparisons and contrasts, these attributes would be evaluated, revised and polished to provide more precise measures of the analytical concepts that define the institutional structure of the property market across different urban contexts. In this sense, the initial categories may be discarded and others may emerge through synthesis and reorganisation on the basis of new evidence. However, as urban socio-economic systems are dynamically evolving and new evidence constantly emerges, both the characteristics and the envisaged relations should continually be revisited, and revised if necessary, as they can never be either fully completed or entirely confirmed. Validation in this respect consists of refining and expanding the model further on the basis of empirical evidence and explaining/verifying additional cases.

Clearly, this process of concept and model validation presents certain challenges. The most obvious challenge concerns the analytical definition of institutions: recognising the difficulties in drawing clear boundaries for their empirical specification. In particular, these difficulties involve the distinction between property-specific and wider environment institutions, between formal and informal institutions, and between structural (or generalisable) and contingent (or local) institutional aspects. These complexities can be attributed to the intricacy of institutional mechanisms, the interwoven nature of institutions, their socio-cultural embeddedness and their dynamic character, all of which reinforce claims for additional in-depth, 'explanatory' case studies.

6.4 Epilogue and the way forward

Before closing this chapter, we must stress, once again, the significance of the current project. As discussed, urban and regional economics has generally ignored or undervalued the pivotal role that the property market plays in the urban economy. The present study has explicitly addressed this issue, placing the property market process at the core of explanations of urban economic change and development. In particular, it has developed a holistic research programme to advance understanding and analysis of the complex institutional structures, mechanisms and processes through which the built environment is provided, and to explore their emergence, development and evolution with reference to the wider institutional conditions and dynamics. To carry out such an analysis the study has provided a rich ontological and epistemological framework and a pluralistic, but critically eclectic, methodological perspective.

The programme put forward is holistic, evolutionary and realistic. It is holistic because it analyses property market institutions with reference to the overall institutional environment within which they exist. In this sense, urban economic explanations explicitly take account of both the property market process and the wider institutional conditions and dynamics. It is evolutionary because it espouses a historical and dynamic view of the property market as an institution. As such, it facilitates understanding of the casual forces (and contingent conditions) behind institutional change and builds this into a wider picture of continuity and evolution. Finally, it is realistic because it takes into appropriate consideration the structural imperfections, institutional characteristics and dynamic nature of the property market to develop a concept for property market efficiency that is pragmatic and fruitful.

In contrast with other approaches, the research programme developed here offers a richer account of the property market process and its institutional environment. This has implications on various fronts. It helps market analysts and active property actors to understand the organisational structure and dynamic nature of the property market and thereby to explain observed patterns of property market activity and performance over time, as well as to identify strategies and boundaries of effective involvement in all market sectors (including use, investment and development as well as property service provision). This is particularly important given the increasing internationalisation of property markets, the substantial complexity of the market institutions at the local level and the subsequent necessity for an in-depth understanding of the institutional peculiarities of each local context.

Similarly, the value of the developed research programme to government and policy-making is also apparent, as it provides a basis for assessing the ability of the property market process to deliver the products that the economy requires with reference to the wider urban institutional conditions and dynamics. This ability has certain economic implications in terms of development potential and the enhancement of urban competitiveness. These are the grounds for claiming that the current research programme offers a rich understanding of the property market institutions and their relations, clarifies thinking in terms of policy choices (i.e. the possibilities for and consequences of specific intervention in the market) and enables economic potential to be supported.

In addition, the study has implications pertinent to the institutional school in economics. First, it demonstrates that it is both feasible and legitimate to integrate key elements from all strands of institutionalist thought. This was made possible through the provision of a unifying philosophical framework (informed by critical realist ontological and epistemological arguments) that dictates appropriate methodologies for concrete institutional analysis. Second, a rich institutionalist perspective on urban economic development and built environment provision is developed. In this sense, the conceptualisation of the property market as an institution is advanced, its relation to the overall institutional environment and the urban economy is explored, and a sound basis for empirical exploration of the issues is established.

Given the theoretical orientation of this book, it is argued that detailed empirical investigation along the lines of HCIA is imperative and should be given high priority. Two stages of empirical work are envisaged. First, a number of exploratory case studies should be undertaken to further refine the analytical indicators and to improve their validity, reliability and generalisability. Second, a set of additional case studies should be conducted to scrutinise the envisaged relations, organise evidence into a coherent and generalised explanatory pattern model, and establish the validity, reliability and generalisability of both the methodological framework and its associated research design. In particular, comparative analysis across time and across markets will provide the basis to elucidate further the relation between the property market as an institution and its wider institutional environment and might also make possible the designation of independent and measurable criteria of purpose efficiency that would enable the concept to be empirically explored and verified.

This book has laid down an agenda for a much deeper understanding of urban economic change and development through the study of the institutional structure and dynamics of the property market. The promise is there. Hopefully, additional studies will follow. Although definitive answers to urban economic questions may never be found, I believe that urban theory will certainly enrich the understanding of the processes and dynamics behind spatial and economic change.

Notes

1 In the context of this research, these are: methodological individualism, rational economic behaviour and the equilibrium state of the economy (see discussion in Chapter 2).

2 It should be stressed once again that the current approach, in contrast with others, places such considerations at the centre of explanation, to emphasise questions related to how well and how quickly institutions adapt to current pressures.

3 That is, the production, distribution, use, exchange and maintenance of land and built structures.

4 Such a case is made in terms of the heterogeneity, indivisibility and illiquidity of the property product, the externalities associated with land and property markets, as well as the transaction costs and information deficiencies associated with trade in property.

5 As has been argued throughout this study, institutions' functional role is to reduce uncertainty. On this basis, the level of remaining uncertainty becomes the yardstick to evaluate their quality.

6 Note, once again, that this does not imply that theories can be discarded simply because expected empirical patterns do not materialise.

7 Quantitative research works mainly at the level of events helping to identify stylised facts, demi-regs and empirical patterns of any sort in relation to the research questions. These patterns suggest the operation of causal mechanisms and are better explicated through qualitative research which provides contextual richness, depth and density.

Appendices

I Property market institutional structure and institutionalised variety

This is a list of themes under which the most essential institutional characteristics of the property market can be organised. As a result of the interwoven nature of institutions, there is a degree of overlap between the themes.

Diversity in use and investment objectives

- Diversity in user demand. The users' requirements in terms of property (e.g. type, quality and location) and an assessment of whether they are prepared or willing to pay accordingly for these qualities.
- Diversity in the investment market. The investment vehicles which are available and an assessment of their quality and degree of enforceability. (Particular attention should be paid to the indirect property investment vehicles, e.g. publicly quoted property companies, property trusts or funds, property securitisation).
- Divisibility and separability of legal interests (e.g. differentiation between the ownership right and the right to build).
- Degree of establishment of distinct property submarkets (differentiated, for example, in terms of sector or location).

Market openness and transparency

- Degree and range of involvement of non-domestic actors and funds.
- Degree and range of involvement in the market of non-property (i.e. other asset) actors.
- Formal restrictions and controls on ownership, use, investment and development (especially for non-domestic actors).
- Degree of market liquidity. The institutional mechanisms that facilitate actors' entrance to, and exit, from the property market.
- Degree of market transparency. The specific instruments or procedures that safeguard transparency in the property market. The quality of information flow regarding property supply and prices.

- Degree of functional flexibility of actors (for instance, if users consider the investment aspects of their property holdings, or if developers build for their own portfolio purposes).

Market flexibility

- Degree of market responsiveness to external and internal conditions in both the short and long run.
- The regulating systems (e.g. the tax system, the incentives regime) and the extent to which they constrain or facilitate the property market. With reference to the tax system, the taxes involved in holding or exchanging property.
- The land use planning system and the way it affects (constrains/facilitates) the operation of the property market. Aspects include:
  - the key legislation that affects the operation of the planning system and the process of development control;
  - the tiers of the planning system (national, regional, local), their function and the existence of conflict between them;
  - the enforcement mechanisms of the planning system and the degree of violation or abuse of the planning rules and procedures;
  - the degree of flexibility of the planning system.

Information flow and research activity

- Issues of information quality, availability and variety. In particular:
  - the availability of historical data, the establishment of information databases and the development of indices;
  - the existence of official publications provided by state organisations/ institutions or by the private sector;
  - the costs associated with the acquisition of information;
  - the degree of centralisation and the means of dissemination of information;
  - the importance of informal networks in the generation and provision of information.
- Issues of property market research (type, quantity, quality) and the role of the organisations involved (e.g. universities, public sector, professional bodies, private firms).
- The degree of uniformity or consensus between actors with regard to market conditions and the interpretation of information.

Property rights and transaction costs

- Forms of ownership and restrictions imposed upon them.
- Forms of tenure. Specification of the prevailing lease structure, including issues, e.g. lease length, rent review timing, rent review basis, actors' obligations and rent payment practices.
- The obligations of occupation (e.g. repairs or insurance).
- Issues of security with reference to tenure, income stream and property rights.
- The costs involved in property transactions (e.g. transactions/acquisition costs, agency fees, legal costs, taxes and transaction delays).
- The degree of flexibility and security in trading property, including issues of market transparency and liquidity.

Standardisation of market practices

- The structure of formal practices in the market process. In particular:
    - their origins;
    - their degree of transparency;
    - their enforcement characteristics, including the role of professional bodies, the public sector or private actors (e.g. property firms) in defining, implementing or modifying them.
- The nature and degree of development of informal practices (their origins, degree of transparency and enforcement characteristics).
- The social character and cultural embeddedness of these practices. In particular, how immutable established practices are and the extent to which market norms lead to conservative, inflexible or rigid responses.

Flexibility in cultural traits

- The prevailing conventions and habits related to property market process (e.g. attitude to property ownership or to the informal provision of information, the importance attached to personal/social networks, the degree of establishment of clientelistic or nepotistic relations and practices).
- The cultural attitudes related to property. The social status related to property ownership, investment and development (e.g. ownership of the premises a company occupies is perceived in some countries as a factor of the company's commercial success).

Plurality of immediate actors

- The organisational structure of the market (i.e. the composition of the market in terms of the key participant actors in the use, investment and development sectors). In particular:

  - the degree of their organisational complexity or sophistication (e.g. in the development sector, the existence of special purpose agencies, public–private partnerships; in the investment market, the form of financial institutions and the investment aspect of owner-occupancy);
  - the relations between them;
  - their power characteristics (e.g. the lobbying power of small retailers to oppose specific retail developments).

- The degree and range of involvement of non-domestic actors in property use, investment and development.

Diversity of financial service provision

- The composition and structure of the market in terms of the key participant actors in property finance.
- The nature of involvement and importance of non-domestic institutions and capital.
- The role of financial institutions. In particular, the role and degree of involvement of pension funds, insurance companies, investment entities and banks.
- The main practices of raising capital from or for property: the flexibility, responsiveness or restrictiveness of these practices and the quality, quantity and diversity of the financial instruments available.

Plurality of property service providers and professionalisation of the market

- The professional bodies. In particular:

  - their role in property matters (e.g. if professional membership is required for involvement in the market);
  - their professional rights and degree of professional protectionism;
  - their manpower;
  - the form and nature of their regulation (e.g. self-regulated, legal/statutory regulated);
  - their entrance requirements and their control procedures;
  - their social status and power characteristics.

- The property service providers. In particular:

  - the type and quantity of 'property experts' operating in the market (e.g. brokers, consultants, valuers);
  - their role in the market (e.g. in areas such as valuation, brokerage, consultancy, research) and the nature of their involvement (e.g. neutral mediation versus serving the interests of specific actors);
  - the degree of demarcation of their professional functions or separation of their professional rights;

- their origins (local, national or international) and affiliations;
- their social status and power characteristics.

- The educational and knowledge base of the professionals (including issues such as overspecialisation on property issues and interdisciplinary education). The range, quality and diversity of educational programmes (vocational versus academic) and the qualifications they provide.
- The degree of development and function of informal networks related to market operation.

II Wider urban institutional environment and institutional uncertainty

The following elements reflect institutional uncertainty with reference to the economic, political, legal and socio-cultural structures as well as the overall urban environment.

1 Economic uncertainty

- Key economic events and their consequences (e.g. accession to the EU).
- Urban economic performance through time (e.g. growth and volatility of GDP, employment, unemployment, inflation, interest rates), including assessments of the capacity of the urban economy to achieve sustained economic growth (usually referred to as 'competitiveness').
- The risk associated with the overall urban macroeconomic performance or with the business environment ('economic risk' and 'business environment risk', respectively).
- Degree of 'economic freedom', i.e. an assessment of the constraints imposed on the economic system beyond the provision of institutions necessary for citizens to protect and maintain liberty itself.
- Frequency of internet searches.
- Degree of entrepreneurship, risk-taking behaviour and innovation potential (measured, for instance, by the degree of development of R&D activities).
- The existence, form and organisational structure of the underground economy ('black markets').
- Degree of diversity of local economic activity (e.g. diversity of the service sector).
- The strength of the endogenous economic activity, including the extent of dependency of the local economy on the flow of international capital and investment and the degree of control of the economy by foreigners.
- The structure of the business environment, including:
  - the organisation and development of asset, financial and investment markets;
  - the magnitude and performance of the stock market;

- the availability of finance (especially with reference to plurality and the quality of the financial vehicles available);
- the plurality of economic actors, their origins (i.e. local, national, international), as well as their role and importance in the local economy;
- the restrictions imposed on both the entrance or exit of the market and on capital movements (exchange controls), especially with reference to international actors;
- the tax regime and incentives available;
- issues of government control and market liberalisation (e.g. in the labour market, the existence of minimum wages, labour unionisation, alternative employment structures, such as part-time or teleworking).

2 *Political uncertainty*

- Key political events and their consequences (e.g. the establishment of autocratic or democratic regimes).
- Political risk. This describes the level of security and quality of administration and is associated with a government action taken against foreign actors or even against its own citizens. Relevant measures take into account corruption levels, as well as nationalisation and expropriation incidents.
- Issues of political pluralism (as indicated by plurality in political parties) and participant democracy.
- The structure of local, regional and national governments, and the degree of conflict between them.
- Stability of the governments.
- The structure, role and power of pressure groups (as well as repressed minorities).
- Degree of participation in international blocs (e.g. European Union) and networks (e.g. city networks).

3 *Legal uncertainty*

- Key legal events and their consequences (e.g. the establishment of a constitution).
- The structural basis of the legal system (i.e. common or civil law). The existence of a written constitution at a national or regional level.
- The hierarchy of the legal structures and the organisational and institutional aspects at each level.
- The judicial structure.
- Quality of justice (at various sectors/levels, e.g. civil, criminal, administrative).
- Issues of legal security and certainty, including:
    - degrees of protection of (intellectual) property rights;
    - levels of bribery and corruption;
    - possibility of arbitrary expropriation.
- Degree of influence of non-national law (e.g. European laws and directives).

4 Socio-cultural uncertainty

- Key social events or cultural changes and their consequences (e.g. waves of immigration).
- Degree of socio-cultural diversity (e.g. ethnic, linguistic or with reference to religion and faith).
- Strength of social values (e.g. in relation to freedom or equality) and cultural attributes (e.g. in relation to religion, sexes or family). Local attitudes towards racial minorities and foreigners. The degree of hostility between local people and people from different regions of the same country.
- Structure and nature of social differentiation (e.g. social classes).
- The structure of the education system and the quality of education. For instance, the number of higher educational institutions as well as the percentage of the population classified as illiterate or having higher degrees.
- Work and business ethics, including attitudes towards welfare benefits and retirement ethics.
- Quality of life (e.g. crime rates, life expectancy, social security, social justice).
- Trust, social capital and social networks (e.g. measures of 'generalised trust',[1] membership in organisations and groups, voluntary contributions to charity and degrees of altruistic behaviour).

III Quantitative indicators of institutional quality

1 The Fraser Institute's Economic Freedom Index

The Fraser Institute's Economic Freedom Index is an attempt to assess economic freedom[2] for more than a hundred countries over a period spanning three decades. As Table A.1 illustrates, the index comprises twenty-five components reflecting various categorical characteristics in five major areas. Each subcomponent is weighted and placed on a scale from zero to ten to produce a component index describing the overall level of economic freedom in each country (ten signifies the highest economic freedom). The areas covered are as follows:

1. Size of government and structure of the economy, which indicates the extent to which countries rely on individual choice and markets rather than the political process to allocate resources, goods and services.
2. Legal structure and security of property rights, which reflects the level of protection that individuals and their property enjoy.
3. Access to sound money, which describes the quality and stability of the monetary system.
4. Freedom to exchange with foreigners, which measures the restraints in international exchange (e.g. tariffs, quotas, price controls, hidden administrative restraints) and the degree of the country's trade openness.
5. Regulations of credit, labour and business, which assesses the quality of available capital and finance, labour markets, as well as the whole business environment.

Table A.1 Components of the Fraser Institute's Economic Freedom Index

I	**Size of government (expenditures, taxes and enterprises) and structure of economy**		
	I-A	General government consumption spending as a percentage of total consumption	
	I-B	Transfers and subsidies as a percentage of GDP	
	I-C	Government enterprises and investment as a percentage of GDP	
	I-D	Top marginal tax rate (and income threshold to which it applies)	
II	**Legal structure and security of property rights**		
	II-A	Judicial independence (the judiciary is not subject to interference by the government or parties in disputes)	
	II-B	Impartial courts (a trusted legal framework exists for private businesses to challenge the legality of government actions or regulation)	
	II-C	Protection of intellectual property	
	II-D	Military interference in rule of law and the political process	
	II-E	Integrity of the legal system	
	II-F	Legal security of private ownership rights (risk of confiscation)	
	II-G	Viability of contracts (risk of contract repudiation by the government)	
	II-H	Rule of law (legal institutions, including access to a non-discriminatory judiciary, that are supportive of rule of law principles)	
III	**Access to sound money**		
	III-A	Average annual growth of the money supply in the last five years minus average annual growth of real GDP in the last ten years	
	III-B	Standard inflation variability in the last five years	
	III-C	Recent inflation rate	
	III-D	Freedom to own foreign currency bank accounts domestically and abroad	
IV	**Freedom to exchange with foreigners**		
	IV-A	Taxes on international trade	
		(i)	Revenue from taxes on international trade as a percentage of exports plus imports
		(ii)	Mean tariff rate
		(iii)	Standard deviation of tariff rates
	IV-B	Regulatory trade barriers	
		(i)	Hidden import barriers
		(ii)	Costs of importing (the combined effect of import tariffs, licence fees, bank fees and the time required for administrative red tape)

IV-C Actual size of trade sector compared with expected size

IV-D Difference between official exchange rate and black market rate

IV-E International capital market controls

- (i) Access of citizens to foreign capital markets and foreign access to domestic capital markets
- (ii) Restrictions on the freedom of citizens to engage in capital market exchange with foreigners

IV-F Trade openness

V Regulation of credit, labour and business

V-A Credit market regulations

- (i) Ownership of banks (percentage of deposits held in privately owned banks)
- (ii) Competition (domestic versus foreign banks)
- (iii) Extension of credit (percentage of credit extended to private sector)
- (iv) Avoidance of interest rate controls and regulations that lead to negative real interest rates
- (v) Interest rate controls on bank deposits and/or loans

V-B Labour market regulations

- (i) Impact of minimum wage
- (ii) Hiring and firing practices (are they determined by private contract or law?)
- (iii) Share of labour force whose wages are set by centralised collective bargaining
- (iv) Unemployment benefits (degree at which the system preserves the incentive to work)
- (v) Use of conscripts to obtain military personnel

V-C Business regulations

- (i) Price controls (extent to which businesses are free to set their own prices)
- (ii) Administrative conditions and start of new businesses
- (iii) Time spent dealing with government bureaucracy
- (iv) Difficulty in starting a new business
- (v) Irregular, additional payments (connected with import and export permits, business licences, exchange controls, tax assessments, police protection or loan applications)

2 The Heritage Foundation Index of Economic Freedom

Another measure of the quality of the economic environment is provided by the Heritage Foundation. In particular, this institution has developed since 1995 a yearly measurement of 'economic freedom' for over 160 countries, combining fifty equally weighted independent variables that fall into ten broad categories, or factors, of economic liberty. Both the factors and the composite index are scored according to a grading scale that runs from one to five, where one signifies an environment that is most conductive to economic freedom (and, by extension, less uncertain). The examined factors are:

1 Trade policy (protectionism). This measures the degree to which government hinders the free flow of foreign commerce, taking into account issues such as the extent of imposed tariffs (i.e. tariff rates), import quotas and other non-tariff barriers, as well as the level of corruption in the customs service.
2 Fiscal burden of government. This places emphasis on the tax rates (arguing that higher tax rates interfere with the ability of individuals to pursue their economic goals) and the level of government expenditures (which reflects the true cost of government in the economy and the society in general, as resources may be drained away from more efficient uses).
3 Government intervention in the economy. This factor comprises both government consumption and production variables to assess government's direct use of scare resources for its own purposes and government's control of resources through ownership.
4 Monetary policy. Focusing on the economic significance of inflation (which not only confiscates wealth, but also distorts pricing, misallocates resources and undermines a free economy), the influence of monetary policy on economic freedom is gauged through analysis of the inflation rate over a period of time.
5 Capital flows and foreign investment policy (imposed restrictions). Based on the argument that restrictions of foreign investment limit the inflow of capital, and thus hamper economic freedom, this factor scrutinises the country's policies towards foreign investment.[3] This analysis also helps to develop an overall picture of the country's investment climate.
6 Banking and finance (imposed restrictions). This factor examines the degree of openness of, and the extent of governmental regulation in, the banking and financial system,[4] providing a description of the country's financial climate. It is argued that although some type of state supervision is required to ensure the safety and soundness of the financial system, governments' burdensome interference in the market provision of financial services restricts economic freedom and reduces economic potential.
7 Wage and price controls. This examines the extent to which the market itself is allowed to set wages and prices without governmental influences. It is asserted that government control over wages and prices restricts economic activity and curtails economic freedom.
8 Regulation. This factor measures how easy or difficult it is to open and operate a business. The more regulations are imposed on licensing and

business, the harder it is for economic activity and entrepreneurship to thrive. The factor also examines the degree of corruption within the bureaucracy and whether regulations are applied uniformly to all businesses.

9 Black market activity. This factor measures the extent of black market activity in the production, distribution or consumption of goods and services, utilising information on smuggling, piracy of intellectual property and black market labour. For the purposes of this index, the higher the level of black market activity, the lower the level of economic freedom. Moreover, this analysis captures the effects of problematic economic organisation not fully measured elsewhere.[5]

10 Property rights. This factor examines the degree by which property rights are protected, taking into consideration whether laws are properly enforced and whether private property is safe from expropriation. In addition, it analyses the independence of the judiciary, the existence of corruption within the judiciary and the ability of individuals and businesses to enforce contracts.

3 The Polity IV Project

The Polity IV Project, available from the Centre for International Development and Conflict Management at the University of Maryland (USA), is an attempt to assess the stability and quality of the political environment for over 150 countries covering a period of 200 years (from 1800 to 2011). This data set consists of coded annual information on the regimes' structural characteristics, institutional changes and the directionality of political changes, recording patterns of conventional authority characteristics and providing assessments of the degree of democracy, autocracy and power concentration. Table A.2 provides the scoring system and full description of the variables used. These are:

1 XRREG: analyses the institutionalised procedures governing the transfer of executive power.

2 XRCOMP: considers the extent to which the executive is chosen through competitive elections.

3 XROPEN: reviews whether it is possible for non-elites to attain executive office.

4 XCONST: examines the operational (de facto) independence of the country's chief executive.

5 PARREG: indicates the degree of development of institutional structures for political expression.

6 PARCOMP: regards the extent to which non-elites are able to access institutional structures for political expression.

7 DEMOC and AUTOC: measure the degrees of openness or closeness of political institutions, respectively. Both are ten-point composited indices constructed from the scores of the authority characteristics.

8 DURABLE: is an indicator of polity durability based on the number of years since the last regime transition.

Table A.2 Variables of the Polity IV Project

Variable	*Score*	*Description*
XRREG	1	Unregulated: changes in chief executives occur through forceful seizure of power
	2	Designation: chief executives are chosen by designation within the political elite, but without formal competition
	3	Regulated: chief executives are determined by hereditary succession or in competitive elections
XRCOMP	0	Unregulated: when power transfers are coded as ‘unregulated’ on XRREG
	1	Selection: chief executives are chosen by hereditary succession, designation or combination of both (e.g. when prime minister is chosen by king or court)
	2	Dual/transitional: hereditary succession plus electoral selection of prime minister
	3	Election: chief executives are chosen in or through competitive elections matching two or more major parties or candidates
XOPEN	0	Unregulated: when power transfers are coded as ‘unregulated’ on XRREG
	1	Closed: chief executives are determined by hereditary succession
	2	Dual/designation: hereditary succession of executive or court selection of the chief minister
	3	Dual/election: hereditary succession plus electoral selection of the chief minister
	4	Open: chief executives are chosen by elite designation, competitive election or transitional arrangements between designation and election
XCONST	1	Unlimited authority: no regular limitations on the executive’s actions
	2	Intermediate category
	3	Slight to moderate limitations: there are some real, but limited, constraints on the executive
	4	Intermediate category
	5	Substantial limitations: the executive has more effective authority than any accountable group, but is subject to substantial constraints by them
	6	Intermediate category
	7	Executive parity or subordination: accountable groups have effective authority equal to or greater than the chief executive in most areas of activity

PARREG	1	Unregulated: political participation is fluid, there are no enduring national political organisations and no systematic regime controls on political activity
	2	Factional/transitional: there are relatively stable and enduring political groups which compete for political influence at the national level, but competition among them is intense, hostile and frequently violent
	3	Factional/restricted: polities which oscillate more or less regularly between intense factionalism and restriction (when one group secures power it restricts its opponents' political activities until it is displaced in turn)
	4	Restricted: some organised political participation is permitted without intense factionalism, but significant group, issues and/or types of conventional participation are regularly excluded from the political process
	5	Regulated: relatively stable and enduring political groups regularly compete for political influence and positions with little use of coercion. No significant groups, issues or types of conventional political action are regularly excluded from the political process
PARCOMP	0	Unregulated: when power transfers are coded as 'unregulated' on XRREG
	1	Suppressed: no significant oppositional activity is permitted outside the ranks of the regime and ruling party
	2	Restricted/transitional: some organised political competition occurs outside government, without serious factionalism, but the regime sharply limits its form, extent or both in ways that exclude substantial groups from participation
	3	Factional: polities with factional or factional/restricted patterns of competition
	4	Transitional: any transitional elements from Restricted or Factional patterns to fully Competitive patterns, or vice versa
	5	Competitive: there are relatively stable and enduring political groups which regularly compete for political influence at the national level. Competition among them seldom causes widespread violence or disruption

4 The Corruption Perception Index

Mainly reflecting the functioning of political and legal institutions, this indicator attempts to assess the extent to which public officials are involved in corrupt practices. Developed by the non-governmental organisation Transparency International the Corruption Perception Index (CPIx) estimates the level at which corruption is perceived by business people, country experts, risk analysts and the general public as impacting on the commercial, political and social life of a country. Corruption can be differentiated in terms of type (e.g. political, administrative, judiciary, private sector), form (e.g. nepotism, favouritism, kickbacks, extortion, bribery) and extent (e.g. with regard to frequency of incidents, financial magnitude, proportion of people involved, overall gain achieved). The CPIx addresses most of these dimensions, although corruption is principally understood with close reference to public sector activities (note that it is defined as the abuse of public power for private gains[6]) and therefore less attention is paid to private sector analysis.

The CPIx is a composite index drawing on numerous equally weighted surveys undertaken over a three year period reflecting the perceptions of international business people, analysts and the general public. On this basis, the collected data do not necessarily reflect the actual level of corruption, but reflect the subjective opinions of people. Nevertheless, perceptions can have important consequences on the way business is conducted and the degree of generated uncertainty within a socio-economy. It can be argued that high corruption is associated with a high level of uncertainty (Brunetti and Weder 1997). The scores used in the CPIx range from ten (country perceived as virtually corruption-free) down to close to zero (country perceived as almost totally corrupt). However, no country has ever scored an outright zero. In an attempt to improve the reliability and quality of the index, an indication of the variance of rankings is also provided. Generally, the greater the variance, the greater is the difference in opinion about a country's corruption, whereas a low variance indicates greater unanimity regarding scores.

According to Transparency International, each year's index must be seen as a result of the sum of reputable sources available at the time. On these grounds, comparisons with the views collected in previous years may be problematic and so caution is required when undertaking dynamic analysis, as differences in a country's score from year to year may not be simply a reflection of changing corruption perceptions, but changing samples and methodologies. Important parameters that must be considered are the number of surveys on which data are based and the variance of the index score.

5 The Freedom House indices

With particular focus on the political, legal and social environments, the Freedom House provides annual indicators (since 1972) evaluating the quality of democracy, civil rights and information freedom throughout the world. The assessments are based on standard surveys exploring the fundamentals of democracy and freedom which individuals should enjoy in each country on three fronts: political rights, civil liberties and press freedom. In a free society, political rights enable people to participate freely in the political process, including enjoying the right to vote and compete for public office and to elect representatives who have a decisive vote on public policies. Civil liberties include the freedom to develop views, institutions and personal autonomy without interference from the state. For this to be achieved, people should be able to seek, receive and impart information and ideas through any media regardless of frontiers.

Countries are assigned a particular rating on the basis of the individual survey author's responses to a series of checklist questions (see Table A.3) and the judgements of the survey team which provide the basis for final adjustments. To reach its conclusions, the Freedom House employs a broad range of sources of information, including foreign and domestic news reports, non-governmental organisation publications, 'think-tank' and academic analyses, and individual professional contacts. Basically, the survey assigns each country under consideration two numerical ratings, one for political rights and one for civil liberties.[7] These are measured on a scale of one to seven, with one representing the highest degree of freedom and seven the lowest. These two ratings are then averaged to determine an overall status of 'Free' (range between one and three), 'Partly Free' (range between three and five and a half) or 'Not Free' (range between five and a half and seven).

With regard to information freedom, the assessment provided is the sum of four scores reflecting four sets of press freedom characteristics. The first concerns the structure of the news delivery system as functioning under the country's laws and administrative decisions. The second considers the degree of political influence or control over the content of the news. The third examines the economic influences on news content as exerted either by the government (e.g. funding pressures, licensing, quotas) or the private sector (i.e. the negative impact of market competition). Finally, the fourth captures actual press freedom violations (including murder, physical attack, harassment and censorship). The first three categories (laws, political and economic factors) are scored from zero to thirty, the fourth from zero to ten, in which the lower the number, the freer the media.

Table A.3 Freedom House checklist questions

Political rights questions

Basic

1 Is the head of state and/or head of government or other chief authority elected through free and fair elections?

2 Are the legislative representatives elected through free and fair elections?

3 Are there fair electoral laws, equal campaigning opportunities, fair polling and honest tabulation of ballots?

4 Are the voters able to endow their freely elected representatives with real power?

5 Do the people have the right to organise in different political parties or other competitive political groupings of their choice, and is the system open to the rise and fall of these competing parties or groupings?

6 Is there a significant opposition vote, de facto opposition power and a realistic possibility for the opposition to increase its support or gain power through elections?

7 Are the people free from domination by the military, foreign powers, totalitarian parties, religious hierarchies, economic oligarchies or any other powerful group?

8 Do cultural, ethnic, religious and other minority groups have reasonable self-determination, self-government, autonomy or participation through informal consensus in the decision-making process?

Discretionary

1 For traditional monarchies that have no parties or electoral process, does the system provide for consultation with the people, encourage discussion of policy and allow the right to petition the ruler?

2 Is the government or occupying power deliberately changing the ethnic composition of a country or territory so as to destroy a culture or tip the political balance in favour of another group?

Civil liberties questions

A *Freedom of expression and belief*

1 Are there free and independent media and other forms of cultural expression?

2 Are there free religious institutions and is there free private and public religious expression?

B *Association and organisational rights*

1 Is there freedom of assembly, demonstration and open public discussion?

2 Is there freedom of political or quasi-political organisation? (This includes political parties, civic organisations and ad hoc issue groups)

3 Are there free trade unions and peasant organisations or equivalent, and is there effective collective bargaining? Are there free professional and other private organisations?

C *Rule of law and human rights*

1 Is there an independent judiciary?

2 Does the rule of law prevail in civil and criminal matters? Is the population treated equally under the law? Are police under direct civilian control?

3 Is there protection from political terror, unjustified imprisonment, exile or torture, whether by groups that support or oppose the system? Is there freedom from war and insurgencies?

4 Is there freedom from extreme government indifference and corruption?

D *Personal autonomy and economic rights*

1 Is there open and free private discussion?

2 Is there personal autonomy? Does the state control travel, choice of residence or choice of employment? Is there freedom from indoctrination and excessive dependency on the state?

3 Are property rights secure? Do citizens have the right to establish private businesses? Is private business activity unduly influenced by government officials, the security forces or organised crime?

4 Are there personal social freedoms, including gender equality, choice of marriage partners and size of family?

5 Is there equality of opportunity, including freedom from exploitation by, or dependency on, landlords, employers, union leaders, bureaucrats or other types of obstacles to a share of legitimate economic gains?

Notes

1 That is, interpersonal trust which reflects the general level of trustworthiness in a community.
2 As discussed in Chapter 5, economic freedom is defined as the absence of constraints in the economic system beyond the institutions required for the protection and maintenance of liberty itself.
3 Variables examined include the presence of a foreign investment code that defines the country's investment laws and procedures, whether the government encourages foreign investment through the fair and equitable treatment of investors, whether there are restrictions on access to foreign exchange, whether foreign firms are treated the same as domestic firms under the law, the presence of restrictions on payments, transfers and capital transactions, and whether specific industries are closed to foreign investment.
4 In particular, it examines whether foreign banks and financial service firms are able to operate freely, how difficult it is to open domestic banks and other financial service firms, how heavily regulated the financial system is, the presence of state-owned banks, whether the government influences the allocation of credit and whether banks are free to provide customers with insurance and invest in securities.
5 It is argued that black markets are the direct result of some kind of improper government intervention in the marketplace, as excessive or shadowy regulation in one area may create the condition for the development of a black market in another (e.g. inefficient property rights protection for items such as intellectual property encourage the piracy and theft of these products).
6 Corruption has also been defined by some researchers (e.g. Baro, 1997) as a particular public reaction to political/administrative behaviour, rather than as a real misbehaviour as such. From that perspective a high degree of observed corruption may be associated with sound ethical standards, but rigidity in the development and adaptability of rules. In any case, however, one should not disregard the fact that corruption relates to illegitimate behaviour that is culturally conditioned (Lambsdorff, 2007) and, in general, it has significant implications on the social life of a people. On these grounds, it also reflects the levels of uncertainty attributed to the social environment.
7 The highest possible score for political rights is thirty-two points, the total of up to four points for each of eight questions. The highest possible score for civil liberties is fifty-six points, the total of up to four points for each of fourteen questions.

References

Acemoglu, D., Johnson, S. and Robinson, J. (2002) "Reversal of fortune: geography and institutions in the making of the modern world income distribution", *Quarterly Journal of Economics*, **117**(4): 1231–94.

Acemoglu, D., Johnson, S. and Robinson, J. (2005) "Institutions as the fundamental cause of long-run growth", in Aghion, P. and Durlauf, S. (eds) *Handbook of Economic Growth.* Amsterdam: North-Holland, pp. 385–472.

Ache, P., Andersen, H.T., Maolutas, T., Raco, M. and Tasan-Kok, T. (eds) (2008) *Cities between Competitiveness and Cohesion. Discourses, Realities and Implementation.* Dordrecht: Springer.

Adair, A., Allen, S., Berry, J. and McGreal, S. (2006) "Central and Eastern European property investment markets: issues of data and transparency", *Journal of Property Investment and Finance*, **24**(3): 211–20.

Adair, A.S., Berry, J.N., Deddis, B., McGreal, S.W., Keogh, G. and Key, T. (1998) "Barriers to data sharing in the surveying profession: implications for the commercial property market", *Journal of Property Research*, **15**(4): 331–46.

Adair, A.S., Berry, J.N. and McGreal, S.W. (1994) "Investment decision making: a behavioural perspective", *Journal of Property Finance*, **5**(4): 32–42.

Adair, A.S., Berry, J.N. and McGreal, S.W. (1997) "Comparative analysis of market performance in European cities", *Journal of Property Valuation and Investment*, **15**(4): 323–35.

Adams, D.C. (1994) *Urban Planning and the Development Process.* London: University College London Press.

Adams, J. (1993) "Institutions and economic development: structure, process, and incentive", in Tool, M.R. (ed.) *Institutional Economics: Theory, Method, Policy.* Boston: Kluwer Academic, pp. 245–69.

Addis, L. (1999) "Methodological holism", in Audi, R. (ed.) *The Cambridge Dictionary of Philosophy*, 2nd edn. Cambridge: Cambridge University Press, p. 566.

Aglietta, M. (1979) *A Theory of Capitalist Regulation: the US Experience*. London: New Left Books.

Aji, A.M. (1995) "Intra-metropolitan productivity variations of selected manufacturing and business service sectors: what can we learn from Los Angeles?", *Urban Studies*, **32**(7): 1081–96.

Akcomak, I.S. (2008) *The Impact of Social Capital on Economic and Social Outcomes.* Maastricht: Universitaire Pers.

Akerlof, G.A. (1970) "The market for 'lemons': quality uncertainty and the market mechanism", *Quarterly Journal of Economics*, **84**(3): 488–500.

Akerlof, G.A. and Shiller, R.J. (2009) *Animal Spirits: How Human Psychology Drives the Economy and Why it Matters for Global Capitalism*. Princeton, NJ: Princeton University Press.

Alchian, A.A. and Demsetz, H. (1972) "Production, information costs and economic organization", *American Economic Review*, **62**(5): 777–95.

Alchian, A.A. and Demsetz, H. (1973) "The property right paradigm", *Journal of Economic History*, **33**(1): 16–27.

Alesina, A. and Rodrik, D. (1994) "Distributive politics and economic growth" *Quarterly Journal of Economics*, **109**(2): 465–90.

Alexander, E.R. (2001) "A transaction-cost theory of land use planning and development control: towards the institutional analysis of public planning", *The Town Planning Review*, **72**(1): 45–75.

Allen, J. (1983) "Property relations and landlordism: a realist approach", *Environment and Planning D: Society and Space*, **1**(2): 191–203.

Alonso, W. (1964) *Location and Land Use: Towards a General Theory of Land Rent*. Cambridge: Harvard University Press.

Alt, J.E. and Shepsle, K.A. (1998) "Rules, restrictions, constraints: structure and process in the new institutional economics", *Journal of Institutional and Theoretical Economics*, **154**(4): 735–43.

Althusser, L. (1969) *For Marx*. Harmondsworth: Penguin.

Ambrose, P. and Colenutt, B. (1975) *The Property Machine*. London: Penguin.

Amin, A. (1999) "An institutionalist perspective on regional economic development", *International Journal of Urban and Regional Research*, **23**(2): 365–78.

Amin, A. and Thrift, N. (1994) "Living in the global", in Amin, A. and Thrift, N. (eds) *Globalisation, Institutions and Regional Development in Europe*. Oxford: Oxford University Press, pp. 1–22.

Amin, A. and Thrift, N. (1995) "Globalisation, institutional 'thickness' and the local economy" in Healey, P., Cameron, S., Davoudi, S., Graham, S. and Madani-Pour, A. (eds) *Managing Cities, the New Urban Context*. Chichester: Wiley, pp. 91–108.

Anas, A., Arnott, R. and Small, K.A. (1998) "Urban spatial structure", *Journal of Economic Literature*, **36**(3): 1426–64.

Anderson, R.I., Lewis, D. and Springer, T.M. (2000) "Operating efficiencies in real estate: a critical review of the literature", *Journal of Real Estate Literature*, **8**(1): 3–18.

Andrews, R.B. (1953) "Mechanics of the urban economic base: historical development of the base concept", *Land Economics*, **29**(2): 161–7.

Archer, M.S. (1995) *Realist Social Theory: the Morphogenetic Approach*. Cambridge: Cambridge University Press.

Archer, M.S. (2000) *Being Human: the Problem of Agency*. Cambridge: Cambridge University Press.

Archer, M.S., Bhaskar, R., Collier, A., Lawson, T. and Norrie, A. (eds) (1998) *Critical Realism, Essential Readings*. London: Routledge.

Arnsperger, C. and Varoufakis Y. (2006) "What is neoclassical economics? The three axioms responsible for its theoretical oeuvre, practical irrelevance and, thus, discursive power", *Panoeconomicus*, **53**(1): 5–18.

Artelaris, P., Arvanitidis, P. and Petrakos, G. (2011) "Explaining knowledge-based economic growth in the world economy", in Nijkamp, P. and Siedschlag, I. (eds) *Innovation, Growth and Competitiveness*. Berlin, Heidelberg: Springer-Verlag, pp. 41–59.

Arvanitidis, P. (2013) "Critical realism: the philosophical underlabourer of heterodox economics", *Bulletin of Political Economy*, **7**(2): 199–221.

Arvanitidis, P. and Kyriazis, N. (2013) "Democracy and public choice in classical Athens", *Peace Economics, Peace Science, and Public Policy*, **19**(2): 213–48.

Arvanitidis, P. and Petrakos, G. (2006) "Understanding economic change in the cities: a review of evidence and theory", *European Spatial Research and Policy*, **13**(2): 97–122.

Atkinson, G.W. and Oleson, T. (1996) "Institutional inquiry: the search for similarities and differences", *Journal of Economic Issues*, **30**(3): 701–18.

Atkinson, R. (2001) "The emerging 'urban agenda' and the European spatial development perspective: towards an EU urban policy?", *European Planning Studies*, **9**(3): 385–406.

Audi, R. (ed.) (1999) *The Cambridge Dictionary of Philosophy*, 2nd edn. Cambridge: Cambridge University Press.

Ayres, C.E. (1921) "Instinct and capacity I: the instinct of belief-in-instincts", *Journal of Philosophy*, **18**(21): 561–5.

Ayres, C.E. (1951) "Institutional economics: the co-ordinates of institutionalism", *American Economic Review*, **41**(May): 47–55.

Ayres, C.E. (1961) *Towards a Reasonable Society.* Austin: University of Texas Press.

Ayres, C.E. (1962) *The Theory of Economic Progress: a Study of the Fundamental Economic Development and Cultural Change*, 2nd edn. New York: Schocken.

Ayres, C.E. (1966) "The nature and significance of institutionalism", *The Antioch Review*, **26**(1): 70–90.

Bailly, A., Jensen-Butler, C. and Leontidou, L. (1996) "Changing cities: restructuring, marginality and policies in urban Europe", *European Urban and Regional Studies*, **3**(2): 161–76.

Ball, M. (1986) "The built environment and the urban question", *Environment and Planning D: Society and Space*, **4**(4): 447–64.

Ball, M. (1998) "Institutions in British property research: a review", *Urban Studies*, **35**(9): 1501–17.

Ball, M. (2002) "Cultural explanation of regional property markets: a critique", *Urban Studies*, **39**(8): 1453–69.

Ball, M. (2003) "Markets and the structure of the housebuilding industry: an international perspective", *Urban Studies*, **40**(5–6): 897–916.

Ball, M. (2004) "Co-operation with the community in property-led urban regeneration", *Journal of Property Research*, **21**(2): 119–42.

Ball, M. (2006) *Markets and Institutions in Real Estate and Construction.* Oxford: Blackwell.

Ball, M. and Wood, A. (1996) "Does building investment affect economic growth?", *Journal of Property Research*, **13**(2): 99–114.

Ball, M., Lizieri, C. and MacGregor, B.D. (1998) *The Economics of Commercial Property Markets.* London: Routledge.

Ball, M., Morrison, T. and Wood, A. (1996) "Structures investment and economic growth: a long-term international comparison", *Urban Studies*, **33**(9): 1687–706.

Baro, R.J. (1997) *Determinants of Economic Growth: a Cross-Country Empirical Study.* Cambridge, MA: Massachusetts Institute of Technology Press.

Barras, R. (1983) "A simple theoretical model of the office development cycle", *Environment and Planning A*, **15**(10): 1381–94.

Barras, R. (1994) "Property and the economic cycle: building cycles revisited", *Journal of Property Research*, **11**: 183–97.

Batten, D.F. (1995) "Network cities: creative urban agglomerations for the 21st century", *Urban Studies*, **32**(2): 313–27.

Beauregard, R.A. (1994) "Capital switching and the build environment: United States 1970–89", *Environment and Planning A*, **26**(5): 715–32.

Bedau, M.A. and Humphreys, P.E. (eds) (2008) *Emergence: Contemporary Readings in Philosophy and Science.* Cambridge, MA: MIT Press.

Begg, I. (1999) "Cities and competitiveness", *Urban Studies*, **36**(5–6): 795–809.

Begg, I. (2002) "Investability: the key to competitive regions and cities?", *Regional Studies*, **36**(2): 187–200.

Berg, L. van der, Braun, E. and Winden, W. van (2001) "Growth clusters in European cities: an integral approach", *Urban Studies*, **38**(1): 185–205.

Berg, L. van der, Drewett, R., Klaassen, L.H., Rossi, A. and Vijverberg, C.H.T. (1982) *Urban Europe: a Study of Growth and Decline.* Oxford: Pergamon Press.

Bergstrom, T.C. (2002) "Evolution of social behavior: individual and social selection", *Journal of Economic Perspectives*, **16**(2): 67–88.

Bertinelli, L. and Black, D. (2004) "Urbanization and growth", *Journal of Urban Economics*, **56**(1): 80–96.

Bhaskar, R. (1975) *A Realist Theory of Science.* Leeds: Leeds Books.

Bhaskar, R. (1979) *The Possibility of Naturalism: a Philosophic Critique of the Contemporary Human Sciences.* Brighton: Harvester.

Bhaskar, R. (1986) *Scientific Realism and Human Emancipation.* London: Verso.

Bhaskar, R. (1989) *Reclaiming Reality: a Critical Introduction to Contemporary Philosophy.* London: Verso.

Black, J. (1997) *A Dictionary of Economics.* Oxford: Oxford University Press.

Blackburn, S. (1996) "Metaphysics", in Bunnin, N. and Tsui-James, E.P. (eds) *The Blackwell Companion to Philosophy.* Oxford: Blackwell, pp. 64–89.

Blanchard, O. (2006) "European unemployment: the evolution of facts and ideas", *Economic Policy*, **21**(45): 5–59.

Blaug, M. (1980) *Economic Theory in Retrospect*, 3rd edn. Cambridge: Cambridge University Press.

Blaug, M. (1992) *The Methodology of Economics or How Economics Explain,* 2nd edn. Cambridge: Cambridge University Press.

Bloom, D.E., Canning, D. and Fink, G. (2010) "Implications of population ageing for economic growth", *Oxford Review of Economic Policy*, **26**(4): 583–612.

Blotevogel, H.H. and King, R. (1996) "European economic restructuring: demographic responses and feedbacks", *European Urban and Regional Studies*, **3**(2): 133–59.

Boddy, M. (1981) "The property sector in late capitalism: the case of Britain" in Dear, M.J. and Scott, A.J. (eds) *Urbanisation and Urban Planning in Capitalist Society.* London: Methuen.

Boddy, M. (1999) "Geographical economics and urban competitiveness: a critique", *Urban Studies*, **36**(5–6): 811–42.

Bosman, J. and de Smidt, M. (1993) "The geographical formation of international management centres in Europe", *Urban Studies*, **30**(6): 967–80.

Bourdieu, P. (1986) "The forms of capital", in Richardson, J.G. (ed.) *Handbook of Theory and Research for the Sociology of Education.* New York: Greenwood, pp. 241–58.

Bovaird, T. (1992) "Local economic development and the city", *Urban Studies*, **29**(3/4): 343–68.

Bovaird, T. (1993) "Analysing urban economic development", *Urban Studies*, **30**(4/5): 631–58.

Boyer, R. (1990) *The Regulation School: a Critical Introduction.* New York: Columbia University Press.

Boyer, R. and Saillard, Y. (eds) (2002) *Regulation Theory: the State of the Art*. London: Routledge.

Brannen, J. (ed.) (1992) *Mixing Methods: Qualitative and Quantitative Research*. Aldershot: Avebury.

Breit, W. (1973) "The development of Clarence Ayres's theoretical institutionalism", *Social Science Quarterly*, **54**(2): 244–57.

Brenner, R. and Glick, M. (1991) "The regulation approach: theory and history", *New Left Review*, **188**(July/August): 45–119.

Bromley, D.W. (1994) "Institutional economics, Wisconsin School of", in Hodgson, G.M., Samuels, W.J. and Tool, M.R. (eds) *The Elgar Companion to Institutional and Evolutionary Economics, A–K*. Aldershot: Edward Elgar, pp. 386–92.

Bromley, D.W. (2006) *Sufficient Reason: Volitional Pragmatism and the Meaning of Economic Institutions*. Princeton: Princeton University Press.

Bruhl, M. and Lizieri, C. (1994) "Centralism vs federalism, implications for regional diversification", *Journal of Property Valuation and Investment*, **12**(1): 59–73.

Brunetti, A. and Weder, B. (1997) *Investment and Institutional Uncertainty*. Washington DC: World Bank.

Brunetti, A. and Weder, B. (1998) "Investment and institutional uncertainty: a comparative study of different uncertainty measures", *Weltwirtschaftliches Archiv*, **134**(3): 513–33.

Brunetti, A., Kisunko, G. and Weder, B. (1997) *Credibility of Rules and Economic Growth, Evidence from a Worldwide Survey of the Private Sector*. Washington, DC: World Bank.

Bryman, A. (1992) *Quantity and Quality in Social Research*. London: Routledge.

Bryman, A. (2001) *Social Research Methods*. Oxford: Oxford University Press.

Budd, L. (1995) "Globalisation, territory and strategic alliances in different financial centres", *Urban Studies*, **32**(2): 345–60.

Budd, L. (1998) "Territorial Competition and globalisation: scylla and charybdis of European cities", *Urban Studies*, **35**(4): 663–85.

Buitelaar, E. (2004) "A transaction-cost analysis of the land development process", *Urban Studies*, **41**(13): 2539–53.

Buitelaar, E. (2007) *The Cost of Land Use Decisions: Applying Transaction Cost Economics to Planning and Development*. Oxford: Blackwell.

Bunnin, N. and Tsui-James, E.P. (eds) (1996) *The Blackwell Companion to Philosophy*. Oxford: Blackwell.

Bush, P.D. (1987) "The theory of institutional change", *Journal of Economic Issues*, **21**(3): 1075–116.

Bush, P.D. (1991) "Reflections on the twenty-fifth anniversary of AFEE: philosophical and methodological issues in institutional economics", *Journal of Economic Issues*, **25**(2): 321–46.

Bush, P.D. (1993) "The methodology of institutional economics: a pragmatic instrumentalist perspective" in Tool, M.R. (ed.) *Institutional Economics: Theory, Method, Policy*. Boston: Kluwer Academic Publishers, pp. 59–107.

Bush, P.D. (1994) "Social change, theory of", in Hodgson, G.M., Samuels, W.J. and Tool, M.R. (eds) *The Elgar Companion to Institutional and Evolutionary Economics, L–Z*. Aldershot: Edward Elgar, pp. 291–6.

Bush, P.D. (2008) "Culture, values and institutions", in Davis, J.B. and Dolfsma, W. (eds) *The Elgar Companion to Social Economics*. Cheltenham: Edward Elgar, pp. 153–70.

Cairncross, F. (1997) *The Death of Distance: How the Communications Revolution Will Change Our Lives*. London: Orion.

Callinicos, A. (1989) "Anthony Giddens: a contemporary critique", in Callinicos, A. (ed.) *Marxist Theory*. Oxford: Oxford University Press, pp. 105–47.

Camagni, R. (1999) "The city as a milieu: applying GREMI's approach to urban evolution", *Revue d'Economie Régionale et Urbaine*, **3**: 591–606.

Camic, C. (1986) "The matter of habit", *American Journal of Sociology*, **91**(5): 1039–87.

Carbonaro, G. and D'Arcy, E. (1993) "Key issues in property-led urban restructuring: a European perspective", *Journal of Property Valuation and Investment*, **11**(4): 339–53.

Castellacci, F. (2006) "A critical realist interpretation of evolutionary growth theorising", *Cambridge Journal of Economics*, **30**(6): 861–80.

Castells, M. (1977) *The Urban Question: a Marxist Approach*. London: Edward Arnold.

Castells, M. (1989) *The Informational City*. Oxford: Basil Blackwell.

Castells, M. (1993) "European cities, the information society, and the global economy", *Tijdschrift Voor Economische En Sociale Geografie*, **84**(4): 247–57.

Castells, M. (1996) "The informational mode of development and the restructuring of capitalism", in Fainstein, S.S. and Campbell, S. (eds) *Readings in Urban Theory*, Oxford: Blackwell, pp. 73–101.

Champion, A. (2001) "A changing demographic regime and evolving polycentric urban regions: consequences for the size, composition and distribution of city populations", *Urban Studies*, **38**(4): 657–77.

Chang, H.-J. (2002) "Breaking the mould: an institutionalist political economy alternative to the neo-liberal theory of the market and the state", *Cambridge Journal of Economics*, **26**(5): 539–59.

Chang, H.-J. (ed.) (2007) *Institutional Change and Economic Development*. London: Anthem.

Chang, H.-J. (2011) "Institutions and economic development: theory, policy and history", *Journal of Institutional Economics*, **7**(4): 473–98.

Charney, I. (2001) "Three dimensions of capital switching within the real estate sector: a Canadian case study", *International Journal of Urban and Regional Research*, **25**(4): 740–58.

Chavance, B. (2009) *Institutional Economics*. London: Routledge.

Cheng, C.-P. (2005) "Critical realism and institutionalism: integrating the scientific method of John R. Commons and Douglass C. North", *Soochow Journal of Economics and Business*, **51**: 297–318.

Cheshire, P. (1990) "Explaining the recent performance of the European Community's major urban regions", *Urban Studies*, **27**(3): 311–33.

Cheshire, P. (1991) "Problems of regional transformation and deindustrialisation in the European Community", in Rodwin, L. and Sazanami, H. (eds) *Industrial Change and Regional Economic Transformation, the Experience of Western Europe*. London: Harper Collins Academic, pp. 237–67.

Cheshire, P. (1995) "A new phase of urban development in Western Europe? The evidence for the 1980s", *Urban Studies*, **32**(7): 1045–63.

Cheshire, P. (1999) "Cities in competition: articulating the gains from integration", *Urban Studies*, **36**(5–6): 843–64.

Cheshire, P. and Carbonaro, G. (1996) "Urban economic growth in Europe: testing theory and policy prescriptions", *Urban Studies*, **33**(7): 1111–28.

Cheshire, P. and Gordon, I. (eds) (1995) *Territorial Competition in an Integrating Europe*. Aldershot: Avebury.

Cheshire, P. and Gordon, I. (1996) "Territorial competition and the predictability of collective (in)action", *International Journal of Urban and Regional Research*, **20**(3): 383–99.

Cheshire, P. and Hay, D. (1989) *Urban Problems in Western Europe – an Economic Analysis*. London: Unwin Hyman.

Cheshire, P., Carbonaro, G. and Hay, D. (1986) "Problems of urban decline and growth in EEC countries: or measuring degrees of elephantness", *Urban Studies*, **23**(2): 131–49.

Chin, H. and Dent, P. (2005) "An analysis of the level of maturity in South East Asian property markets", *Pacific Rim Property Research Journal*, **11**(4): 355–72.

Chin, W., Dent, P. and Roberts, C. (2006) "An exploratory analysis of barriers to investment and market maturity in Southeast Asian cities", *Journal of Real Estate Portfolio Management*, **12**(1): 49–57.

Chinitz, D. (2013) "The special interdisciplinary contribution of institutional economics", *Health Economics, Policy and Law*, **8**(3): 387–96.

Chong, A. and Calderon, C. (2000) "Causality and feedback between institutional measures and economic growth", *Economics and Politics*, **12**(1): 69–81.

Clark, B. (1998) *Principles of Political Economy: a Comparative Approach*. Westport, CT: Praeger.

Clark, J.M. (1918a) "Economics and modern psychology I", *Journal of Political Economy*, **26**(1): 1–30.

Clark, J.M. (1918b) "Economics and modern psychology II", *Journal of Political Economy*, **26**(2): 136–66.

Clark, N.G. and Juma, C. (1987) *Long-Run Economics: an Evolutionary Approach to Economic Growth*. London: Pinter.

Clayton, J. (1998) "Further evidence on real estate efficiency", *Journal of Real Estate Research*, **15**(1/2): 41–57.

Cloke, P., Philo, C. and Sadler, D. (1991) *Approaching Human Geography, an Introduction to Contemporary Theoretical Debates*. London: Paul Chapman.

Coase, R.H. (1937) "The nature of the firm", *Economica*, **4**(16): 386–405.

Coase, R.H. (1960) "The problem of social cost", *Journal of Law and Economics*, **3**(1): 1–44.

Coase, R.H. (1998) "The new institutional economics", *American Economic Review*, **88**(2): 72–4.

Coffey, W. and Bailly, A. (1996) "Economic restructuring: a conceptual framework", in Lever, W.F. and Bailly, A. (eds) *The Spatial Impact of Economic Change in Europe*. Aldershot: Avebury, pp. 13–39.

Colander, D. (2000) "The death of neoclassical economics", *Journal of the History of Economic Thought*, **22**(2): 127–44.

Colander, D., Holt, R.P.F. and Rosser, B.J. (2004a) *The Changing Face of Economics: Conversations with Cutting Edge Economists*. Ann Arbor, MI: University of Michigan Press.

Colander, D., Holt, R.P.F. and Rosser, B.J. (2004b) "The changing face of mainstream economics", *Review of Political Economy*, **16**(4): 485–99.

Coleman, J.S. (1990) *Foundations of Social Theory*. Cambridge: Belknap.

Combes, P.P., Duranton, G. and Overman, H.G. (2005) "Agglomeration and the adjustment of the spatial economy", *Papers in Regional Science*, **84**(3): 311–49.

Commons, J.R. (1924) *Legal Foundations of Capitalism*. New York: Macmillan.

Commons, J.R. (1931) "Institutional economics", *American Economic Review*, **21**(December): 648–57.

Commons, J.R. (1934) *Institutional Economics: its Place in Political Economy*. New York: Macmillan.

Commons, J.R. (1950) *The Economics of Collective Action*. New York: Macmillan.

Cordes, C. (2005) "Veblen's 'instinct of workmanship', its cognitive foundations, and some implications for economic inquiry", *Journal of Economic Issues*, **39**(1): 1–20.

Cordes, C. (2007) "The role of 'instincts' in the development of corporate cultures", *Journal of Economic Issues*, **41**(3): 747–64.

Coulson, A. and Ferrario, C. (2007) " 'Institutional thickness': local governance and economic development in Birmingham, England", *International Journal of Urban and Regional Research*, **31**(3): 591–615.

Cox, K.R. (2013) "Notes on a brief encounter: critical realism, historical materialism and human geography", *Dialogues in Human Geography*, **3**(1): 3–21.

Crampton, G.R. (1999) "Urban unemployment in the EU, tertiary-sector employment growth and urban size", *Urban Studies*, **36**(12): 2121–33.

Creswell, J.W. (1994) *Research Design: Qualitative and Quantitative Approaches*, Thousand Oaks: Sage.

Crosby, N., Gibson, V. and Murdoch, S. (2003) "UK commercial property lease structures: landlord and tenant mismatch", *Urban Studies*, **40**(8): 1487–516.

Cruickshank, J. (ed.) (2003) *Critical Realism: the Difference it Makes*. London: Routledge.

Cumbers, A., MacKinnon, D. and McMaster, R. (2003) "Institutions, power and space: assessing the limits to institutionalism in economic geography", *European Urban and Regional Studies*, **10**(4), pp. 325–42.

D'Arcy, E. and Keogh, G. (1997) "Towards a property market paradigm of urban change", *Environment and Planning A*, **29**(4): 685–706.

D'Arcy, E. and Keogh, G. (1998) "Territorial competition and property market process: an explanatory analysis", *Urban Studies*, **35**(8): 1215–30.

D'Arcy, E. and Keogh, G. (1999) "The property market and urban competitiveness: a review", *Urban Studies*, **36**(5–6): 917–28.

D'Arcy, E. and Keogh, G. (2002) "The market context of property development activity", in Guy, S. and Henneberry, J. (eds) *Development and Developers: Perspectives on Propert*. Oxford: Blackwell, pp. 19–34.

D'Arcy, E. and Lee, S. (1998) "A real estate portfolio strategy for Europe: a review of the options", *Journal of Real Estate Portfolio Management*, **4**(2): 113–23.

D'Arcy, E., McGough, T. and Tsolacos, S. (1997a) "National economic trends, market size and city growth effects on European office rents", *Journal of Property Research*, **14**(4): 297–308.

D'Arcy, E., McGough, T. and Tsolacos, S. (1997b) "An empirical investigation of retail rents in five European cities", *Journal of Property Valuation and Investment*, **15**(4): 308–22.

Dale, P. (1997) "Land tenure issues in economic development", *Urban Studies*, **34**(10): 1621–33.

Danermark, B., Jakobsen, L., Karlsson, J.C. and Ekstrom, M. (2002) *Explaining Society: an Introduction to Critical Realism in the Social Sciences*. London: Routledge.

Darrat, A.F. and Glascock, J.L. (1993) "On the real estate market efficiency", *Journal of Real Estate Finance and Economics*, **7**(1): 55–72.

David, P.A. (1985) "Clio and the economics of QWERTY", *American Economic Review*, **75**(2): 332–7.

David, P. and Rosenbloom, J. L. (1990) "Marshallian factor market externalities and the dynamics of industrial location", *Journal of Urban Economics*, **28**(3): 349–70.

Davidsen, B.-I. (2010) "Towards a critical realist-inspired economic methodology", *The Journal of Philosophical Economics*, **3**(2): 74–96.

Davis, J.B. (2006) "The turn in economics: neoclassical dominance to mainstream pluralism", *Journal of Institutional Economics*, **2**(1): 1–20.

Davis, J.B. (2008) "The turn in recent economics and return of orthodoxy", *Cambridge Journal of Economics*, **32**(3): 349–66.

Dear, M.J. and Moos, A.I. (1986) "Structuration theory in urban analysis: 2. Empirical application", *Environment and Planning A*, **18**(3): 351–73.

DeGregori, T.R. (1977) "Technology and ceremonial behavior: aspects of institutionalism", *Journal of Economic Issues*, **11**(4): 861–70.

Delaney, C.F. (1999) "Dewey, John" in Audi, R. (ed.) *The Cambridge Dictionary of Philosophy*, 2nd edn. Cambridge: Cambridge University Press, pp. 229–31.

Demsetz, H. (1967) "Towards a theory of property rights", *American Economic Review*, **57**(2): 347–59.

Demsetz, H. (1997) "The firm in economic theory: a quiet revolution", *American Economic Review*, **87**(2): 426–9.

Dennis, K. (1994) "Formalism in economics", in Hodgson, G.M., Samuels, W.J. and Tool, M.R. (eds) *The Elgar Companion to Institutional and Evolutionary Economics, A–K*. Aldershot: Edward Elgar, pp. 251–6.

Denscombe, M. (1998) *The Good Research Guide: for Small-scale Social Research Projects*. Buckingham: Open University Press.

Dequech, D. (2008) "Neoclassical, mainstream, orthodox, and heterodox economics", *Journal of Post Keynesian Economics*, **20**(2): 279–302.

Dewey, J. (1891) *Psychology*, 3rd edn. New York: Harper.

Dewey, J. (1922) *Human Nature and Conduct: an Introduction to Social Psychology*. New York: Holt.

Dewey, J. (1929) *The Quest for Certainty: a Study of the Relation of Knowledge and Action*. New York: Minton, Balch.

Dewey, J. (1939a) *Logic: The Theory of Inquiry*. London: George Allen and Unwin.

Dewey, J. (1939b) *Theory of Valuation*. Chicago: University of Chicago Press.

Dicken, P. and Oberg, S. (1996) "The global context: Europe in a world of dynamic economic and population change", *European Urban and Regional Studies*, **3**(2): 101–20.

DiPasquale, D. and Wheaton, W.C. (1996) *Urban Economics and Real Estate Markets*. New Jersey: Prentice-Hall.

Djankov, S. and Murrell, P. (2002) "Enterprise restructuring in transition: a quantitative survey", *Journal of Economic Literature*, **40**(3): 793–837.

Djankov, S., La Porta, R., Lopez-de-Silanes, F. and Shleifer, A. (2002) "The regulation of entry", *Quarterly Journal of Economics*, **1017**(1): 1–37.

Dokko, Y. and Edelstein, R.H. (1992) "Towards a real estate land use modeling paradigm", *Journal of American Real Estate and Urban Economics Association*, **20**(1): 199–209.

Dollery, B. and Leong, W.H. (1998) "Measuring the transaction sector in the Australian economy, 1911–1991", *Australian Economic History Review*, **38**(3): 207–31.

Dosi, G. (1988) "Institutions and markets in a dynamic world", *The Manchester School*, **56**(2): 119–46.

Dow, S.D. (2002) *Economic Methodology: an Inquiry*, Oxford: Oxford University Press.

Downward, P. (ed.) (2003) *Applied Economics and the Critical Realist Critique*. London: Routledge.

Downward, P. and Mearman, A. (2007) "Retroduction as mixed-methods triangulation in economic research: reorienting economics into social science", *Cambridge Journal of Economics*, **31**(1): 77–99.

Downward, P., Dow, S.C. and Fleetwood, S. (2006) "Transforming economics through critical realism: themes and issues", *Journal of Critical Realism*, **5**(1): 151–82.

Downward, P., Finch, J.H. and Ramsay, J. (2002) "Critical realism, empirical methods and inference: a critical discussion", *Cambridge Journal of Economics*, **26**(4): 481–500.

Dugger, W.M. (1979) "Methodological differences between institutional and neoclassical economics", *Journal of Economic Issues*, **13**(4): 899–909.

Dugger, W.M. (1980) "Property rights, law, and John R. Commons", *Review of Social Economy*, **38**(April): 41–53.

Dumais, G., Ellison, G. and Glaeser, E.L. (2002) "Geographic concentration as a dynamic process", *Review of Economics and Statistics*, **84**(2):193–204.

Dunford, M. (1990) "Theories of regulation", *Environment and Planning D: Society and Space*, **8**(3): 297–321.

Dzielinski, M. (2012) "Measuring economic uncertainty and its impact on the stock market", *Finance Research Letters*, **9**(3): 167–75.

Easterly, W. and Levine, R. (1997) "Africa's growth tragedy: policies and ethnic divisions", *Quarterly Journal of Economics*, **112**(4): 1203–50.

Easton, G. (2010) "Critical realism in case study research", *Industrial Marketing Management*, **39**(1): 118–28.

Edel, M. (1992) *Urban and Regional Economics – Marxist Perspectives*. Chur: Harwood Academic.

Edel, M. (1996) "Urban and regional economics – Marxist perspectives", in Arnott, R. (ed.) *Regional and Urban Economics*. Amsterdam: Harwood Academic, pp. 1051–200.

Edie, L.D. (1922) *Principles of the New Economics*. New York: Thomas Cromwell.

Egert, B. and Mihaljek, D. (2007) "Determinants of house prices in Central and Eastern Europe", *Comparative Economic Studies*, **49**(3): 367–88.

Eggertsson, T. (1990a) *Economic Behaviour and Institutions*. Cambridge: Cambridge University Press.

Eggertsson, T. (1990b) "The role of transaction costs and property rights in economic analysis", *European Economic Review*, **34**(2–3): 450–7.

Elsner, W. (2012) *Microeconomics of Interactive Economies: Evolutionary, Institutional, and Complexity Perspectives*. Cheltenham: Edward Elgar.

Engels, F. (1946 [1886]) *Ludwig Feuerbach and the End of Classical German Philosophy*, transcription Taylor, P. [first published in German 1886 in *Die Neue Zeit*, issues 4 and 5]. Moscow: Progress.

Engels, F. (1947 [1876–1878]) *Anti-Dühring, Herr Eugen Dühring's Revolution in Science*, tr. Burns, E. [first published in German 1877–1878 in *Vorwärts*; first published as a book in German 1878 by Genossenschaftsbuchdruckerei, Leipzig]. Moscow: Progress.

Engels, F. (1964 [1925]) *Dialectics of Nature*, 3rd rev. edn, tr. Dutt, C. [first published in German and Russian 1925 by the Marx-Engels Institute, *Archives of Marx and Engels, Book 2*, ed. Riazanov, D.B.]. Moscow: Progress.

EOS Gallup Europe (2000) *Entrepreneurship*. Brussels: European Commission, Directorate General Education and Culture.

European Commission (1997) *Towards an Urban Agenda in the European Union*. Brussels: European Commission.

Evans, A.W. (1985) *Urban Economics, an Introduction*. Oxford: Blackwell.

Evans, A.W. (1995) "The property market: ninety per cent efficient?", *Urban Studies*, **32**(1): 5–29.

Evans, A.W. (2008) *Economics, Real Estate and the Supply of Land*. Oxford: Blackwell.

Fainstein, S.S. and Campbell, S. (eds) (1996) *Readings in Urban Theory*. Oxford: Blackwell.

Falkenbach, H. (2009) "Market selection for international real estate investments", *International Journal of Strategic Property Management*, **13**(4): 299–308.

Fama, E.F. (1970) "Efficient capital markets: a review of theory and empirical work", *Journal of Finance*, **25**(2): 383–417.

Farole, T., Rodríguez-Pose, A. and Storper, M. (2011) "Cohesion policy in the European Union: growth, geography, institutions", *Journal of Common Market Studies*, **49**(5): 1089–111.

Favereau, O. and Lazega, E. (eds) (2003) *Conventions and Structures in Economic Organization: Markets, Networks and Organizations*. Cheltenham: Edward Elgar.

Feagin, J.R. (1987) "The secondary circuit of capital: office construction in Houston, Texas", *International Journal of Urban and Regional Research*, **11**(2): 172–92.

Fereidouni, H.G., Al-Mulali, U. and Mohammed, M.A.H.B. (2013) "The effects of transaction costs, landlord and tenant practices and property rights on foreign real estate investment", *Margin: the Journal of Applied Economic Research*, **7**(3): 351–70.

Field, A.J. (1994) "North, Douglass C.", in Hodgson, G.M., Samuels, W.J. and Tool, M.R. (eds) *The Elgar Companion to Institutional and Evolutionary Economics, L–Z*. Aldershot: Edward Elgar, pp. 134–8.

Fielding, A.J. (1994) "Industrial Change and Regional Development in Western Europe", *Urban Studies*, **31**(4/5): 679–704.

Finch, J.H. and McMaster, R. (2002) "On categorical variables and non-parametric statistical inference in the pursuit of causal explanations", *Cambridge Journal of Economics*, **26**(6): 753–72.

Fischer, C.C. (1986) "Institutionalism versus orthodoxy: the articulation of methodological alternatives", *American Journal of Economics and Sociology*, **45**(3): 359–72.

Fisher, P. (2005) "The property development process: case studies from Grainger Town", *Property Management*, **23**(3): 158–75.

Fleetwood, S. (ed.) (1999) *Critical Realism in Economics, Development and Debate*. London: Routledge.

Fleetwood, S. (2001) "Causal laws, functional relations and tendencies", *Review of Political Economy*, **13**(2): 201–20.

Flick, U. (2009) *An Introduction to Qualitative Research*, 4nd edn. London: Sage.

Foster, F.J. (1981) "The papers of J. Fagg Foster", *Journal of Economic Issues*, **14**(4): 857–1007.

Foster, J. (1988) *Evolutionary Macroeconomics*. London: Allen and Unwin.

Frankfort-Nachmias, C. and Nachmias, D. (1992) *Research Methods in the Social Sciences*, 4th edn. London: Edward Arnold.

Fraser, W.D. (1993) *Principles of Property Investment and Pricing*, 2nd edn. Basingstoke: Macmillan.

Friedman, M. (1953) "The methodology of positive economics" in Friedman, M. (ed.) *Essays in Positive Economics*. Chicago: Chicago University Press, pp. 3–43.

Fujita, M. and Krugman, P. (2004) "The new economic geography: past, present and the future", *Papers in Regional Science*, **83**(1): 139–64.

Fujita, M. and Mori, T. (2005) "Frontiers of the new economic geography", *Papers in Regional Science*, **84**(3): 377–405.

Fujita, M. and Thisse, J.-F. (1996) "Economics of agglomeration", *Journal of the Japanese and International Economics*, **10**(4): 339–78.

Fujita, M., Krugman, P.R. and Venables, A. (1999) *The Spatial Economy: Cities, Regions, and International Trade*. Cambridge, MA: Massachusetts Institute of Technology Press.

Furubotn, E.G. and Richter, R. (2005) *Institutions and Economic Theory: the Contribution of the New Institutional Economics*, 2nd edn. Michigan: University of Michigan Press.

Fusfeld, D.R. (1977) "The development of economic institutions", *Journal of Economic Issues*, **11**(4): 743–84.

Ganderton, P. (1994) "Modeling the land conversion process: a realist perspective", *Environment and Planning A*, **26**(5): 803–19.

Gaspar, J. and Glaeser, E.L. (1998) "Information technology and the future of cities", *Journal of Urban Economics*, **43**(1): 136–56.

Gatzlaff, D.H. and Tirtiroglu, D. (1995) "Real estate market efficiency: issues and evidence", *Journal of Real Estate Literature*, **3**(2): 157–89.

Gau, G.W. (1987) "Efficient real estate markets: paradox or paradigm?", *Journal of American Real Estate and Urban Economics Association*, **15**(2): 1–12.

Gee, A.J.M. (1991) "The neoclassical school" in Mair, D. and Miller, A.G. (eds) *A Modern Guide to Economic Thought, an Introduction to Comparative Schools of Thought in Economics*. Aldershot: Edward Elgar, pp. 71–108.

Geertz, C. (1973) *The Interpretation of Cultures: Selected Essays*. New York: Basic Books.

Gertler, M.S. (2010) "Rules of the game: the place of institutions in regional economic change", *Regional Studies*, **44**(1): 1–15.

Geurts, T.G. and Jaffe, A.J. (1996) "Risk and real estate investment: an international perspective", *Journal of Real Estate Research*, **11**(2): 117–29.

Gibb, K. and Hoesli, M. (2003) "Developments in urban housing and property markets", *Urban Studies*, **40**(5–6): 887–96.

Gibson, V. (2000) "Property portfolio dynamics: the flexible management of inflexible assets", *Facilities*, **18**(3/4): 150–4.

Gibson, V. (2003) "Flexible working needs flexible space? Towards an alternative workplace strategy", *Journal of Property Investment and Finance*, **21**(1): 12–22.

Gibson, V. and Lizieri, C. (1998) *The Real Estate Implications of Business Reorganisation and Working Practice, Right Space: Right Price? A Study of the Impact of Changing Business Patterns on the Property Market*. London: Royal Institution of Chartered Surveyors.

Gibson, V. and Lizieri, C. (1999) "New business practices and the corporate property portfolio: how responsive is the UK property market?", *Journal of Property Research*, **16**(3): 201–18.

Gibson, V. and Lizieri, C. (2001) "Friction and inertia: business change, corporate real estate portfolios and the U.K. office market", *Journal of Real Estate Research*, **22**(1/2): 59–79.

Giddens, A. (1979) *Central Problems in Social Theory*. Berkeley: University of California Press.

Giddens, A. (1981) *A Contemporary Critique to Historical Materialism, Vol 1: Power, Property and the State*. London: Macmillan.

Giddens, A. (1984) *The Constitution of Society: Outline of the Theory of Structuration*. Cambridge: Policy Press.

Giussani, B., Hsia, M. and Tsolacos, S. (1993) "A comparative analysis of the major determinants of office rental values in Europe", *Journal of Property Valuation and Investment*, **11**(2): 157–73.

Glaeser, E.L. and Gottlieb, J.D. (2009) "The wealth of cities: agglomeration economies and spatial equilibrium in the United States", *Journal of Economic Literature*, **47**(4): 983–1028.

Glaeser, E., Kallal, H., Scheinkman, J. and Shleifer, A. (1992) "Growth in cities", *Journal of Political Economy*, **100**(6): 1126–52.

Goel, R.K. and Ram, R. (2013) "Economic uncertainty and corruption: evidence from a large cross-country data set", *Applied Economics*, **45**(24): 3462–8.

Goldberg, M.A. (2004) "Local property markets and effective flexible market institutions", in Seabrooke, W., Kent, P. and How, H.H.H. (eds) *International Real Estate: an Institutional Approach*, Oxford: Blackwell, pp. 96–129.

Goodall, B. (1972) *The Economics of Urban Areas*. Oxford: Pergamon Press.

Gordon, I. (1999) "Internationalisation and urban competition", *Urban Studies*, **36**(5–6): 1001–16.

Gordon, I.R. and McCann, P. (2000) "Industrial clusters: complexes, agglomeration and/or social networks?", *Urban Studies*, **37**(3): 513–32.

Gordon, J., Mosbaugh, P. and Canter, T. (1996) "Integrating regional economic indicators with the real estate cycle", *Journal of Real Estate Research*, **12**(3): 469–501.

Gottdiener, M. (1987) "Space as a force of production: contribution to the debate on realism, capitalism and space", *International Journal of Urban and Regional Research*, **11**(3): 405–16.

Graff, M. (2008) "Law and finance: common law and civil law countries compared – an empirical critique" *Economica*, **75**(297): 60–83.

Graff, R.A. and Webb, J.R. (1997) "Agency costs and inefficiency in commercial real estate", *Journal of Real Estate Portfolio Management*, **3**(1): 19–36.

Granato, J., Inglehart, R. and Leblang, D. (1996) "The effect of cultural values on economic development: theory, hypotheses, and some empirical tests", *American Journal of Political Science*, **40**(3): 607–31.

Granovetter, M. (1985) "Economic action and social structure: the problem of embeddedness", *American Journal of Sociology*, **91**(3): 481–510.

Granovetter, M. (1992) "Economic institutions as social constructions: a framework for analysis", *Acta Soliologica*, **35**(1): 3–11.

Granovetter, M. (2005) "The impact of social structure on economic outcomes", *Journal of Economic Perspectives*, **19**(1): 33–50.

Greif, A. (1998) "Historical and comparative institutional analysis", *American Economic Review*, **88**(2): 80–4.

Greif, A. (2006) *Institutions and the Path to the Modern Economy: Lessons from Medieval Trade*. New York: Cambridge University Press.

Grossman, S.J. and Stiglitz, J.E. (1980) "On the impossibility of informationally efficient markets", *American Economic Review*, **70**(2): 393–408.

Groth, N.B. (2000) "Urban systems between policy and geography", *Regional Studies*, **34**(6): 571–80.

Gruffyd-Jones, B. (2006) *Explaining Global Poverty: a Critical Realist Approach*. New York: Routledge.

Guimaraes, P., Figueiredo, O. and Woodward, D. (2000) "Agglomeration and the location of foreign direct investment in Portugal", *Journal of Urban Economics*, **47**(1): 115–35.

Guntermann, K.L. and Norrbin, S.C. (1991) "Empirical tests of real estate market efficiency", *Journal of Real Estate Finance and Economics*, **4**(3): 297–313.

Guy, S. and Harris, R. (1997) "Property in a global-risk society: towards marketing research in the office sector", *Urban Studies*, **34**(1): 125–40.

Guy, S. and Henneberry, J. (2000) "Understanding urban development processes: integrating the economic and the social in property research", *Urban Studies*, **37**(13): 2399–416.

Guy, S. and Henneberry, J. (2002a) "Bridging the divide? Complementary perspectives on property", *Urban Studies*, **39**(8): 1471–8.

Guy, S. and Henneberry, J. (eds) (2002b) *Development and Developers: Perspectives on Property*. Oxford: Blackwell.

Gwartney, J., Lawson, R. and Block, W. (1996) *Economic Freedom of the World, 1975–1995*. Vancouver, BC: Fraser Institute.

Gwartney, J., Lawson, R. and Gartzke, E. (2005) *Economic Freedom of the World, 2010 Annual Report*. Vancouver, BC: Fraser Institute.

Gwartney, J., Lawson, R. and Hall, J. (2010) *Economic Freedom of the World, 2010 Annual Report*. Vancouver, BC: Fraser Institute.

Gwartney, J., Lawson, R. and Hall, J. (2013) *Economic Freedom of the World, 2013 Annual Report*. Vancouver, BC: Fraser Institute.

Hadar, Y. and Pines, D. (2004) "Population growth and its distribution between cities: positive and normative aspects", *Regional Science and Urban Economics*, **34**(2): 125–54.

Hall, J.C. (2013) "Economic freedom and regional economics: an introduction to a special issue", *Journal of Regional Analysis and Policy*, **43**(1): 1–2.

Hall, P. (1993) "Forces shaping urban Europe", *Urban Studies*, **30**(6): 883–98.

Hall, P. (1997a) "Modelling the post-industrial city", *Futures*, **29**(4/5): 311–22.

Hall, P. (1997b) "The future of the metropolis and its form", *Regional Studies*, **31**(3): 211–20.

Hall, P. (1999) "The future of cities", *Computers, Environment and Urban Systems*, **23**(3): 173–85.

Hall, P. and Hay, D. (1980) *Growth Centres in the European Urban System*. London: Heinemann Educational.

Hamel, J., Dufour, S. and Fortin, D. (1993) *Case Study Methods*. Newbury Park: Sage.

Hamilton, D. (1953) "Veblen and Commons: a case of theoretical convergence", *Southern Social Science Quarterly*, **34**(September): 43–50.

Hamilton, M., Lim, L.C. and McCluskey, W. (2006) "The changing pattern of commercial lease terms: evidence from Birmingham, London, Manchester and Belfast", *Property Management*, **24**(1): 31–46.

Hamilton, W.H. (1919) "The institutional approach to economic theory", *The American Economic Review, Supplement, Papers and Proceeding of the Fifty-First Annual Meeting of the American Economic Association*, **4**(1): 309–18.

Hamilton, W.H. (1932) "Institution", in Seligman, E.R.A. and Johnson, A. (eds) *Encyclopaedia of the Social Sciences*, Vol. 7. New York: Macmillan, pp. 84–9.

Hansen, E.R. (1990) "Agglomeration economies and industrial decentralization – the wage-productivity trade-offs", *Journal of Urban Economics*, **28**(2): 140–59.

Hargreaves-Heap, S.P. (1994) "Rationality and maximization" in Hodgson, G.M., Samuels, W.J. and Tool, M.R. (eds) *The Elgar Companion to Institutional and Evolutionary Economics, L–Z*. Aldershot: Edward Elgar, pp. 215–19.

Harris, N. (1997) "Cities in a global economy: structural change and policy reactions", *Urban Studies*, **34**(10): 1693–703.

Harris, R. (2001) "From fiefdom to service: the evolution of flexible occupation", *Journal of Corporate Real Estate*, **3**(1): 7–16.

Harvey, D. (1973) *Social Justice and the City*. Baltimore: Johns Hopkins University Press.

Harvey, D. (1978) "The urban process under capitalism: a framework for analysis", *International Journal of Urban and Regional Research*, **2**(1–4): 101–31.

Harvey, D. (1982) *The Limits to Capital*. Oxford: Basil Blackwell.

Harvey, D. (1985) *The Urbanization of Capital*. Oxford: Basil Blackwell.

Harvey, D. (1987) "Three myths in search of a reality in urban studies", *Environment and Planning D: Society and Space*, **5**(4): 367–76.

Harvey, D. (2008) "The right to the city", *New Left Review*, **53**(September/October): 23–40.

Harvey, D. (2010) *The Enigma of Capital*. London: Profile.

Harvey, D. (2012) *Rebel Cities: From the Right to the City to the Urban Revolution*. London: Verso.

Harvey, J. (1996) *Urban Land Economics*, 4th edn. London: Macmillan.

Hausner, V. (1987) *Urban Economic Change, Five City Studies*. Oxford: Oxford University Press.

Hayter, R. (2004) "Economic geography as dissenting institutionalism: the embeddedness, evolution and differentiation of regions", *Geografiska Annaler*, **86**B(2): 95–115.

Healey, P. (1991a) "Models of the development process: a review", *Journal of Property Research*, **8**(3): 219–38.

Healey, P. (1991b) "Urban regeneration and the development industry", *Regional Studies*, **25**(2): 97–110.

Healey, P. (1992) "An institutional model of the development process", *Journal of Property Research*, **9**(1): 33–44.

Healey, P. (1994) "Urban policy and property development: the institutional relations of real-estate development in an old industrial region", *Environment and Planning A*, **26**(2): 177–98.

Healey, P. (1995) "The institutional challenge for sustainable urban regeneration", *Cities*, **12**(4): 221–30.

Healey, P. (1997) *Collaborative Planning*. Basingstoke: Macmillan.

Healey, P. (1998) "Building institutional capacity through collaborative approaches to urban planning", *Environment and Planning A*, **30**(9): 1531–46.

Healey, P. (2002) "On creating the 'city' as a collective resource", *Urban Studies*, **39**(10): 1777–92.

Healey, P. and Barrett, S.M. (1990) "Structure and agency in land and property development process: some ideas for research", *Urban Studies*, **27**(1): 89–104.

Heiner, R.A. (1983) "The origin of predicable behavior", *American Economic Review*, **73**(4): 560–95.

Henderson, J.V. (1986) "Efficiency of resource usage and city size", *Journal of Urban Economics*, **19**(1): 47–70.

Henderson, J.V. (2003) "The urbanization process and economic growth: the so-what question", *Journal of Economic Growth*, **8**(1): 47–71.

Henderson, J.V. (2007) "Understanding knowledge spillovers", *Regional Science and Urban Economics*, **37**(4): 497–508.

Henisz, W.J. (2000) "The institutional environment for economic growth", *Economics and Politics*, **12**(1): 1–31.

Henneberry, J. (1999) "Convergence and difference in regional office development cycles", *Urban Studies*, **36**(9): 1439–65.

Henneberry, J. and Rowley, S. (2000) *Property Market Processes and Development Outcomes in Cities and Regions*. London: Royal Institution of Chartered Surveyors.

Hirst, P. and Zeitlin, J. (1991) "Flexible specialization versus post-Fordism: theory, evidence and policy implications", *Economy and Society*, **20**(1): 1–55.

Hjalmarsson, E. and Hjalmarsson, R. (2009) "Efficiency in housing markets: which home buyers know how to discount?", *Journal of Banking and Finance*, **33**(11): 2150–63.

Hodge, D. (2008) "Economics, realism and reality: a comparison of Maki and Lawson", *Cambridge Journal of Economics*, **32**(2): 163–202.

Hodgson, G.M. (1988) *Economics and Institutions*. Oxford: Polity.

Hodgson, G.M. (1989) "Institutional rigidities and economic growth", *Cambridge Journal of Economics*, **13**(1): 79–101.

Hodgson, G.M. (1993a) "Institutional economics: surveying the 'old' and the 'new'", *Metroeconomica*, **44**(1): 1–28.

Hodgson, G.M. (1993b) "Commentary", in Tool, M.R. (ed.) *Institutional Economics: Theory, Method, Policy*. Boston: Kluwer Academic, pp. 108–18.

Hodgson, G.M. (1993c) *Economics and Evolution, Bringing Life Back into Economics*. Cambridge: Polity.

Hodgson, G.M. (1994a) "Methodological individualism", in Hodgson, G.M., Samuels, W.J. and Tool, M.R. (eds) *The Elgar Companion to Institutional and Evolutionary Economics, L–Z*. Aldershot: Edward Elgar, pp. 63–7.

Hodgson, G.M. (1994b) "Institutional economic thought in Europe" in Hodgson, G.M., Samuels, W.J. and Tool, M.R. (eds) *The Elgar Companion to Institutional and Evolutionary Economics, A–K*. Aldershot: Edward Elgar, pp. 374–8.

Hodgson, G.M. (1994c) "The return of institutional economics", in Smelser, N.J. and Swedberg, R. (eds) *The Handbook of Economic Sociology*. Princeton: Princeton University Press, pp. 58–76.

Hodgson, G.M. (1996) "An evolutionary theory of long-term economic growth", *International Studies Quarterly*, **40**(3): 391–410.

Hodgson, G.M. (1997) "The ubiquity of habits and rules", *Cambridge Journal of Economics*, **21**(6): 663–84.

Hodgson, G.M. (1998a) "The approach of institutional economics", *Journal of Economic Literature*, **36**(1): 166–92.

Hodgson, G.M. (1998b) "Emergence", in Davis, J.B., Hands, W.D. and Maki, U. (eds) *The Handbook of Economic Methodology*. Cheltenham: Edward Elgar, pp. 156–60.

Hodgson, G.M. (1999a) "Structures and institutions: reflections on institutionalism, structuration theory and critical realism", *Unpublished Mimeo*, University of Hertfordshire.

Hodgson, G.M. (1999b) *Evolution and Institutions, On Evolutionary Economics and the Evolution of Economics*. Cheltenham: Edward Elgar.

Hodgson, G.M. (2000) "What is the essence of institutional economics?", *Journal of Economic Issues*, **34**(2): 317–29.

Hodgson, G.M. (2001) *How Economics Forgot History: the Problem of Historical Specificity in Social Science*. London: Routledge.

Hodgson, G.M. (2002) "Darwinism in economics: from analogy to ontology", *Journal of Evolutionary Economics*, **12**(3): 259–81.

Hodgson, G.M. (2003) "The hidden persuaders: institutions and individuals in economic theory", *Cambridge Journal of Economics*, **27**(2): 159–75.

Hodgson, G.M. (2004a) *The Evolution of Institutional Economics: Agency, Structure and Darwinism in American Institutionalism*. London: Routledge.

Hodgson, G.M. (2004b) "Reclaiming habit for institutional economics", *Journal of Economic Psychology*, **25**(5): 651–60.

Hodgson, G.M. (2006) "What are institutions?", *Journal of Economic Issues*, **40**(1): 1–25.

Hodgson, G.M. (2007) "Evolutionary and institutional economics as the new mainstream?", *Evolutionary and Institutional Economics Review*, **4**(1): 7–25.

Hodgson, G.M. and Jiang, S. (2007) "The economics of corruption and the corruption of economics: an institutionalist perspective", *Journal of Economic Issues*, **41**(4): 1043–61.

Hodgson, G.M. and Samuels, W.J. (1994) "Marx, Karl", in Hodgson, G.M., Samuels, W.J. and Tool, M.R. (eds) *The Elgar Companion to Institutional and Evolutionary Economics, L–Z.* Aldershot: Edward Elgar, pp. 56–60.

Hodgson, G.M., Samuels, W.J. and Tool, M.R. (eds) (1994a) *The Elgar Companion to Institutional and Evolutionary Economics, A–K.* Aldershot: Edward Elgar.

Hodgson, G.M., Samuels, W.J. and Tool, M.R. (eds) (1994b) *The Elgar Companion to Institutional and Evolutionary Economics, L–Z.* Aldershot: Edward Elgar.

Hohenberg, P.M. (2004) "The historical geography of European cities", in Henderson, V.J. and Thisse, J.-F. (eds) *Handbook of Regional and Urban Economics, Vol. 4, Cities and Geography*. Amsterdam: Elsevier, pp. 3021–52.

Hoksbergen, R. (1994) "Postmodernism and institutionalism: toward a resolution of the debate on relativism", *Journal of Economic Issues*, **28**(3): 679–713.

Hoksbergen, R. (1998) "Postmodernism and institutionalism: a reply to Klein and Samuels", *Journal of Economic Issues*, **32**(3): 844–8.

Hollis, M. (1996) "Philosophy of social science", in Bunnin, N. and Tsui-James, E.P. (eds) *The Blackwell Companion to Philosophy*. Oxford: Blackwell, pp. 358–87.

Holmes, T.J. (1999) "Localisation of industry and vertical disintegration", *Review of Economics and Statistics*, **81**(2), 314–25.

Honderich, T. (ed.) (1995) *The Oxford Companion to Philosophy*. Oxford: Oxford University Press.

Hooper, A.J. (1992) "The construction of theory: a comment", *Journal of Property Research*, **9**(1): 45–8.

Hudson, R. (1994) "Institutional change, cultural transformation and economic regeneration: myths and realities from Europe's old industrial areas", in Amin, A. and Thrift, N. (eds) *Globalisation, Institutions and Regional Development in Europe*. Oxford: Oxford University Press, pp. 196–216.

Hulsen, P. (1998) "Back to basics: a theory of the emergence of institutional facts", *Law and Philosophy*, **17**(3): 271–99.

Hutchings, D. (1997) "Real estate and a single currency", *Journal of Property Valuation and Investment*, **15**(4): 372–83.

Ilbery, B.W. (1990) *Western Europe, a Systematic Human Geography*, 2nd edn. Oxford: Oxford University Press.

Imrie, R. and Thomas, H. (1993) "The limits of property-led regeneration", *Environment and Planning C: Government and Policy*, **11**(1): 87–102.

Jaffe, A.J. (1996) "On the role of transaction costs and property rights in housing markets", *Housing Studies*, **11**(3): 425–34.

Jaffe, A.J. and Louziotis, D. Jr. (1996) "Property rights and economic efficiency: a survey of institutional factors", *Journal of Real Estate Literature*, **4**(2): 137–59.

James, W. (1890) *The Principles of Psychology*, Vols I, II. New York: Henry Holt.

James, W. (1907) *Pragmatism: a New Name for Some Old Ways of Thinking*. New York: Longman Green.

Jensen, H.E. (1994) "Human nature, theory of", in Hodgson, G.M., Samuels, W.J. and Tool, M.R. (eds) *The Elgar Companion to Institutional and Evolutionary Economics, A–K*. Aldershot: Edward Elgar, pp. 338–42.

Jensen, M.C. (1978) "Some anomalous evidence regarding market efficiency", *Journal of Financial Economics*, **6**(2): 95–101.

Jensen-Butler, C., Shachar, A. and van Weesep, J. (eds) (1997) *European Cities in Competition*. Aldershot: Avebury.

Jessop, B. (1990) "Regulation theories in retrospect and prospect", *Economy and Society*, **19**(2): 153–216.

Jessop, B. (1994) "Regulation theory, French", in Hodgson, G.M., Samuels, W.J. and Tool, M.R. (eds) *The Elgar Companion to Institutional and Evolutionary Economics, L–Z*. Aldershot: Edward Elgar, pp. 233–8.

Jessop, B. (1997) "The regulation approach", *Journal of Political Philosophy*, **5**(3): 287–326.

Jiang, Y. and Shen, J. (2010) "Measuring the urban competitiveness of Chinese cities in 2000", *Cities*, **27**(5): 307–14.

Johnson, B. and Nielsen, K. (1998) "Introduction: institutions and economic change" in Nielsen, K. and Johnson, B. (eds) *Institutions and Economic Change, New Perspectives on Markets, Firms and Technology*. Cheltenham: Edward Elgar, pp. xiii–xxviii.

Johnston, R.J. (1986) *Philosophy and Human Geography*. London: Edward Arnold.

Johnston, R.J. (1997) *Geography and Geographers, Anglo-American Human Geography since 1945*. New York: Arnold.

Johnston, R.J., Gregory, D., Pratt, G. and Watts, M. (2000) *The Dictionary of Human Geography*, 4th edn. Oxford: Blackwell.

Joireman, S.F. (2004) "Colonization and the rule of law: comparing the effectiveness of common law and civil law countries", *Constitutional Political Economy*, **15**(4): 315–38.

Jones Lang Wootton (1992) *Real Estate Investment in the Changing European Environment, Positioning for Long Term Performance*. Reading: British Council for Offices.

Jones, A. and Murphy, J.T. (2010) "Theorizing practice in economic geography: foundations, challenges, and possibilities", *Progress in Human Geography*, **35**(3): 366–92.

Jones, C. (1996) "Urban regeneration, property development, and the land market", *Environment and Planning C: Government and Policy*, **14**(2): 269–79.

Jones, C. and Watkins, C. (1996) "Urban regeneration and sustainable markets", *Urban Studies*, **33**(7): 1129–40.

Jones, E.L. (1995) "Economic adaptability in the long term" in Killick, T. (ed.) *The Flexible Economy*. London: Routledge, pp. 79–110.

Kahneman, D. (1994) "New challenges to the rationality assumption", *Journal of Institutional and Theoretical Economics*, **150**(1): 18–36.

Kaiser, R. (1997) "The long cycle in real estate" *Journal of Real Estate Research*, **14**(3): 233–56.

Kanemoto, Y., Ohkawara, T. and Suzuki, T. (1996) "Agglomeration economies and a test for optimal city sizes in Japan", *Journal of the Japanese and International Economics*, **10**(4): 379–98.

Kapp, W.K. (1968) "In defence of institutional economics", *Swedish Journal of Economics*, **70**(March): 1–18.

Kapp, W.K. (1976) "The nature and significance of institutional economics", *Kyklos*, **29**(2): 209–32.

Katouzian, H. (1980) *Ideology and Method in Economics*. London: Macmillan.

Katznelson, I. (1992) *Marxism and the City*. Oxford: Oxford University Press.

Kauko, T. (2012) "Recreating residential property values in the inner city – an adapted 'old' institutional approach", *Journal of Property Research*, **29**(2): 153–76.

Kazepov, Y. (ed.) (2005) *Cities of Europe: Changing Contexts, Local Arrangements, and the Challenge to Social Cohesion*. Oxford: Blackwell.

Keivani, R., Parsa, A. and McGreal, S. (2002) "Institutions and urban change in a globalising world: the case of Warsaw", *Cities*, **19**(3): 183–93.

Keogh, G. (1994) "Use and investment markets in British real estate", *Journal of Property Valuation and Investment*, **12**(4): 58–72.

Keogh, G. and D'Arcy, E. (1994) "Market maturity and property market behaviour: a European comparison of mature and emergent markets", *Journal of Property Research*, **11**(3): 215–35.

Keogh, G. and D'Arcy, E. (1999) "Property market efficiency: an institutional economics perspective", *Urban Studies*, **36**(13): 2401–14.

Keynes, J.M. (1921) *A Treatise on Probability*. London: Macmillan.

Keynes, J.M. (1936) *The General Theory of Employment, Interest and Money*. London: Macmillan.

Khalil, E.L. (1994) "Rules", in Hodgson, G.M., Samuels, W.J. and Tool, M.R. (eds) *The Elgar Companion to Institutional and Evolutionary Economics, L–Z*. Aldershot: Edward Elgar, pp. 253–64.

Kholdy, S., and Sohrabian, A. (2008) "Capital gain expectations and efficiency in the real estate markets", *Journal of Business and Economics Research*, **6**(4): 43–52.

Killick, T. (1995a) "Flexibility and economic progress", *World Development*, **23**(5): 721–34.

Killick, T. (ed.) (1995b) *The Flexible Economy*. London: Routledge.

Kilminster, R. (1991) "Structuration theory as a world-view" in Bryant, C.G.A. and Jary, D. (eds) *Giddens' Theory of Structuration: a Critical Appreciation*. London: Routledge, pp. 75–115.

Kim, J. (1999) "Making sense of emergence", *Philosophical Studies*, **95**(1), 3–36.

Kim, J.H. (2011) "Linking land use planning and regulation to economic development: a literature review", *Journal of Planning Literature*, **26**(1): 35–47.

King, R.J. (1989) "Capital switching and the role of ground rent: 2. Switching between circuits and switching between submarkets", *Environment and Planning A*, **21**(6): 711–38.

Kleiman, R.T., Payne, J.E. and Sahu, A.P. (2002) "Random walks and market efficiency: evidence from international real estate markets", *Journal of Real Estate Research*, **24**(3): 279–97.

Klein, P.A. (1977) "An institutionalist view of development economics", *Journal of Economic Issues*, **11**(4): 785–807.

Kliesen, K.L. and Ricketts, L.R. (2013) "Uncertainty and the economy", *The Regional Economist*, April, 1–3.

Kloosterman, R.C. and Musterd, S. (2001) "The polycentric urban region: towards a research agenda", *Urban Studies*, **38**(4): 623–33.

Knack, S. and Keefer, P. (1995) "Institutions and economic performance: cross-country tests using alternative institutional measures" *Economics and Politics*, **7**(3): 207–27.

Knack, S. and Keefer, P. (1997) "Does social capital have an economic payoff? A cross-country investigation", *Quarterly Journal of Economics*, **112**(4): 1251–88.

Knight, F.H. (1921) *Risk, Uncertainty and Profit*. Boston: Houghton Mifflin.

Knight, R.V. (1995) "Knowledge-based development: policy and planning implications for cities", *Urban Studies*, **32**(2): 225–60.

Krabben, E. van der (1995) *Urban Dynamics: a Real Estate Perspective, an Institutional Analysis of the Production of the Built Environment.* Amsterdam: Tilburg University.

Krabben, E. van der (2009) "A property rights approach to externality problems: planning based on compensation rules", *Urban Studies*, **46**(13): 2869–90.

Krabben, E. van der and Boekema, F. (1994) "Missing links between urban economic growth theory and real estate development processes: economic growth and building investment in city of 's-Hertogenbosch", *Journal of Property Research*, **11**(2): 111–29.

Krabben, E. van der and Lambooy, J.G. (1993) "A theoretical framework for the functioning of the Dutch property market", *Urban Studies*, **30**(8): 1381–97.

Kratke, S. (1999) "A regulationist approach to regional studies", *Environment and Planning A*, **31**(4): 683–704.

Kresl, P.K. (2013) "Empirical approaches to urban competitiveness analysis", in Kresl P.K. and Sobrino, J. (eds) *Handbook of Research Methods and Applications in Urban Economies*. Cheltenham: Edward Elgar, pp. 32–59.

Kresl, P.K. and Singh, B. (1999) "Competitiveness and the urban economy: twenty-four large US metropolitan areas", *Urban Studies*, **36**(5–6): 1017–27.

Krugman, P.R. (1991a) *Geography and Trade*. Cambridge, MA: Massachusetts Institute of Technology Press.

Krugman, P.R. (1991b) "Increasing returns and economic geography", *Journal of Political Economy*, **99**(3): 483–99.

Kunzmann, K.R. (1996) "Euro-megalopolis or Themepark Europe? Scenarios for European spatial development", *International Planning Studies*, **1**(2): 143–63.

La Porta, R., Lopez-de-Silanes, F., Shleifer, A. and Vishny, R.W. (1999) "The quality of government", *Journal of Law, Economics and Organisation*, **15**(1): 222–79.

Lambooy, J.G. (1993) "The European city: from carrefour to organisational nexus", *Tijdschrift Voor Economische En Sociale Geografie*, **84**(4): 258–68.

Lambooy, J.G. and Moulaert, F. (1996) "The economic organization of cities: an institutional perspective", *International Journal of Urban and Regional Research*, **20**(2): 218–37.

Lambsdorff, J.G. (2007) *The Institutional Economics of Corruption and Reform: Theory, Evidence and Policy*. Cambridge: Cambridge University Press.

Langlois, R.N. (1986a) "The new institutional economics: an introductory essay", in Langlois, R.N. (ed.) *Economics as a Process, Essays in the New Institutional Economics*. Cambridge: Cambridge University Press, pp. 1–25.

Langlois, R.N. (1986b) "Rationality, institutions, and explanation", in Langlois, R.N. (ed.) *Economics as a Process, Essays in the New Institutional Economics*. Cambridge: Cambridge University Press, pp. 225–55.

Langlois, R.N. (ed.) (1986c) *Economics as a Process, Essays in the New Institutional Economics*. Cambridge: Cambridge University Press.

Langlois, R.N. (1986d) "Coherence and flexibility: social institutions in a world of radical uncertainty" in Kirzner, I.M. (ed.) *Subjectivism, Intelligibility, and Economic Understanding*. Basingstoke: Macmillan, pp. 171–91.

Lawson, C., Peacock, M. and Pratten, S. (1996) "Realism, underlabouring and institutions", *Cambridge Journal of Economics*, **20**(1): 137–51.

Lawson, J. (2006) *Critical Realism and Housing Studies*. London: Routledge.

Lawson, T. (1985) "Uncertainty and economic analysis", *Economic Journal*, **95**(380): 909–27.

Lawson, T. (1989) "Abstraction, tendencies and stylised facts: a realist approach to economic analysis", *Cambridge Journal of Economics*, **13**(1): 59–78.

Lawson, T. (1994) "Realism, philosophical", in Hodgson, G.M., Samuels, W.J. and Tool, M.R. (eds) *The Elgar Companion to Institutional and Evolutionary Economics, L–Z.* Aldershot: Edward Elgar, pp. 219–25.

Lawson, T. (1995) "A realist perspective on contemporary 'economic theory'", *Journal of Economic Issues*, **29**(1): 1–32.

Lawson, T. (1997a) *Economics and Reality*. London: Routledge.

Lawson, T. (1997b) "Situated rationality", *Journal of Economic Methodology*, **4**(1): 101–25.

Lawson, T. (1998a) "Tendencies", in Davis, J.B., Hands, W.D. and Maki, U. (eds) *The Handbook of Economic Methodology*. Cheltenham: Edward Elgar, pp. 493–8.

Lawson, T. (1998b) "Transcendental realism" in Davis, J.B., Hands, W.D. and Maki, U. (eds) *The Handbook of Economic Methodology*. Cheltenham: Edward Elgar, pp. 504–10.

Lawson, T. (1999) "Feminism, realism and universalism", *Feminist Economics*, **5**(2): 25–59.

Lawson, T. (2003) *Reorienting Economics*. London: Routledge.

Lawson, T. (2006) "The nature of heterodox economics", *Cambridge Journal of Economics*, **30**(4): 483–505.

Lawson, T. (2012) "Ontology and the study of social reality: emergence, organisation, community, power, social relations, corporations, artefacts and money", *Cambridge Journal of Economics*, **36**(2): 345–85.

Lawson, V.A. and Staeheli, L.A. (1990) "Realism and the practice of geography", *Professional Geographer*, **42**(1): 13–20.

Lees, L. and Wyly, E.K. (eds) (2010) *The Gentrification Reader*. London: Routledge.

Lees, L., Slater, T. and Wyly, E.K. (2008) *Gentrification*. London: Routledge.

Lefebvre, H. (1991) *The Production of Space*. Oxford: Blackwell.

Leitner, H. (1994) "Capital markets, the development industry, and urban office market dynamics: rethinking building cycles", *Environment and Planning A*, **26**(5): 779–802.

Lesmand, D.A., Ogden, J.P. and Trzcinka, C.A. (1999) "A new estimate of transaction costs", *Review of Financial Studies*, **12**(5): 1113–41.

Lever, W.F. (1999) "Competitive cities in Europe", *Urban Studies*, **36**(5–6): 1029–44.

Lever, W.F. and Bailly, A. (1996) *The Spatial Impact of Economic Change in Europe*. Aldershot: Avebury.

Levine, R. and Ahmed, S. (1998) "The legal environment, banks, and long-run economic growth", *Journal of Money, Credit and Banking*, **30**(3): 596–620.

Lewis, A.W. (1955) *The Theory of Economic Growth*. London: George Allen & Unwin.

Lewis, P.A. (1996) "Metaphor and critical realism", *Review of Social Economy*, **54**(4): 487–506.

Lewis, P.A. (2004) *Transforming Economics: Perspectives on the Critical Realist Project*. London: Routledge.

Lewis, P.A. (2011) "On the merits of critical realism and the 'ontological turn' in economics: reply to Steele", *Critical Review: a Journal of Politics and Society*, **23**(1–2): 207–30.

Lincoln, Y.S. and Guba, E.G. (1985) *Naturalistic Inquiry*. Beverly Hills, CA: Sage.

Lind, H. (1993) "The myth of institutionalist method", *Journal of Economic Issues*, **27**(1): 1–17.

Lipietz, A. (1992) *Towards a New Economic Order: Postfordism, Ecology and Democracy*. Cambridge: Polity.

Lizieri, C. (1991) "The property market in a changing world economy", *Journal of Property Valuation and Investment*, **9**(3): 227–46.

Lizieri, C. (1992) "The property crisis, international investment criteria", *Estates Gazette*, **9227**: 110–11.

Lizieri, C. (1997) "Editorial", *Journal of Property Valuation and Investment*, **15**(4): 302–5.

Lizieri, C.M. (2003) "Occupier requirements in commercial real estate markets", *Urban Studies*, **40**(5–6): 1151–69.

Lizieri, C., Baum, A., Williams, N. and Oughton, M. (2000) *Space Race: the Contribution of Property Markets to the Competitiveness of London and Frankfurt*. Reading: University of Reading and Development Securities plc.

Luithlen, L. (1992) "Marxian concepts, capital accumulation and office property", *Journal of Property Research*, **9**(3): 227–46.

Luithlen, L. (1993) "Capital accumulation and office development in Leicester, 1967–90", *Journal of Property Research*, **10**(1): 27–48.

Luker, B., Luker, B. Jr, Cobb, S.L. and Brown, R. (1998) "Postmodernism, institutionalism, and statistics: considerations for an institutionalist statistical method", *Journal of Economic Issues*, **32**(2): 449–56.

Lutz, W., Sanderson, W. and Scherbov, S. (2008) "The coming acceleration of global population ageing", *Nature*, **451**(7179): 716–19.

MacKinnon, D., Cumbers, A., Pike, A., Birch, K. and McMaster, R. (2009) "Evolution in economic geography: institutions, political economy, and adaptation", *Economic Geography*, **85**(2):129–50.

Magalhaes, C.S. de (2001) "International property consultants and the transformation of local markets", *Journal of Property Research*, **18**(1): 99–121.

Magnus, B. (1999) "Postmodern", in Audi, R. (ed.) *The Cambridge Dictionary of Philosophy*, 2nd edn. Cambridge: Cambridge University Press, pp. 725–6.

Mahoney, J. and Rueschemeyer, D. (eds) (2003) *Comparative Historical Analysis in the Social Sciences*. Cambridge: Cambridge University Press.

Mahoney, P.G. (2001) "The Common law and economic growth: Hayek might be right", *Journal of Legal Studies*, **30**(2): 503–25.

Maier, G. and Herath, S. (2009) "Real estate market efficiency: a survey of literature", *SRE Discussion Paper 2009–07*. Available at http://epub.wu.ac.at/402/.

Maillat, D. and Lecoq, B. (1992) "New technologies and transformation of regional structures in Europe: the role of milieu", *Entrepreneurship and Regional Development*, **4**(1): 1–20.

Maki, U., Gustafsson, B. and Knudsen, C. (1993) *Rationality, Institutions and Economic Methodology*. London: Routledge.

Mandel, E. (1975) *Late Capitalism*. London: New Left Books.

Mano, Y. and Otsuka, K. (2000) "Agglomeration economies and geographical concentration of industries: a case study of manufacturing sectors in postwar Japan", *Journal of Japanese and International Economics*, **14**(3): 189–203.

Marshall, A. (1920) *Principles of Economics*. London: Macmillan.

Martin, R. (2000) "Institutional approaches in economic geography" in Sheppard, E. and Barnes, T.J. (eds) *A Companion to Economic Geography*. Malden: Blackwell, pp. 77–94.

Marx, K. (1959 [1844]) *Economic and Philosophical Manuscripts of 1844*, tr. Mulligan, M. [first published in German 1932 by the Institute of Marxism-Leninism in the USSR]. Moscow: Progress.

Marx, K. (1970 [1859]) *A Contribution to the Critique of Political Economy*, tr. Ryazanskaya, S.W., ed. Dobb. M. [first published in German 1859 by F. Duncker, Berlin]. Moscow: Progress.

Marx, K. (1973 [1857–1861]) *Grundrisse, Foundation of the Critique of Political Economy*, tr. Nicolaus, M. [first published in German 1931–1941 by the Marx-Engels Institute in Moscow]. London: Penguin.

Marx, K. (1976 [1867, 1885, 1894]) *Capital, Vols I, II and III*, tr. Fowkes, B. (Vol. I) and Fernbach, D. (Vols II and III) [first published in German 1867, 1885, 1894 by Verlag von Otto Meisner]. Harmondsworth: Penguin Books.

Marx, K. and Engels, F. (1956 [1844]) *The Holy Family*, tr. Dixon, R. [first published in German 1845 in Frankfurt am Main]. Moscow: Foreign Languages.

Marx, K. and Engels, F. (1970 [1846]) *The German Ideology*, tr. Arthur, C.J. [first published in German 1932 by D. Riazanov through the Marx-Engels Institute, Moscow]. London: Lawrence and Wishart.

Massey, D. and Catalano, A. (1978) *Capital and Land: Landownership by Capital in Great Britain*. London: Edward Arnold.

Massey, D.B. (1984) *Spatial Divisions of Labour: Social Structures and the Geography of Production*. Basingstoke: Macmillan.

Matthews, R.C.O. (1986) "The economics of institutions and the sources of growth", *The Economic Journal*, **96**(384): 903–18.

May, T. (1997) *Social Research: Issues, Methods, Process*, 2nd edn. Buckingham: Open University Press.

Mayhew, A. (1987) "Culture: core concept under attack", *Journal of Economic Issues*, **11**(4): 871–95.

Mayhew, A. (1994) "Culture", in Hodgson, G.M., Samuels, W.J. and Tool, M.R. (eds) *The Elgar Companion to Institutional and Evolutionary Economics, A–K*. Aldershot: Edward Elgar, pp. 115–19.

McCann, P. (1995) "Rethinking the economics of location and agglomeration", *Urban Studies*, **32**(3): 563–77.

McCann, P. (2008) "Globalization and economic geography: the world is curved, not flat", *Cambridge Journal of Regions, Economy and Society*, **1**(3): 351–70.

McCann, P. and Sheppard, S. (2003) "The rise, fall and rise again of industrial location theory", *Regional Studies*, **37**(6&7): 649–63.

McCarthy, L. (2000) "European integration, urban economic change, and public policy responses", *Professional Geographer*, **52**(2): 193–204.

McEvoy, D. (2006) "A critical realist rationale for using a combination of quantitative and qualitative methods", *Journal of Research in Nursing*, **11**(1): 66–78.

McGreal, S., Parsa, A. and Keivani, R. (2002) "Evolution of property investment markets in Central Europe: opportunities and constraints", *Journal of Property Research*, **19**(3): 213–30.

McGuirk, P.M. (2000) "Power and policy networks in urban governance: local government and property-led regeneration in Dublin", *Urban Studies*, **37**(4): 651–72.

McIntosh, A. (1997) *Towns and Cities, Competing for Survival*. London: E & FN Spon.

McMaster, R. and Watkins, C. (2006) "Economics and underdetermination: a case study of urban land and housing economics", *Cambridge Journal of Economics*, **30**(6): 901–22.

Mearman, A (2006) "Critical realism in economics and open-systems ontology: a critique", *Review of Social Economy*, **64**(1): 47–75.

Meijer, M. (1993) "Growth and decline of European cities: changing positions of cities in Europe", *Urban Studies*, **30**(6): 981–90.

Meijers, E. (2005) "Polycentric urban regions and the quest for synergy: is a network of cities more than the sum of the parts?", *Urban Studies*, **42**(4): 765–81.

Menard, C. (1995) "Markets as institutions versus organisations as markets? Disentangling some fundamental concepts", *Journal of Economic Behavior and Organization*, **28**(2): 161–82.

Menard, C. (2001) "Methodological issues in new institutional economics", *Journal of Economic Methodology*, **8**(1): 85–92.

Menard, C. and Shirley, M.M. (eds) (2005) *Handbook of New Institutional Economics*. Dordrecht: Springer.

Miller, E.S. (1978) "Institutional economics: philosophy, methodology and theory", *The Social Science Journal*, **15**(1): 13–25.

Miller, E.S. (1998) "Veblen and Commons and the concept of community", in Samuels, W.J. (ed.) *The Founding of Institutional Economics, the Leisure Class and Sovereignty*. London: Routledge, pp. 14–29.

Mills, E.S. (1972) *Urban Economics*. Glenview: Scott, Foresman.

Mingers, J.C. (2006) *Realising Systems Thinking: Knowledge and Action in Management Science*. New York: Springer.

Mingione, E. (1995) "Social and employment change in the urban arena" in Healey, P., Cameron, S., Davoudi, S., Graham, S. and Madani-Pour, A. (eds) *Managing Cities, the New Urban Context*, Chichester: John Wiley, pp. 195–208.

Mirowski, P. (1987) "The philosophical bases of institutional economics", *Journal of Economic Issues*, **21**(3): 1001–38.

Mitchell, C.J.A. (2004) "Making sense of counterurbanization", *Journal of Rural Studies*, **20**(1): 15–34.

Mitchell, W.C. (1910) "The rationality of economic activity II", *The Journal of Political Economy*, **18**(3): 197–216.

Moomaw, R.L. (1981) "Productivity and city size: a critique of the evidence", *Quarterly Journal of Economics*, **96**,(4): 675–88.

Moomaw, R.L. (1985) "Firm location and city size: reduced productivity advantages as a factor in the decline of manufacturing in urban areas", *Journal of Urban Economics*, **17**(1): 73–89.

Moos, A.I. and Dear, M.J. (1986) "Structuration theory in urban analysis: 1. Theoretical exegesis", *Environment and Planning A*, **18**(2): 231–52.

Morgan, G., Campbell, J., Crouch, C., Pedersen, O.K. and Whitley, R. (eds) (2010) *The Oxford Handbook of Comparative Institutional Analysis*. Oxford: Oxford University Press.

Moulaert, F. and Swyngedouw, E.A. (1989) "Survey 15. A regulation approach to the geography of flexible production systems", *Environment and Planning D: Society and Space*, **7**(3): 327–45.

Munro, M. (1995) "Homo-economicus in the city: towards an urban socio-economic research agenda", *Urban Studies*, **32**(10): 1609–21.

Murdoch, J. (1995) "Actor-networks and the evolution of economic forms: combining description and explanation in theories of regulation, flexible specialization, and networks", *Environment and Planning A*, **27**(5): 731–57.

Musole, M. (2009) "Property rights, transaction costs and institutional change: conceptual framework and literature review", *Progress in Planning*, **71**(2): 43–85.

Musterd, S. and Murie, A. (eds) (2011) *Making Competitive Cities*. Chichester: Wiley-Blackwell.

Mutch, A. (2002) "Actors and networks or agents and structures: towards a realist view of information systems", *Organization*, **9**(3): 477–96.

Myrdal, G. (1958) *Value in Social Theory: a Selection of Essays on Methodology*. London: Routledge & Kegan Paul.

Myrdal, G. (1970) *Objectivity in Social Research.* London: Gerald Duckworth.

Nabarro, R. (1990) "The investment market in commercial and industrial development: some recent trends", in Healey, P. and Nabarro, R. (eds) *Land and Property Development in a Changing Context.* Aldershot: Gower, pp. 47–59.

Naess, P. and Jensen, O.B. (2002) "Urban land use, mobility and theory of science: exploring the potential for critical realism in empirical research" *Journal of Environmental Policy and Planning*, **4**(4): 295–311.

Nagle, G. and Spencer, K. (1996) *A Geography of the European Union, A Regional and Economic Perspective.* Oxford: Open University Press.

Neale, W.C. (1987) "Institutions", *Journal of Economic Issues*, **21**(3): 1177–206.

Needham, B. (1994) "Comment", *Journal of Property Research*, **11**(1): 65–7.

Needham, B. (2006) *Planning, Law and Economics: the Rules We Make for Using Land.* London: Routledge.

Needham, B. and de Kam, G. (2004) "Understanding how land is exchanged: co-ordination mechanisms and transaction costs", *Urban Studies*, **41**(10): 2061–76.

Needham, B., Segeren, A. and Buitelaar, E. (2011) "Institutions in theories of land markets: illustrated by the Dutch market for agricultural land", *Urban Studies*, **48**(1): 161–76.

Nelson, R.R. (1994) "Evolutionary theorizing about economic change", in Smelser, N.J. and Swedberg, R. (eds) *The Handbook of Economic Sociology.* Princeton: Princeton University Press, pp. 108–36.

Nelson, R.R. and Sampat, B.N. (2001) "Making sense of institutions as a factor shaping economic performance", *Journal of Economic Behavior and Organization*, **44**(1): 31–54.

Neuman, L.W. (1994) *Social Research Methods, Qualitative and Quantitative Approaches*, 2nd edn. Boston: Allyn and Bacon.

Ni, P. (2012) *The Global Urban Competitiveness Report – 2011.* Cheltenham: Edward Elgar.

Nielsen, P. (2002) "Reflections on critical realism in political economy", *Cambridge Journal of Economics*, **26**(6): 727–38.

Nilsson, J.-E. and Schamp, E.W. (1996) "Restructuring of the European production system", *European Urban and Regional Studies*, **3**(2): 121–31.

Nooteboom, B. (2007) 'Social capital, institutions and trust" *Review of Social Economy*, **65**(1): 29–53.

North, D.C. (1981) *Structure and Change in Economic History.* New York: Norton.

North, D.C. (1986) "The new institutional economics", *Journal of Institutional and Theoretical Economics*, **142**(1): 230–7.

North, D.C. (1990) *Institutions, Institutional Change and Economic Performance.* Cambridge: Cambridge University Press.

North, D.C. (1991) "Institutions", *Journal of Economic Perspectives*, **5**(1): 97–112.

North, D.C. (1993a) "Institutions and credible commitment", *Journal of Institutional and Theoretical Economics*, **149**(1): 11–23.

North, D.C. (1993b) "Institutions and economic performance", in Maki, U., Gustafsson, B. and Knudsen, C. (eds) *Rationality, Institutions and Economic Methodology.* London: Routledge, pp. 242–61.

North, D.C. (1994) "Economic Performance Through Time: The Limit to Knowledge", *American Economic Review*, **84**(3): 359–68.

North, D.C. (2005) *Understanding the Process of Economic Change.* Princeton: Princeton University Press.

North, D.C. and Thomas, R.P. (1970) "An economic theory of the growth of the western world", *The Economic History Review*, **23**(1): 1–17.

Northover, P. (1999) "Evolutionary growth theory and forms of realism", *Cambridge Journal of Economics*, **23**(1): 33–63.

O'Driscoll, G.P. Jr, Holmes, K.R. and Kirkpatrick, M. (2000) *2000 Index of Economic Freedom*, Washington, DC: Heritage Foundation.

O'Hara, P.H. (2000) *Marx, Veblen, and Contemporary Institutional Political Economy: Principles and Unstable Dynamics of Capitalism*. Cheltenham: Edward Elgar.

O'Sullivan, A. (2012) *Urban Economics*, 8th edn. Boston: McGraw-Hill.

Oatley, N. (ed.) (1998) *Cities, Economic Competition and Urban Policy*. London: Paul Chapman.

Organization for Economic Cooperation and Development (OECD) (2000) *The Service Economy*. Paris: OECD.

Organization for Economic Cooperation and Development (OECD) (2005) *Enhancing the Performance of the Services Sector*. Paris: OECD.

Orlean, A. (ed.) (2004) *Analyse économique des Conventions*. Paris: Presses Universitaires de France – Quadrige.

Ostrom, E. (2007) "Challenges and growth: the development of the interdisciplinary field of institutional analysis", *Journal of Institutional Economics*, **3**(3): 239–64.

Ottaviano, G. and Puga, D. (1998) "Agglomeration in the global economy: a survey of the "new economic geography", *The World Economy*, **21**(6): 707–31.

Ottaviano, G. and Thisse, J.-F. (2004) "Agglomeration and economic geography", in Henderson, V.J. and Thisse, J.-F (eds) *Handbook of Regional and Urban Economics, Vol. 4, Cities and Geography*. Amsterdam: Elsevier, pp. 2563–608.

Outhwaite, W. (1990) "Realism, naturalism and social behaviour", *Journal for the Theory of Social Behaviour*, **20**(4): 365–77.

Parker, C.H. (1918) "Motives in economic life", *American Economic Review*, **8**(1): 212–31.

Paraskevopoulos, C.J. (1998) "Social capital and the public-private divide in Greek regions", *West European Politics*, **21**(2): 154–77.

Parsa, A.R. and Keivani, R. (1999) "Development of real estate markets in Central Europe: the case of Prague, Warsaw, and Budapest", *Environment and Planning A*, **31**(8): 1383–400.

Parsons, S.D. (1999) "Economics and reality: a philosophical critique of transcendental realism", *Review of Political Economy*, **11**(4): 455–66.

Peet, R. (1998) *Modern Geographical Thought*. Oxford: Blackwell.

Peirce, C.S. (1877) "The fixation of belief", *Popular Science Monthly*, **12**(November): 1–15.

Peirce, C.S. (1878) "How to make our ideas clear", *Popular Science Monthly*, **12**(January): 286–302.

Peirce, C.S. (1905) "What pragmatism is", *The Monist*, **15**(2): 161–81.

Peng, W., Tam, D.C. and Yiu, M.S. (2008) "Property market and the macroeconomy of mainland China: a cross region study", *Pacific Economic Review*, **13**(2): 240–58.

Phelps, N.A. and Ozawa, T. (2003) "Contrasts in agglomeration: proto-industrial, industrial and post-industrial forms compared", *Progress in Human Geography*, **27**(5): 583–604.

Philip, L.J. (1998) "Combining quantitative and qualitative approaches to social research in human geography – an impossible mixture?", *Environment and Planning A*, **30**(2): 261–76.

Philo, C. (1984) "Reflections on Gunnar Olsson's contribution to the discourse of contemporary human geography", *Environment and Planning D: Society and Space*, **2**(2): 217–40.

Phipps, A.G. (2001) "Empirical applications of structuration theory", *Geografiska Annaler, Series B: Human Geography*, **83**(4): 189–204.

Pinkstone, B. (2002) "Persistent demi-regs and robust tendencies: critical realism and the Singer–Prebisch thesis", *Cambridge Journal of Economics*, **26**(5): 561–83.

Piore, M. and Sabel, C. (1984) *The Second Industrial Divide: Possibilities for Prosperity*. New York: Basic Books.

Polanyi, K. (1944) *The Great Transformation: the Political and Economic Origins of our Time*. New York: Rinehart.

Polanyi, K. (1957) "The economy as instituted process", in Polanyi, K., Arensberg, C. M. and Pearson H.W. (eds) *Trade and Market in the Early Empires, Economies in History and Theory*. New York: Free Press, pp. 243–70.

Porter, M.E. (1990) *The Competitive Advantage of Nations*. New York: Free Press.

Porter, M.E. (1996) "Competitive advantage, agglomeration economies and regional policy", *International Regional Science Review*, **19**(1–2): 85–90.

Porter, M.E. (2003) "The competitive advantage of regions", *Regional Studies*, **6**(7): 549–78.

Posner, R.A. (2004) "Law and economics in common-law, civil-law, and developing nations", *Ratio Juris*, **17**(1): 66–79.

Pratt, A.C. (1995) "Putting critical realism to work: the practical implications for geographical research", *Progress in Human Geography*, **19**(1): 61–74.

Pratten, S. (2013) "Critical realism and the process account of emergence", *Journal for the Theory of Social Behaviour*, **43**(3): 251–79.

Przeworski, A. and Limongi, F. (1993) "Political regimes and economic growth", *Journal of Economic Perspectives*, **7**(3): 51–69.

Putnam, R. (2000) *Bowling Alone: the Collapse and Revival of American Community*, New York: Simon & Schuster.

Qian, Z. (2007) "Institutions and local growth coalitions in China's urban land reform: the case of Hangzhou high-technology zone" *Asia Pacific Viewpoint*, **48**(2): 219–33.

Raco, M. (1998) "Assessing 'institutional thickness' in the local context: a comparison of Cardiff and Sheffield", *Environment and Planning A*, **30**(6): 975–96.

Raco, M. (1999) "Competition, collaboration and the new industrial districts: examining the institutional turn in local economic development", *Urban Studies*, **36**(5–6): 951–68.

Rafiqui, P.S. (2009) "Evolving economic landscapes: why new institutional economics matters for economic geography", *Journal of Economic Geography*, **9**(3): 329–53.

Ramstad, Y. (1986) "A pragmatist's quest for holistic knowledge: the scientific methodology of John R. Commons", *Journal of Economic Issues*, **20**(4): 1067–105.

Randall, A. (1978) "Property institutions and economic behavior", *Journal of Economic Issues*, **12**(1): 1–21.

Rauch, J.E. (1993) "Productivity gains from geographic concentration of human capital: evidence from the cities", *Journal of Urban Economics*, **34**(3): 380–400.

Redmond, W.H. (2006) "Instinct, culture, and cognitive science", *Journal of Economic Issues*, **40**(2): 431–8.

Renaud, B. (1997) "The 1985 to 1994 global real estate cycle: an overview", *Journal of Real Estate Literature*, **5**(1): 13–44.

Richter, R. (2005) "The new institutional economics: its start, its meaning, its prospects", *European Business Organization Law Review*, **6**(2): 161–200.

Rivera-Batiz, F.L. (1988) "Increasing returns, monopolistic competition, and agglomeration economies in consumption and production", *Regional Science and Urban Economics*, **18**(1): 125–53.

Rodríguez-Pose, A. (2013) "Do institutions matter for regional development?", *Regional Studies*, **47**(7): 1034–47.

Rodríguez-Pose, A. and Storper, M. (2006) "Better rules or stronger communities? On the social foundations of institutional change and its economic effects", *Economic Geography*, **82**(1): 1–25.

Rodrik, D. (2008) *One Economics, Many Recipes: Globalization, Institutions, and Economic Growth*. Princeton: Princeton University Press.

Rogerson, R.J. (1999) "Quality of life and city competitiveness", *Urban Studies*, **36**(5–6): 969–85.

Ronald, R. (2004) "Home ownership, ideology and diversity: re-evaluating concepts of housing ideology in the case of Japan", *Housing, Theory and Society*, **21**(2): 49–64.

Rosenbaum, E.F. (2000) "What is a market? On the methodology of a contested concept", *Review of Social Economy*, **58**(4): 455–82.

Rosenthal, L. (2006) "Efficiency and seasonality in the UK housing market 1991–2001", *Oxford Bulletin of Economics and Statistics*, **68**(3): 289–317.

Rosenthal, S.S. and Strange, W.C. (2001) "The determinants of agglomeration", *Journal of Urban Economics*, **50**(2): 191–229.

Rosenthal, S.S. and Strange, W.C. (2004) "Evidence on the nature and sources of agglomeration economies" in Henderson, V.J. and Thisse, J.-F. (eds) *Handbook of Regional and Urban Economics, Vol. 4, Cities and Geography*. Amsterdam: Elsevier, pp. 2119–71.

Royal Institution of Chartered Surveyors (RICS) (1994) *Economic Cycles and Property Cycles*. London: RICS.

Rozenblat, C. and Pumain, D. (1993) "The location of multinational firms in the European urban systems", *Urban Studies*, **30**(10): 1691–709.

Rutherford, M.C. (1981) "Clarence Ayres and the instrumental theory of value", *Journal of Economic Issues*, **15**(3): 657–73.

Rutherford, M.C. (1983) "J.R. Commons's institutional economics", *Journal of Economic Issues*, **17**(3): 721–44.

Rutherford, M.C. (1994a) *Institutions in Economics: the Old and the New Institutionalism*. Cambridge: Cambridge University Press.

Rutherford, M.C. (1994b) "Commons, John R." in Hodgson, G.M., Samuels, W.J. and Tool, M.R. (eds) *The Elgar Companion to Institutional and Evolutionary Economics, A–K*. Aldershot: Edward Elgar, pp. 63–9.

Rutherford, M.C. (1998) "Institutionalism", in Davis, J.B., Hands, W.D. and Maki, U. (eds) *The Handbook of Economic Methodology*. Cheltenham: Edward Elgar, pp. 249–53.

Sajor, E.E. (2005) "Professionalisation or hybridisation? Real estate brokers in Metro Cebu, the Philippines, during the boom of the 1990s", *Urban Studies*, **42**(8): 1321–43.

Samuels, W.J. (1977) "Technology vis-à-vis institutions in the JEI: a suggested interpretation", *Journal of Economic Issues*, **11**(4): 871–95.

Samuels, W.J. (1990) "Institutional economics and the theory of cognition", *Cambridge Journal of Economics*, **14**(2): 219–27.

Samuels, W.J. (1995) "The present state of institutional economics", *Cambridge Journal of Economics*, **19**(4): 569–90.

Samuels, W.J. (1998a) "Comment on 'Postmodernism and Institutionalism'", *Journal of Economic Issues*, **32**(3): 823–32.

Samuels, W.J. (1998b) "Methodological pluralism", in Davis, J.B., Hands, W.D. and Maki, U. (eds) *The Handbook of Economic Methodology*. Cheltenham: Edward Elgar, pp. 300–3.

Samuels, W.J. (1999) "Theories of property", *Journal of Economic Issues*, **33**(1): 183–8.

Samuels, W.J. (2000) "Institutional economics after one century", *Journal of Economic Issues*, **34**(2): 305–5.

Sassen, S. (2001) *The Global City: New York, London, Tokyo*, 2nd edn. Princeton, NJ: Princeton University Press.

Sato, Y. and Yamamoto, K. (2005) "Population concentration, urbanisation, and demographic transition", *Journal of Urban Economics*, **58**(1): 45–61.

Saunders, P. (1981) *Social Theory and the Urban Question*. London: Hutchinson.

Sayer, A. (1992) *Method in Social Science: a Realist Approach*. London: Routledge.

Sayer, A. (2000) *Realism and Social Science*. New York: Sage.

Schiller, F.C.S. (1907) *Studies in Humanism*. London: Macmillan.

Schmid, A.A. (2008) *Conflict and Cooperation: Institutional and Behavioral Economics*. Malden, MA: Blackwell.

Schmidt, C. (ed.) (1996) *Uncertainty in Economic Thought*. Cheltenham: Edward Elgar.

Schotter, A. (1981) *The Economic Theory of Social Institutions*. Cambridge: Cambridge University Press.

Schulte, K.W., Rottke, N. and Pitschke, C. (2005) "Transparency in the German real estate market", *Journal of Property Investment and Finance*, **23**(1): 90–108.

Scott, A.G. (1991) "Marxian and radical economics" in Mair, D. and Miller, A.G. (eds) *A Modern Guide to Economic Thought, an Introduction to Comparative Schools of Thought in Economics*. Aldershot: Edward Elgar, pp. 233–62.

Scott, A.J. (1988) *New Industrial Spaces: Flexible Production Organization and Regional Development in North America and Western Europe*. London: Pion.

Scully, G.W. (1988) "The institutional framework of economic development", *Journal of Political Economy*, **96**(3): 652–62.

Seabrooke, W., Kent, P. and How, H.H.H. (eds) (2004) *International Real Estate: an Institutional Approach*. Oxford: Blackwell.

Searle, J.R. (2005) "What is an institution?", *Journal of Institutional Economics*, **1**(1): 1–22.

Shiller, R.J. (1990) "Market volatility and investor behaviour", *The American Economic Review, Supplement, Papers and Proceedings*, **80**(1): 58–62.

Shiller, R.J. (2005) *Irrational Exuberance*, 2nd edn. Princeton, NJ: Princeton University Press.

Shleifer, A. and Vishny, R.W. (1993) "Corruption", *Quarterly Journal of Economics*, **108**(3): 599–617.

Short, J.R. (1996) *The Urban Order, an Introduction to Cities, Culture, and Power*. Oxford: Blackwell.

Silverman, D. (2000) *Doing Qualitative Research, a Practical Handbook*, London: Sage.

Simon, H.A. (1982) *Models of Bounded Rationality*. Cambridge, MA: Massachusetts Institute of Technology Press.

Simon, H.A. (1991) "Organizations and markets", *Journal of Economic Perspectives*, **5**(2): 25–44.

Singh, A., Jain-Chandra, S. and Mohommad, A. (2012) *Inclusive Growth, Institutions, and the Underground Economy*. Washington: International Monetary Fund.

Smart, A. and Lee, J. (2003) "Housing and regulation theory, domestic demand and global financialization", in Forrest, R. and Lee, J. (eds) *Housing and Social Change: East West Perspectives*. London: Routledge, pp. 87–107.

Smidt, M. de and Marc, R. van der (1991) "European metropolises in competition for offices: the functional network of cities and real estate indicators", *GeoJournal*, **24**(3): 247–56.

Smith, N. (1984) *Uneven Development: Nature, Capital and the Production of Space*. Oxford: Blackwell.

Soja, E.W. (1980) "The socio-spatial dialectic", *Annals of the Association of American Geographers*, **70**(2): 207–25.

Soja, E.W. and Hadjimichalis, C. (1979) "Between geographical materialism and spatial fetishism: some observations on the development of Marxist spatial analysis", *Antipode*, **11**(3): 3–11.

Sperry, R.W. (1991) "In defence of mentalism and emergent interaction", *Journal of Mind and Behavior*, **12**(2): 221–46.

Sproull, L.S. and Tamuz, M. (1999) "Learning from samples of one or fewer", in March, J.G. (ed.) *The Pursuit of Organizational Intelligence*. Oxford: Blackwell, pp. 137–55.

Stanfield, J.R. (1980) "The institutional economics of Karl Polanyi", *Journal of Economic Issues*, **14**(3): 593–614.

Stanfield, J.R. (1999) "The scope, method, and significance of original institutional economics", *Journal of Economic Issues*, **33**(2): 231–55.

Steele, G.R. (2005) "Critical thoughts about critical realism", *Critical Review*, **17**(1–2): 133–54.

Storper, M. (1995) "The resurgence of regional economies, ten years later the region as a nexus of untraded interdependencies", *European Urban and Regional Studies*, **2**(3): 191–221.

Storper, M. (1997) *The Regional World: Territorial Development in a Global Economy*. London: Guilford Press.

Storper, M. (2005) "Society, community, and economic development", *Studies in Comparative International Development*, **39**(4): 30–57.

Storper, M. and Venables, A.J. (2004) "Buzz: face-to-face contact and the urban economy", *Journal of Economic Geography*, **4**(4), 351–70.

Suarez-Villa, L. and Walrod, W. (1997) "Operational strategy, R&D and intra-metropolitan clustering in a polycentric structure: the advanced electronics industries of the Los Angeles Basin", *Urban Studies*, **34**(9): 1343–80.

Sugiura, K. (1999) "Institutional economics needs interdisciplinary studies of social sciences", *Journal of Economic Issues*, **33**(2): 257–64.

Svensson, J. (1998) "Investment, property rights and political instability: theory and evidence", *European Economic Review*, **42**(7): 1317–41.

Sweeney, F.M. (1993) "Mapping a European property investment strategy", *Journal of Property Valuation and Investment*, **11**(3): 259–67.

Swyngedouw, E., Moulaert, F. and Rodriguez, A. (eds) (2003) *The Globalized City: Economic Restructuring and Social Polarization in European Cities*. Oxford: Oxford University Press.

Syrquin, M. (1995) "Flexibility and long-term economic development", in Killick, T. (ed.) *The Flexible Economy, Causes and Consequences of the Adaptability of National Economies*. London: Routledge, pp. 34–63.

Tabuchi, T. (1998) "Urban agglomeration and dispersion: a synthesis of Alonso and Krugman", *Journal of Urban Economics*, **44**(3): 333–51.

Thevenot, L. (2001) "Organized complexity: conventions of coordination and the composition of economic arrangements", *European Journal of Social Theory*, **4**(4): 405–25.

Thompson, J.B. (1984) *Studies in the Theory of Ideology*. Cambridge: Polity Press.

Thornhill, N.W., Cosmides, L., Maryanski, A.M., Meyer, P., Tooby, J. and Turner, J.H. (1997) "Evolutionary theory and human social institutions: psychological foundations", in Weingart, P., Mitchell, S.D., Richerson, P.J. and Maasen, S. (eds) *Human by Nature: Between Biology and the Social Sciences*. Mahwah, NJ: Lawrence Erlbaum, pp. 212–53.

Thorns, D.C. (2002) *The Transformation of Cities, Urban Theory and Urban Life*. Basingstoke: Palgrave Macmillan.

Thrift, N. (1983) "On the determination of social action in space and time", *Environment and Planning D: Society and Space*, **1**(1): 23–57.

Tickell, A. and Peck, J.A. (1992) "Accumulation, regulation and the geographies of post-Fordism: missing links in regulationist research", *Progress in Human Geography*, **16**(2): 190–218.

Tickell, A. and Peck, J.A. (1995) "Social regulation after Fordism: regulation theory, neo-liberalism and the global-local nexus", *Economy and Society*, **24**(3): 357–86.

Tilman, R. (1996) *The Intellectual Legacy of Thorstein Veblen: Unresolved Issues*. Westport, CN: Greenwood Press.

Tooby, J. and Cosmides, L. (1992) "The psychological foundations of culture", in Barkow, J.H., Cosmides, L. and Tooby J. (eds) *The Adapted Mind: Evolutionary Psychology and the Generation of Culture*. New York: Oxford University Press, pp. 19–136.

Tool, M.R. (1986) *Essays in Social Value Theory: a Neoinstitutionalist Contribution*. New York: M.E. Sharpe.

Tool, M.R. (1988) *Evolutionary Economics, Vol I: Foundations of Institutional Thought, Vol II: Institutional Theory and Policy*. New York: M.E. Sharpe.

Tool, M.R. (ed.) (1993) *Institutional Economics: Theory, Method, Policy*. Boston: Kluwer Academic.

Tool, M.R. (1994a) "Ayres, Clarence E.", in Hodgson, G.M., Samuels, W.J. and Tool, M.R. (eds) *The Elgar Companion to Institutional and Evolutionary Economics, A–K*. Aldershot: Edward Elgar, pp. 16–21.

Tool, M.R. (1994b) "Instrumental value theory" in Hodgson, G.M., Samuels, W.J. and Tool, M.R. (eds) *The Elgar Companion to Institutional and Evolutionary Economics, A–K*. Aldershot: Edward Elgar, pp. 406–12.

Trigilia, C. (1992) [Development without autonomy: perverse effects of policies in the Mezzogiorno]. Bolonga: Il Mulino [in Italian].

Trochim, W.M. and Donnelly, J.P. (2008) *The Research Methods Knowledge Base*, 3rd edn. Mason, OH: Cengage Learning.

Tsang, E.W.K. and Kwan, K.M. (1999) "Replication and theory development in organizational science: a critical realist perspective", *Academy of Management Review*, **24**(4): 759–80.

Tugwell, R.G. (1922) "Human nature in economic theory", *Journal of Political Economy* **30**(3): 317–45.

Tugwell, R.G. (1930) "Human nature and social economy I, II", *Journal of Philosophy*, **27**(17, 18): 449–57, 477–92.

Turok, I. (1992) "Property-led urban regeneration: panacea or placebo", *Environment and Planning A*, **24**(3): 361–79.

Turok, I. (2004) "Cities, regions and competitiveness", *Regional Studies*, **38**(9): 1069–83.

Turok, I. and Mykhnenko, V. (2007) "The trajectories of European cities, 1960–2005", *Cities*, **24**(3): 165–82.

Turok, I. and Mykhnenko, V. (2008) "Resurgent European cities?", *Urban Research and Practice*, **1**(1): 54–77.

Tversky, A. and Kahneman, D. (1986) "Rational choice and the framing of decisions", *Journal of Business*, **59**(4): S251–78.

Twomey, P. (1998) "Reviving Veblenian economic psychology", *Cambridge Journal of Economics*, **22**(4): 433–48.

Van Staveren, I. (1999) "Chaos theory and institutional economics: metaphor or model?", *Journal of Economic Issues*, **33**(1): 141–67.

Veblen, T. (1898a) "Why is economics not an evolutionary science", *The Quarterly Journal of Economics*, **12**(4): 373–97.

Veblen, T. (1898b) "The beginning of ownership", *American Journal of Sociology*, **4**(3): 352–65.

Veblen, T. (1899) *The Theory of the Leisure Class: an Economic Study of Institutions*. London: Macmillan.

Veblen, T. (1904) *The Theory of the Business Enterprise*. New York: Charles Scribners.

Veblen, T. (1914) *The Instinct of Workmanship, and the State of the Industrial Arts*. New York: Augustus Kelley.

Veblen, T. (1918a) *Imperial Germany and the Industrial Revolution*. New York: Huebsch.

Veblen, T. (1918b) *The Higher Learning in America: a Memorandum on the Conduct of Universities by Business Men*. New York: Augustus Kelley.

Veblen, T. (1919a) *The Place of Science in Modern Civilisation and Other Essays*. New York: Huebsch.

Veblen, T. (1919b) *The Vested Interests and the Common Man*. London: Macmillan.

Veblen, T. (1934) *Essays on Our Changing Order*. New York: Viking Press.

Vigar, G., Healey, P., Hull, A. and Davoudi, S. (2000) *Planning, Governance and Spatial Strategy in Britain: an Institutionalist Analysis*. Basingstoke: Macmillan.

Walker, D.A. (1977) "Thorstein Veblen's economic system", *Economic Inquiry*, **15**(2): 213–37.

Walker, D.A. (1979) "The institutionalist economic theories of Clarence Ayres", *Economic Inquiry*, **17**(4): 519–38.

Wallace, J. and Williamson, I. (2006) "Building land markets", *Land Use Policy*, **23**(2): 123–35.

Waller, W. (1994) "Veblenian dichotomy and its critics" in Hodgson, G.M., Samuels, W.J. and Tool, M.R. (eds) *The Elgar Companion to Institutional and Evolutionary Economics, L–Z*. Aldershot: Edward Elgar, pp. 368–72.

Waller, W.T. Jr (1982) "The evolution of Veblenian dichotomy: Veblen, Hamilton, Ayres, and Foster", *Journal of Economic Issues*, **16**(3): 757–71.

Waller, W.T. Jr (1988a) "Radical institutionalism: methodological aspects of the radical tradition", *Journal of Economic Issues*, **22**(3): 667–74.

Waller, W.T. Jr (1988b) "The concept of habit in economic analysis", *Journal of Economic Issues*, **22**(1): 113–26.

Wallis, J.J. and North, D.C. (1986) "Measuring the transaction sector in the American economy, 1870–1970", in Engerman, S.L. and Gallman, R.E. (eds) *Long-Term Factors in American Economic Growth*. Chicago: University of Chicago Press, pp. 95–161.

Watkins, C. (2001) "The definition and identification of housing submarkets", *Environment and Planning A*, **33**(12): 2235–53.

Watkins, C. (2008) "Microeconomic perspectives on the structure and operation of local housing markets", *Housing Studies*, **23**(2): 163–77.

Weber, M. (1930) *The Protestant Ethic and the Spirit of Capitalism*. London: Allen & Unwin.

Webster, C.J. and Lai, L.W.C. (2003) *Property Rights, Planning and Markets: Managing Spontaneous Cities*. Cheltenham: Edward Elgar.

Webster, J.G. (2011) "The duality of media: a structurational theory of public attention", *Communication Theory*, **21**(1): 43–66.

Whalen, C.J. (1996) "A note on 'The myth of institutionalist method' ", *Journal of Economic Issues*, **30**(1): 279–82.

Wheaton, W.C. (1999) "Real estate 'cycles': some fundamentals", *Real estate economics*, **27**(2): 209–230.

Whittington, R. (1992) "Putting Giddens into action: social systems and managerial agency", *Journal of Management Studies*, **25**(6): 521–36.

Wilber, C.K. and Harrison, R.S. (1978) "The methodological basis of institutional economics: pattern model, storytelling, and holism", *Journal of Economic Issues*, **12**(1): 61–89.

Williamson, O.E. (1975) "Markets, hierarchies, and the modern corporation, an unfolding perspective", *Journal of Economic Behavior and Organization*, **17**(3): 335–52.

Williamson, O.E. (1985) *The Economic Institutions of Capitalism*. New York: Free Press.

Williamson, O.E. (1993) "Transaction cost economics and organization theory", *Industrial and Corporate Change*, **2**(2): 107–56.

Williamson O.E. (1996) *The Mechanisms of Governance*. Oxford: Oxford University Press.

Williamson, O.E. (2000) "The new institutional economics: taking stock, looking ahead", *Journal of Economic Literature*, **38**(3): 595–913.

Wisman, J.D. and Rozansky, J. (1991) "The methodology of institutionalism revisited", *Journal of Economic Issues*, **25**(3): 709–37.

Wolfl, A. (2005) "The service economy in OECD countries", in *Enhancing the Performance of the Services Sector*. Paris: OECD, pp. 27–61.

Wolozin, H. (2005) "Thorstein Veblen and human emotions: an unfulfilled prescience". *Journal of Economic Issues*, **39**(3): 727–40.

Wood, B. and Williams, R. (1992) *Industrial Property Markets in Western Europe*. London: E & FN Spon.

Wood, G.A. and Parr, J.B. (2005) "Transaction costs, agglomeration economies, and industrial location", *Growth and Change*, **36**(1): 1–15.

Woodside, A.G. (2010) *Case Study Research: Theory, Methods, Practice*. Bingley: Emerald.

World Bank (2002) *World Development Report 2002: Building Institutions for Markets*, New York: Oxford University Press for the World Bank.

Worzala, E. and Bernasek, A. (1996) "European economic integration and commercial real estate markets: an analysis of trends in market determinants", *Journal of Real Estate Research*, **11**(2): 159–81.

Yeung, W.H. (1997) "Critical realism and realist research in human geography: a method or a philosophy in search of a method?", *Progress in Human Geography*, **21**(1): 51–74.

Yin, R.K. (1998) "The abridged version of case study research" in Bickman, L. and Rog, D.J. (eds) *Handbook of Applied Social Research Methods*. Thousand Oaks: Sage, pp. 229–59.

Yin, R.K. (2003) *Case Study Research, Design and Methods*, 3rd edn. Thousand Oaks: Sage.

Young, P.H. (1996) "The economics of conventions", *Journal of Economic Perspectives*, **10**(2): 105–22.

Zak, P.J. and Knack, S. (2001) "Trust and growth", *Economic Journal*, **111**(470): 295–321.

Zhu, J. (2005) "A transitional institution for the emerging land market in urban China", *Urban Studies*, **42**(8): 1369–90.

Zingler, E.K. (1974) "Veblen vs. Commons: a comparative evaluation", *Kyklos*, **27**(2): 322–44.

Index

Page numbers in **bold** denote figures.